Contents

Heinemann Educational Publishers
Halley Court, Jordan Hill, Oxford OX2 8EJ
a division of Reed Educational & Professional Publishing Ltd

OXFORD   FLORENCE   PRAGUE   MADRID
ATHENS   KUALA LUMPUR   JOHANNESBURG   MELBOURNE
AUCKLAND   SINGAPORE   TOKYO   IBADAN   NAIROBI
GABORONE   KAMPALA   PORTSMOUTH NH (USA)
CHICAGO   MEXICO CITY   SAO PAULO

© Martin Coles 1997

First published 1997
2000 99 98 10 9 8 7 6 5 4 3 2 1
A catalogue record for this book is available from the British
Library on request.

ISBN 0 435 455265
Designed by Roger Denning
Typeset by TechType, Abingdon, Oxon
Printed by Bath Press Ltd, Bath

Acknowledgements

The author would like to thank the following:
Jan Nikolic and Margaret Berriman at Heinemann Educational
for their contributions and advice in the publication of this book;
neglected family and friends for their understanding; Brian Coles
for proofreading; and particularly his partner Judith Nelson, for
her patience and support.

The author and publishers would like to thank the following for
permission to reproduce photographs and other copyright
materials:

The Economist
Format
Honda UK
Chris Honeywell, Working Images
Marks and Spencer plc
Tesco Photographic Unit
UK AEA Technology, Imaging Centre

Introduction

This book has been written primarily for the BTEC finance core and option modules leading to the award of HND and HNC in Business and Finance. The book is also suitable for other students who are studying finance topics as part of a general business course, such as BTEC CMS, and the first year of undergraduate courses leading to degrees in business studies and business administration. A matrix at the end of this Introduction summarises how the contents of this book relate to the BTEC HND specifications.

What does the term financial management mean?

The focus of finance in the business context is on the maximisation of wealth. Despite widespread discussion concerning the importance of the stakeholder approach (which holds that business has obligations to a wide range of interested parties), business policy is decided in the interest of the business owner. If finance is about wealth creation, then it is a discipline that permeates all business activities.

The word finance is often taken to be synonymous with terms such as cash, money, funds and wealth. However, it is clear that while many businesses are worth considerable amounts of money they may have little cash in the bank. So what is meant by the various terms? An entrepreneur who pays £1000 into the bank of a new business venture is clearly providing cash measured in money terms (a currency). The business is said to have been financed or funded with £1000 and the owner's interest in the business (called capital) is valued in money terms to the extent of the same £1000.

If the business subsequently receives a bank loan of £500, this too is a source of finance that provides the funds for items to be purchased. Clearly a loan is not owner's capital, although it is part of the total stock of capital to be utilised. A supplier who supplies goods on credit terms has provided the goods, and in the short term at least, also the means by which they are funded or financed.

However, financial management is not solely concerned with raising finance to fund business operations. Financial management aims to assist operational management to achieve the financial objectives of the business and to report financial results to investors, managers and other parties interested in the business.

Because money can be used as a common unit of measurement to record financial transactions, finance is the language used for communicating business performance. Business activity is quantified in money terms and decisions are based on this quantitative information. Hence financial management encompasses three main disciplines:

1 *treasury management* – concerned with making financial transactions and planning how the business should be funded to pay for the resources it requires;

2 *financial accounting* – concerned with the recording of financial transactions and the preparation of financial reports to communicate past financial performance;

3 *management accounting* – looking to the future, using a knowledge of past performance where relevant to aid the management of the business.

In recognising that financial information is a valuable resource for managing the business, this book also considers the nature of the management information systems in which it is used. Managing information and managing finance are both important enablers. Finance enables resources to be acquired and data to be generated. From this data, management information systems create meaningful management information.

The first chapter of this book is an introduction to managing financial resources, and is followed by a description of the main financial statements and how they may be interpreted. Chapter 3 examines the needs for financial information and how financial reporting is influenced by regulatory pressures. Chapters 4 –11 describe the preparation of financial reports, and Chapters 12–18 explain the accounting and statistical techniques that are used to prepare management information. Chapter 19 examines the context in which management information systems operate and the main considerations in implementing such a system.

The following case study, based on an article in *The Economist*, highlights the important roles of financial management and information systems.

Case study

Selling PCs like bananas

from *The Economist*, 5 October 1996

Making personal computers used to be a war of engineers, each seeking a cleverer way to solder circuit boards. Now often it is the accountants who rule the battlefield. With PC manufacturing largely reduced to snapping together pre-assembled parts, the distance between market winner and loser is measured more often in inventory turns and stock management than megahertz and kilobytes.

That helps explain why Dell Computer is now the darling of Wall Street. Since January, the PC maker's share price has risen by more than 250 per cent. Its profits in the latest quarter were up nearly 60 per cent over a year earlier. Although the company claims the usual advantages for its technology and management, Dell's success really boils down to one thing: while most PC makers sell through shops, resellers, and system integrators, Dell sells directly to customers, mostly by telephone.

The advantage of direct sales is more than eliminating the middleman's mark-up. It can also eliminate the two months or more of delay in which a PC typically languishes in warehouses and on store shelves waiting to be sold. This is more important than it might seem: when it comes to inventory, PCs are like ripe fruit not bent metal.

About 80 per cent of the cost of a PC is made up of components, such as the processor chip, that fall in price by an average of 30 per cent a year. Each day those parts sit on the shelf, they become a worse deal. In the best of times, too much inventory leaves a PC maker with machines that are priced higher than speedier competitors. At the worst of times, when a manufacturer is caught on the cusp of a big change in technology – such as the transition from the 486 chip to the Pentium – it can be left with millions of dollars of out of date PCs. It then either has to compensate stores to unload the white elephants at a loss, or ship them to the developing world to sell on the cheap.

Direct sales also help Dell around one of the trickiest bits of the industry: forecasting. Because some 500 000 customers call Dell's operators each week, it can gauge trends in demand more quickly – and so plan more efficiently – than firms that get their data indirectly from stores.

The combination of these two advantages allows Dell to run one of the tightest manufacturing operations in the industry. It turns its inventory every 14 days on average, compared to about 50 days for Compaq, the best of the indirect PC makers. Goldman Sachs, an investment bank, says this alone gives Dell a 3 per cent cost advantage over Compaq, and over twice that over more typical indirect makers, whose inventory is often 100 days.

Lower costs allow Dell to charge lower prices, which is largely why customers are willing to take a chance on buying a PC unseen. Throughout 1995 and 1996 Dell has been growing at nearly 50 per cent a year in a market growing at just 20 per cent.

Tasks

1 *What are the two main financial benefits for Dell in selling direct to customers?*
2 *How has managing finance and managing information enabled Dell to focus on winning marketing strategies?*

Student guide to contents of HND modules

Chapter	Core Module 4	Option Module 1	Option Module 2	Option Module 3	Option Module 4
1 Managing finance	◆				
2 Financial performance	◆				
3 Needs for financial information		◆		◆	
4 Recording financial information		◆		◆	
5 Preparing financial reports		◆			
6 Company accounts		◆			
7 Preparing reports for different industry sectors		◆			
8 Partnership accounts				◆	
9 Incomplete records				◆	
10 Published accounts for companies				◆	
11 Cash flow statements		◆		◆	
12 Cost measurement			◆		
13 Handling costing data			◆		
14 Costing systems			◆		
15 Costing techniques			◆		
16 Financial planning framework					◆
17 Information for planning and control					◆
18 Quantitative aids to planning					◆
19 Managing information	◆				

1 Managing finance

On completion of this chapter students should be able to:

- identify and analyse organisational financial resources
- identify and evaluate alternative sources of finance
- report on the impact of different methods of raising finance on the gearing of the business.

For businesses to operate they need resources. These include physical items such as property, equipment and materials but also less tangible resources in the form of services from employees and other businesses.

Finance is required to fund these resources so it is possible to state that:

$$\text{Financial resources utilised} = \text{Sources of finance}$$

This simple statement forms the basis for reporting the financial affairs of the business.

Although financial resources and sources of finance can be valued at a point in time, their precise form is not a static one. Business resources change from day to day as people are employed, equipment is purchased and stock is sold. A financial resource in its most liquid form is cash. The flow of financial resources is similar to the water cycle. They are transformed from a liquid (flexible) resource into other assets like property, equipment and stocks, etc. These assets help to generate income from customers and result in cash being received back at the bank ready to continue the cycle. Like the life-giving qualities of water, finance is essential for a business to survive and so it is vital that the receipts and payments of cash are properly monitored and controlled.

Figure 1.1 Finance levels

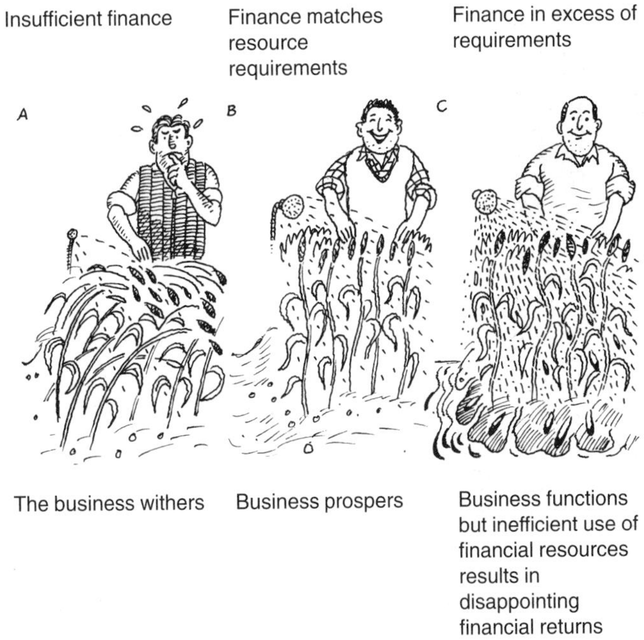

Insufficient finance	Finance matches resource requirements	Finance in excess of requirements
A	B	C
The business withers	Business prospers	Business functions but inefficient use of financial resources results in disappointing financial returns

But just as a farmer requires neither too little nor too much water to sustain his crops, businesses require just so much finance to operate efficiently.

Resources

The identification of resources to be used by a business is an important starting point in determining the finance requirements of the business.

Some of the resources will have a continuing value that can be used time and again, such as a building. Expenditure on these lasting items is called **capital expenditure** and it provides the physical infrastructure to enable the business to operate. Apart from very small items (such as an office stapler) these resources are called **fixed assets**.

Other resources are changing and are being consumed with business activity. Expenditure on these items is called **revenue expenditure**. Revenue expenditure can be classified as a **cost** (or an expense) if it has no continuing value, or a **current asset** if it has continuing value. Wages for shop assistants and electricity for the accounts office have no continuing value and are expenses of running the business. Stocks purchased for resale are costs if they have been sold, as they also have no continuing value. However stocks that remain unsold are considered a current asset because they relate to a future sale.

Other items that may have value in the short term are also classified as current assets. When sales are made on credit, valuable resources have been expended on providing the goods or service but nothing tangible has been received in their place. However, the customer's obligation to pay is in itself an asset as cash will be received eventually. Customers who owe money are called **debtors**. The cash held at a bank is another example of a current asset. The money tied up in these short-term assets is often called **working capital**. Part of this working capital may be funded by suppliers who have provided resources on credit terms. Suppliers who are owed money are called **creditors** and, because they usually require payment within one year, are classified as **current liabilities**. A bank overdraft is another example of a current liability. Working capital can therefore be defined as current assets less current liabilities.

Exercise 1.1   Expenditure analysis

Consider the resources required by the following businesses and analyse them into the categories of capital and revenue expenditure.

1   A college
2   Stagecoach plc (a public transport company).

Careful budgeting for the purchase of capital items is the focus of many new business start-ups, but it is inadequate planning for working capital requirements that causes most business failures. For a trading or manufacturing business, the investment in stocks can be very large and that investment continues for as long as it takes for the customer to pay for them. Hence an item that stays in stock for a month before being sold to a customer who then takes one month credit actually requires financing for two months. In addition there are the selling and administrative expenses incurred in the meantime.

Nature of income

Like expenditure, cash receipts can be divided into capital and revenue items. Receipts from investors are classified as capital and receipts from customers are considered as revenue.

Revenue receipts depend on the type of business and are variously described as income, sales or turnover. Income can be the sum of many individual transactions, such as for a retailer; whereas other businesses enjoy a consistent flow of income resulting from ongoing arrangements, such as an office cleaning contract or a rent agreement. For reporting purposes income is often analysed into two categories: operating income and investment income.

Operating income:

- sales of goods
- provision of services
- commissions for agency work
- royalties for patents held
- admission charges to leisure and tourism facilities
- rental income, e.g. car hire.

Figure 1.2   Classification of expenditure

Business	Capital expenditure	Revenue expenditure
Window cleaner	■ Motor vehicle ■ Ladder	■ Vehicle running expenses ■ Cleaning materials

Clothes shop	■ Premises
	  (if purchased)
	■ Shop fittings
	■ Cash till
	■ Office computer
		■ Premises (if rented)
		■ Stock for resale
		■ Wages
		■ Utility expenses
		■ Legal and accountancy
		  fees
		■ Advertising expenditure

Investment income:

- interest and dividends received on investments.

Exercise 1.2   Business income

Identify the nature of operating income for the following organisations:

- Natural History Museum
- Estate agency
- Computer system supplier
- Manchester United
- Garage
- Hilton Hotel.

Flow of financial resources

The flow of financial resources can be considered with the aid of the following cycles:

1   working capital cycle
2   capital expenditure cycle
3   finance cycle.

Working capital cycle

The working capital cycle follows the processes of normal trading activity. For a manufacturing business the cycle starts with the purchase of materials, continues through the making of the product, and finishes with the receipt of cash from customers.

For any product going through this cycle, funds are being invested to increase its value until the customer finally pays.

Figure 1.3   Working capital cycle

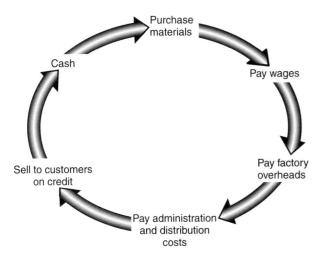

Figure 1.4   Investment in working capital

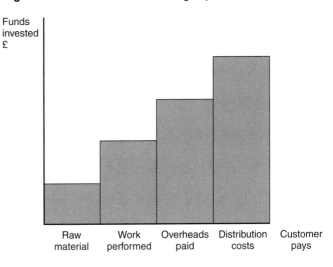

The greater the number of products being produced the greater the amount of funds that are required. There may come a point where a business is too successful in generating sales volume in relation to its working capital. **Overtrading** describes the situation where a business has run into financial difficulties because its demand for resources has outstripped the funding it has available.

Illustration – Overtrading

Jasmine Patel commenced trading in January 19X7 with £3 000 in the bank. She knew that her suppliers had to be paid cash on delivery, despite the fact that her customers would demand one month's credit. She forecast her first month's sales would be £1 800 which would represent her costs of £1 500 plus a 20 per cent mark-up.

Jasmine's business proved highly successful and her sales increased by roughly 50 per cent a month. At the end of June 19X7 she owed £4 434. How could she have run into cash problems when things were going so well?

Jasmine's profit and loss account demonstrates how well the business has performed:

Jasmine Patel Profit and loss account
for the six months ended 30 June 19X7

	January (£)	February (£)	March (£)	April (£)	May (£)	June (£)
Sales	1 800	2 700	4 050	6 075	9 112	13 668
Costs	1 500	2 250	3 375	5 063	7 593	11 390
Profit	300	450	675	1 012	1 519	2 278
Cumulative profit	300	750	1 425	2 437	3 956	6 234

Jasmine made £6 234 in profit but her cash flow was less impressive:

Jasmine Patel Cash flow statement
for the six months ended 30 June 19X7

	January (£)	February (£)	March (£)	April (£)	May (£)	June (£)
Sales receipts	0	1 800	2 700	4 050	6 075	9 112
Payment for stock purchases	1 500	2 250	3 375	5 063	7 593	11 390
Receipts less payments	−1 500	−450	−675	−1 013	−1 518	−2 278
Balance at the start of the month	3 000	1 500	1 050	375	−638	−2 156
Balance at the end of the month	1 500	1 050	375	−638	−2 156	−4 434

The cash problem arose because Jasmine had to wait a month to receive sales revenues but had to pay costs immediately. Whilst this was manageable in the first three months, sales growth meant that payments were always greater than sales receipts.

The working capital cycle does not always result in a consistent flow of cash and it is important to recognise the effect of two operating cycles.

The extent to which products use up or generate cash will depend on the point reached in their **product life cycle**. During product development cash will flow out of the business but none will flow in. However, later in the cycle, cash receipts should exceed cash payments. For the financial wellbeing of a business that is subject to marked product life cycles, it is important that a balanced portfolio of products is maintained where sufficient funds are being generated for the development of new products.

The size of the net cash flows and the duration of each phase will obviously depend on the product, with some products not necessarily conforming to this archetypal time-series curve. For example, a fresh round of

Figure 1.5 Cash flows during the product life cycle

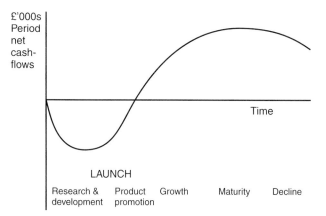

development and promotional expenditure may be incurred at later stages of the product life cycle to allow a further period of sales growth. On the other hand, cash flows may increase markedly during the maturity stage if no further development expenditure is incurred. Products in this situation are 'cash cows' that can be 'milked' to generate funds to develop new products.

Many businesses experience specific times of the year when trading activity is particularly high or low. Examples of **seasonal businesses** include: building and gardening materials, power generation, travel and leisure industries, clothing, farming and products bought for gifts. It is usual for more cash to be tied up in the operating cycle at times of increased business activity, as more resources have been purchased but the business is awaiting payment from its customers.

Case study

Seasonal cash flow at Thorntons

Results for 1996 showed a pre-tax loss of £13.8 million on turnover of £97.6 million. Comment by the *Investors Chronicle* 18 October 1996:

Twelve weeks of the year, which include Christmas and Easter, account for 54% of sales. During this period sales were buoyant, but they were down 4% in the rest of the year. New products are being introduced, including chocolate bars and children's sweets to boost non-seasonal sales.

Tasks

For seasonal businesses and others that experience peak periods, the need to boost off-peak sales is often acute. Suggest how the following businesses may be able to smooth out business activity:

1 garden centres
2 seaside resorts
3 colleges
4 trains.

Capital expenditure cycle

Although the amount of funds tied up in working capital does vary, the **capital expenditure cycle** fluctuates even more. Some periods may experience heavy expenditure on fixed assets while others experience none at all.

Figure 1.6 The fluctuations of the capital expenditure cycle

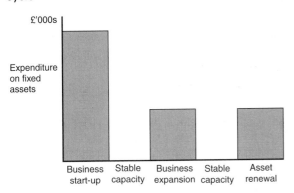

For those industries where capital expenditure requirements can be very large, businesses have to forecast cash flows many years in advance, for example shipping companies and power generation plants.

While in the normal course of business fixed assets result in an out-flow of funds, businesses undergoing reorganisation may decide to raise funds from the sale of fixed assets. This may be to:

- pay for past operating losses;
- lower overheads and become 'fitter and leaner' for the future;
- relinquish funds for more efficient use on other assets, for example selling under-used factory space to pay for a new production process.

Finance cycle

The finance cycle is by definition the flow of funds required to finance the other cycles. If the funds available are inadequate to finance the resources desired, then, at the very least, business performance will be affected. Where finance cannot match the resources actually

Figure 1.7 Finance and financial returns

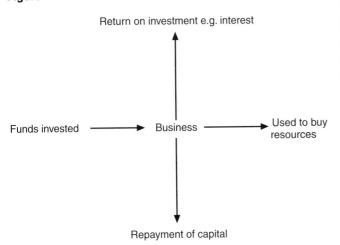

consumed then the business will become insolvent. Funds provided by the business owners are referred to as **capital**. Funds provided by other sources of finance (such as banks) are **liabilities** that will have to be repaid at some future date.

Periodically the providers of finance will expect a return on their investment. Cash or goods transferred to the owner(s) of a sole-trader or a partnership are called **drawings** whereas a distribution of profits to the shareholders of a limited company is in the form of a **dividend**.

Case study

Tottenham Hotspur Football Club

Investors Chronicle 18 October 1996 commenting on the club's results for the year ended 31 July 1996.

> New sponsorship deals lifted that source of profit-rich income from £3 million to £4.7 million, and merchandising jumped £1 million to £3.8 million. Gate and television receipts rose 12 per cent to £2.5 million. The cash pile [£12m] arises from April's rights issue and is ear-marked for rebuilding the North Stand, which should be completed by the end of next season. That will mark the end of the post-Taylor-report stadium upgrading, at a total cost of £27 million.

Tasks

1 *Analyse the various cash flows described into the categories: operating activities, capital expenditure and financing.*
2 *Would paying a transfer fee for a player constitute capital or revenue expenditure?*
3 *Produce a list of six revenue expenditure items that a football club might incur.*

Cash budget

The cash budget (or forecast cash flow statement) is a valuable tool for managing the finances of a business. It is used to forecast all cash receipts and payments.

Basic format:

Business name

Cash Budget

For the 5 months ending 31 May 19X9

	January	February	March	April	May	Total
Capital	10 000					10 000
Loan	10 000					10 000
Sales receipts	2 000	5 000	7 000	10 000	12 000	36 000
Total receipts	22 000	5 000	7 000	10 000	12 000	56 000
Payments:						
Salaries and wages	2 000	3 000	3 000	4 000	4 000	16 000
Rent and rates	3 000			3 000		6 000
Power				500		500
Purchase of materials	4 500	3 000	2 000	4 000	4 000	17 500
Equipment	5 500					5 500
Drawings				1 000	1 000	2 000
Total payments	15 000	6 000	5 000	12 500	9 000	47 500
Receipts minus payments	7 000	(1 000)	2 000	(2 500)	3 000	8 500
Balance brought forward	0	7 000	6 000	8 000	5 500	0
Balance carried forward	7 000	6 000	8 000	5 500	8 500	8 500

Guidelines for preparing a cash budget:

- Use headings that are appropriate to the business.
- The statement can be for any division of time – weekly, quarterly – and for any number of periods.
- The closing cash balance for one period is the opening balance for the next period.
- The total period covered by the statement depends on the purpose of the forecast. A forecast that indicates a continuing cash deficit after six months should continue into future periods to identify the duration for which additional finance is required. It is not unusual for a new business venture to prepare a cash flow statement for its first three years of operations. The first year should be analysed on a monthly basis, with the second and third years possibly analysed on a quarterly basis.
- Capital and loans that have been agreed should be included in the cash receipts section for the relevant period.
- Positive carried forward balances indicate cash in the bank.
- Negative carried forward balances indicate that finance arrangements are insufficient to pay for all the forecast commitments. Arrangements have to be made to cover the deficit, perhaps by applying for an overdraft facility if it is seen as a temporary situation.
- Where the cycles experienced by a business are particularly marked, it may be necessary to prepare a cash forecast for a longer period than would be required for a business that enjoys stable demand.

Exercise 1.3 Simple cash flow statement

Spinning Discs is a music retailer with estimated cash sales of £11 000 per month. The business will incur the following costs over the next six months to 30 September:

	April (£)	May (£)	June (£)	July (£)	August (£)	September (£)
Salaries and wages	3 000	3 000	3 000	3 000	3 000	3 000
Rent and rates	2 000			2 000		
Power		400			400	
Purchase of stock	6 000	5 000	4 000	5 000	5 000	6 000
Equipment						1 000

The shop owner is about to visit the bank manager to renew an overdraft facility. The overdraft on 1 April was £3 600.

Tasks

1 *Prepare a cash budget to find the forecast cash balance at the end of each month.*
2 *Advise the shop owner as to the size and duration of the overdraft facility required.*

It is important to identify the point when cash is actually received or paid. This may require the cash flows to be *phased* to allow for credit transactions. Where customers are allowed up to 30 days credit before they need to pay for supplies, then the sales for month 1 will not be received until month 2. Likewise it may be possible to delay the payment to suppliers.

Illustration

Race Machines Ltd sells goods to suppliers on 60 day credit terms. Its forecast sales for the next six months are:

	April (£)	May (£)	June (£)	July (£)	August (£)	September (£)
Sales	30 000	45 000	40 000	50 000	52 000	46 000

Sales were £35 000 in February and £40 000 in March.

The budgeted cash receipts for the six months to September are therefore:

	April (£)	May (£)	June (£)	July (£)	August (£)	September (£)
Sales	35 000	40 000	30 000	45 000	40 000	50 000

Exercise 1.4 Phased cash flows

Flame is a partnership that has just started trading as a fashion boutique. The shop sells for cash only but the partners have negotiated a 30 day credit period with their clothes suppliers. All other costs are for immediate payment. Forecast sales and costs are shown below:

Tasks

1 *Prepare a cash budget for the first six months of trading.*
2 *What additional finance does the partnership require?*

Exercise 1.5 Cash budget

Patricia Nelson is a children's nurse who has recently completed a catering and hospitality management course on a part-time basis. She wishes to change career and set up in business as a mobile caterer for business and social functions. The various events she has catered for have won her high praise and she believes the time is now right to make the change.

Before she can start, Patricia needs to purchase a van for £5 000 and equip a spare room as a commercial kitchen at a cost of £8 000. She forecasts her sales and other costs to be as follows:

	April (£)	May (£)	June (£)	July (£)	August (£)	September (£)
Sales	1 000	1 500	2 000	2 500	3 000	4 000
Costs:						
Wages						500
Materials	500	650	800	1 000	1 300	1 700
Other costs	300	100	100	100	200	200

Patricia estimates that one half of her business will come from commercial organisations that will take one month to pay for her services. Other customers will be expected to pay on delivery. All costs and expenses will be paid promptly except for the butcher, who is a friend of Patricia. He will extend her a month's credit on supplies that will make up 40 per cent of her material costs.

Patricia has £15 000 of her own money to put into the venture but she will have to draw £900 every month to pay her living costs.

	July (£)	August (£)	September (£)	October (£)	November (£)	December (£)
Sales	5 000	7 000	9 000	9 000	12 000	18 000
Costs:						
Clothes	15 500	3 500	4 500	4 500	8 000	8 000
Rent	3 000			3 000		
Utilities				1 000		
Equipment	4 500					
Wages	1 000	1 200	1 500	1 500	2 000	3 000

The business partners paid £5 000 into the business bank account on 1 July.

Tasks

1 *Prepare a cash budget for Patricia for the six months to 30 September 19X9.*
2 *Comment on the adequacy of Patricia's financial resources.*
3 *How sensitive is the budget to inaccuracies in the sales forecast?*

Sources of finance

The sources of available finance depend crucially on the size of the business. Small businesses rely heavily on the personal resources of those participating directly in the firm with a valuable top up from the banking sector.

Larger businesses, which are too big for a few individuals to finance, make more use of the financial institutions that make up the financial markets. The financial institutions pool the wealth of the general public by selling them financial products such as pension plans, savings schemes and unit trusts. These funds are then invested in businesses under financial arrangements that provide the fund managers with an appropriate level of financial return, risk and liquidity. Liquidity is important because it allows the fund manager to sell investments to meet the fund's obligations, e.g. to pensioners.

The financial markets match the expectations of individual investors with the needs of business. Individuals often save on a short-term basis, whereas businesses require permanent funds. Without banks and other financial institutions, individuals would have nowhere to save and invest for the future and businesses would find it practically impossible to obtain the long term finance they require. The financial markets therefore serve two main purposes:

1 they pool the savings of individuals to enable the financing of the largest business project, and
2 they enable short-term savings to be invested long term.

Finance for business is provided by the following sources:

- individuals – founders, employees, general public
- financial institutions including banks, pension funds and insurance companies
- suppliers
- government
- profits retained in the business.

The arrangements under which finance is provided are the subject of the next few sections.

Figure 1.8   Financial markets

Owner's capital

The business's owners are the ultimate risk takers, as they receive a return on their investment only if the business proves to be profitable. Compared with other investors, owners benefit most when the firm is successful but stand to lose the most if it fails.

Unincorporated businesses, which comprise sole traders and partnerships, are simple to set up but are not recognised in law as being separate from their owners. This means the owners may be forced to transfer more of their personal wealth into the firm if the business cannot generate enough funds to pay its debts. Although one advantage of a partnership is the opportunity to raise funds from a number of individuals, there are often problems for raising funds from sources outside the working partners. An interest in a partnership is not easily marketable and is therefore of limited appeal to institutional investors.

Incorporated businesses are legally recognised as being separate from their owners and managed in accordance with the companies acts. The capital contributed by the owners of the business is divided into **shares**. The purchaser of shares is called a **shareholder**. Once issued, share capital is a permanent source of capital and only under special circumstances will capital be returned to the shareholders. Subsequent buying and selling of shares by the shareholders results in cash transfers between the individuals concerned and not the company. The advantage for the business is that the company's ability to trade is unaffected by changes in its ownership. In addition, because shares are tradable securities, it is usually easier for a company to attract outside investors who wish to tie up funds for only a finite period of time.

Unlike owners of unincorporated businesses, shareholders enjoy limited liability. The maximum amount they can lose in the business venture is the amount they paid for the shares they hold. Shareholders receive benefits from profits earned in the form of cash dividends and an increase in the value of the shares they hold.

There are two types of limited company. A **public limited company** that uses the suffix 'plc' as part of its name can offer its shares to the general public. A **private limited company** that uses the suffix 'ltd' is restricted in the manner in which it can sell shares as it cannot advertise its shares generally.

Public limited companies may have their shares listed on the stock exchange, although it is not a requirement. To be listed the company will have to conform with additional financial reporting requirements as well as ensuring that at least 25 per cent of its shares are held by the general public. One danger for the business's founders is the risk of losing control to a corporate predator. The London Stock Exchange also requires a minimum market valuation of £1 million. Despite these obligations a quoted company gains a number of advantages.

- It becomes easier to raise more funds as a market already exists for the company's shares.
- The reputation of the company is enhanced.
- The ability to motivate employees with share schemes is enhanced. Share schemes operate more satisfactorily where shares are marketable and an up-to-date price is available to monitor capital gains.
- A ready market increases the value of the company's shares as shareholders can liquidate their holding if they require funds at short notice.

Shares can be issued with different rights to dividend and capital repayment. The types of shares issued and the rules governing them will be decided by the company's founders who signed the memorandum of association, but typically they fall into two main categories.

An **ordinary shareholder** shares in the profits of the business after all other investors have been paid their dues. The shareholder is able to vote at General Meetings of the company, including the appointment of the board of directors. A company's wealth attributable to ordinary shareholders is often referred to as **equity**.

As with other forms of finance, there is a cost associated with the use of shareholder funds. Shareholders suffer an opportunity cost in having invested in a particular business, i.e. the return they have forgone by not investing elsewhere. As company directors are directly responsible to the ordinary shareholders they should not invest in a new project unless the increased profits are at least equivalent to the return that shareholders could earn on investments of similar risk.

Preference shareholders are entitled to receive a dividend out of profits even when there may be insufficient profits to pay ordinary shareholders. However, they have few voting rights and hence less influence on company policy.

The cost of preference share capital is measured by the fixed dividend that shareholders are entitled to receive.

This is usually measured in percentage terms, e.g. 8 per cent £1 preference shares would entitle the holder to 8p per year for each share held. Therefore the shares have limited appeal for investors looking for capital appreciation.

There are usually fewer preference shares than ordinary shares and some companies have none at all. A large proportion of capital in the form of preference shares may lead to the undesirable effects of gearing (discussed later).

Issued share capital is the number and nominal value of the shares that the shareholders must pay for. **Authorised share capital** is the maximum number of shares the directors can issue according to the memorandum of association. The existing shareholders may give their approval for the limit to be increased if they agree with the need for additional share capital. Authorised share capital protects shareholder interests, especially when 50 per cent plus one of issued shares gives control of the business.

Shares in companies are purchased by a range of financial institutions including pension funds, insurance companies, unit and investment trusts and venture capitalists (often subsidiaries of banks). Other businesses will also purchase shares, either to develop strategic alliances or for short-term capital gain. Individuals are not usually the largest source of capital for public limited companies, although of course they are often the major shareholders in private limited companies.

Methods of issuing shares for a PLC

1 *Issue by prospectus* – invites offers from the general public in the form of a newspaper advertisement giving information about the company and its future prospects.
2 *Offers for sale* – the company sells all of the shares to an issuing house, which then publishes a prospectus as above. The success of the issue is more certain by this method but the issuing house takes a profit.
3 *Placing* – blocks of shares are sold to private investors, pension funds, unit trusts, investment trusts and others via a financial intermediary, such as a stock broker or issuing house.
4 *Rights issue* – gives existing shareholders the right to buy new shares in the company in proportion to their existing holding, usually at a favourable price.

The Private Limited Company is unable to issue shares to the general public – so relies on methods 3 and 4.

Case study

The Alternative Investment Market (AIM)

The AIM is an alternative stock market for smaller companies and is supervised by the London Stock Exchange. It was launched in June 1995 as a stock market for small public limited companies that needed to raise more cash to grow. AIM itself has grown from nothing to a serious alternative to the finance provided by venture capitalists. After just one year, 150 companies were quoted on AIM with most companies seeking to raise between £1 million and £10 million.

The real attraction compared with a full stock exchange listing is that there is no minimum capitalisation limit, nor is there a need to have a three-year trading history. And for existing shareholders who do not want a significant dilution in their holdings, AIM companies do not have to observe the minimum of 25 per cent shares that have to be available to the general public. In addition, having marketable shares with prices quoted by market makers provides many of the advantages of a full listing. However, the procedures for obtaining a listing do entail significant costs when compared to other sources of finance, such as a placing of shares with venture capitalists. A launch on AIM may cost in excess of £100 000 together with the need to retain a nominated advisor and stockbroker. Other disadvantages include ongoing obligations to publish annual and interim accounts, to observe restrictions on share dealings and to make announcements of events that affect the progress of the company.

Tasks

1 Obtain the latest annual report for a company that has been launched on AIM in the last two years.
2 Ascertain how much money was raised by the share launch and to what purpose it was put.
3 Why was the AIM listing an appropriate way of raising finance for the company?

Exercise 1.6   Cost of issuing shares

For a public limited company the cost of issuing shares can be high. Consider these figures:

Company	Year to:	Type of issue	Value of issue £'000	Cost of issue £'000
Quality Software	Dec. 94	Placing	1 653	78
Tadpole Technology	Sept. 95	Placing	2 513	16
Filtronic Comtex	May 95	Placing at initial flotation	15 000	1 397
Wyko	Apr. 95	Rights issue	8 473	363
Precoat International	Apr. 95	Placing at initial flotation	2 000	390
Games Workshop	May 95	Placing at initial flotation	8 000	952

Tasks

1 Calculate the percentage cost of each issue in relation to the amount of finance raised.
2 Comment on the relative costs of each type of issue.

Exercise 1.7   Who owns British business?

Many public limited companies publish an analysis of their ordinary shareholders.

In its 1996 accounts, the food company Unigate plc stated that the number of shares in issue could be analysed: 27.04 per cent pension funds, 22.34 per cent investment/unit trusts, 17.68 per cent insurance companies, 11.93 per cent individuals, 8.30 per cent overseas holders and 12.71 per cent others.

Tasks

1 From the annual report of two further companies, find a similar analysis of shareholders.
2 Using this small sample determine the biggest shareholders in British business.
3 Identify the people who ultimately benefit from business ownership.

Long-term loans

For sole traders and partnerships, the opportunity to arrange long-term loans is often limited to the individuals and their families who are actively participating in the business. For a company, long-term loans are usually in the form of **debentures**. They may alternatively be described as bonds or loan stock and are evidenced by a document stamped with the company's common seal. The debenture document confirms that the holder has made a loan to the company and hence has the advantage of being a tradable security. Redeemable debentures have to be purchased back by the company at a specified price on a particular date, whereas there is no obligation to repay the capital on irredeemable debentures. It is possible for debentures to be 'secured' on the assets of the business and this entitles the debenture holder to take possession and sell the assets if interest payments or repayment of capital are not made on the agreed dates. If the company is listed on a stock exchange its debentures can be traded in the same way as its shares.

The debentures are purchased by financial institutions and individual investors who require a relatively low-risk investment. The holders receive a financial return in the form of a fixed rate of interest that must be paid irrespective of the level of profits generated by the business. As with preference shares, the amount of finance to be raised by loan stock will depend on the desired level of financial gearing (gearing is examined later).

Case study

Tesco

Tesco plc uses loan stock to finance its activities, and the following figures have been extracted from the company's annual report for the year ended 24 February 1996.

£77 million	4 per cent unsecured deep discount loan stock 2006 redeemable for £125 million in 2006
£200 million	10.375 per cent bonds redeemable at par in 2002
£200 million	8.75 per cent bonds redeemable at par in 2003

Tasks

1 *Explain the following terms: unsecured, redeemable and par.*
2 *Describe, with the help of the £77 million loan stock details, the features of deep discount loan stock.*
3 *Explain the factors that will have determined the different interest rates for the three loan stock issues.*
4 *What will have been considered when determining the redemption dates?*

Banks and other financial institutions

Merchant banks and the main clearing banks are substantial investors in business. **Bank loans** are for a fixed period, repayment either being in instalments or in full at the end of the agreed term. Banks are reluctant to lend for periods of more than 7 years, primarily because they receive deposits on short notice terms. Short pay-back from business also tends to reduce the risk of bad debts.

Bank overdrafts are popular because they offer greater flexibility than a straight loan. An arrangement is made to allow the business to overdraw on its current account up to a specified limit. Interest is only charged when the facility is used, and so an overdraft will prove to be cheaper than a bank loan when finance needs fluctuate.

Banks will want to see a detailed business plan demonstrating that the business can generate the cash flow necessary to meet interest payments and capital repayments. They are usually unwilling to lend more than the owners themselves are putting into the business. In particular, the banks need to be convinced of the owners' commitment to the enterprise before they will pledge their own funds.

Interest rates are usually variable, with the rate quoted in terms of a premium to the bank base rate. For example, '3 per cent over base' when base rates are 6 per cent will result in a 9 per cent charge. In addition, there may be arrangement fees and a security fee (if the loan is secured on personal or business assets).

Finance houses (often subsidiaries of the clearing banks or equipment suppliers) provide **hire purchase** facilities. Providers include Lombard Tricity Finance Ltd, RoyScot Trust plc and Ford Motor Credit Co. Ltd. Hire purchase (HP) allows the business to use an asset without having immediately to find the money to pay for it. A finance house buys the asset from the supplier and retains ownership of it during the period of the hire purchase agreement. The business pays a deposit and then further payments to the finance house as stipulated in the agreement. At the end of the HP agreement, ownership of the asset is passed to the business.

The cost of hire purchase is implicit in the agreement terms which results in payments in excess of the cash price of the asset.

Leasing an asset provides similar benefits to hire purchase. Finance houses, such as Lombard North Central plc and Anglo Leasing plc (**lessors**) allow the business (**lessee**) to use an asset without having to buy it outright. The real distinction between the two forms of finance is that leasing does not confer an automatic right to eventual ownership of the asset. It is a popular form of finance for company vehicles, office equipment and factory machinery. There are two types of lease.

An **operating lease** is a rent agreement allowing the lessee to use the asset for a period that is shorter than the asset's useful life. For example, two-year agreements for motor cars are fairly typical. The finance house makes a profit by charging more than the asset's fall in value over the period of the agreement. A **finance lease** tends to run for longer periods than an operating lease. The agreement will run for most of the asset's economic life and so requires payments under the agreement to be in excess of the cash price of the asset. Because the asset has relatively little value at the end of the lease term, the agreement often allows the lessee to continue leasing on a 'peppercorn' rent or to purchase the asset for a nominal sum.

The different nature of the two types of lease is reflected in other terms to the agreement. Under an operating lease the finance house is concerned that the asset retains a high resale value. So to ensure maintenance is carried out, these costs are often borne by the lessor (although they will of course have been considered when setting the lease terms). Under a finance lease, the risk of ownership is largely transferred to the lessee who usually has to maintain the asset.

HP and lease agreements ensure that ownership of the asset remains with the finance house until the final payment has been made. However, before entering into an agreement they will want reassurance that the business has a good payment record on past debt arrangements.

Factors are finance houses that specialise in providing finance against a business's trade debtors. Examples include Alex Lawrie Factors Ltd, RoyScot Factors Ltd and Lombard NatWest Commercial Services Ltd. Factoring may be particularly appropriate for fast growing businesses and businesses that experience volatile sales, perhaps affected by seasonal sales. The amount of finance provided will grow automatically in line with the growth in debtors and so satisfies a major element of working capital needs when sales are growing. Factors provide two types of service.

Invoice factoring describes a situation where the factor undertakes to collect amounts due from the business's debtors and advances immediately up to 80 per cent of the value of the invoices outstanding. This enables the business to receive payment quickly on debts that might otherwise take 30–90 days to collect. The other advantage is that the task of debt collection is passed to the factor. As the monies are received from the debtors, the factor pays the business the balance of the debtors transferred less its charges. Many factors also provide cover for bad debts under 'non-recourse' agreements. **Invoice discounting** also allows an advance of cash against trade debtors, but responsibility for debt collection remains with the business. The debtors are requested to pay the factor for amounts due and so, as with invoice factoring, the customer is aware that the debt has been passed to a factor. Another form of this type of financing is called **confidential invoice discounting**. This allows debtors to continue paying their debts to the business, but turnover must be at least £1 million per annum.

Factors will charge interest, typically at 1–3 per cent over base rates on amounts advanced, so this procedure is similar in cost to a bank overdraft. For invoice factoring, a further charge of up to 3 per cent of the value of debtors is charged for sales ledger administration.

Minimum annual turnover of £100 000 is required for factoring and around £1 million for discounting arrangements. Otherwise, this form of finance is only limited by the balance of acceptable debtor balances as finance houses will not wish to purchase debtors that are likely to contain substantial bad debts.

A **commercial mortgage** is a loan secured on land and buildings and can either be used to finance the purchase of the property, or to provide security for a loan applied to some other purpose. It is a long term financing arrangement of typically 10–30 years.

Mortgages can be arranged with a bank and for larger amounts insurance companies and pensions funds may provide funds.

Under a **sale and lease back** arrangement the firm sells its freehold property to an investment company, and then leases it back. This releases funds for other purposes in the business without incurring further debt. A major disadvantage is the loss of capital appreciation in times of rising property prices.

Case study

Tamaris plc

The nursing home operator Tamaris uses sale and leaseback to finance its ambitious expansion plans. In mid-1996 the company took the number of beds it had under management to 1 000. With occupancy rates of over 90 per cent the only way to increase profits further was to acquire more nursing homes. The directors planned to have over 3 000 beds by the end of 1997. Future deals would be largely financed through further sale and lease back arrangements as the company already had high levels of debt.

Tasks

1 *Why are sale and lease back arrangements a particularly attractive method of financing for a company such as Tamaris?*
2 *Identify two other types of business where sale and lease back would be appropriate.*

Government

In return for a 2.5 per cent p.a. premium, the UK's Department of Employment **Loan Guarantee Scheme** will repay 70–80 per cent of a medium-term bank loan on which a business has defaulted. The scheme enables banks to lend money to otherwise unattractive, high-risk businesses provided they have fewer than 200 employees.

There exist a number of institutions of the **European Union** that can provide finance for business. The European Investment Bank provides loans or loan guarantees for investment projects in industry to improve an area's infrastructure. The European Social Fund can finance schemes that improve employment opportunities, such as training. The European Regional Development Fund makes grants for one-off development projects as opposed to ongoing subsidy to help redress regional economic imbalance.

Suppliers

Suppliers are a valuable source of finance for many businesses. Just as the business may give credit to its own customers, it may be able to negotiate credit terms with its suppliers. Credit terms are typically 30 days from date of supply, or for payment at the end of the month following delivery, i.e. 30–60 days.

The great attraction of trade credit is that it is often free. However, where the business over-extends the agreed credit period, the trading relationship may become strained and so affect the level of service and goodwill between supplier and customer. In addition, where settlement discounts are offered, failure to take them can be expensive relative to other forms of finance.

Retained earnings

Probably the most important ongoing source of finance is the retention of profits. Instead of distributing all of the profits to owners, some of the wealth created each year is invested in further assets to increase earnings potential for the future.

For business owners, retained profits involve them in opportunity costs as they have to forgo returns on alternative investments.

Financial planning

How a business is financed is often subject to constraints dictated by the financial market. However, where possible the financing strategy should be decided after due regard to:

- *duration* – how long the finance is required
- *cost* – relative to alternative sources of finance
- *gearing* – the proportion of fixed return finance to equity capital.

Other considerations include:

- *security* – assets pledged to the investor in the event that operating cash flow is inadequate to finance capital repayments and/or finance charges
- *government intervention* – incentives from government agencies such as grants and loan guarantee schemes.

Duration

In the same way that individuals do not purchase houses with bank overdrafts or finance home computers with a 25 year mortgage, businesses should match the source of finance with the need for finance. This makes sense for:

- *the business* – as it ensures finance is guaranteed for as long as the need exists;
- *the investor* – as it ensures adequate security can be obtained for the duration of the loan, for example a 20

year loan may be secured against property that will continue to have value in 20 years' time.

The main sources of finance can be analysed according to the period of finance they provide:

Source of finance	Duration	
Ordinary share capital	Long term	Permanent
Preference share capital	Long term	Specified date of redemption or permanent
Retained earnings	Long term	Permanent until distributed as dividends
Commercial mortgage	Long term	Typically 10 to 30 years
Debentures	Medium/long term	Specified date of redemption or permanent
Bank finance – lease, HP and loan	Medium term	Typically 1 to 7 years
Bank overdraft	Short term	Repayable on demand
Debt factor	Short term	Depending on credit periods
Trade credit	Short term	Typically 7 to 60 days

For medium-term finance, small businesses are almost entirely reliant on bank finance. This situation is not new, having been identified in the 1960s, but it is a major issue which successive governments have sought to rectify. The problem is less acute for larger companies, which can issue medium-term debentures.

The financing of a business is not an exact science – finance and expenditure cannot be matched precisely. Generally, the cash flows of a typical business are quite complex and financing requirements can change on a daily basis. It is important, however, that the business's financial structure is generally appropriate to the make-up of its assets and the pattern of its cash flows.

Some items of expenditure seem quite short term, but business is a continuous process of similar short-term transactions. There is usually a job to start on just as another is being finished. Hence working capital, for such things as materials, wages and overheads, will continue to be a long-term requirement. It is necessary to identify what minimum level of permanent finance is required and ensure this is properly funded. Short-term fluctuations should then be accommodated, as they arise, with appropriate sources of short-term finance. Finance has a cost so it is essential not to pay unnecessarily for more finance than is needed. Taking out a loan that results in a healthy bank balance is not good financial management.

In Figure 1.9, the dotted line MM indicates the forecast minimum level of finance required. It would seem appropriate, therefore, for at least some of the current assets to be financed by long-term finance to ensure continuity of business even when credit facilities may become difficult to obtain, say line LL. The difference between the total finance required and MM should, if possible, be financed by a flexible source where finance charges are only incurred when the finance is actually required, e.g. a bank overdraft or factoring.

Cost of finance

Raising finance invariably results in a cost and so it follows that the financial benefits arising from a particular project should outweigh the cost of using the funds. Unfortunately it is not always possible to identify specific sources with specific needs, and so it becomes necessary to calculate the average cost of capital for the business as a whole.

Illustration

A company has shareholder funds of £200 000 and debentures of £50 000 at 10 per cent. If the shareholders require a return of 15 per cent, what is the required return from the average business activity?

Weighted average cost of capital

$$= \frac{\text{Total finance returns required}}{\text{Total finance employed}} \times 100\%$$

$$= \frac{(200\,000 \times 15\%) + (£50\,000 \times 10\%)}{£250\,000} \times 100\%$$

$$= 14.0\%$$

Figure 1.9 Financing needs

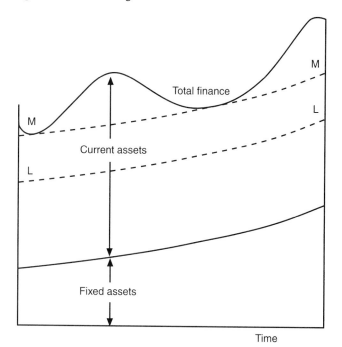

Gearing

Gearing is the term used to describe the relationship between finance that enjoys a fixed rate of return and equity (capital that enjoys profit related returns). Fixed return finance is the sum of preference shares and net debt, where net debt comprises all interest bearing finance (such as loans and leases) less cash holdings. The equity of a company includes ordinary share capital, retained earnings and other reserves.

$$\text{Gearing ratio} = \frac{\text{preference shares} + \text{net debt}}{\text{equity}}$$

Ratios in excess of 1 indicate highly geared companies.

Illustration – The effects of gearing

Consider three companies that employ £100 000 of capital and that generate annual pre-interest profits that vary between £5 000 and £20 000. The composition of the capital structure will greatly affect the returns that ordinary shareholders receive.

	Company A Very high gearing (£)	Company B High gearing (£)	Company C Low gearing (£)
Capital structure:			
Ordinary shares	10 000	50 000	90 000
Debentures at 10% p.a.	90 000	50 000	10 000
	100 000	100 000	100 000
Returns on profits of £5 000			
Shares (receives the balance)	–4 000	0	4 000
Debentures 10% p.a.	9 000	5 000	1 000
	5 000	5 000	5 000
Returns on profits of £20,000			
Shares	11 000	15 000	19 000
Debentures 10% p.a.	9 000	5 000	1 000
	20 000	20 000	20 000

Irrespective of profit levels, debenture holders will always receive 10 per cent of the value of debentures. However, the percentage return enjoyed by ordinary shareholders varies widely, depending on the level of profits and extent of financial gearing. Where gearing is low, ordinary shareholders receive returns of between 4.4 per cent (£4 000/£90 000) and 21.1 per cent (£19 000/£90 000).

Summary of percentage returns to ordinary shareholders:

	Gearing		
	High	Medium	Low
On profits of £5 000 (%)	–40	0	4.4
On profits of £10 000 (%)	10	10	10.0
On profits of £20 000 (%)	110	30	21.1
Range of returns (%)	150	30	16.7

The range of percentage returns to ordinary shareholders increases as gearing increases. Therefore gearing can be said to increase the risk of not attaining a particular return. In addition, as can be seen from this illustration, there is a risk that interest paid on fixed-rate capital may result in losses for ordinary shareholders. Business losses are eventually bad news for everybody so the level of gearing is of interest to the providers of all types of finance.

It is difficult to generalise about preferred levels of gearing. The main issue is the extent to which financial risk is affected by gearing. The more volatile the level of business profits, the more marked are the effects of gearing. In the case of the three companies above (which do experience volatile profits) Company C with low gearing would appear to have the most appropriate capital structure. However, if the businesses could expect a narrower range of profits a higher level of gearing may offer benefits for shareholders.

Exercise 1.8   Gearing ratio

1   Recalculate the financial returns to the ordinary shareholders of companies A, B and C assuming annual profits ranged between £9 000 and £13 000.
2   Evaluate the figures calculated.

Interest cover

Another valuable measure of financial risk is the relationship of interest payments to the profits generated by the business.

$$\text{Interest cover} = \frac{\text{profit before interest}}{\text{interest payments}}$$

A low-interest cover ratio indicates that interest payments are a burden. The larger the profits earned in relation to interest commitments, the less risk there is of interest payments pushing the business into a loss situation.

Businesses that are heavily influenced by economic cycles, such as capital goods suppliers, would not normally wish to be highly geared. On the other hand stable industries, such as food producers, may be able to provide adequate interest cover at all stages of the economic cycle. They are unlikely to make losses for ordinary shareholders even if highly geared.

Figure 1.10 Financial risk

	Stable operating profits	Volatile operating profits
High gearing	Medium financial risk	High financial risk
Low gearing	Low financial risk	Medium financial risk

Exercise 1.9 Gearing and interest cover

The following companies are from the same industry:

	Red	Green	Orange
Profits before interest	£120 000	£120 000	£120 000
Capital structure:			
Ordinary share capital	£800 000	£600 000	£400 000
Debentures @ 10 %	£200 000	£400 000	£600 000

Forecasts indicate profits may fall by 50 per cent for all three companies during the next year.

Tasks

1 *Calculate the current year gearing ratio for each company.*
2 *Calculate the current year's interest cover for each company.*
3 *Repeat the interest cover calculations for the forthcoming year.*
4 *Evaluate the companies' financial structures on the basis of the ratios calculated.*

Case study

Capital structure of Stagecoach Holdings plc

Following the privatisation of bus services, the industry has seen significant consolidation with companies like Stagecoach buying out regional operators. For Stagecoach, growth and operating efficiencies have also come from a massive investment in new buses and coaches. The company reported the following financial results and finance structure in its interim results to 14 October 1995.

	6 months to 14 Oct. 95 £'000	12 months to 30 Apr. 95 £'000
Profit before interest	26 225	40 978
Interest payable	5 542	8 363
Profit on ordinary activities	20 683	32 615
Capital employed:		
Shareholders' funds	94 410	83 467
Bank loans	62 224	59 807
Loan stock	4 968	8 774
HP and lease obligations	72 808	58 369
Cash	(3 751)	(8 442)
Total capital employed	230 659	201 975

Tasks

1 *Calculate the company's gearing ratio and interest cover for both sets of figures.*
2 *Evaluate the appropriateness of the company's capital structure in relation to the nature of its business, in particular the relatively high level of HP and lease finance.*

The investor's perspective

The willingness of investors to provide finance will depend on the risk and financial return of their investment. Some investors may wish to participate in the profits of the business by becoming shareholders, while others will want a safer investment with a fixed rate of return. In addition, they will be interested in how easy it is to sell out when they want to.

The financing plan will have to accommodate a range of investors' expectations. One way would be to offer debenture holders and preference shareholders fixed redemption dates or the option to convert into ordinary shares once the business has proved successful. Of course, the offer of reassurances and options that reduce the risk for one group of investors correspondingly increases the risk and reduces the potential returns for other groups.

Return on investment

Other things being equal, investors are looking for the highest possible returns on their investment and will compare the returns of various investment opportunities.

Fixed returns on preference shares and debentures are easy to compare, but for ordinary share capital there is much more uncertainty.

Return on investment in ordinary shares

$$= \frac{\text{Dividend per share} + \text{Share price movement}}{\text{Market price of share}}$$

Risk

It is not possible to consider the rate of return without considering the risk attached to it. Risk can take two forms:

1 commercial risk, i.e. whether it is a financially viable business;
2 financial risk depending on the capital structure of the business (gearing) and the rights of the particular security (share or debenture).

There is often a trade off between rate of return and risk. Government bonds yield an unexciting rate of return but are considered risk free. At the other end of the scale, business start-ups often fail in the first three years of trading, so whilst there may be potential for making big profits, investors must recognise that they may lose all of the capital invested.

Security

With the knowledge that a business may default on its obligations to pay interest and make capital repayments, investors can reduce their risk of loss by obtaining security for the funds advanced. The finance agreement will give the right to claim beneficial ownership of specific assets if certain conditions have been broken. The asset or assets pledged as security may belong to the business or may be personal assets of the business's owner, such as the family home.

Duration

The duration for which finance is available will depend upon the needs of the various investors. Many entrepreneurs have no desire to leave the business they have set up whereas other investors may want to take their profits as soon as possible. It is not unusual for venture capitalists, who are providing some of the funds to get a business started, to obtain assurances that the business will float on the stock exchange within five years. With a planned exit date, investment fund managers can ensure sufficient liquidity in their investment portfolios to repay fund obligations and to invest in new opportunities.

Case studies

Sources of finance

Palmer Software Ltd required £50 000 for computer hardware to re-equip its programming facilities with the latest personal computers.

Task

■ *Identify appropriate sources to finance the purchase.*

Sinclair and Symons Ltd ran into temporary cash flow problems when disruption to work flow was caused by a delay in the introduction of a new production line. The situation was aggravated by unpaid creditors who stopped supplying materials.

Task

■ *What measures could have resolved the short-term situation?*

Fortnum and Mason trades from just one shop which has limited the company's sales growth. In 1996 the company decided to buy the building next door, adding 23 per cent to floor area. The £11.7 million move was partly financed by a £5.1 million rights issue.

Tasks

1 *What is a rights issue?*
2 *Suggest other sources of finance for the remaining £6.6 million that was needed.*

Eurotunnel's ordinary shares were worth £1 billion in November 1996 but because of cost over-runs in building the Channel Tunnel it owed its bankers £9 billion. Such high gearing left the company with interest payments it could not afford to pay.

Tasks

1 *Explain what the term gearing means.*
2 *What type of new finance was needed to reduce the company's gearing ratio?*

British Biotech announced a £143 million rights issue in June 1996 to continue the development of its potential blockbuster drug Marimastat. This followed the announcement of a £25.1 million loss on sales of £8.5 million.

1 *Why was an issue of shares an appropriate source of finance?*
2 *What would be the problems with debt finance, such as a debenture issue or a bank loan?*

Case study

Oasis

Oasis offers an exclusive range of clothing and accessories to the 18–35 age group. The fashion company is on a fast growth path having been bought out in 1991 by experienced retailers Michael and Maurice Bennett. In 1986 they sold to Freemans the Warehouse chain they founded with designer Jeff Banks. From that experience they learnt that success came from an eye for detail and good systems for doing things. Their aim is 'to produce good design, quality and recognisable value complemented by an attractive store environment and knowledgeable and friendly service'.

The business reported a turnover of £60 million in the year to January 1996, having expanded in 1995 with seven new stores and eight new concessions in the UK. Since then, more stores have opened, including a fifth store in Ireland. Further afield, Oasis is developing its brand in selected overseas markets. The format looks right with good progress in Germany, the Middle East and the Far East.

Other product ideas are being looked at, including the teenage market. But with an ever widening product range, many existing stores are too small to stock all Oasis merchandise. This means store relocations, use of stock room space or acquisition of adjacent stores. However, property leases of five years or more sometimes makes expansion difficult.

With turnover and profits growing at an annual rate of 20–30 per cent, much of the finance required has come from retained profits. The company has no debt.

Despite a dividend yield at a modest 2 per cent on the share price, the shares have done well. Since being launched on the stock exchange in June 1995, the shares soared from £1.48 to £2.61 by January 1996. On hearing the company's results for the year to 27 January 1996, the shares raced ahead again during April 1996 to £4.00.

Financial affairs as at 27 January 1996:

Assets	Value £'000s	Source of finance	Value £'0002
Property	2 137	Ordinary share capital	5 246
Fixtures and fittings	7 605	Retained profit	10 148
Stocks	5 153	Amounts owed to creditors	10 368
Investments	391		
Debtors	2 778		
Cash at bank	7 698		
	25 762		25 762

Tasks

1 *Explain the advantages and disadvantages of debt finance.*
2 *Describe what is meant by the following two statements: 'No debt – a missed opportunity' and 'No debt – potential for growth'.*
3 *The investment in a new store requires finance for premises, fixtures and fittings and stock. Suggest ways in which finance could be raised without asking ordinary shareholders for more cash.*
4 *Why are investors interested in a share that yields less from dividends than a bank deposit rate?*
5 *Why is a buoyant share price good news for the business?*

Case study

National Express Group plc

Since privatisation in 1988 and its launch on the stock market in 1992, National Express has changed dramatically from the staid coach operator it once was. As the directors look to apply their skills and knowledge to other areas of mass passenger transport, the company has branched out into railways and airports. National Express owns East Midlands and Bournemouth Airports, and in 1995 took over West Midlands Travel to add a network of local bus routes to its product portfolio.

By early 1996 the company had turned its attention to railways. For £11 million the company bought into London & Continental (L&C), the consortium charged with supervising the construction of the £3 billion Channel Tunnel rail link to London. This move into trains was followed by a successful bid to run the Gatwick Express rail route and in April 1996 the go-ahead was given to run trains between London and the Midlands. Expansion of train services will be good for other parts of the group as links with buses and airports are made.

The number of people using public transport is rising steadily in all divisions. West Midlands is turning in good profits and with the introduction of 300 new buses, operating costs are set to fall. During 1995 company profits increased by 173 per cent, adding £18.0 million to reserves and generating £33 million in operating cash flow after interest payments and tax.

The company has ambitious plans and intends to strengthen its market position with organic growth and acquisitions. A strong financial base from which to grow is essential.

Financial affairs as at 31 December 1995:

Assets	Value £ million	Source of finance	Value £ million
Property	147.0	Share capital and reserves	106.0
Vehicles	39.6	Bank loans	43.9
Plant	12.9	Bank overdraft	5.4
Investment in other businesses	1.8	Other loans	15.5
Stock	2.5	Finance leases	12.5
Debtors	26.2	Owed to creditors (including	
Investments – short term	8.6	income received in advance)	94.9
Cash	39.6		
	278.2		278.2

Analysis of borrowings:

Due to be repaid:	Bank loans £ million	Bank loans £ million	Other loans £ million	Finance leases £ million	Total £ million
0–1 years	11.4	5.4	6.0	3.5	26.3
1–2 years	9.9	0.0	1.6	2.9	14.4
2–5 years	22.6	0.0	2.3	6.1	31.0
after 5 years	0.0	0.0	5.6	0.0	5.6
	43.9	5.4	15.5	12.5	77.3

Tasks

1 *Calculate the financial gearing ratio for National Express.*
2 *In relation to the assets being employed, evaluate the financial structure of the company.*
3 *The repayment of borrowings is carefully planned. Explain in outline the cash budgeting process.*
4 *The group had expansion plans that required significant financial resources. Suggest how the expansion could have been financed if the company had planned the following expenditure during 1996: £30 million in property, £30 million in vehicles, £10 million in debtors and £10 million in revenue expenditure to start up further train franchises.*

Summary

Financial resource needs are identified within revenue and capital expenditure categories. Sources of finance are required to satisfy financial resource needs to the extent that these are not funded by income receipts. The need for finance is quantified with the use of a cash budget which identifies all cash receipts and payments of the business for some defined future period. The sources of finance should be adequate and appropriate to the business's needs with particular consideration given to relative costs, financial gearing and duration of the financing need.

Further reading

Management Accounting, published monthly by the Chartered Institute of Management Accountants.

Robert W. Hutchinson, *Corporate Finance: Principles of Investment, Financing and Valuation*, Stanley Thornes, 1995.

Robert W. Kolb and Ricardo Jo Rodriguez, *Financial Markets*, Blackwell, 1996.

Alan Parkinson, *Managerial Finance*, Butterworth Heinemann, 1994.

John Watts, *Accounting in the Business Environment*, 2nd edition, Pitman, 1996.

2 Financial performance

On completion of this chapter students should be able to:

- evaluate the financial performance of organisations.

Financial statements

Business financial performance is reported using a set of well-defined financial statements. The primary financial statements are:

- a balance sheet
- a profit and loss account
- a cash flow statement
- a statement of total recognised gains and losses.

These statements enable the relative financial performance of different organisations to be evaluated. Comparability across the range of business organisations is achieved through regulatory influences, which are particularly demanding for limited companies. Those who prepare company accounts have to comply with regulations stipulated by the Companies Acts and the Accounting Standards Board.

This chapter is concerned with the evaluation of financial performance, primarily using the published results of public limited companies. The preparation of the financial statements referred to, and further details concerning the underpinning principles, are described in later chapters.

Balance sheet

Chapter 1 introduced the basic concept of the balance sheet where the firm's sources of capital were considered in relation to the financial resources employed in the business. The balance sheet shows how these financial resources have been deployed at a specified point in time; for annual accounts this is on the last day of the company's financial year.

The balance sheet shows the nature and value of:

- the assets employed in the business
- the liabilities to others
- the capital provided by the business owners.

The basic accounting equation is based on the principle that the resources used in the business must have been funded by a source of finance. The accounting equation is:

Assets = owner's capital + liabilities.

Liabilities include borrowings such as bank loans and debentures, in addition to amounts owed to creditors in respect of goods and services that have not yet been paid for. Rearranging the accounting equation gives:

Assets − liabilities = owner's capital.

This equation provides the basic structure of the balance sheet, which is usually prepared in a vertical format:

	(£)
Assets	50 000
Less liabilities	20 000
Net assets	30 000
Financed by:	
Owner's capital	30 000

This format is common to most businesses although it may vary in detail depending on the nature and legal type of the business. The net assets of the business (total assets less total liabilities) represent the owners' investment in the business.

An example of a balance sheet for a public limited company:

Tesco plc
Balance sheet
as at 24 February 1996

	1996 £ million	1995 £ million
Fixed assets:		
Tangible fixed assets	5 466	5 204
Investments	19	10
	5 485	5 214
Current assets:		
Stocks	559	415
Debtors	80	104
Investments	54	131
Cash at bank and in hand	38	44
	731	694
Creditors: amounts falling due within one year	2 002	1 781
Net current liabilities	(1 271)	(1 087)
Total assets less current liabilities	4 214	4 127
Creditors: amounts falling due after more than one year		
Convertible capital bonds	0	200
Other	598	721
Provisions for liabilities and charges	22	93
	3 594	3 113

Capital and reserves:		
Called up share capital	108	103
Share premium account	1 383	1 152
Other reserves	40	40
Profit and loss account	2 057	1 809
Equity shareholders' funds	3 588	3 104
Minority equity interests	6	9
	3 594	3 113

Assets are presented in order of liquidity (how easily they can be converted to cash) starting with fixed assets which are the least liquid. Fixed assets may be classified into intangible, tangible and long term investments.

Intangible assets are assets that do not have a physical form. Examples include: the goodwill which is included in the purchase of another business where the amount paid was greater than the value of the net assets acquired; and expenditure on developing new products or processes which will provide benefit in future periods. **Tangible assets** include property, plant and motor vehicles.

In published accounts for companies, liabilities are described as 'creditors' and are analysed according to whether they are repayable within one year or after one year. The main financial statements are accompanied by **notes to the accounts** which provide valuable additional information. The following example explains the nature of the creditor balances in the balance sheet for Tesco plc:

Tesco plc
Creditors falling due within one year

	1996 £ million	1995 £ million
Borrowings (loans, bank overdrafts, HP, leases and debentures)	335	327
Trade creditors	764	723
Other creditors (incl. taxation and dividends)	903	731
	2 002	1 781

The capital and reserves section of the balance sheet equates to owners' equity (their capital interest in the business). The balance on the profit and loss account represents the profits retained in the business to fund future expansion.

Profit and loss account

Profit is the difference between revenue income and costs. An item sold for £5 that cost the business £3 has created a profit of £2, which is a measure of the wealth created for the business owners.

It is important to appreciate the accounting concept of **matching** that relates to income and costs. Income and costs are not just those that have passed through the business's bank account; owner's capital can be represented by assets other than cash. The profit calculation considers income earned rather than cash received. Likewise, costs relate to resources used, not necessarily those paid for in the accounting period. If in the above example the item was sold on credit for £5 and this amount had not yet been received, £2 profit would still have been made. It is just that in the balance sheet the £5 asset will be represented by a debtor of £5 and not £5 in cash.

In complying with the matching concept, preparers of business accounts use accounting conventions that measure the value of goods or services actually provided to customers, together with the related costs of resources actually consumed. A major issue that has to be addressed concerns fixed assets which are purchased for use over a number of years. In order to reflect properly the consumption of the business's resources the cost of these items should be spread over the years in which they will be used. The cost allocated to a particular accounting period is called **depreciation**.

For example, a motor vehicle purchased for £6 000 is to be used for three years before being scrapped. The depreciation charge would be £2 000 per annum based on a straight line basis. After one year the vehicle will have a net book value of £4 000 which represents the cost to be allocated to future periods. This will be included in the balance sheet as a fixed asset.

The published profit and loss account of a company is prepared on an annual basis and its basic format deducts the cost of resources consumed from the value of goods or services provided.

Profit and loss account
Pro forma

	(£)
Sales	1 000
Cost of sales	500
Gross profit	500
Distribution costs	150
Administration expenses	100
Operating profit	250
Interest payments	50
Net profit before taxation	200
Corporation tax @ 25%	50
Profit after taxation	150
Dividends	75
Retained profit for the year	75
Retained profit at the start of the year	180
Retained profit at the end of the year	255

The cost of the goods sold or services provided, whether purchased from a supplier or made in house, are deducted in order to arrive at a gross profit. Other costs are described as the 'expenses' of running the business and are often analysed between **distribution costs** and **administration expenses**.

In addition there is a clear distinction between those items of income and expenditure that relate to the operations of the business, and financial items arising from investments and the need to raise debt finance. Operating profit measures operating performance before deducting the costs relating to finance.

The net profit of a company is appropriated in three ways: corporation tax (based on a percentage of taxable profit), dividends to shareholders, and the remainder retained in the business to help it grow.

Figure 2.1 Analysis of sales and profit

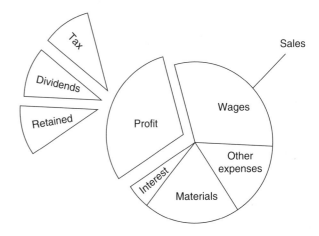

Like the balance sheet, the published profit and loss account for a company is accompanied by additional disclosures in notes to the accounts. For example, from the accounts of Tesco plc:

Tesco plc
Profit on ordinary activities is stated after charging:

	1996 £ million	1995 £ million
Employment costs:		
Wages and salaries	1 065	899
Social security costs	73	64
Other pension costs	46	38
	1 184	1 001
Depreciation	285.0	247.0
Operating lease costs	114.0	96.0
Audit	0.5	0.4

The cash flow statement

Unlike the cash budget which is used to assess future financing needs, the published cash flow statement of companies is concerned with reviewing past cash movements. The cash flow statement shows the ability of the business to generate cash flows and gives a fresh insight into the quality of profits earned and the ability of the business to remain solvent.

The basic format of the cash flow statement

	£'000	£'000
Net cash inflow from operating activities		500
Returns on investment and servicing of finance:		
Dividend paid	−200	
Interest received:	100	−100
Taxation		−100
Investing activities:		
Purchase of tangible fixed assets	−200	
Proceeds on sale of tangible fixed assets	50	−150
Net cash inflow before financing		150
Financing		
Bank loan repaid		−100
Increase in cash and cash equivalents		50

All figures relate to actual cash flows and are unaffected by adjustments made in the profit and loss account to comply with the matching concept. They correspond closely to the main cash cycles described in Chapter 1.

Net cash inflow (outflow) from operating activities relates to actual cash receipts from customers less revenue payments to employees and suppliers of revenue goods and services. **Returns on investment and servicing of finance** are revenue receipts and payments relating to financial items, including interest and dividends. **Taxation** relates to corporation tax. **Investing activities** are the cash flows for the purchase or sale of assets whether tangible, intangible or investments. This section shows the extent to which cash has been invested to maintain and expand the future earnings capacity of the business. **Financing** shows how the financing needs of the business have been met, for example share issues or new leases.

Change in cash and cash equivalents is the total of all the above cash flows resulting in a movement on cash holdings or cash equivalents. Cash equivalents include short term investments and debt.

Inter-relationship of financial reports

The three financial reports described so far come from the same base information. The balance sheet is concerned with balances at a point in time. The profit and loss account and cash flow statements are concerned with describing how the profit and cash balances have changed over the accounting period.

Figure 2.2 Inter-relationship of financial reports

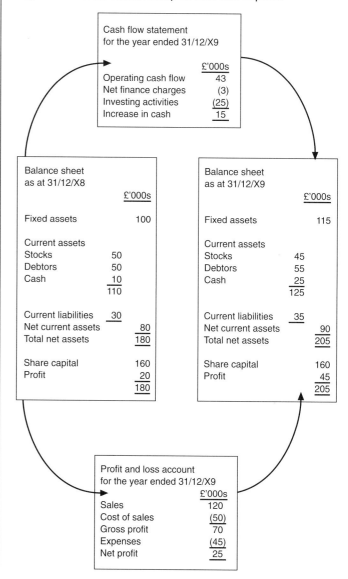

Interpretation of accounts

The process used to evaluate financial statements should identify the significant issues affecting financial performance. A valuable overview of company performance can be obtained simply by reading the annual report containing the company accounts, and comparing the current year's results with those of the previous year. However, the use of accounting ratios provides the financial analyst with a scientific approach that can use a number of benchmarks against which to measure performance.

Absolute money values are of little use unless they are set in the context in which they arose. For example, all other things being equal, financial performance will be improved if wage costs can be reduced. But businesses are not equal – as demonstrated by the wage bill at W H Smith, which is far greater than that for a small newsagent chain. Only by comparing costs with some measure of business activity, such as the level of sales, can an opinion be formed concerning *relative* financial performance.

An **accounting ratio** compares the value of one item with that of another. For example, a retailer who buys an item for £25 and then sells it for £50 enjoys a gross profit to sales ratio of 50 per cent (£25/£50) on that product line. This gross profit per cent can be evaluated by comparison with appropriate benchmarks, for example ratios relating to:

- *a previous period* – is performance improving or deteriorating?
- *budget* – to compare actual performance with expected performance
- *a similar business* – to show relative performance
- *different divisions of the same firm* – to show responsibility for performance
- *different product lines or different markets of the same firm* – to identify the most lucrative activities in which to deploy financial resources.

Investment ratios

The use of investment ratios will be illustrated using the results of Tesco plc (food retailer) and Oasis plc (fashion retailer).

	Tesco Year to 24 February 96 £'000	Oasis Year to 27 January 96 £'000
Operating profit	718 000	8 991
Interest receivable	63 000	906
Interest payable	−106 000	−30
Profit on ordinary activities before tax	675 000	9 867
Tax	209 000	3 811
Profit for the financial year	466 000	6 056
Dividends	206 000	1 799
Retained profit	260 000	4 257
Average number of shares	2 095 million	52.5 million
Dividend paid per share	9.6 p	3.33 p
Share price at 23 August 1996	311.5 p	383.0 p

From a business owner's perspective a very important measure of financial performance is the relationship of profits earned to the amount invested in the equity of the business. Just as a bank or building society account can be compared on the basis of interest rates, companies can be compared on the basis of their **earnings yield**. For a company with shares quoted on a stock exchange this is calculated by comparing business profits to the share price.

$$\text{Earnings yield} = \frac{\text{Earnings per share}}{\text{Share price}} \times 100\%$$

where:

Earnings per share

$$= \frac{\text{Net profit (after tax and preference dividend)}}{\text{Average number of ordinary shares}}$$

	Tesco	Oasis
Earnings per share (pence)	22.2	11.5
Earnings yield (%)	7.1	3.0

Tesco's earnings yield is more than double that of Oasis. On the basis of current profits Tesco, therefore, looks the more attractive investment.

The same figures are often inverted to calculate the price–earnings (PE) ratio, which in simple terms represents how many years it will take current profits to pay back the share price.

$$\text{Price–earnings (PE) ratio} = \frac{\text{Market price of share}}{\text{Earnings per share}}$$

	Tesco	Oasis
Price earnings ratio	14.0	33.3

The share price and price–earnings ratio for quoted companies are regularly listed in the *Financial Times*. Oasis' PE ratio is higher than that for Tesco because the ratio is calculated with reference to historical profits. The financial markets clearly perceive that Oasis will increase its profits at a greater rate than Tesco in future years. Tesco is profitable but is operating in a fiercely competitive marketplace where overall growth will be limited. Oasis, on the other hand, is a fairly new company with a product that has been well received by young, fashion-conscious consumers. Although there is competition, Oasis has plenty of scope for expansion in the UK and is also actively extending its operations into Europe and the Far East.

A high PE ratio shows market confidence in a company's future growth prospects. An investor will buy shares in a company that apparently has a low PE ratio in relation to its earnings growth potential. As more investors take the same view, the share price will rise, so the PE ratio will become comparable to other companies with the same growth potential.

Exercise 2.1 PE ratios

Using a recent copy of the *Financial Times,* ascertain the PE ratios for the following companies: Barclays Bank, ICI, PowerGen, Tate and Lyle, BSkyB, Next, British Airways and Anglian Water.

With regard to the companies' respective industry sectors, suggest possible reasons for the differences in their PE ratios.

Earnings yield includes profits retained in the business but some investors are particularly interested in the **dividend yield** because they require a certain level of regular income from their investments.

$$\text{Dividend yield} = \frac{\text{Gross dividend per share}}{\text{Market price of share}} \times 100\%$$

where:

$$\text{Gross dividend per share} = \text{Net dividend} \times \frac{100}{80} \times 100\%$$

Note:

Dividends are paid net of tax and are received by shareholders accompanied by a tax credit currently calculated at 20 per cent of the gross dividend. The 100/80 adjustment to gross up dividends allows investors to compare the dividend yield with other investment opportunities, with returns stated in gross terms.

	Tesco	Oasis
Dividend per share (pence)	12.0	4.1625
Dividend yield (%)	3.9	1.1

Tesco provides a dividend yield similar to that earned on some savings accounts and is therefore appropriate for those investors looking for a reasonable income level. Oasis gives a low dividend yield partly because its growth potential has inflated the current share price. However, Oasis is also pursuing a financing strategy based on retained profits to fund its expansion plans. The proportion of profits distributed as dividends is measured by the **dividend cover** ratio.

$$\text{Dividend cover} = \frac{\text{Net profit (after tax and interest before dividends)}}{\text{Dividends}}$$

	Tesco	Oasis
Dividend cover	2.3	3.4

Profits exceed dividends by 2.3 times for Tesco and 3.4 times for Oasis. A company that has few opportunities to expand should be returning a high proportion of profit to shareholders and this gives a low dividend cover. However, the ratio is also a measure of risk attached to the current dividend payout. Tesco shareholders can be reassured that their 3.9 per cent income is covered more than twice by available profits. Profits would have to fall by a large amount before the company had to reduce its dividend payout.

Management ratios

Management's attention should be focused on those aspects of the business that impinge on shareholder wealth. Management ratios are relevant to the operations of the business and provide the conceptual framework to support investors expectations.

Management uses the capital actually paid into the business, not the current market capitalisation. For example the market value (share price × number of shares) of Oasis plc on 23 August 1996 was £200.9 million compared with total shareholder funds of £15.4 million in the balance sheet.

	Tesco at 24 February 96 £'000	Oasis at 27 January 96 £'000
Share capital	108 000	5 246
Other reserves	1 423 000	0
Profit and loss account	2 057 000	10 148
	3 588 000	15 394

The share price is the transfer value from one owner to another and does not affect the business directly. The remaining £185.5 million is the amount of wealth created for shareholders by an increase in the share price – reflecting goodwill not recorded in the company's accounting records. As a tool to monitor the management's effective use of the funds actually entrusted to them, management performance is more appropriately measured by comparing profitability with the balance sheet equity balance.

Return on ordinary shareholder funds

$$= \frac{\text{Net profit before tax (after pref. div.)}}{\text{Ordinary shares and reserves}} \times 100\%$$

	Tesco	Oasis
Return on shareholder funds =	$\frac{675\,000}{3\,588\,000} \times 100\%$	$\frac{9\,867}{15\,394} \times 100\%$
	18.8%	64.1%

Although Tesco makes a very acceptable return, clearly the outstanding figures for Oasis reflects the considerable market potential for its products and store format.

By using other sources of finance, management are able to increase the capital they employ in the business. The effective use of this enlarged capital base can be measured by comparing profits before interest charges to total capital employed.

$$\text{Return on capital employed (ROCE)} = \frac{\text{Operating profit}}{\text{Capital employed}} \times 100\%$$

where

Capital employed

= Shareholders funds + Borrowings – Cash not used

	Tesco at 24 February 96 £'000	Oasis at 27 January 96 £'000
Shareholder funds	3 588 000	15 394
Borrowings (including loans, bank overdrafts, HP, leases and debentures)		
Creditors due within one year	335 000	
Creditors due after more than one year	570 000	
Less cash balance	–38 000	–7 698
Total capital employed	4 455 000	7 696

		Tesco	Oasis
Return on capital employed (ROCE)	=	$\frac{718000}{4455000} \times 100\%$	$\frac{8991}{7696} \times 100\%$
	=	16.1%	116.8%

ROCE is considered the primary measure of operating performance. The ROCE for Oasis is considerably higher than the return on shareholders funds because the company has actually used less capital in its operations than it has available to invest. Whereas Tesco is in a net debt situation, Oasis has net cash. But for Oasis' shareholders the £7.7 million excess funds have earned them relatively little interest compared to profits from operating activities. It is in their interest for the cash to be invested in more shops sooner rather than later.

Subsidiary ratios

When analysing the return on capital employed, a pyramid structure of subsidiary ratios can show how profit has been generated and how the capital employed has been used (see Figure 2.3).

Figure 2.3 Profitability ratios

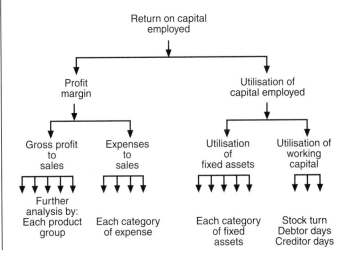

The return on capital employed is a function of two items: profit and capital employed. The ratio may change because of a change in one or both of these items, for example a fall in ROCE may be the result of a fall in profits and/or an increase in capital employed.

To examine the mechanics of the ROCE ratio, consider the following example, which is illustrated in Figure 2.4.

Illustration

A business with turnover of £100 and capital employed of £200 currently generates a profit of £50. From this information the return (£50) on capital employed (£200) is 25 per cent. However, the same result has also been achieved by another firm in the same line of business which has doubled its sales volume by reducing its selling price by £25 (assuming unit costs and capital employed are also the same).

Figure 2.4 ROCE for two firms

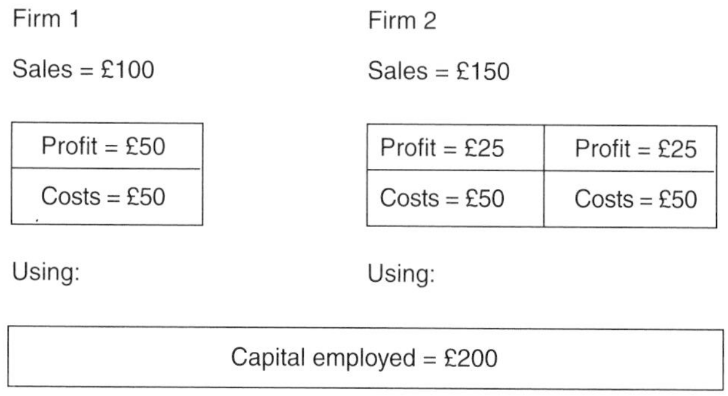

Firm 1

Sales = £100

| Profit = £50 |
| Costs = £50 |

Using:

Firm 2

Sales = £150

| Profit = £25 | Profit = £25 |
| Costs = £50 | Costs = £50 |

Using:

| Capital employed = £200 |

Despite having the same ROCE, the businesses have achieved the result using different marketing strategies. One has tried to protect high profit margins, the other has followed a 'pile them high, sell them cheap' strategy. Both are of course valid marketing approaches and businesses do use price levels as part of a strategy to increase profitability. The crucial point is that if prices are reduced, sales volumes must be increased to make the same financial return. Ratio analysis can be used to measure the effect of changes in profit margin and sales volume on ROCE.

The profit margin measures operating profit as a proportion of sales:

$$\text{Profit margin} = \frac{\text{Operating profit}}{\text{Sales}} \times 100\%$$

Utilisation of capital employed is a measure of business activity in relation to the capital employed:

$$\frac{\text{Utilisation of}}{\text{capital employed}} = \frac{\text{Sales}}{\text{Average capital employed}}$$

For the example above:

	Firm 1	Firm 2
Profit margin	50%	33.3%
Utilisation of capital employed	0.5	0.75
Return on capital employed	25%	25%

The relationship between these two ratios and ROCE can be confirmed by stating:

Return on capital
= Profit margin × Utilisation of capital employed,

i.e. 25 per cent in both cases.

In this example, different marketing strategies were used to achieve the same financial result, a return on capital employed of 25 per cent. Businesses should strive to maximise the return on capital employed by finding the optimum mix of unit profitability and capital utilisation.

Exercise 2.2 ROCE and subsidiary ratios

Complete the matrix of ratios for the following firms:

Firm	Return on capital employed	Profit margin	Utilisation of capital employed
A	?	6%	3.5
B	30%	20%	?
C	25%	?	5.0
D	?	15%	1.6
E	20%	?	2.50
F	8%	10%	?

Case study

Tesco plc and Kwiksave Group plc

Both Tesco and Kwiksave are large retailers operating in the fiercely competitive food sector.

Kwiksave's annual accounts for its financial year to 26 August 1995 showed on operating profit of £134.1 million on a turnover of £3 228.1 million. Shareholders' funds amounted to £435.5 million, debt was £48.4 million and cash £19.5 million.

Tesco's annual accounts for its financial year to 24 February 1996 showed an operating profit of £718 million on a turnover of £12 094 million. Capital employed was £4 455 million.

Tasks

1 *Calculate Kwiksave's capital employed.*
2 *Calculate for each company: ROCE, profit margin and utilisation of capital employed.*
3 *Evaluate the relative financial performance of the two companies.*

Illustration

The most commonly used management ratios will now be demonstrated using the accounts of Magenta plc. The financial statements have been prepared for internal purposes, and are not in a form suitable for publication.

Magenta plc
Profit and loss account
for the year ended 31 December 19X2

	Year 2 (£'000)		Year 1 (£'000)	
Sales:		5 850		5 525
Opening stock	545		525	
Purchases	4 088		3 611	
	4 633		4 136	
Closing stock	655		545	
Cost of sales		3 978		3 591
Gross profit		1 872		1 934
Distribution costs		540		510
Administration expenses		890		725
Operating profit		442		699
Interest paid		220		205
Profit before taxation		222		494
Taxation		70		150
Profit after tax		152		344
Dividends		100		150
Retained profit		52		194

Magenta plc
Balance sheet
as at 31 December 19X2

	Year 2 (£'000)		Year 1 (£'000)	
Fixed assets		3 987		3 545
Current assets				
Stocks	655		545	
Trade debtors	710		672	
Cash	0		50	
	1 365		1 267	
Creditors due within one year				
Trade creditors	423		345	
Bank overdraft	410		0	
	833		345	
Net current assets		532		922
		4 519		4 467
Creditors due in more than one year				
Debentures		2 000		2 000
		2 519		2 467
Share capital		500		500
Profit and loss account		2 019		1 967
		2 519		2 467

Cash flow statement extract:

	Year 2	Year 1
Operating cash flow	772	923

Before calculating the accounting ratios it is worth scanning the financial statements for major changes or differences to ensure the analysis has some focus. Some features to note from these accounts are that:

1 profits have fallen despite higher sales;
2 the bank balance has gone from being an asset to a substantial overdraft.

The evaluation should address both these issues.

Solution

$$\text{Return on capital employed (ROCE)} = \frac{\text{Operating profit}}{\text{Capital employed}} \times 100\%$$

ROCE for Magenta plc:

	Year 2	Year 1
Return on capital employed	$=\dfrac{442}{(2\,519 + 2\,000 + 410)} \times 100\%$	$\dfrac{699}{(2\,467 + 2\,000 - 50)} \times 100\%$
	$= \quad 9.0\%$	15.8%

The return on capital employed has deteriorated markedly in year 2. A fall in profits and an increase in capital employed have both contributed to the deterioration in Magenta's ROCE.

Profit margin ratios

$$\text{Profit margin} = \frac{\text{Operating profit}}{\text{Sales}} \times 100\%$$

	Year 2	Year 1
Profit margin	7.6%	12.7%

A 5.1 per cent fall in profit margin for Magenta plc is very significant and should be analysed using further profitability ratios.

Most businesses should expect to make **gross profit to sales** of 40–60 per cent if they are to make a profit after paying for other expenses. Lower gross profits may be satisfactory if the business achieves high sales volumes.

$$\text{Gross profit to sales} = \frac{\text{Gross profit}}{\text{Sales}} \times 100\%$$

	Year 2	Year 1
Gross profit to sales =	32.0%	35.0%

Over half of the drop in profit margin is accounted for by a 3 per cent fall in gross profits. This could either be due to a fall in selling prices or an increase in unit costs. The reasons should be ascertained by further analysis, which should perhaps also consider the gross profit percentage for individual product lines and market segments.

The **expenses to sales** ratios can be calculated for total expenses, a functional breakdown of expenses and by individual expense heading, e.g. wages to sales.

$$\text{Expenses to sales} = \frac{\text{Expenses}}{\text{Sales}} \times 100\%$$

	Year 2	Year 1
Distribution costs to sales	9.2%	9.2%
Administration expenses to sales	15.2%	13.1%

The ratio of administration expenses to sales has increased by 2.1 per cent during year 2. Further investigation should identify the reasons for the increase in expenditure and identify whether the increase was a one-off item or a factor that should be controlled in the future.

The 5.1 per cent fall in profit margin can now be broken down into 3.0 per cent arising from gross profit and 2.1 per cent from administration expenses. This is despite there being good reason to expect the profit margin to rise as sales increase. Where some cost items, such as rent, remain stable in absolute terms, an increase in sales means that some costs become a smaller proportion of sales. It follows that for Magenta plc, either selling prices actually fell in year 2 or some costs rose by an amount that could not be passed onto customers.

Utilisation of capital

Utilisation of capital employed

$$= \frac{\text{Sales}}{\text{Average capital employed}}$$

		Year 2	Year 1
Utilisation of capital employed	=	$\dfrac{5\,850}{4\,929}$	$\dfrac{5\,525}{4\,417}$
	=	1.19	1.25

Wherever possible, the figures used should be for the average capital employed. These may be either simple averages or averages based on monthly figures. Where averages cannot be calculated for all sets of accounts being analysed, it is important to be consistent and use year-end balances for both periods. Despite an increase in sales in absolute terms, Magenta's sales have grown by less than the increase in capital employed, resulting in a 4.8 per cent fall in utilisation. Reasons should be sought and corrective action taken if necessary. One step in the investigative process is to calculate further ratios for the items constituting capital employed.

$$\text{Utilisation of fixed assets} = \frac{\text{Sales}}{\text{Average fixed assets}}$$

		Year 2	Year 1
Utilisation of fixed assets	$=$	$\dfrac{5850}{3987}$	$\dfrac{5525}{3545}$
	$=$	1.47	1.56

An increase in fixed assets should be accompanied by a proportionate increase in sales but for Magenta the utilisation rate has fallen. Perhaps expenditure was required for non-revenue earning assets, such as those required to conform to health and safety regulations. Another possibility is that the extra capacity has yet to be fully utilised, suggesting possible future growth.

The use of net current assets can be examined by performing the following calculation for the utilisation of working capital.

Utilisation of working capital =

$$\frac{\text{Sales}}{\text{Average net current assets (excluding debt and cash)}}$$

		Year 2	Year 1
Utilisation of working capital	$=$	$\dfrac{5850}{(532+410)}$	$\dfrac{5525}{(922-50)}$
	$=$	6.21	6.34

A slight decline in the utilisation of working capital has occurred although it is not significant. It might still be useful, however, to look at individual items within working capital in case poor control of one item has been masked by tighter control on another.

In general, the greater the level of business activity, the greater the level of stocks needed to service customer demand. **Stock turn** measures the efficiency of stock control.

$$\text{Stock turn} = \frac{\text{Annual cost of sales}}{\text{Average stock}}$$

The resulting ratio indicates how many times a year the stock balance is turned over.

		Year 2	Year 1
Stock turn for Magenta	$=$	$\dfrac{3978}{(545+655)/2}$	$\dfrac{3591}{(525-545)/2}$
$=$		6.63 times per year	6.71 times per year

To find the average amount of time taken to sell a stock item, divide 365 days by the stock turn. This gives 55.1 days for year 2 and 54.4 days for year 1. There has been a slight fall in stock turnover.

A calculation of **debtor days** measures the average credit period taken by customers to pay their debts. For the external analyst it is not always possible to determine the value of sales on credit, in which case a general measure of credit extended to customers could be calculated based on total sales. Care must also be taken when extracting the debtor figure from the accounts. The term **trade debtors** relates specifically to credit sales and this can be found in a note to the accounts if it is not on the face of the balance sheet itself. It is preferable to use an average debtor balance to minimise the risk of using an unrepresentative figure. Unfortunately there is insufficient information for Magenta plc to calculate an average for both years, so for consistency the calculations are based on the year end debtor balances.

$$\text{Debtor days} = \frac{\text{Average trade debtors}}{\text{Credit sales}} \times 365 \text{ days}$$

		Year 2	Year 1
Debtor days $=$		$\dfrac{710}{5850} \times 365 \text{ days}$	$\dfrac{672}{5525} \times 365 \text{ days}$
	$=$	44.3 days	44.4 days

Standard credit terms for many industries are in the range of 30–60 days so these figures do not look unreasonable. A final judgement should be based on an aged debtor analysis, as average debtor days do not highlight problems on individual customer accounts. Average debtor days should also be compared with industry norms to ensure funds are not unnecessarily tied up in debtor balances.

A **creditor days** analysis will show to what extent the firm uses suppliers to finance its business. Supplier credit should be maximised where possible because trade credit is free provided no settlement discounts are lost. As with debtor days, care should be taken to ensure the information extracted from the accounts results in correct and consistent calculations for both periods. For Magenta, period end balances will have to suffice again.

$$\text{Creditor days} = \frac{\text{Average trade creditors}}{\text{Credit purchases}} \times 365 \text{ days}$$

	Year 2	Year 1
Creditor days $= $	$\dfrac{423}{4\,088} \times 365$ days	$\dfrac{345}{3\,611} \times 365$ days
$=$	37.8 days	34.9 days

Magenta appears to be taking a little longer to pay its suppliers and this will have helped to keep working capital levels down. Magenta's suppliers would probably wish to confirm that this is a result of tight financial control rather than a sign of cash flow problems, particularly as the firm is now running a large bank overdraft.

Solvency ratios

The **current ratio** is a measure of financial liquidity. It compares liabilities that are payable in the near future with cash and other short term assets.

$$\text{Current or working capital ratio} = \frac{\text{Current assets}}{\text{Current liabilities}}$$

		Year 2	Year 1
Current or working capital ratio	$=$	$\dfrac{1\,365}{833}$	$\dfrac{1\,267}{345}$
	$=$	1.64	3.67

Businesses must have sufficient resources to pay short-term liabilities, and so a ratio of around 2 is often recommended. However, this is an arbitrary figure and some financially strong businesses have ratios that are significantly less. For example, the current ratio for Tesco plc as at 24 February 1996 was only 0.37. The food retailers have relatively low stocks and debtors, but enjoy strong and stable cash flows from which to pay current liabilities. Clearly different industries can justify different ratios. However, for Magenta plc, the fall in the value of the ratio from 3.67 to 1.64 is of real concern and measures need to be taken to halt a further decline.

The **acid** or **quick test ratio** is a more stringent test of liquidity than the current ratio as it excludes stocks from the calculation. Stocks are less liquid than other current assets because they have to be sold before money can be collected (perhaps on credit terms) and so may not provide funds soon enough to repay short-term liabilities.

$$\text{Acid or quick test ratio} = \frac{\text{Current assets} - \text{stock}}{\text{Current liabilities}}$$

		Year 2	Year 1
Acid or quick test ratio	$=$	$\dfrac{710}{833}$	$\dfrac{722}{345}$
	$=$	0.85	2.09

Like the current ratio, an appropriate quick ratio will depend upon the type of business. A ratio of 0.85 is therefore not of particular concern in itself; what is more worrying is the fact that the ratio has more than halved during year 2. It is a symptom of the reversal of the cash balance into a bank overdraft.

The **operating cash to operating profit ratio** demonstrates a firm's ability to turn profits into cash. Profits combined with strong operating cash flow are considered to be better quality than mere book profits as the business is less likely to run into liquidity problems. An expanding business with a low operating cash to operating profit ratio (because of an increase in working capital) can actually run into cash flow problems (see 'Overtrading' in Chapter 1).

$$\text{Operating cash to operating profit} = \frac{\text{Operating cash}}{\text{Operating profit}}$$

A business with stable sales should achieve a ratio in excess of 1, depending on the amount of depreciation charged in operating profit. A capital-intensive business will certainly require a ratio in excess of 1 if it is to generate sufficient funds to invest in new fixed assets.

		Year 2	Year 1
Operating cash to operating profit	$=$	$\dfrac{722}{442}$	$\dfrac{923}{699}$
	$=$	1.75	1.32

An improving operating cash ratio confirms that changes in working capital are not the reason for the Magenta's deteriorating cash balance.

Comparing short-term liabilities to operating cash flow shows how long it would take the business to repay current debts (solvency days).

$$\text{Solvency days} = \frac{\text{Creditors due within one year}}{\text{Operating cash}} \times 365 \text{ days}$$

		Year 2	Year 1
Solvency days	$=$	$\dfrac{833}{772} \times 365$ days	$\dfrac{345}{923} \times 365$ days
	$=$	394 days	136 days

At the current rate of cash generation, it would take Magenta 394 days just to clear the debts that are due within one year, assuming the bank overdraft had to be repaid. Of course, in reality the business will be afforded ongoing credit by its suppliers and the bank is unlikely to insist on a repayment of the overdraft unless the business did get into serious financial difficulties. However, the deterioration in solvency days does confirm the company's growing liquidity problems.

The results of the Magenta analysis in summary

Magenta's return on capital employed has fallen principally as a result of a drop in profits. This has arisen because of a fall in gross profit and an increase in administration expenses. The sizeable bank overdraft has occurred because the capital employed has increased from £4 417k to £4 929k with no other finance being raised other than the £52k retained profits for the year. Most of the increase in capital employed is the result of a significant investment in fixed assets. To improve the situation, management must improve profitability without increasing capital employed in the coming year. With no further information to suggest otherwise, tight control of costs and capital expenditure would appear appropriate. Cash forecasts may indicate that additional longer term finance is required to ensure the firm is not reliant on the bank overdraft.

Summary of accounting ratios:

	Calculation	Measure	Preferred level
Investment ratios Earnings yield	$\dfrac{\text{Earnings per share}}{\text{Share price}} \times 100\%$	Per cent	High
Earnings per share	$\dfrac{\text{Net profit (after tax and preference dividend)}}{\text{Number of ordinary shares}}$	Pence	High
Price earnings (P/E) ratio	$\dfrac{\text{Market price of share}}{\text{Earnings per share}}$	Number	High
Dividend yield	$\dfrac{\text{Dividend per share (gross)}}{\text{Market price of share}} \times 100\%$	Per cent	High
Dividend cover	$\dfrac{\text{Net profit (after tax and interest, before dividends)}}{\text{Dividends}}$	Number	High
Gearing ratio	$\dfrac{\text{Preference share} + \text{debt} - \text{cash at bank}}{\text{Equity}}$	Number	Less than 1
Interest cover	$\dfrac{\text{Profit (before interest and tax)}}{\text{Interest payable for year}}$	Number	High

	Calculation	Measure	Preferred level
Primary management ratios Return on ordinary shareholders' funds	$\dfrac{\text{Net profit before taxation (less pref. div.)}}{\text{Average equity}} \times 100\%$	Per cent	High
Return on capital employed (ROCE)	$\dfrac{\text{Operating profit}}{\text{Average capital employed}} \times 100\%$	Per cent	High

	Calculation	Measure	Preferred level
Profitability ratios			
Profit margin	$\dfrac{\text{Operating profit}}{\text{Sales}} \times 100\,\%$	Per cent	High
Gross profit to sales	$\dfrac{\text{Gross profit}}{\text{Sales}} \times 100\,\%$	Per cent	High
Expenses to sales (in total and by expense type)	$\dfrac{\text{Expenses}}{\text{Sales}} \times 100\,\%$	Per cent	Low

Utilisation of resources			
Utilisation of capital employed	$\dfrac{\text{Sales}}{\text{Average capital employed}}$	Number	High
Utilisation of fixed assets	$\dfrac{\text{Sales}}{\text{Average fixed assets}}$	Number	High
Utilisation of working capital	$\dfrac{\text{Sales}}{\text{Average net current assets}}$	Number	High
Debtor days	$\dfrac{\text{Average trade debtors}}{\text{Credit sales}} \times 365$	Days	Low
Creditor days	$\dfrac{\text{Average trade creditors}}{\text{Credit purchases}} \times 365$	Days	High
Stock turn	$\dfrac{\text{Average cost of sales}}{\text{Average stock}}$	Number	High

Liquidity ratios			
Current or working capital ratio	$\dfrac{\text{Current assets}}{\text{Current liabilities}}$	Number	Usually 2 or more
Acid or quick test ratio	$\dfrac{\text{Current assets} - \text{stock}}{\text{Current liabilities}}$	Number	Usually 1 or more
Operating cash to operating profit	$\dfrac{\text{Operating cash}}{\text{Operating profit}}$	Number	High
Solvency days	$\dfrac{\text{Creditors due within one year}}{\text{Operating cash}} \times 365$	Days	Low

Information is rarely complete, so it is important that ratios are calculated consistently. It may not be possible to use the precise ratios planned because similar information is not available for all periods or for all businesses being compared. For example, see the debtor and creditor calculations for Magenta.

Exercise 2.3 Ratio analysis

The financial statements below are the latest results of two companies, Alpha Ltd and Beta Ltd. One company is a food retailer, the other an engineering firm.

Profit and loss accounts

	Alpha ('000)	Beta (£'000)
Sales	1 200	1 300
Cost of sales	930	600
Gross profit	270	700
Distribution costs	80	200
Administration expenses	40	200
Profit before taxation	150	300
Taxation	50	100
Profit after tax	100	200
Dividends	50	75
Retained profit	50	125

Balance sheets

	Alpha (£'000)	Beta (£'000)
Fixed assets	250	325
Current assets		
Stocks	60	120
Trade debtors	5	210
Cash	10	20
	75	350
Creditors due within one year	50	90
Net current assets	25	260
	275	585
Share capital	100	200
Profit and loss account	175	385
	275	585

Tasks

1 *You are required to calculate the following accounting ratios:*
   - *return on capital employed*
   - *profit margin*
   - *utilisation of capital employed*
   - *gross profit margin*
   - *stock turnover*
   - *debtor days.*
2 *Identify, using the ratios you have calculated, which business is the food retailer and which the engineering firm.*

Exercise 2.4 Ratio analysis

The management of Silton Sand and Gravels are concerned about the company's recent decline in financial performance. They had hoped to finish the year with £300 000 in the bank so that they could buy replacement plant in 19X7 without resorting to bank borrowing.

Task

Evaluate Silton's profitability and solvency for the year ended 31 December 19X6.

The following financial information has been prepared by the firm's accountant.

Silton Sand and Gravels
Profit and loss account
for the year ended 31/12/X6

| | Actual | | Budget | | Actual | |
	19X6 £'000s	19X6 £'000s	19X6 £'000s	19X6 £'000s	19X5 £'000s	19X5 £'000s
Sales		3 250		3 500		3 100
Cost of sales		1 625		1 700		1 600
Gross profit		1 625		1 800		1 500
Depreciation	200		210		190	
Salaries and wages	780		720		650	
Hire of plant	325		305		245	
Bad debts	150		50		45	
Other expenses	125		125		100	
Total expenses		1 580		1 410		1 230
Net profit		45		390		270

Silton Sand and Gravels
Balance sheet
as at 31/12/X6

| | Actual | | Budget | | Actual | |
	19X6 £'000s	19X6 £'000s	19X6 £'000s	19X6 £'000s	19X5 £'000s	19X5 £'000s
Fixed assets		1 200		1 250		1 100
Current assets						
Stocks	360		450		420	
Debtors	390		300		350	
Bank and cash	70		285		100	
	820		1 035		870	
Creditors due within one year						
Trade creditors	280		200		275	
Net current assets		540		835		595
		1 740		2 085		1 695
Share capital		1 000		1 000		1 000
Profit and loss account		740		1 085		695
		1 740		2 085		1 695

The following accounting ratios are averages for the industry.

Return on capital employed	21.0%
Gross profit to sales	50.0%
Profit margin	12.0%
Utilisation of capital employed	1.75

Segmental reporting

There can be problems in interpreting the financial performance of companies involved in more than one type of business and/or which operate in more than one geographical area. From the profit and loss account it is possible to determine the average profit margin on each £1 of sales, but different parts of the business may achieve significantly different results. The *Companies Act 1989* requires a segmental analysis of business performance for turnover and profit before taxation. For public companies and the larger private limited companies, Statement of Standard Accounting Practice 25 requires separate disclosure for each market or class of business in respect of the following:

- turnover
- profit before taxation (and before interest if this is difficult to allocate to the segments)
- net assets.

A segment is a class of business or a geographical area. A geographical analysis shows the places in the world from which the company operates (analysis by origin).

Turnover must additionally be analysed by the geographical markets supplied (analysis by destination) if this is different. The analysis shows users of the accounts the relative sizes, performance and risk of the company's various business activities.

The categories used to analyse the business activities are a matter of judgement for the company. The overriding factor is to ensure that the users of the accounts are fully able to appreciate the implications of a number of major influences:

- the rates of return on investment
- the past growth and potential for future development
- the degree of risk
- the nature of the supply of goods or services
- the organisation of the company's activities
- the markets served and the channels of distribution.

The geographical analysis provides an insight into the external environment including:

- the economic climate
- the stability and nature of political regimes
- foreign currency exchange rate fluctuations and foreign exchange control regulations.

Case study in segmental reporting

First Leisure Corporation plc

First Leisure operates a wide ranges of leisure facilities for which it provides segmental reporting. Its activities are described under the following headings:

- *dancing* – night clubs
- *sports* – Super Bowls, Arena One, health and fitness suites, snooker and pool halls
- *resorts* – Blackpool Tower and Central Pier, Brannigans music bar, Trecco Bay Caravan Park
- *bingo* – Riva Clubs
- *theatres* – landlord for two West End theatres that generate no trading turnover but do contribute to operating profit.

The company's financial results for the four years to 1995 were as follows:

	Year to 31.10.95 (£m)	Year to 31.10.94 (£m)	Year to 31.10.93 (£m)	Year to 31.10.92 (£m)
Turnover:				
Resorts	44.6	45.7	41.9	40.1
Dancing	57.1	50.1	44.5	38.2
Sports	41.5	36.2	32.1	30.2
Bingo	15.5	9.8	3.3	0
	158.7	141.8	121.8	108.5
Operating profit:				
Resorts	12.2	12.9	11.7	12.3
Dancing	20.4	17.3	14.5	12.5
Sports	13.1	11.2	13.7	14.1
Bingo	2.5	2.8	0.9	0
Theatres	0.6	0.6	0.4	0.2
Administration expenses and misc. items	−8.7	−7.3	−5.9	−5.8
	40.1	37.5	35.3	33.3

	Year to 31.10.95 (£m)	Year to 31.10.94 (£m)	Year to 31.10.93 (£m)	Year to 31.10.92 (£m)
Net assets:				
Resorts	90.5	82.8	84.9	106.7
Dancing	80.1	77.6	71.7	100.9
Sports	90.3	89.1	82.0	89.5
Bingo	34.7	19.5	13.5	0
Theatres	7.4	7.1	6.7	6.4
Administration	7.6	6.1	4.1	3.6
	310.6	282.2	262.9	307.1

First Leisure started 1996 with an aggressive expansion plan. Organic growth was to be funded from operating cash flow, and with gearing set at just 18 per cent, from borrowing facilities if required. Investment programmes were (i) to build on the strength in the Dancing and Bingo divisions; (ii) to open more health and fitness centres; and (iii) to export the format of Blackpool's Brannigans music bar to other parts of the country.

Tasks

1 Calculate the following financial ratios for each segment of the business (excluding theatres): return on capital employed, utilisation of net assets and profit margin.
2 Analyse trends and evaluate the financial performance of the different segments.
3 How can these accounting ratios be used for appraising an expansion proposal?

Business changes

Where businesses have undergone significant changes in business activities, Financial Reporting Standard 3 requires an analysis of the items making up operating profit. The analysis must show how operating profit can be attributed to continuing and discontinuing activities. Where activities have been discontinued, the comparative figures for the previous year must be restated to show the earlier performance of those activities.

In addition, items of exceptional size or type also require highlighting either on the face of the profit and loss account or in a note to the accounts.

These additional disclosure requirements provide valuable information for the evaluation of financial performance. The financial analyst is now able to calculate ratios including or excluding exceptional items depending on what is considered most appropriate.

Case study

B Elliot plc

B Elliot is a medium-sized engineering company quoted on the London Stock Exchange. In November 1996 the company reported interim results showing a loss before tax of £1.1 million compared to a profit of £2.4 million in the first half of the previous year. The directors' report sounded upbeat about future prospects following plans to reorganise the company's activities.

Profit and loss account
for the 26 weeks to 29 September 1996

	1996			1995		
	Continuing ('000)	Discontinued (£'000)	Total (£'000)	Continuing (£'000)	Discontinued (£'000)	Total (£'000)
Turnover	55 618	1 028	56 646	54 326	3 314	57 640
Cost of sales	(38 301)	(1 448)	(39 749)	(37 470)	(2 749)	(40 219)
Gross profit	17 317	(420)	16 897	16,856	565	17 421
Distribution costs	(5 603)	(257)	(5 860)	(5 090)	(279)	(5 369)
Administration expenses	(8 806)	(213)	(9 019)	(8 808)	(211)	(9 019)
Operating profit	2 908	(890)	2 018	2 958	75	3 033
Exceptional item:						
Provision for loss on disposal		(2 444)	(2 444)			
Profit before interest	2 908	(3 334)	(426)	2 958	75	3 033
Financing costs, net			(716)			(609)
Profit before tax			(1 142)			2 424
Capital employed			30 905			28 503

Tasks

1 *Evaluate B Elliot's financial performance as far as the information allows.*
2 *What evidence is there to support the directors' confidence in the future?*

Narratives in annual reports

Accounts for limited companies are contained in an annual report that also includes a directors' report. It is not unusual for companies also to provide other reports, perhaps from the chairman or the managing director. These reports provide a valuable narrative to the events behind the financial figures. A commentary is often supplied, describing trading conditions and the factors affecting profit margins. Other significant events may include programmes for buying or selling fixed assets, new financing arrangements or changes in accounting policy.

Using computers

For those involved in the interpretation of accounts on a regular basis, computers can be invaluable for calculating accounting ratios. Specialist modelling programs can be used, but spreadsheets are also effective and flexible. Once a standard template has been created, subsequent sets of data need only be keyed in.

Exercise 2.5 Spreadsheet

Create a spreadsheet model to calculate a full range of accounting ratios and demonstrate its use using the published accounts of a public company.

Absolute versus relative values

For the interpretation of financial performance, accounting ratios are not infallible. Sometimes a decision that results in the deterioration of a ratio actually produces a better result in absolute terms.

As an example, a business that has a cost of capital of 10 per cent p.a. currently earns operating profits of £2 million on share capital of £10 million. An expansion to the business requiring capital of £5 million would generate an extra operating profit of £700,000.

Summary of performance

	Present £'000	Expanded £'000
Profits	2 000	2 700
Capital employed	10 000	15 000
Return on capital employed	20%	18%

Despite the return on capital employed falling by 2 per cent, the business would generate an extra £200 000 profit in excess of the minimum required by the providers of finance. This is because profits would increase by £700 000 but the cost of capital would increase by only £500 000.

It is important to be aware that in some circumstances absolute values are more important than relative ones.

Limitations of financial performance indicators

Accounting ratios are often criticised for generating a particularly mechanistic view of business. Because they are used widely by investment analysts, ratios place a greater emphasis on short-term results, where a slip in an otherwise long-term increase in earnings can be punished with a severe fall in the share price.

Whilst shareholder ratios such as earnings per share and return on capital employed are valid for measuring the efficient use of capital, they are subject to accounting conventions that could deter policies which might otherwise make commercial sense in the long run. For example, most expenditure on research and development and on staff welfare, such as training, are charged against the current year's profits even though some or all of the benefits might accrue in subsequent years. The management of companies listed on the stock market have to balance the long-term needs of the business with the short-term expectations of the stock market.

Other limitations of financial performance indicators are:

- *A lack of up to date information* – the external analyst has to use information that is at least several months old.
- *Different business activities* – the results of different businesses are difficult to compare as they rarely undertake identical activities.
- *Price inflation* – some values may have been affected more than others by changes in price levels. For example, comparisons between items in the profit and loss account which have occurred during the past year and items in the balance sheet which may have arisen many years previously will be particularly affected. Where property values are involved, comparability will be enhanced if the accounts incorporate independent asset revaluations. Otherwise the danger is for low property valuations to increase artificially the stated returns on capital employed.
- *Accounting policies* – reported profits and the value of net assets will be affected by the accounting policies

adopted by the various businesses. Where different businesses are being compared the accounts of each should be restated to be consistent on such matters as the depreciation of fixed assets, the capitalisation of research and development expenditure and the valuation of stocks.

Case study

Quality Software Products Holdings plc

Quality Software Products (QSP) made an operating profit of £1 246 295 on sales of £21 385 842 during its financial year ended 31 December 1995 (£3 234 848 and £16 494 732 in 1994). Its net assets at the end of the year were £20 735 336 (1994 – £15 028 088) which included £16 784 616 (1994 – £13 650 661) in respect of product development expenditure that had been capitalised.

During the year development costs of £6 321 105 (1994 – £5 923 281) were capitalised and added to net assets. Past development costs were amortised (depreciated) and the charge reduced profits by £3 187 150 (1994 – £2 374 575).

Tasks

1 *Calculate the following ratios for QSP based on its reported results: return on capital employed, sales utilisation of capital employed and profit margin.*
2 *Many businesses in the software industry charge product development costs against profits as they are incurred. Restate the profits and net assets of QSP on this basis.*
3 *Recalculate the ratios in (1) on these restated figures.*
4 *What are the implications of this case study for the comparison of the financial performance of different businesses?*

Summary

Financial performance is reported using four primary financial statements. The three described in this chapter were: the profit and loss account, the balance sheet and the cash flow statement. The profit and loss account and cash flow statement summarise the various transactions that have occurred during a financial year. The balance sheet is a statement of the financial affairs of the business on the last day of the financial year.

Despite their limitations, the use of accounting ratios to evaluate financial performance can be a catalyst for management action. Accounting ratios do not provide immediate answers but they do provoke searching questions that should result in tighter control and a better understanding of the business.

Further reading

Geoffrey Holmes and Alan Sugden, *Interpreting Company Reports and Accounts*, 5th edition, Prentice Hall, 1996.
Roger Oldcorn, *Company Accounts*, 3rd edition, Macmillan, 1996.
Peter Walton, *Corporate Reports: Their Interpretation and Use in Business*, 2nd edition, Stanley Thornes, 1994.
John Watts, *Accounting in the Business Environment*, 2nd edition, Pitman, 1996.

3 Needs for financial information

On completion of this chapter students should be able to:

- identify and explain the factors influencing the reporting process
- examine the needs of different user groups
- evaluate and illustrate the requirements of regulatory bodies.

Information needs

For the wide range of individuals and organisations who may be affected by a particular business, relevant information can reduce risk and maximise opportunities. The different stakeholders in the business will each have their own particular areas of concern and as a result have their own information needs. To satisfy these needs the government and other regulatory bodies impose reporting requirements on businesses. In addition, many businesses choose to provide further information voluntarily.

Owners

The interests and priorities of business owners are varied, for example sole traders and partners are more likely to be involved in the daily management of the business, so their interests may be more akin to those of an employee. It is also true that these small business owners will rely less on a formal reporting system to know how well the business is doing. However, the concerns of company shareholders as detailed below are universal to all business owners, even if they do possess informal information channels. Shareholders require information concerning:

- *profitability* – whether the business makes efficient use of resources to provide the desired financial return
- *liquidity* – whether the business has the ability to generate cash to ensure continued trading and to make dividend payments
- *state of financial affairs* – the nature of the business's assets and liabilities
- *financial structure* – the nature and value of the business's prior charge capital (e.g. preference shares and loans) in relation to equity
- *future prospects* – an evaluation of the business's future prospects, having regard to the firm's external environment and its adaptability to change.

Case study

Tobacco companies

from *Financial Times*, 24/25 August 1996

Cigarette companies are proving bad for your wealth. Profits are surging, aided by growing sales in emerging markets; but against a backdrop of legal and political threats in the US, investors are steering clear. Since the industry lost its second case two weeks ago, the Western world's big three have lost close to 20 per cent of their stock market value. Thursday's scares only confirmed tobacco's status as a pariah sector.

Legal actions against the tobacco industry usually fail, leaving the anti-smoking groups with huge legal bills. Legal history was made in Florida on 9 August 1996 when an ex-smoker received $750,000 in damages, signalling the go ahead for hundreds of similar cases.

Tasks

1 *Identify the UK companies that have exposure to the tobacco industry.*
2 *To what extent are their financial results dependent on smokers?*
3 *Informed investment decisions can clearly only be made if the nature of a firm's business is known. From the annual accounts of two public limited companies, find the descriptions of their principal trading activities. Describe the opportunities and risks arising from their respective operating environments.*

Lenders

The primary concern of **lenders** is the ability of the firm to pay interest and make repayments on the loans advanced. Although the information needs of lenders will be similar to those of owners, of particular interest will be information concerning cash flow and the relationship of outstanding debt to marketable assets.

Management

Financial information is important for the effective management of a business. Information concerning the recent past is used to monitor and control operations, and financial projections are a vital component of the decision making process.

Suppliers

Before making supplies on credit terms, a supplier should ensure that the customer's business is financially secure and that it generates sufficient cash flow to pay its creditors.

Case study

Facia

Facia, 100% owned by Sheffield businessman Mr Hinchcliffe, crashed in mid-1996 owing creditors £70 million. The Facia group of companies grew from nothing to become the UK's second largest private retailer in just two years. It acquired 850 shops at rock bottom prices, included such well-known names as Sock Shop, Freeman Hardy Willis, Salisbury, Torq, Oakland, Contessa and Red or Dead. All were ailing high street stores that the bigger public limited companies had wanted to sell off.

Previous business deals had already brought Mr Hinchcliffe to the attention of the Department of Trade and Industry but now the Serious Fraud Office are also involved. Commenting on the appointment of liquidators, the *Independent on Sunday* stated on 27 October 1996: 'It is also likely to lead to further legal action against Mr Hinchcliffe's web of private companies to recover disputed payments of more than £10 million. These include £2 million in "finders" fees for Facia's deals and a corporate jet and £430 000 of helicopter expenses to Chase Montagu, Mr Hinchcliffe's master private company.'

The first set of Facia accounts for the year ended January 1995 were due to be filed by the end of November 1995, but they remained outstanding one year later. The liquidators of Facia have indicated that ordinary creditors may receive about 10p for every £1 owed. Too little and too late for some suppliers.

Tasks

1 *Existing suppliers to the Facia shops were used to being paid when the owners included big names like Sears and Courtaulds. But even if a manufacturer had reservations about Facia, suggest why normal credit control procedures may have been allowed to lapse.*
2 *What information should creditors obtain before extending credit to a customer?*

Customers

Customers are concerned about the financial affairs of their suppliers for two main reasons:

■ where long-term trading relationships are desired, a

supplier must be able to demonstrate financial stability for the foreseeable future; however

■ high profits may be a sign of market exploitation.

The accounts of companies with dominant market positions, including those recently privatised, have their accounts analysed by consumer groups and industry watchdogs. It is difficult for businesses with a large market share to satisfy shareholder expectations without attracting attention from regulatory bodies.

Case study

Utility regulation

from *The Economist*, 24 August 1996

Together, the privatised telecoms, gas, electricity, and water industries serve 25m customers and have annual sales of £51 billion, representing 8 per cent of Britain's GDP. So it is hardly surprising that the regulators who determine what prices these industries can charge have become controversial public figures. ...

Why? The privatised utilities are hugely unpopular because they earn juicy profits. But high profits in the short term are the quid pro quo for lower prices in the long term. That is because the regulator sets the price cap at a level that should allow the utility a reasonable profit if it performs reasonably efficiently, and far bigger profits if it performs more efficiently than the regulator expects. When the regulator next reviews the price cap, the greater efficiency achieved by the firm is then taken into account, resulting in lower prices. ...

Instead of whingeing about utility profits, or regulators, both Labour and Tories ought to explain more clearly to the public how the incentives in the current system operate, so that utility profits are seen in context, rather than undermining a system that is working well.

Tasks

1 *Using press reports, describe how the financial results of a privatised utility were received by the various interested parties: the city, consumer groups, politicians and the industry regulator.*

2 *Research information provided by the utilities to show the value for money they give customers.*

Employees

Employees are concerned about job security and opportunities for personal advancement. Important sources of information for individuals and employee groups (such as unions) are financial reports that have either been published for public consumption or have been compiled as part of an employee information pack. Of particular concern will be the business's financial solvency – to maintain operations – and long-term profitability – to support progressive wage claims.

Government agencies

The government requires financial information to assess and collect taxes. The Inland Revenue is concerned about payments to employees and sub-contractors and taxes on the level of business profits. Customs and Excise monitor the value of sales and purchases that attract VAT. Financial returns are also an important source of information for the compilation of economic statistics that can help the government plan economic and industrial policy.

Figure 3.1 Information needs

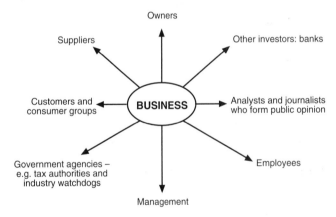

The need for regulation

Although different stakeholders' needs for financial information may be slightly different, the nature of the information required is essentially the same. It must be timely, relevant and sufficiently accurate for the evaluation of the business's financial performance and of its financial affairs. **Comparability** of the information provided will be particularly important. Users will wish to compare current financial results with the past results of the same business, in order to establish **trends**, and with results of similar businesses, in order to monitor **performance**. Without any guiding framework for the preparer of accounting information, there would be no consistency between financial statements and hence they would be of little help to the user of those statements.

In addition, because most shareholders are remote from the day-to-day activities of the business, the reporting framework must provide information to monitor whether the directors are acting in the shareholders' interests. For example, the directors own shareholdings and their salaries have to be disclosed.

It is more difficult for a business to deceive interested parties if there are rules concerning how accounts are prepared and presented. For the user of financial statements it is important that the underlying assumptions are disclosed. If accountants use the same conventions when reporting, it facilitates comparisons and meaningful conclusions; hence the need for accounting regulations.

Illustration

Julie Covy set up in business providing a taxi service in her local town. She bought a car for £12 000 and in its first year the business achieved takings of £20 000 with vehicle expenses of £4 500. How much profit has the business made?

Without some guiding principles on how to account for the cost of the car, Julie's profits could range between £15 500 and £3 500.

Regulatory influences

In the UK, regulations influencing the financial reporting of companies to external stakeholders originate primarily from two sources:

- government legislation, currently in the form of the *Companies Act 1985* as modified by the *Companies Act 1989*
- accounting standards issued by the Accounting Standards Board.

Legislation

The companies acts lay down requirements concerning:

- the content of accounts
- accounting principles
- valuation rules.

The companies acts relate to financial statements prepared for limited companies. However, members of the main accountancy bodies are under an obligation to use best accounting practice in the preparation of all accounts intended to give a 'true and fair' view of a business's trading performance and financial position. In practice this means that all business accounts are prepared according to generally accepted accounting concepts and valuation rules.

Outwardly, however, the accounts for unincorporated and incorporated organisations do look significantly different as the content rules of the companies acts have been drafted with the responsibility structure of limited companies in mind. The requirement for directors to report on their stewardship of company resources is the overriding emphasis of the disclosure rules. Within 10 months of the end of an accounting period (normally one year) for a private limited company and seven months for a public limited company, the following information must be issued:

- a balance sheet
- a profit and loss account
- a statement of total recognised gains and losses (from FRS 3)
- a cash flow statement (from FRS 1)
- 'notes to the accounts' that describe the company's accounting policies and provide an analysis of certain items contained in the financial reports
- an auditors report that confirms that the financial reports are consistent with the company's accounting records and that they do provide a 'true and fair' view of its trading performance and state of financial affairs
- a directors report that describes amongst other things the development of the business over the year and the prospects for future growth.

This information is filed with the Registrar of Companies and is available for public inspection. Failure to conform to these reporting requirements leads to financial penalties for the company and the risk of criminal prosecution for the company's directors, resulting in fines and possible disqualification.

Content of published company accounts

The law prescribes certain information that must be disclosed in the accounts of a limited company and the manner in which it must be presented. Various formats are prescribed for the presentation of the profit and loss account and balance sheet although most companies conform with 'format 1' (for detailed requirements see Chapter 10).

Directors and other employees

The directors manage the business on behalf of the shareholders and so it is important that the accounts report on matters which the directors have a personal interest. The *Companies Act 1985* requires disclosure of payments to directors and other employees.

In the case of directors the following payments should be disclosed:

■ emoluments and benefits
■ transactions in which the directors have a personal interest.

Directors' emoluments (salaries and benefits) should clearly distinguish between amounts receivable for:

■ services as a director and
■ other services (including salaries for executive directors).

For directors of group companies or where total directors' emoluments are over £60 000 the following additional information must be given:

■ the emoluments of chairman and highest paid director
■ the number of other directors falling in £5 000 pay bands.

For all employees (and stating whether executive directors are included) the following should be disclosed:

1 the average number of employees (full time equivalents) with an analysis by function
2 emoluments analysed by:
   ■ wages and salaries,
   ■ social security costs,
   ■ other pension costs.

Illustration

Payskip Ltd has incurred the following payroll costs during the year.

Name	Position	Gross pay	Employer's NI	Directors fees included in gross pay
		(£)	(£)	(£)
David Lewis	Managing Director	35 000	3 500	
Dawn Johnson	Marketing Director	27 000	2 700	
Kevin Smith	Sales co-ordinator	14 000	1 400	
Kylie Jones	Production co-ordinator	14 000	1 400	
Robin Hod	Chairman	5 000	500	5 000
Sylvia Rose	Production supervisor	13 000	1 300	
Betty Booth	Operator	9 000	900	
Kurt Lawrie	Part time accountant	4 000	400	
Rupert Redding	Production artist	15 000	1 500	
Casual workers	4 Operators (18 hrs/week)	18 000	1 800	
Total		154 000	15 400	5 000

Solution

The notes to the accounts are:

Note: Staff costs including executive directors

	(£)
Wages and salaries	149 000
Social security costs	14 900
	163 900

Note: Number of employees by function

	(£)
Production	6
Marketing and selling	2
Administration (accountant less than 0.5)	1
	9

Note: Directors' emoluments

	(£)
Services as a director	5 000
Emoluments for other services	62 000
	67 000

The chairman's emoluments were £5 000 and those of the highest paid director were £35 000. One other director received emoluments within the following band:

(£)	Number
25 001–30 000	1

Exercise 3.1 Pay notes

Exposure Ltd has incurred the following payroll costs during the year.

Name	Position	Gross pay	Employer's NI
		(£)	(£)
Gordon Brown	Finance director	30 000	3 000
Tony Blair	Chairman and M.D.	50 000	5 000
John Cunningham	Sales director	30 000	3 000
Robin Cook	Sales manager	35 000	3 500
Harriet Harman	Stores manager	21 000	2 100
Bryan Gould	Export manager	23 000	2 300
Tony Benn	Warehouse assistant	12 000	1 200
Jack Straw	Clerk	11 000	1 100
John Prescott	Operations director	40 000	4 000
Total		252 000	25 200

All directors' emoluments were in respect of executive duties.

Task

Prepare the notes to Exposure's accounts for employee and director details.

Business size

To apply the same reporting requirements to all companies would be disproportionately burdensome for small companies. Hence small and medium size companies (as defined by the companies acts) are relieved of some of the disclosure requirements applied to large businesses.

A business is classified as being either small or medium sized if it can satisfy two of the three criteria used to measure company size.

	Small – no more than	Medium – no more than
Sales	£2 800 000	£11 200 000
Balance sheet total net assets	£1 400 000	£5 600 000
Number of employees	50	250

Small companies need only file with the Registrar of Companies an abbreviated balance sheet and a special auditor's report. Medium-sized companies can file an abbreviated profit and loss account but must provide a full balance sheet, a special auditor's report and a director's report. There is a requirement for all companies to provide a full set of accounts to the shareholders of the company if requested.

Valuation

All items in financial accounts are measured in money terms but a choice has to be made as to which of the following valuation rules is used:

- *historical cost* – the value placed on an item or transaction at the time it arose
- *alternative cost* – a valuation based on current cost having made an adjustment for the changing value of money.

Some assets used in the business may have a current value that bears little resemblance to the amounts paid for them at the time of purchase. In particular, property acquired say 20 or 50 years ago may be worth significantly more in today's terms than the historical cost. This change in value over time can seriously mis-state the value of resources being used in the business, and in times of high inflation this also applies to working capital items.

The application of inflation accounting was an important item on the accountancy profession's agenda during the 1970s when inflation in the UK was running at over 20 per cent per year. Since then inflation has been curbed in most industrialised countries and so the complexity of alternative cost accounts has been largely shelved. As a result most accounts are prepared on an historical cost basis, although many companies do take the opportunity to include more up-to-date valuations of land and buildings.

The valuation basis should be disclosed with the other accounting policies of the company.

Accounting standards

The preparation of accounts is also subject to accounting guidelines issued by the Accounting Standards Board (ASB). The ASB reports to the Financial Reporting Council (FRC) which oversees the accounting standards process. Its members are appointed by the Governor of the Bank of England, the Secretary of State for Trade and Industry and various interested organisations including the users and preparers of company accounts.

The ASB took over the work of the previous standard-setting regime called the Accounting Standards Committee (ASC) which was largely composed of accountants who actually prepared the accounts. It was felt that a more independent standard-setting process was necessary.

The ASB issues accounting standards in the form of Financial Reporting Statements (FRSs) and final draft versions of proposed standards in the form of Financial Reporting Exposure Drafts (FREDs). The accounting standards produced by the previous ASC are called 'Statements of Standard Accounting Practice' (SSAPs).

Accounting standards are to be applied to all financial statements intended to give a 'true and fair' view of the financial affairs of a business and of its performance for a particular accounting period. There is an obligation on the part of members of the main professional accounting bodies to comply with accounting standards in cases where they either prepare accounts or are required to audit them. Non-compliance should be disclosed in the notes to the accounts, or failing this, in the auditors' report. However, they are not so prescriptive that they should be applied where they would undermine the true and fair view. In addition, it is not necessary to comply with accounting standards for items that are not of a material value.

The process for creating a new accounting standard starts with the Accounting Standards Board identifying an area of accounting practice which requires guidelines to ensure appropriate and consistent treatment.

There is a consultative period during which the ASB invites comments from individuals and organisations who are interested in the subject area under review. Those consulted would include both preparers and users of financial statements.

After the ASB has sufficiently defined the problem under review and has come to an opinion on the accounting treatment required, it will issue a FRED. Interested parties may make further submissions to the ASB as a result of the FRED and these will be considered before the final Financial Reporting Standard is issued.

For the time being the ASB has accepted many of the accounting guidelines issued by the previous ASC and the list of current accounting standards is detailed here.

FRS 1	Cash Flow Statements
FRS 2	Accounting for Subsidiary Undertakings
FRS 3	Reporting Financial Performance
FRS 4	Capital Instruments
FRS 5	Reporting the Substance of Transactions
FRS 6	Acquisitions and Mergers
FRS 7	Fair Values in Acquisition Accounting
FRS 8	Related party disclosures
SSAP 1	Accounting for the Results of Associated Companies
SSAP 2	Disclosure of Accounting Policies
SSAP 3	Earnings per Share (amended by FRS 3)
SSAP 4	The Accounting Treatment of Government Grants
SSAP 5	Accounting for Value Added Tax
SSAP 8	The Treatment of Taxation under the Imputation System in the Accounts of Companies
SSAP 9	Stocks and Long-term Contracts
SSAP 12	Accounting for Depreciation
SSAP 13	Accounting for Research and Development
SSAP 15	Accounting for Deferred Taxation
SSAP 17	Accounting for Post Balance Sheets Events
SSAP 18	Accounting for Contingencies
SSAP 19	Accounting for Investment Properties
SSAP 20	Foreign Currency Translation
SSAP 21	Accounting for Leases and Hire Purchase Agreements
SSAP 22	Accounting for Goodwill
SSAP 24	Accounting for Pension Costs
SSAP 25	Segmental Reporting

Some of the accounting standards relate to only a proportion of companies as they are quite specialised, whereas others affect most companies. For example, all companies that use fixed assets and maintain a stock of materials will be affected by SSAP 9 and SSAP 12.

Several standards are described in more detail in Chapters 10 and 11.

Case study
Softbank – is the success of this acquisitive Japanese firm based on software engineering or financial engineering?

from *The Economist*, 18 May 1996

A feature of Softbank's acquisitive strategy is its aggressive accounting techniques. Each time Mr Son buys a company, almost all the value is in 'goodwill' (the difference between the purchase price and the firm's net assets). Softbank depreciates this goodwill over 30 years, some six times the usual depreciation period for Japanese firms. This helps the company's earnings, because the acquisition costs are spread out over three decades, while the profits show up immediately. On the other hand, many of Softbank's American purchases are fickle, people businesses, where the 'goodwill' could leave tomorrow.

Tasks

1 *In accounting terms, what is goodwill?*
2 *Why is the accounting method for goodwill important?*
3 *Investigate and describe the main provisions of the UK accounting standard that deals with goodwill. In particular, what is prescribed if goodwill 'walked-out' one day?*
4 *If Softbank had been a UK company, how would its results have been affected by this standard?*

Urgent Issue Task Force (UITF) statements

Sometimes accounting problems arise that require guidelines before the ASB can complete the normal standard setting process. The ASB therefore asks the UITF to produce an 'abstract' to give guidance to accountants until the area is covered in an FRS.

The UITF also issues 'abstracts' for areas of reporting that are covered by legislation or an accounting standard but where some controversy or confusion has arisen when the methods of accounting described have been applied to specific cases. These pronouncements, therefore, tend to be focused on issues of a specialised nature.

Conceptual framework for accounting

The *Companies Act 1985* specifies certain basic concepts that should be applied when preparing a set of financial reports. The four main concepts are prudence, matching (accrual), going concern and consistency.

SSAP 2 gives guidance on the application of these fundamental accounting concepts, identifying the possibility that there may be a range of acceptable **accounting bases** on which a business may base its specific **accounting policies**.

Financial statements, apart from varying periods at the start or termination of a business, are always prepared for periods of one year if for publication; and often on a monthly basis for internal use within the business. For the profit and loss account to report accurately what has happened in the period, it is important to apply the **matching** concept to identify:

1 The actual value of work supplied to customers.
2 The value of resources consumed while making these supplies.

Many business transactions do not result in a simultaneous receipt or payment of cash, so accounts cannot be reliably prepared from records of cash transactions alone. Common problems at an accounting period end include:

- credit sales to customers remain unpaid
- work has been started for a customer and costs have been incurred, but payment cannot be requested until the work is complete
- materials have been purchased for stock to satisfy future sales orders
- materials have been purchased on credit and not been paid for
- equipment purchased in the current year will continue to give good service in the future
- equipment purchased in a previous year has given good service but is not worth as much at the end of the year as it was at the beginning.

When a business buys assets, whether for use in the business or for resale, it is usually on the basis that they will provide a future benefit in excess of their cost. Taking the case of stock for resale, SSAP 9 states that it should be valued in the balance sheet at the lower of: (i) its cost or (ii) its net realisable value (market value less costs of selling) under *normal market conditions*. The accounts are prepared on the assumption that the business will continue in operation for the foreseeable future – the **going concern** principle. If the business had to stop trading and its assets were liquidated, then the market value of the fixed assets and stock, under these conditions, may be significantly less than normal. If the business cannot be assumed to be a going concern then the assets would have to be valued at net realisable values under distress conditions, e.g. auction values for bankrupt stock. Confirmation that the going concern concept can legitimately be applied is an important reassurance to users of financial reports.

As a result of the Cadbury Committee's Report, all companies listed on the stock exchange must include statements from the company's directors and its auditors regarding corporate governance. Both directors and auditors must state whether in their opinion the company has the financial resources to continue as a going concern in the foreseeable future.

Items of a similar nature should be accounted for on a **consistent** basis from one period to the next. For example, if it has been accounting policy to depreciate (i.e. spread the cost) of motor vehicles over 4 years then it would be inconsistent to depreciate over 6 years in the next accounting period. This is important so that the reported performance of one period can be properly compared with that of another.

Financial statements are prepared on a **prudent** basis. Gains will only be recognised when they are reasonably certain and losses will be provided for as soon as they are known.

It is important to distinguish between *total recognised gains* and the profit as stated in the profit and loss account. For example, where a business property has increased in value, the potential gain cannot be included in the profit and loss account unless the property has been sold and the gain has been *realised*. If, however, it is desired that property values should be revalued to give the users of the accounts a more complete picture of the value of net assets, then the gain is reflected in a revaluation reserve.

Balance sheets	Assets revalued (£)	Assets at cost (£)
Assets	80 000	70 000
Less liabilities	25 000	25 000
	55 000	45 000
Financed by:		
Share capital	30 000	30 000
Revaluation reserve	10 000	
Profit and loss account	15 000	15 000
	55 000	45 000

The uplifted value of the property has the dual effect of a £10 000 balance on a revaluation reserve. The revaluation reserve is part of the shareholders' capital but is an unrealised gain.

A potential loss is accounted for in a different way. If an asset's value to the business were to fall below its value in the balance sheet, then the profit and loss account would be charged with the deficit and the value of the asset would be written down.

Despite their reputation for fastidiousness, accountants do try to be realistic in their quest for accurate accounts. There is a need for quantitative accuracy which sometimes requires considerable time and cost. However, it is often qualitative judgements which most influence reported figures. Whether an issue becomes a point of contention between the preparers and the auditors of accounts will depend upon the item's **materiality.** A material item is one which has a value that is large relative to other items, and is something that is likely to alter the true and fair view of a set of accounts.

Take for example the classification of research and development expenditure. According to SSAP 13, development expenditure can only be deferred and treated as an intangible asset in the balance sheet if certain rules are satisfied to demonstrate that the expenditure will give future benefits, such as a commercially viable new product. If a business with a sales turnover of £1m incurs £50 000 development expenditure, then the treatment of the expenditure is a material issue and should be accounted for in strict accordance with the accounting standard. However, if GEC, with a turnover in excess of £9 billion pounds, were to defer £500 000 of research expenditure incorrectly, then that would not be considered material to the understanding of the performance of the business.

There can be instances where there is tension between the various concepts, and it will be a matter of judgement to determine a fair balance between their different requirements. In general, the prudence concept prevails over the accruals concept if the two conflict.

Accounting bases are the different methods used to apply the accounting concepts to practical situations. Different bases have evolved in response to the needs of a diverse range of business activities, and include the methods used for accounting for depreciation and the valuation of stock for resale.

Illustration – Fixed assets and depreciation

The purpose of depreciation is to apply the matching concept to capital expenditure, i.e. the cost of a fixed asset should be spread over the periods that will benefit from its use. One method of calculating depreciation simply spreads the cost evenly over the years involved. For example, a machine that costs £10 000 and is to be used for 4 years before being scrapped would result in a depreciation charge of £2 500 per annum. Another method, if the information is available, would be to spread the cost in proportion to the asset's usage over its economic life. Hence if the same £10 000 machine's life is estimated to be 10 000 hours and it is used for 2 000 hours in its first year, the first year's depreciation charge would be £10 000 × 2 000/10 000 = £2 000.

Accounting policies are the specific accounting bases adopted by the business. The choice of bases will depend upon the nature of the asset, and the asset renewal policy adopted by the business. Once chosen, an accounting policy should be applied consistently from one accounting period to another.

Accounting policies must be disclosed in a note to the accounts as different accounting bases will affect the reported profit (as demonstrated in the depreciation illustration above).

Case study

Tesco plc – Accounting policies

for the year ended 24 February 1996

Fixed assets and depreciation

Fixed assets include amounts in respect of interest paid, net of taxation, on funds specifically related to the financing of assets in the course of construction.

Depreciation is provided on an equal annual instalment basis over the anticipated useful working lives of the assets, after they have been brought into use, at the following rates:

■ Land premiums paid in excess of the alternative use value on acquisition – at 4 per cent of cost.

- Freehold and leasehold buildings with greater than 40 years unexpired – 2.5 per cent on cost.
- Leasehold properties with less than 40 years unexpired are amortised by equal annual instalments over the unexpired period of the lease.
- Plant, equipment, fixtures and fittings and motor vehicles – at rates varying from 10 to 33 per cent.

Tasks

1 *Obtain the annual reports of three companies and highlight the differences in accounting policy in respect of depreciation.*
2 *How will the policy differences affect reported profits?*
3 *Suggest reasons for the different policies.*

Accounting standard requirements – stocks

The accounting for stock and long term contracts is guided by SSAP 9. **Stocks** comprise all materials held for eventual resale, whether these be raw materials, work in progress or stocks of finished goods. Long-term contracts are major projects involving work in progress extending over more than one year and are the subject of a contractual agreement with a particular customer. An example would be a major civil engineering project, such as bridge building.

The accounting principles of SSAP 9 apply equally to stock and contracts, although long-term contracts do introduce added practical problems. This section will concentrate on the accounting treatment of stocks.

The overriding requirement of SSAP 9 is that stocks and long term contracts *should be valued at whichever is the lower of cost or net realisable value.*

SSAP 9 defines **cost** as: 'that expenditure which has been incurred in the normal course of business in bringing the product or service to its present location and condition'. For a trading business such as a retailer, cost will therefore be the purchase price plus the cost of delivery to the retail store. For a manufacturing business, the cost of finished goods will be the direct costs of labour, materials and expenses, and in addition will include factory overheads absorbed into product costs (see Chapter 12 on absorption costing). Costs should also relate to normal business conditions. If costs are increased because of inefficient working or abnormal waste then these should be excluded. Similarly, overheads should be absorbed at normal production rates and should not be influenced by volume variations that result in overheads being under- or over-absorbed.

Net realisable value is the selling price of the stock less all further costs to be incurred before a sale is completed.

An accounting concept stipulated by the *Companies Act 1985* but not described by SSAP 2 is the rule of **no offset**. When accounting for stock, this rule means that a loss on one item of stock, cannot be offset against a gain on another. In practice it may prove too onerous to perform the lower of cost or net realisable value test to every single item held in stock as some stores hold thousands of different items. However, the test should be performed for each main category of stock.

SSAP 9 allows a number of accounting bases for determining the cost of a stock item. Stock may be valued on a 'first-in first-out' or average cost basis, or a

Figure 3.2 The conceptual framework for depreciation

Concepts	Going concern	Prudence	Accrual	Consistency
	The business should be capable of making use of the asset in the future	Rate and method used should not burden future periods with charges in excess of the benefit to be derived from the asset's use	Spread the cost of the asset over the periods that receive economic benefit	Same rate and method every year
Accounting bases – acceptable methods	Straight line	Reducing balance	Usage	Asset valuation
Accounting policy		The business chooses appropriate bases for each category of fixed assets		

reasonable approximation of these, such as standard costs, provided these are a true reflection of the actual cost during the accounting period (see Chapter 12 for details of material costing systems).

Illustration – Stock valuation

A firm has four different products in stock that it has manufactured. The following details of unit costs have been extracted from the firm's records:

	Case 01 (£)	Case 02 (£)	Case 03 (£)	Case 04 (£)
Direct materials	5.50	7.50	10.00	11.00
Direct wages	7.00	8.00	9.00	10.00
Direct expenses	1.00	1.00	1.00	1.00
Prime cost	13.50	16.50	19.00	22.00
Factory overhead – 100% of direct wages	7.00	8.00	9.00	10.00
Total factory cost	20.50	24.50	28.00	32.00
Administration expenses – 20% of factory cost	4.10	4.90	5.60	6.40
Total cost	24.60	29.40	33.60	38.40
Number in stock	500	600	250	300
Current selling price	£32.50	£28.00	£35.00	£25.00

Case 03 is sold through an agent who receives a 10 per cent commission based on the selling price.

A stock valuation in accordance with SSAP 9 is required.

Solution

	Case 01 (£)	Case 02 (£)	Case 03 (£)	Case 04 (£)
Cost of production per case	20.50	24.50	28.00	32.00
Current selling price	32.50	28.00	35.00	25.00
Less further costs			3.50	
Net realisable value	£32.50	£28.00	£31.50	£25.00
Lower of cost or net realisable value	20.50	24.50	28.00	25.00
Number of cases	500	600	250	300
Stock valuation	£10 250	£14 700	£7 000	£7 500

Total stock valuation is £39 450.

Note that the loss on case 04 cannot be offset against the gains on the other cases because of the rule of no offset.

Exercise 3.2 Stock valuation

Asher Manufacturing has four different products in stock that it has manufactured. The following details of unit costs have been extracted from the firm's records:

	Box A (£)	Box B (£)	Box C (£)	Box D (£)
Direct materials	32.40	29.60	70.20	540.00
Direct wages	45.00	29.00	86.00	326.00
Direct expenses	5.00	0.00	2.50	0.00
Prime cost	82.40	58.60	158.70	866.00
Factory overhead – 50% of prime cost	41.20	29.30	79.35	433.00
Total factory cost	123.60	87.90	238.05	1299.00
Administration expenses – 10% of factory cost	12.36	8.79	23.81	129.90
Total cost	135.96	96.69	261.86	1428.90
Current selling price	160.00	95.00	220.00	1500.00
Number in stock	22 of	12 of	42 of	5 of

It has been found that two Box Ds will require rectification work at a cost of £700.00 each.

Task

Value the stock in accordance with SSAP 9.

Exercise 3.3 Stock valuation

Jason Mills prices the goods in his shop on a 100 per cent mark up basis. On reviewing his stock levels he finds several items are damaged or defective. He believes he will sell all items except the golf umbrellas that were faulty when received. These will be returned for a full refund.

	Footballs (£)	Cricket (£)	Cricket (£)	Golf (£)£
Normal selling price	32.00	43.20	26.00	20.00
Mark down price	18.00	30.00	10.00	

Task

What stock valuation should be placed on each item?

Exercise 3.4 Stock valuation

China Classics specialises in the retailing of discontinued household items. The firm purchases end-of-line goods from manufacturers as well as dealing in second-hand items.

Selling price is calculated to give a 40 per cent profit margin. A recent stock take showed that some items were damaged and a number of others were very slow moving. The proprietor has agreed to some price discounts to get the stock moving.

	Denby – brown (£)	Royal Worcester (£)	Royal Doulton (£)	Dartington Glass (£)
Normal selling price	30.00	24.00	60.00	8.00
Mark down price	15.00	18.00	50.00	2.00

Task

What valuation should be placed on each item?

Exercise 3.5 Stock valuation

Flemings Ltd specialises in sub-contract machining work for the automobile industry. Stock and job cost records give the following balances:

		Cost (£)
Raw materials	Steel sheet	41 250
	Steel strips	10 100
	Wiring	12 650
Work in progress	Job 598 – contract value £7 900	5 850
	Job 599 – contract value £13 500	9 000
	Job 601 – contract value £5 700	4 270
	Job 602 – contract value £9 100	1 385

An inspection of the raw material store has revealed that steel sheet costing £570 is damaged. After the edges are trimmed at a cost of £50, the resulting sheets will be worth just £200. Also it is found that wiring costing £860 is no longer used and its scrap value is £40.

Job costs as a percentage of total cost to completion: Job 598: 90%, Job 599: 75%, Job 601: 70%, Job 602: 20%.

Task

Provide valuations for stock and work in progress in accordance with SSAP 9.

Compliance with accounting standards

The accounting standards issued by the ASB are not directly enforced by law but there are a number of reasons why preparers of accounts feel compelled to comply.

The *Companies Act 1989* requires public and large private companies to state whether their accounts have been prepared in accordance with accounting standards. Non-compliance with an accounting standard must be highlighted and an explanation given.

Company accounts that are filed at Companies House are examined by the Financial Reporting Panel to ensure they comply with accounting standards. Where non-compliance has undermined the 'true and fair' view of the company's financial affairs and financial performance, the panel will ask for the accounts to be revised. If necessary the panel will take court action to compel compliance.

The professional accountancy bodies insist that their members observe the requirements of the accounting standards. This applies to members preparing or auditing accounts and also those acting as company directors who will approve the accounts. The main accountancy bodies are: the Institute of Chartered Accountants of Scotland, the Institute of Chartered Accountants in Ireland, The Institute of Chartered Accountants in England and Wales, the Chartered Institute of Management Accountants, The Chartered Association of Certified Accountants and the Chartered Institute of Public Finance and Accountancy.

The role of auditors

It is required that the accounts of a limited company be audited by a firm of independent accountants who are **registered auditors**. The auditors are asked to verify that the accounting records are accurate and to ensure that the financial statements to be published are consistent with them. The auditors should confirm that the accounts are in accordance with the *Companies Act 1985* and should highlight non-compliance with accounting standards where appropriate. The overriding requirement is for the auditors to confirm that the accounts provide a 'true and fair' view of the valuation of assets and liabilities as at the date of the accounts and of the profit or loss up to that date (usually one year). To fulfil this responsibility, the auditors may actually encourage or concur with a departure from an accounting standard if it is consistent with a 'true and fair' view.

In addition to checking the company's historical performance, the auditors will verify that the going concern concept can be applied to the valuation of its assets. If assets have to be disposed of as a result of a cessation of the business then appropriate (often lower) market values should be used in preparing the accounts. Hence some of the audit will be devoted to the company's future outlook.

Where auditors have difficulty confirming that the accounts give a 'true and fair' view they will issue a 'qualified' audit report. Reasons for a qualified audit report fall into two main categories:

- There might be **uncertainty**. The accounting records may be inadequate for them to carry out a full audit of financial transactions or there may be uncertainty concerning the outcome of a known situation, e.g. a law suit or the applicability of the going concern concept.
- There might be **disagreement**. The accounting records may not be factual or the financial reports may not be in accordance with the accounting records. Non-compliance with relevant legislation and accounting standards may also be a cause for disagreement.

For users of accounts, the reluctance of the auditors to state that the accounts provide a true and fair view seriously undermines their value. But an effective audit of a company's accounts is not cheap, and is paid by the shareholders out of their profits. The audit at Sainsbury's cost £500 000 in 1996, on turnover of £12 billion and an operating profit of £0.8 billion.

Stock exchange requirements

Public limited companies listed on the London International Stock Exchange are required to disclose additional information in accordance with the Exchange's 'Yellow Book'. The provision of information on a more regular basis is considered important for a stock market to operate properly. Therefore one requirement is for companies to issue an interim financial report of performance which should include details of turnover, profit and shareholder dividends.

Figure 3.3 Unqualified Audit Report

Report of the auditors to the shareholders of J Sainsbury plc

We have audited the accounts on pages 9 to 28.

Respective responsibilities of Directors and Auditors
As described above the Company's Directors are responsible for the preparation of accounts. It is our responsibility to form an independent opinion, based on our audit, on those accounts and to report our opinion to you.

Basis of opinion
We conducted our audit in accordance with Auditing Standards issued by the Auditing Practices Board. An audit includes examination, on a test basis, of evidence relevant to the amounts and disclosures in the accounts. It also includes an assessment of the significant estimates and judgements made by the Directors in the preparation of the accounts and of whether the accounting policies are appropriate to the Company's circumstances, consistently applied and adequately disclosed.

We planned and performed our audit so as to obtain all the information and explanations which we considered necessary in order to provide us with sufficient evidence to give reasonable assurance that the accounts are free from material misstatement, whether caused by fraud or other irregularity or error. In forming our opinion we also evaluated the overall adequacy of the presentation of information in the financial statements.

Opinion
In our opinion the accounts give a true and fair view of the state of affairs of the Company and the Group as at 9th March 1996 and of the profit, total recognised gains and cash flows of the Group for the 52 weeks then ended and have been properly prepared in accordance with the Companies Act 1985.

Coopers & Lybrand

Chartered Accountants and Registered Auditors, London, 7th May 1996

Stock exchange requirements have become more stringent in recent years with quoted companies required to state whether they have complied with the Cadbury Committee code of best practice concerning corporate governance. The recommendations by Cadbury concerned: the composition of the board of directors, with non-executive directors playing an independent and stronger role; directors' contracts; and recognition of directors' responsibility for financial reporting and control.

Case study

Global accounting's roadblock

from *The Economist*, 27 April 1996

Accountants may seem like a dull bunch, but their power to move financial markets is awesome. Every day, firms' share prices soar or plummet based on their latest quarterly earnings announcements. The trouble with this simple reward-and-punishment scheme, as any company boss will tell you, is that a firm's reported earnings depend on the way in which its financial accounts are prepared. And this, in turn, depends on which country it is based in. As companies compete ever more fiercely for a chunk of an increasingly global capital market, the battle over accounting standards is heating up.

Few institutional investors doubt that a single rulebook is needed. A desire to diversify across borders has heightened their frustration with incompatible national standards. To make it easier for outsiders to compare their performance with that of other companies, more firms are beginning to report their financial results according to International Accounting Standards (IAS) – a body of rules that has been around since the early 1970s, and which is currently being revised by an international committee of accountants, financial executives and equity analysts. Such a co-operative approach would seem to be an ideal response to global investors' needs.

But there is a hitch. Most big national stock exchanges allow foreign firms that list on them to report their results according to IAS. But a few national regulators – including, crucially, America's Securities and Exchange Commission (SEC) – refuse to accept these standards. If a foreign firm wishes to list its shares on an American exchange, it must publish a second set of accounts that are compatible with America's Generally Accepted Accounting Principles (US GAAP).

Without the SEC's blessing, the IAS have failed to take off as a truly global norm. ... It can be embarrassing. After Daimler Benz listed on the New York Stock Exchange (NYSE) in 1993, the German group's first set of dual accounts showed a £370 million profit under German rules and a $1 billion loss under US GAAP ....

Although there will be some messy battles ahead, the IASC is likely to [satisfy SEC's requirements] by early 1998. When it does, investors will find it far easier to compare firms in different parts of the world ... Not everybody will be pleased, however. Without confusing national standards to hide behind, a boss who cannot deliver consistent profits will be in deeper water than ever.

Tasks

1 *Obtain copies of the UK accounting standards and the comparable IASs relating to stocks and tangible fixed assets (UK SSAP 9 and 12, IAS 2 and 4).*
2 *Compare the requirements of these accounting standards, highlighting the similarities and differences in accounting method and disclosure requirements.*
3 *From your findings, to what extent do you consider the harmonisation of global accounting standards will affect the reporting of UK companies?*

Sole traders and partnerships

Sole traders and partnerships do not have to file accounts for public scrutiny and so there are no legal requirements to prepare accounts other than for taxation purposes. It is the responsibility of the business owners to ensure they receive information that is adequate for the running of the business and to monitor and control their personal interest in the business. Most businesses in this category are small and so the owners of the business are sufficiently involved in its running to be well informed. For partnerships the partnership agreement should specify an appropriate reporting system to ensure all partners are kept informed, even if only on an annual basis.

Despite there being no legislation regarding the accounting of non-incorporated businesses, there is as described above an obligation on reporting accountants who are members of one of the professional accounting bodies to observe the requirements of accounting standards. So whilst the format of accounts may vary between businesses, users of the accounts (such as bankers) can reasonably assume the application of appropriate accounting policies.

Tax authorities will require accounts that facilitate the computation of tax according to tax regulations. For income tax purposes the Inland Revenue will require a profit and loss statement with reasonable detail concerning the analysis of costs to verify they are deductible for tax purposes. Customs and Excise will require all VAT-registered businesses to maintain proper records and documentation for all transactions subject to value added tax regulations.

Financial information for managers

Financial accounts prepared for use by management are called **management accounts**. Their format and content will depend very much on the specific needs of the particular business.

Management accounts are usually prepared to a strict timetable on a monthly basis, often reporting within one week of the period end. The format of the accounts is designed with the needs of the user in mind, often providing a highly detailed analysis of costs and revenues, with a breakdown by department. Comparative figures are usually provided from the budget and the previous year's accounts. The accounts may include a revised forecast of results up to the year end and performance indicators including accounting ratios and operational statistics.

In keeping with the need to provide information that is relevant to the user, the accounts department in large businesses will issue different accounting packs to different managers, depending on their function and level of responsibility.

Summary

The need for financial reporting stems from the demand for information by the various stakeholder groups. For companies these needs have been largely satisfied by a regulatory framework comprising the companies acts and the accounting standards accepted by the Accounting Standards Board. Reporting accountants comply with these requirements because of legal and professional pressures. As this framework explicates best accounting practice it has ramifications for the financial reporting by all business entities.

Further reading

Geoff Black, *Student's Guide to Accounting and Financial Reporting Standards, 1996/7*, DP Publications, 1996.
David Chopping and Len Skerratt, *Apply GAAP 1996/7*, Accountancy Books, 1996.

4 Recording financial information

O n completion of this chapter students should be able to:

■ identify and investigate the systems needed to record financial transactions
■ examine the role of different components within the accounting system
■ apply the appropriate concepts and conventions to the recording of transactions.

Introduction

All businesses should maintain full and accurate accounting records as a means to:

■ satisfy internal and external financial reporting requirements
■ provide the Inland Revenue and Customs and Excise with reliable information on which to establish the amount of taxes due
■ control the financial resources of the business.

Companies are required by law to maintain accounting records of financial transactions. These records should also be adequate to determine the financial position of the company at any point in time. In particular, the records should:

■ analyse the receipts and payments of cash
■ record the assets and liabilities of the business
■ if the company is involved in the buying and selling of goods, the records should show details of period end stock-takes and, for businesses not in the retail sector, details of individual buyers and sellers.

It should be noted that the precise form of accounting records is not prescribed by law because businesses are so diverse. However, the accounting systems of different businesses will be based on common principles.

Accounting equation

For accounting purposes the business is treated as a separate entity from its owners, whether this is legally the case or not. The accounts recognise that the business is in possession of certain assets even if they legally belong to the business owners, as in the case of sole traders and partnerships. This is known as the **entity concept**.

The entity concept leads to the principle of **double entry**. For all goods and services utilised in the business, it should be shown how they were acquired.

Business assets originate from one of two sources:

■ Business owners – capital.
■ Suppliers and investors who have provided resources without receiving payment – liabilities.

This logic underpins the accounting equation, which is:

$$\text{Assets} = \text{capital} + \text{liabilities}$$

Most accounting systems operate using the **double entry** concept that every transaction has two aspects to it.

Illustration – Double entry concept

Mick Jones has decided to set up in business selling stationery to local firms.

Transaction 1 – His first transaction is to pay £5 000 capital into the business bank account.

Mick Jones			
Assets Detail	Amount (£)	Capital and Liabilities Detail	Amount (£)
Bank	5 000	Capital – Jones	5 000

Dual aspect

Assets increase	Bank balance increases by £5 000
Capital increases	Received from M Jones £5 000

Transaction 2 – Mick now purchases on credit terms £3 000 of supplies from Jon Rhodes.
Note: Items purchased for subsequent resale are classified as the asset **stock**.

Mick Jones			
Assets Detail	Amount (£)	Capital and Liabilities Detail	Amount (£)
Bank Stock	5 000 3 000	Capital – Jones Jon Rhodes	5 000 3 000
	8 000		8 000

Dual aspect

Assets increase	Stock increases by £3000
Liabilities increase	Jon Rhodes is owed £3000

Transaction 3 – As a special introductory offer, Mick sells stationery at the cost price of £800 to P Lehman Ltd, who will pay in one month's time.

Note: Although Mick has not received payment, his customer will eventually pay so the debt is treated as an asset.

Mick Jones			
Assets Detail	Amount (£)	Capital and Liabilities Detail	Amount (£)
Bank Stock P Lehman Ltd	5 000 2 200 800	Capital – Jones Jon Rhodes	5 000 3 000
	8 000		8 000

Dual aspect

Assets increase	P Lehman will pay in the future £800
Assets decrease	Stock is depleted by £800

Transaction 4 – Mick pays Jon Rhodes the £3 000 he owes him.

Mick Jones			
Assets Detail	Amount (£)	Capital and Liabilities Detail	Amount (£)
Bank Stock P Lehman Ltd	2 000 2 200 800	Capital – Jones	5 000
	5 000		5 000

Dual aspect

Assets decrease	Bank is depleted by £3 000
Liabilities decrease	The debt payable to Jon Rhodes is extinguished

Transaction 5 – Mick receives cash from P Lehman Ltd

Mick Jones			
Assets Detail	Amount (£)	Capital and Liabilities Detail	Amount (£)
Bank Stock	2 800 2 200	Capital – Jones	5 000
	5 000		5 000

Dual aspect

Assets increase	Bank increases by £800
Assets decrease	P Lehman Ltd no longer has an obligation to pay £800 to Mick

These statements prepared for Mick Jones giving details of his assets and liabilities are examples of balance sheets. They are called balance sheets simply because they are a set of balances that make up the business's net worth at a point in time.

Apart from the initial capital paid into the business, none of the transactions have led to a change in the capital balance. Transactions so far have involved:

Transactions	One aspect	Second aspect
2	Assets increased £3 000	Liabilities increased £3 000
3	Assets increased £800	Assets decreased £800
4	Liabilities decreased £3 000	Assets decreased £3 000
5	Assets increase £800	Assets decrease £800

The net effect of each transaction on the net worth of the business is nil. In the next transaction Mick increases the net worth of the business by making a profit on a transaction.

Transaction 6
Mick sells, for £1 500 cash, stock that cost him £1 000.

Mick Jones			
Assets		Capital and Liabilities	
Detail	Amount (£)	Detail	Amount (£)
Bank	4 300	Capital – Jones	5 500
Stock	1 200		
	5 500		5 500

Dual aspect

Assets increase	Bank increases by £1 500
Assets decrease	Stock falls by £1 000
Capital increases	Owner's net worth increases by £500

This last transaction completes the picture of how owner's capital can change, i.e. when:

1 the owner puts money into or takes money out of the business
2 the business makes a profit or a loss which increases or decreases the difference between the assets and liabilities of the business.

The preparation of statements that report on the financial affairs and the profits or loss of a business is described in the next chapter. At this stage it is only necessary to appreciate the dual aspect of financial transactions.

Exercise 4.1 Dual aspect of accounting

Jo Green finished February 19X9 with the assets, liabilities and capital in the following balance sheet:

Assets	(£)	Capital and liabilities	(£)
Van	10 000	Capital	20 000
Stock	5 000	Creditors	2 000
Debtors	1 000		
Cash	6 000		
	22 000		22 000

Tasks

Identify the dual aspect for each of the following transactions that occurred during the first week of March and prepare a new balance sheet after each.

1 *Stock costing £2 000 is sold for £2 000 in cash.*
2 *Debtors pay their debt of £1 000.*
3 *Stock costing £1 500 is bought on credit.*
4 *Jo pays £2 000 for past supplies received on credit.*
5 *Jo sells stock that cost £500 for £1 000 on credit terms.*

The administrative process of buying and selling

For financial transactions that are settled in cash at the time of sale, the recording process merely requires a listing of cash receipts and payments made. The records maintained should be supported by invoices or receipts that provide evidence of the transaction and the amount of cash involved.

However, in many situations it is impractical for cash to change hands at the point of sale. This is often because buyers and sellers are geographically remote from one another and it would be difficult for the mode of delivery also to be the channel for payment. It would be administratively onerous and physically insecure to expect freight carriers and postmen to collect and account for the value of every item they delivered. In addition, where businesses have, potentially, thousands of transactions with the same trading partner, there needs to be a settlement system to consolidate transactions for a convenient trading period and to allow just one payment to be made to settle amounts owing. For these reasons the vast majority of trade between businesses is made on credit terms, with typically 30–60 day settlement periods.

The process of buying and selling commences with a *purchase order* being sent to a supplier either by hand, post, telephone or electronic means. The purchase order gives details of what is required together with any other pertinent information, such as place of delivery and date required. In larger businesses it is likely that the firm has a specialist purchasing department that has responsibility for placing all orders with other firms. If this is the situation, individuals within the firm will send a *purchase requisition* detailing what is required, and by when, to the purchase department who will then identify the most appropriate supplier and issue a purchase order accordingly.

On receipt of the *purchase order*, the supplying firm may transfer the details of the order onto a *sales order*. This ensures the completeness of the information required for subsequent stages in the sales accounting process. The goods will be delivered together with a form called an *advice note* (or *delivery note*) which the customer will have to sign to confirm that a supply has been made. In the case of having provided a service, such as maintenance of equipment, the engineer will require the customer to sign a *work completed form*. On receipt of goods, it is usual practice for the department receiving the goods (in large organisations, a dedicated goods received department) to complete a *goods received note* (GRN), with copies sent to the person originating the order, the purchase department and the purchase ledger section of the accounts department.

The supplying firm is now in possession of two documents signed by the customer: a request for a supply of goods and services (purchase order) and confirmation that the order has been satisfied (advice note). The supplier can now issue an *invoice* stating the amount payable for the supply. The sales invoice will be recorded on the sales ledger where it will remain outstanding against the customer until payment is received.

The purchasing firm should now be in possession of three documents relevant to the transaction. A purchase order, a GRN and a purchase invoice. If all three documents agree, the purchase invoice can be recorded as a verified debt to the supplier which will be paid at the end of the agreed credit period.

The precise procedures and documents used will depend on the business, but this description illustrates common principles.

Books of prime entry

Every year a business may enter into thousands, or perhaps millions, of financial transactions. Even relatively small businesses with just a few employees can accumulate several thousand accounting documents during the course of a year. Clearly an accounting system that relied on drawing up a balance sheet after every transaction would

Figure 4.1 The administrative process for buying and selling

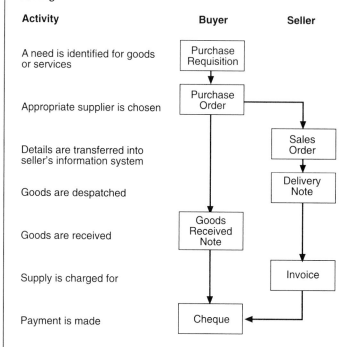

be impractical. In addition, the balance sheet fails to provide details of business activity or an audit trial to establish how balances occurred.

There are a number of source documents from which an accounting system is updated:

1 Credit transactions:

   ■ Invoices to customers (sales invoices)
   ■ Credit notes from customers (sales returns)
   ■ Invoices from suppliers (purchase invoices)
   ■ Credit notes from suppliers (purchase returns)

2 Small cash payments (petty cash vouchers)

3 Bank transactions

   ■ Bank receipts (paying-in slips for manual deposits and bank advices for automated receipts)
   ■ Bank payments (cheques for manual payments and bank advices for automated payments).

The first step in the recording process is to prepare books of prime entry. These are simply totalled lists of each type of financial transaction.

The **sales journal** (or sales day book) is a listing of all the sales invoices prepared in respect of credit sales.

The following transactions were made by Del's Trading Company during September 19X7:

Del's sales day book			
Document no	Customer	Value (£)	Month
567	Allen	1 100	09/X7
568	Diana	900	09/X7
569	Diana	400	09/X7
570	Allen	350	09/X7
571	Diana	1 600	09/X7
	Total	4 350	

Del's purchase day book			
Document no	Customer	Value (£)	Month
341	Liam	180	09/X7
342	Lynne	340	09/X7
343	Lynne	400	09/X7
344	Liam	710	09/X7
	Total	1 630	

The sales journal can, if required, be analysed to provide information concerning the make-up of sales, e.g. with separate columns for different products or different sales locations. As a minimum, the information required for each transaction includes the invoice number, the customer's name and the total value for each transaction. In addition, a computerised system is almost certain to include a customer account number field.

If items that have been sold are returned by customers they are called **returns inwards**. There are two methods for recording these transactions. They are either deducted in the sales journal as a negative sale or, alternatively, they are recorded in a separate **returns inwards journal**. Instead of being referenced by an invoice number, returns are identified with a credit note number.

Del's sales returns day book			
Document no	Customer	Value (£)	Month
125	Allen	150	09/X7
126	Diana	50	09/X7
	Total	200	

The **purchases journal** (or purchase day book) is a listing of all the purchase invoices received in a period relating to credit purchases.

The purchase journal can also be analysed to provide information concerning the make-up of purchases. The minimum information required in the purchases journal for each transaction is a reference number (either the supplier's invoice number or an internally generated number), the name of the supplier and the total value for each transaction.

When items are returned to the supplier they are called **returns outwards**. As with sales there are two methods by which these can be recorded. Either they can be recorded as negative purchases to be deducted in the purchases journal, or they can be recorded in a separate **returns outwards journal**. Returns outwards are referenced with credit note numbers.

The **cash book** is a record of bank receipts and payments. The book can be used to analyse the transactions in some way, although in the illustration from Del's books below, the cash book is just a listing of transactions similar to the sales and purchases journals. However, the cash book can be prepared like a ledger account or with analysis columns similar to the petty cash book (both illustrated later).

Del's cash book – receipts			
Date	Document no	Received from	Value (£)
05/09/X7	5721	Diana	270
15/09/X7	5722	Allen	700
23/09/X7	5723	Diana	900
		Total	1 870

Del's cash book – payments

Date	Document no	Paid to	Nominal account	Value (£)
30/9/X7	741	Liam	Purchase ledger	140
30/9/X7	742	Lynne	Purchase ledger	950
30/9/X7	743	Liam	Purchase ledger	180
30/9/X7	744	Joyce	Rent	500
30/9/X7	745	Local Telegraphic	Telephone	15
30/9/X7	746	Cash	Wages	500
30/9/X7	747	Cash	Petty cash	120
				2 405

Like the other books of prime entry, every cash book transaction should be adequately referenced to enable the source document to be located if necessary. The reference may relate to an internal document such as a cheque requisition form or to the identifying numbers on paying-in slips and cheques.

Petty cash is the term used to describe the cash float held in many offices to cover small payments that can be made more conveniently in cash. The petty cash book is a record of amounts paid out from the petty cash float. It has a columnar analysis of the payments made.

Del's petty cash

Narrative	Reference	Value (£)	Petrol (£)	Cleaner (£)	Postage (£)
1/9/X7 Balance B/F		200			
Payments:					
Petrol	326	30	30		
Cleaner	327	5		5	
Postage	328	50			50
Petrol	329	20	20		
Cleaner	330	15		15	
Total		120	50	20	50
Paid in from bank 30/9/X7		120			
Balance C/F		200			

Most businesses operate an *imprest petty cash system*. The person responsible for custody of the petty cash is given a fixed 'float'. Periodically the petty cash float is replenished to its original level by drawing out of the bank an equal amount of cash to that expended. In the above illustration,

£120 has been paid out during September 19X7. At the end of the month a cheque for £120 has been drawn on the bank (see cash book) to bring the petty cash balance back up to its authorised level of £200.

Nominal ledger accounts

The totals from the books of prime entry are transferred to **nominal ledger accounts**. Every type of transaction and every classification of asset and liability has its own ledger account.

The terms **debit and credit** are used to describe the effect a transaction has on a particular ledger account. It is not adequate to say 'plus this account' and 'minus that account' because the dual aspect of a transaction has to be recognised within the framework of the accounting equation. An increase in assets is not the same as an increase in liabilities, so to avoid confusion the terms debit and credit are used.

Debits and credits affect ledger account balances in different ways depending on the type of account:

Account type	Debit	Credit
Asset	an increase	a decrease
Liability	a decrease	an increase
Capital	a decrease	an increase
Expense	an increase	a decrease
Sales revenue	a decrease	an increase

It can seem confusing trying to remember which account should be debited and which credited. It may be easier to consider the effect of each transaction on the bank account. Cash is an asset so money in the bank is a debit and any further money deposited must result in the bank ledger account being debited. The double entry will be completed by crediting some other ledger account such as sales. (Do not be confused by the use of debit and credit on the bank statement. A credit balance on a bank statement is recognition by the bank that it owes the account holder the net amount paid in.)

Of course not every transaction involves the bank account but even for credit transactions it may help to consider an equivalent cash transaction. For example, if a business sells an item on credit, what are the ledger account entries? A clue can be found by considering the similar position of selling for cash where the receipt of cash would result in the bank account being debited. Sales must still be credited for a credit sale but the debit is recorded against the debtor who owes the business the money (e.g. P Lehman in the earlier illustration).

For Del's business transactions it is now necessary to post the prime book totals to the nominal ledger accounts. The totals to be posted are:

	Total (£)	Accounts to debit	Accounts to credit
Sales	4 350	Sales ledger control account	Sales
Purchases	1 630	Purchases (and various expense accounts)	Purchase ledger control account
Sales returns	200	Sales returns	Sales ledger control account
Bank receipts	1 870	Bank	Sales ledger control account
Bank payments	2 405	Purchase ledger control account (and various expense accounts paid directly in cash)	Bank
Petty cash payments	120	Expense accounts	Petty cash

The ledger account uses a similar format to the simple balance sheets illustrated earlier. Del's nominal ledger accounts for the month of September 19X7:

Sales

Date	Narrative	Debit £	Date	Narrative	Credit £
			1/9/X7	Balance B/F	18 240
30/9/X7	Balance c/f	22 590	30/9/X7	Sales ledger control	4 350
		22 590			22 590
			1/10/X7	Balance B/F	22 590

Purchases

Date	Narrative	Debit £	Date	Narrative	Credit £
1/9/X7	Balance B/F	8 270			
30/9/X7	Purchase ledger control	1 630	30/9/X7	Balance c/f	9 900
		9 900			9 900
1/10/X7	Balance B/F	9 900			

Wages

Date	Narrative	Debit £	Date	Narrative	Credit £
1/9/X7	Balance B/F	5 200			
30/9/X7	Bank	500	30/9/X7	Balance c/f	5 700
		5 700			5 700
1/10/X7	Balance B/F	5 700			

Stock

Date	Narrative	Debit £	Date	Narrative	Credit £
1/9/X7	Balance B/F	3 550	30/9/X7	Balance c/f	3 550
1/10/X7	Balance B/F	3 550			

Telephone

Date	Narrative	Debit £	Date	Narrative	Credit £
1/9/X7	Balance B/F	190			
30/9/X7	Bank	15	30/9/X7	Balance c/f	205
		205			205
1/10/X7	Balance B/F	205			

Rent

Date	Narrative	Debit £	Date	Narrative	Credit £
1/9/X7	Balance B/F	4 500			
30/9/X7	Bank	500	30/9/X7	Balance c/f	5 000
		5 000			5 000
1/10/X7	Balance B/F	5 000			

Bank

Date	Narrative	Debit £	Date	Narrative	Credit £
1/9/X7	Balance B/F	1 525	30/9/X7	Cash book	2 405
30/9/X7	Cash book	1 870	30/9/X7	Balance c/f	990
		3 395			3 395
1/10/X7	Balance B/F	990			

Sales ledger control

Date	Narrative	Debit £	Date	Narrative	Credit £
1/9/X7	Balance B/F	970	30/9/X7	Bank	1 870
30/9/X7	Sales	4 350	30/9/X7	Sales returns	200
			30/9/X7	Balance c/f	3 250
		5 320			5 320
1/10/X7	Balance B/F	3 250			

Purchase ledger control

Date	Narrative	Debit £	Date	Narrative	Credit £
30/9/X7	Bank	1 270	1/9/X7	Balance B/F	1 090
30/9/X7	Balance c/f	1 450	30/9/X7	Purchases	1 630
		2 720			2 720
			1/10/X7	Balance B/F	1 450

Petrol

Date	Narrative	Debit £	Date	Narrative	Credit £
1/9/X7	Balance B/F	560			
30/9/X7	Petty cash	50	30/9/X7	Balance c/f	610
		610			610
1/10/X7	Balance B/F	610			

Capital

Date	Narrative	Debit £	Date	Narrative	Credit £
1/9/X7	Balance c/f	6 755	30/9/X7	Balance B/F	6 755
			1/10/X7	Balance B/F	6 755

Sales returns

Date	Narrative	Debit £	Date	Narrative	Credit £
1/9/X7	Balance B/F	420			
30/9/X7	Sales ledger control	200	30/9/X7	Balance c/f	620
		620			620
1/10/X7	Balance B/F	620			

Cleaning

Date	Narrative	Debit £	Date	Narrative	Credit £
1/9/X7	Balance B/F	620			
30/9/X7	Petty cash	20	30/9/X7	Balance c/f	640
		640			640
1/10/X7	Balance B/F	640			

Postage

Date	Narrative	Debit £	Date	Narrative	Credit £
1/9/X7	Balance B/F	80			
30/9/X7	Petty cash	50	30/9/X7	Balance c/f	130
		130			130
1/10/X7	Balance B/F	130			

Petty cash

Date	Narrative	Debit £	Date	Narrative	Credit £
1/9/X7	Balance B/F	200	30/9/X7	Petty cash	120
30/9/X7	Bank	120	30/9/X7	Balance c/f	200
		320			320
1/10/X7	Balance B/F	200			

The usual convention in the ledger accounts is to record the debits on the left and credits on the right.

Note the balancing off at the end of an accounting period. In the above example for petty cash, the total of cash at the beginning of the period and the receipts made during the period are in excess of the period's payments. It follows that the difference between the two must be the balance of cash left at the end of the period. This is inserted on the side with the lower transactions total, so that both sides of the ledger account can be balanced off to the same column total of £320 (the value itself has no meaning). The final cash balance at 30 September 19X7 is carried forward (c/f) and becomes the brought forward (B/F) balance at 1 October 19X7.

At this stage it is important to be familiar with some accounting terms that have a special meaning for bookkeepers and accountants.

- *Sales* – relate to amounts received or are receivable from customers for supplies made in the normal course of trading. Other receipts of cash, such as bank interest on a deposit account, are not counted as sales. Sales are recorded net of trade discounts given to customers.
- *Purchases* – relate to the acquisition of goods intended for resale, including raw materials used in a manufacturing process. They exclude the buying of fixed assets or items consumed in the business as an overhead. Purchases are recorded net of trade discounts.
- *Carriage in* – the cost of bringing goods into the business.

- *Carriage out* – the cost of delivering goods to customers.
- *Discount received* – discounts given by suppliers for paying promptly (e.g. 3 per cent discount for paying within 7 days). These are settlement discounts that should not be confused with trade discounts given as a percentage off list prices.
- *Discounts allowed* – discounts given by the business to customers for paying promptly.
- *Stock* – the term used to describe those materials and goods purchased for resale but currently remaining unsold.
- *Expenses or overheads* – purchases of goods or services that are consumed in the business within a short time period. Examples include electricity, stationery, repairs to equipment, wages and rent. Various small items (say under £100) such as staplers and hand tools that are considered too small to record as a fixed asset are also treated as an expense.

The trial balance

The total of all account balances is listed to form the 'trial balance'. The trial balance has separate columns for debit and credit balances. It is prepared after the ledger accounts have been 'balanced off'.

Del's trial balance as at 30 September 19X7:

	Debit £	Credit £
Sales		22 590
Purchases	9 900	
Wages	5 700	
Stock 1/1/X7	3 550	
Telephone	205	
Rent	5 000	
Bank	990	
Sales ledger control account	3 250	
Purchase ledger control account		1 450
Petrol	610	
Capital		6 755
Sales returns	620	
Cleaner	640	
Postage	130	
Petty cash	200	
	30 795	30 795

If the double entry principle has been applied accurately, total debits should equal total credits. If the trial balance does not balance, one of the following errors may have been made:

- Only one side of a transaction has been posted, e.g. a debit but no credit.
- Both entries for a transaction have been posted to the same side, e.g. two debits.
- The two sides of a transaction have been posted with different values.
- An arithmetic error, either in the summation of the books of prime entry, in the balancing off of ledger accounts, or in the preparation of the trial balance.

The trial balance is the source of much of the information required to prepare financial reports.

Personal ledger accounts

The nominal ledger records total debtors and creditors, but it is important that the business also maintains records of individual customers and suppliers, to enable payment and to control amounts remaining unpaid. Large organisations may have thousands of customers and suppliers, while some of those that deal with the general public, such as the utility companies and the banks, have millions of customers. Therefore larger businesses have departments dedicated to customer and supplier accounting.

- *The purchase ledger (or creditors' ledger)* comprises separate accounts for debts incurred with individual suppliers.
- *The sales ledger (or debtors' ledger)* comprises separate accounts for amounts owing by individual customers.

The personal ledger accounts are a memorandum record of individual debtor and creditor balances. The total of all personal account balances on each ledger should be reflected by the same balance on the nominal ledger's corresponding control account.

Illustration – Del's accounts

Sales ledger

Allen						
Date	Narrative	Debit £	Date	Narrative		Credit £
1/9/X7	Balance B/F	700	30/9/X7	Bank		700
30/9/X7	Sales	1100	30/9/X7	Returns		150
30/9/X7	Sales	350	30/9/X7	Balance c/f		1300
		2150				2150
1/10/X7	Balance B/F	1300				

Diana						
Date	Narrative	Debit £	Date	Narrative		Credit £
1/9/X7	Balance B/F	270	30/9/X7	Bank		270
30/9/X7	Sales	900	30/9/X7	Bank		900
30/9/X7	Sales	400	30/9/X7	Returns		50
30/9/X7	Sales	1600	30/9/X7	Balance c/f		1950
		3170				3170
1/10/X7	Balance B/F	1950				

Summary of sales ledger balances
Unpaid debtor balances at 30/9/X7

	£
Allen	1300
Diana	1950
	3250

Purchase ledger

Liam						
Date	Narrative	Debit £	Date	Narrative		Credit £
30/9/X7	Bank	140	1/9/X7	Balance B/F		140
30/9/X7	Bank	180	30/9/X7	Purchases		180
30/9/X7	Balance c/f	710	30/9/X7	Purchases		710
		1030				1030
			1/10/X7	Balance B/F		710

Lynne					
Date	Narrative	Debit £	Date	Narrative	Credit £
30/9/X7	Bank	950	1/9/X7	Balance B/F	950
			30/9/X7	Purchases	340
30/9/X7	Balance c/f	740	30/9/X7	Purchases	400
		1690			1690
			1/10/X7	Balance B/F	740

Summary of purchase ledger balances
Unpaid creditor balances at 30/9/X7

	£
Liam	710
Lynne	740
	1450

Note that the totals of the individual ledger account balances do reconcile with the balances on the respective nominal ledger control account (see trial balance).

Figure 4.2 Overview of bookkeeping system for purchases

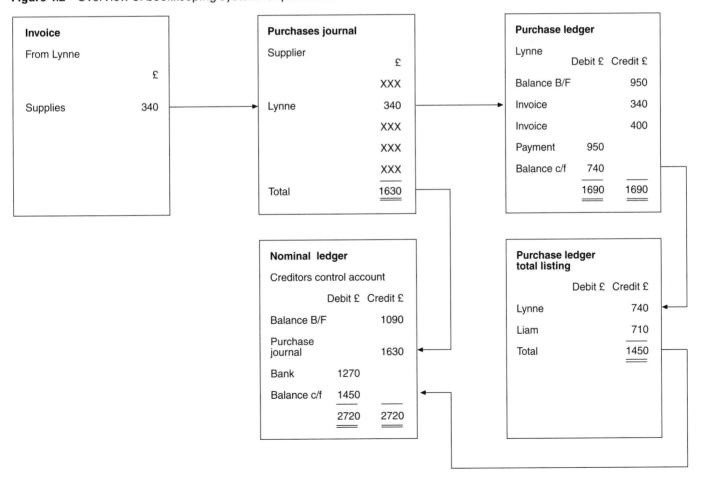

Exercise 4.2   Sales accounting

For the credit sales transactions listed below:

1 Prepare an analysed sales journal.
2 Prepare the individual sales ledger accounts and 'debtors control account'.

Ledger account balances 1/6/X9

Account name	£
Jenkins & Co	560
A Duxbury	45
P Tutty	250

Date	Name	Supply of	Invoice no.	Value (£)
1/6/X9	Jenkins & Co	Computer software	3256	400.00
4/6/X9	P Tutty	Stationery	3257	50.00
7/6/X9	Duxbury Ltd	Computer software	3258	250.00
10/6/X9	P Tutty	Text books	3259	120.00
13/6/X9	Jenkins & Co	Text books	3260	170.00
16/6/X9	P Tutty	Stationery	3261	10.00
19/6/X9	Duxbury Ltd	Text books	3262	65.00
22/6/X9	P Tutty	Text books	3263	75.00
25/6/X9	Duxbury Ltd	Computer software	3264	180.00
28/6/X9	Jenkins & Co	Stationery	3265	35.00

Accounting for stock

Many small businesses do not maintain a system to record stock as it is used. The purchases account in the nominal ledger is the only record relating to stock transactions. The stock account itself is only updated with the periodic valuation of stock following a stock take.

As no details exist of stock issues, the value of stock used has to be deduced as follows:

	(£)
Opening stock (from a stock take)	12 900
Add purchases (nominal ledger account)	84 510
	97 410
Less closing stock (from a stock take)	19 250
Therefore the cost of stock used	78 160

Many small businesses operate on this basis because it requires a minimum of paperwork and is simplé, but it does have shortcomings:

■ in larger stores it is difficult to monitor individual stock balances and the risk of running out of stock is high

■ the cost of materials used cannot be reported to management without a full count and valuation of all the stock in the stores

■ there are no records of stock issues, and hence it is difficult to ascertain economic yet adequate stock levels of individual items

■ there is no information concerning the purpose of the stock issue; this raises a number of questions. Was the stock used for bona fide purposes? Has the customer been charged correctly? How much material did each job require?

To overcome these problems many businesses operate a stock control system that records stock as it is received and issued. With this information the stock balance of individual items is known without having to undertake a stock take. This system is called a **perpetual inventory system**.

A perpetual inventory system is able to produce a listing of all stock issues for a period, which can then be used as a book of prime entry for nominal accounting purposes.

Exercise 4.3   Stock accounting

Casey & Co. operate a perpetual inventory system to control their stocks of automotive parts. To provide a running stock balance all stock movements are posted to a single stock account (a separate purchases account is not used). From the following information prepare a nominal ledger account for stock at 30 June 19X9, showing clearly the current stock balance.

	(£)
Purchase journal	38 100
Returns out journal	3 500
Stock issues	29 300
Stock balance 1 June 19X9	17 700

Physical stock take

Whether a stock recording system is in operation or not, it is important that stock balances are physically verified at least once during an accounting year. Where no stock records are maintained, it is necessary for a stock take to be carried out at the accounting year end. However, if an accurate perpetual inventory system is in operation, the stock record card can be used to value stocks and a full end-of-year stock take will not be needed. In these circumstances, the stock take of items can be carried out on a continuous basis throughout the year without disrupting normal business activities.

Exercise 4.4 Books of prime entry and ledger accounts

Westfield Supplies Ltd has had the following transactions during the month of January 19X9.

Date	Narrative	Value (£)
1/1/X9	Purchased goods for resale from Wells Engineering on credit	1 200
2/1/X9	Paid rent by cheque	3 000
3/1/X9	Components sold on credit to John Bryant	3 500
4/1/X9	Purchased goods for resale from Jason Robards on credit	4 200
5/1/X9	Purchased goods for resale from Corniche Manufacturing on credit	400
8/1/X9	Assemblies sold on credit to Desborough Workshops Ltd	5 400
9/1/X9	Components sold on credit to John Bryant	1 600
10/1/X9	Paid for stationery by cheque	900
11/1/X9	Purchased on credit some office chairs from Phipps & Drew	650
12/1/X9	Purchased goods for resale by cheque	100
15/1/X9	Assemblies sold on credit to Desborough Workshops Ltd	2 400
16/1/X9	Components sold on credit to Willis Bros.	950
17/1/X9	Received cash from John Bryant	2 500
18/1/X9	Components sold on credit to John Bryant	200
19/1/X9	Received cash from Desborough Workshops Ltd	1 600
22/1/X9	Paid Wells Engineering by cheque	2 300
23/1/X9	Assemblies sold on credit to Desborough Workshops Ltd	1 700
24/1/X9	Paid Wells Engineering	1 200
25/1/X9	Paid Corniche Manufacturing	400
26/1/X9	Components sold on credit to Willis Bros.	800
29/1/X9	Paid wages	6 000
30/1/X9	Received cash from Willis Bros.	950
31/1/X9	Assemblies sold on credit to John Bryant	750

- The accounting year runs from 1 October to 30 September.
- The accounting records had the following balances brought forward on 1 January 19X9 being the balances carried forward at 31 December 19X8.

Ledger	Name	Debit £	Credit £
Sales ledger	John Bryant	2 500	
	Desborough Workshops Ltd	1 600	
Purchase ledger	Wells Engineering		2 300
	Corniche Manufacturing		400
Nominal ledger	Office furniture	11 000	
	Bank control account	10 100	
	Debtors control account	4 100	
	Creditors control account		2 700
	Stationery	200	
	Wages	11 650	
	Sales		89 600
	Purchases	40 800	
	Other accounts	14 450	
	Total of nominal accounts	92 300	92 300

Tasks

1 *Enter the month's transactions onto the appropriate book of prime entry and provide an analysis of transactions consistent with the nominal ledger structure.*
2 *Make appropriate postings to the sales ledger, purchase ledger and nominal ledger.*
3 *Ensure that the totals of the personal ledgers do reconcile to the corresponding nominal ledger control account.*

Exercise 4.5 Bookkeeping system

The following transactions were made by Rodneys Trading Company during September 19X7.

Credit sales:

Document no	Customer	Value (£)	Sale / return
1011	Conrad	500	sale
1012	Terrys	100	sale
057	Conrad	100	return
1013	Simon	150	sale
1014	Terrys	150	sale
1015	Conrad	500	sale
1016	Julie	300	sale
058	Julie	100	return
1017	Conrad	100	sale
1018	Julie	50	sale
1019	Simon	400	sale
059	Conrad	200	return

Unpaid debtor balances at 1/9/X7

	(£)
Terrys	165
Simon	220
Julie	110
Conrad	495
	990

Credit purchases:

Document no	Supplier	Value (£)	Transaction type
906	Rowena	150	Motor repair
907	Larrie	1 500	Stock purchase
908	Leila	100	Repairs
909	Rowena	100	Motor service
910	Larrie	200	Stock purchase
911	BT	100	Telephone
912	Larrie	100	Stock purchase
913	Larrie	300	Stock purchase
914	Leila	50	Repairs

Unpaid credit balances at 1/9/X7

	(£)
Rowena	220
Larrie	1 100
Leila	110
	1 430

Cash book

The following receipts were paid into the bank account:

Document no	Received from	Value (£)
451	Terrys	165
452	Simon	220
453	Julie	110
454	Conrad	250
		745

The following payments were made from the bank account:

Document no	Paid to	Narrative	Value (£)
5720	Rowena	Purchase ledger	220
5722	Cherry	Rent	200
5723	Larrie	Purchase ledger	900
5724	Leila	Purchase ledger	110
5725	Karen	Wages	400
5726	Rodney	Drawings	600
5727	Cash	Petty cash	150
5725	Phil	Wages	300
			2 880

Petty cash

The following payments were made out of the petty cash float of £200.

Narrative	Value (£)
Petrol	30
Petrol	30
Cleaner	5
Postage	50
Petrol	20
Cleaner	15
	150

Trial balance as at 31/8/X7.	Debit (£)	Credit (£)
Sales		30 000
Purchases	20 000	
Wages	5 000	
Gas	200	
Stock 1/1/X7	2 000	
Telephone	150	
Rent	1 600	
General repairs	150	
Bank	5 000	
Sales ledger control account	990	
Purchase ledger control account		1 430
Motor repairs	200	
Petrol	400	
Capital		5 260
Sales returns	500	
Cleaner	100	
Postage	200	
Petty cash	200	
	36 690	36 690

Stocks at 30 September 19X7 were £2 900.

Tasks

1 *Prepare the books of prime entry for: sales, sales returns and purchases.*
2 *Prepare sales and purchase ledger accounts and post September's transactions.*
3 *Prepare the nominal ledger accounts and post September's transactions.*
4 *Balance off the nominal and personal ledger accounts as at 30 September 19X7.*
5 *Reconcile the purchase and sales ledger control accounts to the personal ledger accounts.*
6 *Prepare a nominal ledger trial balance as at 30 September 19X7.*

Accounting with computers

The accounting function was the first department in most businesses to use computers extensively. The large volumes of similar transactions are well suited to being computerised. In addition to the efficiency of data handling, computerised systems have facilitated the use of the vast bank of data afforded for management reporting purposes.

For medium to large businesses the accounting software may be bespoke or adapted to cater for the unique requirements of the business. Smaller businesses can utilise low-cost, standardised packages written for personal computers, such as those offered by Sage or Pegasus.

Accounting databases are classified into two types of file:

1 *Master file* – information that identifies the data subject and is common for all transactions, e.g. name and address.
2 *Transaction file* – information concerning each transaction, e.g. date, reference and amount paid.

Computer modules for accounting

Accounting module	Master file details	Transactions	Output
Sales ledger accounting	Details of customers: ■ account number ■ name ■ address ■ bank details ■ credit limit	Sales invoices Cash received ■ date ■ details ■ reference ■ value	Sales invoices Statements of account Sales journal Cash receipts list Analysis of sales by: 1 customer, 2 sales area, 3 product, etc. Age debtor analysis
Purchase ledger accounting	Details of suppliers: ■ account number ■ name ■ address ■ bank details	Purchase invoices Cheque payments ■ date ■ details ■ reference ■ value	Purchase journal Cheques and remittance advices Aged creditor analysis
Stock control	Details of stock: ■ reference number ■ description ■ supplier ■ unit of measure ■ control levels	Quantity and value: ■ receipts ■ issues ■ allocations	Stock movement enquiries Stock valuation lists Reorder lists Stock take lists
Payroll	Employee details: ■ payroll number ■ name ■ address ■ pay rates ■ tax code ■ bank details	Pay details: ■ hours worked ■ wages paid ■ tax and national insurance deducted	Payslip Bank transfer details Payroll summary, analysed by department End of year details P60 Termination – P45
Nominal ledger	Account details: ■ account number ■ name ■ analysis code for reporting	Transactions from: ■ purchases ■ sales ■ payroll ■ stock movements ■ cash transactions ■ journals	Account enquiries Trial balance Financial reports

Data subjects recorded on the master files are referred to using a data key, such as an account number for ledger accounts and a payroll reference number in the case of an employee. Data keys greatly speed up the input of data but also allow ledger accounts to be logically structured for reporting purposes. To ensure all staff are coding transactions correctly and consistently, it is standard practice for the financial accountant to issue an account code list for nominal ledger purposes. This list provides the basic structure for the accounts system and is designed to suit business reporting needs, having regard to business activities and organisation structure.

Typical features include income and expenditure codes that are common across the business, with function or location codes which enable transactions to be analysed by department (alternatively called profit centres or cost centres). Using the code list in Figure 4.3, the full nominal code is obtained by adding the cost centre code to the expenditure code. Hence an invoice for stationery for the sales office would be coded 3006124.

Figure 4.3 Extract from a code list – sales department only

Expenditure code	Description	Cost centre code	Description
3001	Wages and salaries	120	Sales – North
3002	Motor vehicle expenses	121	Sales – South
3003	Subsistence	122	Sales – East
3004	Entertainment	123	Sales – West
3005	Training	124	Sales office
3006	Stationery		
3007	Meetings		
3008	Sundries		

A code structure enables flexible reporting of financial transactions. The total of all codes beginning with 3001 measures the business's total wages bill. The total of all codes with 122 as the last three digits gives the cost of running the sales team operating in the east. Analysing all the transactions by the last three digits enables a printout to be issued each month to every cost centre manager, comparing actual sales and expenditure with budget.

Spreadsheets are used extensively in accounts departments to augment the basic accounting system, particularly for data analysis and flexible reporting. For

whilst most accounting packages offer a range of reports which vary in format, content and output medium, spreadsheets allow the user to handle and present information particularly effectively.

The use of spreadsheets has been accelerated by the introduction of accounting packages that can save data in spreadsheet format. Data files created in this way can then be accessed and used by a compatible spreadsheet package, such as Lotus 123 or Microsoft's Excel. Of real value is the ability to combine data from a number of different sources. In addition to bringing together financial data from different accounting modules, financial data can be combined with non-financial data from operational databases. This provides meaningful information for line management, as money values can be compared with activity times and physical measures such as the number of tonnes of factory output.

Once designed, the basic spreadsheet format can be used time and again for similar problems. The widespread use of spreadsheets within accounts departments testifies to their usefulness.

Summary

This chapter has examined the basic financial recording system, although its precise details in individual businesses will be dependent on the data to be processed and the reporting needs of that business.

1 Financial transactions are evidenced by invoices, credit notes, cheques and counterfoils, etc.
2 Transactions are classified by type and recorded in books of prime entry. The records may be manual books or computer files and comprise listings for credit sales, credit purchases and cash transactions. An additional prime book in respect of stock issues may also be maintained.
3 The totals recorded in each book are periodically posted to the nominal ledger.
4 The sales and purchase ledger accounts for individual customers and suppliers are updated from the detail lines of the books of prime entry.
5 The totals of the purchase and sales ledgers should reconcile to the corresponding nominal ledger control accounts.
6 A listing of the nominal ledger balances is called a trial balance.

Figure 4.4 Overview of the accounting system

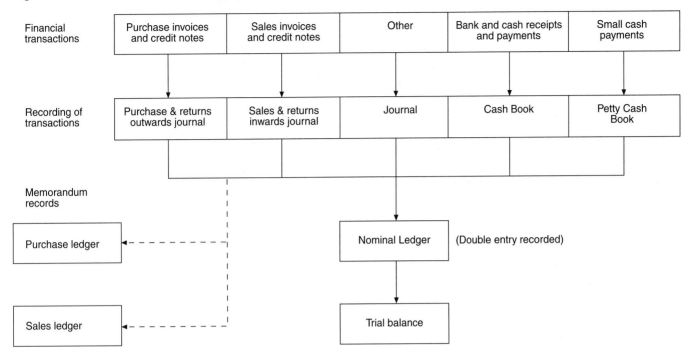

Further reading

R. J. Bull, David A. Harvey and Lindsey M. Lindley, *Accounting in Business*, 6th edition, Butterworth, 1990.

D. Cox, *Success in Bookkeeping and Accounts*, John Murray, 1989.

Paul Gee, *Spicer and Pegler's Bookkeeping and Accounts*, 23rd edition, Butterworth, 1996.

Richard Giles, *A Complete Course in Business Accounting*, Stanley Thornes, 1996.

A.H. Millichamp, *Foundation Accounting*, DPP, 1992.

Margaret Nicholson, *Accounting Skills*, Macmillan, 1989.

Alan Pizzey, *Accounting and Finance – a Firm Foundation*, 3rd edition, Cassell, 1990.

Geoffrey Whitehead, *Bookkeeping*, 4th edition, Butterworth Heinemann, 1993.

Frank Wood and Allan Sangster, *Business Accounting 1*, 7th edition, Pitman Publishing, 1996.

O n completion of this chapter students should be able to:

- identify and illustrate the structure of the main financial statements
- prepare profit and loss accounts and balance sheets from given data incorporating appropriate adjustments.

A major responsibility of the accounts department is the preparation of financial reports. Like other management information, this should be relevant, timely, accurate and well presented.

Financial reporting tends to focus on three principal financial statements, each being modified where necessary for the range of firms in the business sector:

1 the profit and loss account
2 the balance sheet
3 the cash flow statement.

The preparation of the profit and loss account and balance sheet are introduced in this chapter. The cash flow statement is considered in Chapter 11.

Introduction

The trial balance is the main source of information for preparing financial statements.

The accounts listed on the trial balance fall into two categories:

1 those which relate to items of continuing value at the end of the accounting period, i.e. assets, liabilities and capital
2 running totals of transactions that have occurred during the year.

Illustration – Trial balance

AB Engineering
Trial balance
for the year to 31 March 19X9

Account Name	Debit (£)	Credit (£)
Sales		100 000
Purchases	50 000	
Wages	10 000	
Rent	6 000	
Electricity	2 000	
Equipment	10 000	
Stock at 1 April 19X8	20 000	
Debtors	15 000	
Bank and cash	5 000	
Trade creditors		5 000
Capital at 1 April 19X8		13 000
Total	118 000	118 000

The trial balance is often accompanied by additional information which requires the balances to be updated or amended. In particular, where the trial balance has not been updated with prime data concerning stock usage, the minimum information necessary is a period-end stock valuation. The stock take for AB Engineering on 31 March 19X9 valued stock at £10 000.

Each category of items provides the basic information for one of the main financial statements:

1 *the balance sheet* – items of continuing value
2 *the trading and profit and loss account* – a summary of financial transactions.

From the trial balance for AB Engineering it is possible to identify the assets and liabilities of the business at 31 March 19X9:

	(£)	
Assets		
Equipment	10 000	
Stock	10 000	(end of period balance)
Debtors	15 000	
Bank and cash	5 000	
Total	40 000	
Liabilities		
Trade creditors:	5 000	
Total net assets	35 000	

Applying the accounting equation capital = assets – liabilities, the owner's capital invested in the business at 31 March 19X9 can be derived:

Capital	35 000	(£40 000 less £5 000).

This is an example of a balance sheet and is a statement of the business's financial affairs at a point in time, i.e. 31 March 19X9. However, it does not provide a full picture of what happened during the year to 31 March 19X9. From the trial balance it can be ascertained that owner's capital at 1 April 19X8 was £13 000 so during the year it has increased by £22 000. This increase in capital is the result of having made a *profit* during the period.

A profit is made by a business if it charges its customers more than the cost of the resources it consumes. Most of the cost items in the case of AB Engineering would appear to be quite straightforward. The exception is the amount of stock used. It is important to match the cost of stock actually sold to the amounts charged to customers. This is to comply with the *accruals* (or *matching*) *concept*. The calculation of stock used is:

Stock at the beginning of the period	£20 000
Add stock purchased during the period	£50 000
Total amount available for use	£70 000
Less stock at the end of the period	£10 000
Therefore the value of stock sold is	£60 000

It is now possible to calculate AB Engineering's profit for the period using a **trading and profit and loss account**. Its name arises because it is the combination of two ledger accounts:

1 *the trading account* – which derives gross profit by deducting the cost of stock sold from sales revenue.
2 *the profit and loss account* – which deducts expenses from gross profit to arrive at net profit.

AB Engineering
Trading and profit and loss account
for the ended 31 March 19X9

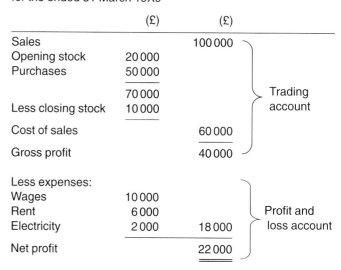

	(£)	(£)	
Sales		100 000	
Opening stock	20 000		
Purchases	50 000		
	70 000		Trading
Less closing stock	10 000		account
Cost of sales		60 000	
Gross profit		40 000	
Less expenses:			
Wages	10 000		
Rent	6 000		Profit and
Electricity	2 000	18 000	loss account
Net profit		22 000	

Note that the net profit explains the £22 000 increase in the owner's capital during the year.

The items in AB Engineering's balance sheet can now be rearranged to conform with a generally accepted format.

AB Engineering
Balance sheet

as at 31 March 19X9	(£)	(£)
Fixed assets:		
Equipment		10 000
Current assets:		
Stocks	10 000	
Debtors	15 000	
Cash at bank and on hand	5 000	
	30 000	
Current liabilities:		
Trade creditors	5 000	
Net current assets		25 000
		35 000
Financed by:		
Capital brought forward		13 000
Profit for the year		22 000
Capital carried forward		35 000

Accounts preparation

A comprehensive illustration will now be used to show how the basic report formats accommodate a range of accounting transactions and balance sheet items.

Illustration – Accounts from a trial balance

Lenny Keats requires a trading and profit and loss account and balance sheet from the following trial balance relating to the year ended 31 December 19X9.

	Debit (£)	Credit (£)
Bank	6 500	
Debtors	12 000	
Creditors		8 100
Sales		94 600
Stock at 1 January 19X9	12 200	
Purchases	53 100	
Rent	6 000	
Wages	9 900	
Drawings	5 500	
Electricity	1 000	
Capital		81 900
Bank loan – repayable in 2 years		20 000
Plant and equipment	21 000	
Land and buildings	68 000	
Carriage in	1 500	
Carriage out	900	
Returns in	1 300	
Returns out		300
Discounts received		500
Discounts allowed	400	
Motor vehicles	5 500	
Motor expenses	600	
	205 400	205 400

Stock at 31 December 19X9 was valued at £900.

Solution

Lenny Keats
Trading and profit and loss account
for the year ended 31 December 19X9

	(£)	(£)	(£)
Sales			94 600
Returns in			(1 300)
			93 300
Opening stock		12 200	
Purchases	53 100		
Returns out	(300)		
Carriage in	1 500	54 300	
		66 500	
Closing stock		900	
Cost of sales			65 600
Gross profit			27 700
Less expenses			
Rent		6 000	
Wages		9 900	
Electricity		1 000	
Carriage out		900	
Discounts allowed		400	
Discounts received		(500)	
Motor expenses		600	18 300
Net profit			9 400

Lenny Keats
Balance sheet
as at 31 December 19X9

	(£)	(£)
Fixed assets		
Land and buildings		68 000
Plant and equipment		21 000
Motor vehicles		5 500
		94 500
Current assets		
Stocks	900	
Debtors	12 000	
Bank	6 500	
	19 400	
Current liabilities		
Creditors	8 100	
Net current assets		11 300
Total assets less current liabilities		105 800
Long term liabilities		
Bank loan		20 000
		85 800
Financed by:		
Capital at 1 January 19X9		81 900
Profit		9 400
Less Drawings		(5 500)
Capital at 31 December 19X9		85 800

Notes:
- *Account headings – Every accounting statement requires an appropriate heading including: name of the business, title of the accounting statement (e.g. trading and profit and loss account or balance sheet), and the date.*
- *Use different columns to help the reader of the accounts appreciate the composition of totals and sub-totals. Figures in columns to the right generally represent totals of figures inset to the left.*
- *Indicate the denomination and currency being used in the accounts. Reports for small businesses may be in round pounds (£) but larger businesses may report in round thousands or even millions of pounds.*
- *Assets are presented in the balance sheet from the least liquid (fixed assets) to cash (highly liquid). Hence debtors are presented before cash but after stocks.*
- *Amounts payable within one year are classified as current liabilities and amounts payable after more than one year are considered long term liabilities.*
- *'Carriage-in' is added to purchases in the trading account because stocks are valued at the cost incurred in bringing the products to their present location and condition (SSAP 9). 'Carriage out' is a distribution expense just like advertising. Hence it is written off in the period to which it relates by treating it as an expense in the profit and loss account.*

- *Drawings relate to cash and other assets taken out of the business by the business owners and so is shown as a reduction in capital.*

A useful first step in the preparation of financial reports is to identify, for each item in the trial balance, whether it relates to the trading and profit and loss account or the balance sheet. For guidance use the following table:

	Debit	Credit
Trading and profit and loss account	Cost or expense	Income
Balance sheet	Asset	Capital or a liability

Here are some common problems because descriptions are not always informative:

Description	Treatment
Bank balance	Is it money in the bank or an overdrawn balance? A debit indicates an asset so it is money in the bank, a credit shows an overdraft.
Returns	Are they returns in or out? 'Returns in' are debits, 'returns out' are credits.
Discounts	Are they discounts received or discounts allowed? Discount allowed is a cost so will be a debit and discount received is income so must be a credit.

Exercise 5.1 Accounts from an unadjusted trial balance

The following trial balance and additional information relates to Anne Collson's business for the year ended 31 December 19X8.

	(£)	(£)
Plant and equipment	24 896	
Stock at 1 January 19X8	15 871	
Sales		56 870
Purchases	28 957	
Repairs and renewals	452	
Rent	3 000	
Wages	7 256	
Other expenses	2 654	
Trade debtors	6 784	
Trade creditors		2 369
Bank	8 741	
Capital at 1 January 19X8		48 372
Drawings	9 000	
	107 611	107 611

Notes:
Stock at 31 December 19X8 has been valued at £20 250.

Task

Prepare for Anne Collson a trading and profit and loss account and balance sheet for the year ended 31 December 19X8.

Exercise 5.2 Accounts from an unadjusted trial balance

The following trial balance and additional information relates to Margaret Seymour's business for the year ended 31 December 19X8.

	(£)	(£)
Plant and equipment	69 654	
Stock at 1 January 19X8	35 124	
Sales		565 477
Purchases	277 981	
Repairs and renewals	2 652	
Rent	26 000	
Wages	154 258	
Bad debts	1 256	
Returns inwards	984	
Returns outwards		125
Carriage in	863	
Carriage out	3 655	
Trade debtors	55 966	
Trade creditors		39 853
Bank		5 647
Capital at 1 January 19X8		35 791
Drawings	18 500	
	646 893	646 893

Notes:
Stock at 31 December 19X8 has been valued at £54 250.

Task

Prepare for Margaret Seymour a trading and profit and loss account and balance sheet for the year ended 31 December 19X8.

Exercise 5.3 Accounts from an unadjusted trial balance

The following trial balance and additional information relates to Justin Miles's business for the year ended 31 December 19X8.

	(£)	(£)
Plant and equipment	28 654	
Stock at 1 January 19X8	32 544	
Sales		154 785
Purchases	65 889	
Utility charges	5 588	
Rent	5 500	
Wages	15 774	
Other expenses	12 658	
Discount received		560
Returns outwards	440	
Carriage in	659	
Carriage out	2 336	
Trade debtors	54 862	
Trade creditors		17 542
Bank	5 694	
Capital at 1 January 19X8		75 711
Drawings	18 000	
	248 598	248 598

Notes:
Stock at 31 December 19X8 has been valued at £18 233.

Task

Prepare for Justin Miles a trading and profit and loss account and balance sheet for the year ended 31 December 19X8.

Adjustments to the trial balance

The necessity to comply with the companies acts and accounting standards was explained in Chapter 3. Unfortunately the trial balance is not necessarily in a form that complies with these regulatory requirements as it is merely a listing of account balances that have been derived from the books of prime entry. These records do not necessarily reflect the services to customers and the cost of resources actually used. For example, electricity is consumed continually by businesses but is invoiced on a monthly or quarterly basis. It is highly unlikely that recent usage has been recorded in the ledger accounts. Similarly, charges may have been received from suppliers for resources not yet consumed, for example insurance is often paid a year in advance.

Four types of adjustments to the trial balance will be considered in this chapter. All adjustments are an attempt to match costs correctly with revenues as required by SSAP 2:

1 *Accruals* – Some costs have not been reflected in the accounting records, such as utility charges as described above. These costs need to be 'accrued' in the accounts.

2 *Prepayments* – Payments for goods or services have been made in advance to their consumption, such as rent paid for future months.

3 *Depreciation* – Fixed assets have been purchased that will give economic benefit in future periods. A mechanism is needed for charging each accounting period with a fair share of the cost of assets used.

4 *Bad and doubtful debts* – It is unfortunate but a fact of business life that some goods sold on credit will never be paid for. The cost of bad debts should be spread over the periods that gave rise to the loss rather than charged to the period in which the debt is actually 'written off' as irrecoverable.

Accruals

An expense accrual is made in recognition that the accounting records currently understate the cost of resources consumed. The dual aspect of the adjustment recognises that suppliers are owed more than the accounting records currently state.

The adjustment is affected by carrying forward a credit balance on the expense account and hence increasing the transfer to the profit and loss account. An illustration is shown below.

The credit balance remaining on the expense account represents the liability to the supplier and is incorporated in the balance sheet as a current liability with the title 'accrual'.

Illustration – Balance sheet extract

Current liabilities	£
Trade creditors	5 000
Bank overdraft	400
Expense accrual	50
	5 450

Where a number of accruals have been made it is acceptable to consolidate them as one figure on the balance sheet (accompanying workings should show the make up of the total figure).

Exercise 5.4   Accruals

Robert Tite started trading on 1 January 19X8 and he is now at the end of his first year of trading. However, certain expenses he has incurred have yet to be invoiced by his suppliers.

Ledger account: Power								
Debit					**Credit**			
Date	Narrative	Ref.	Value £		Date	Narrative	Ref.	Value £
30/4/X8	Bank		200		31/12/X8	Profit and loss		500
31/7/X8	Bank		150					
31/10/X8	Bank		100					
31/12/X8	Balance c/f		50					
			500					500
					1/1/X9	Balance b/f		50

Trial balance as at 31 December 19X8:

	Debit (£)	Credit (£)
Sales		40 500
Purchases	31 500	
Power	800	
Telephone	650	
Stationery	250	
Equipment	2 200	
Bank and cash on hand	5 100	
Trade debtors and creditors	4 550	1 050
Capital		3 500
	45 050	45 050

- Stock at 31 December 19X8 was valued at £6 900
- Power charges for the first three quarters of 19X8 up to 30 September 19X8 were £300, £200 and £300 respectively. Usage for the final quarter to 31 December 19X8 is estimated to be £250.
- Telephone charges for the first three quarters of 19X8 up to September 19X8 were £160, £220 and £270 respectively. Usage for the final quarter to 31 December 19X8 is estimated to be £320.
- At the year end a stationery bill had not been received for an order delivered just before the Christmas holiday. The value of stationery received was £50.

Since the preparation of the trial balance the ledger account for power has been updated:

Ledger account: Power								
Debit					Credit			
Date	Narrative	Ref.	Value £		Date	Narrative	Ref.	Value £
	Bank		300		31/12/X8	Profit and loss		1 050
	Bank		200					
	Bank		300					
31/12/X8	Balance c/f		250					
			1 050					1 050
					1/1/X9	Balance B/F		250

After the accrual adjustment the charge for electricity in the profit and loss account is now £1 050. The cost accrual of £250 will be included with similar adjustments for telephone and motor expenses under current liabilities in the balance sheet.

Tasks

1 *Prepare and balance off the remaining ledger accounts for each expense that requires an accrual adjustment.*
2 *Prepare for Robert Tite his trading and profit and loss account and balance sheet for the period ending 31 December 19X8.*

Exercise 5.5 Accruals

Prepare the trading and profit and loss account and balance sheet for Fiona Fullerdale for the year ended 31 December 19X9 from the information below:

Trial balance

	Debit (£)	Credit (£)
Sales		109 700
Purchases	87 400	
Debtors	1 325	
Creditors		588
Fixed assets	3 984	
Bank	11 982	
Motor expenses	428	
Repairs and renewals	987	
Advertising	547	
Telephone	526	
Capital at 1 January 19X9		2 891
Stock at 1 January 19X9	5 000	
Drawings	1 000	
	113 179	113 179

■ Stock at 31/12/X9 was valued at £12 611.
■ The following items are to be accrued as due: telephone £120, advertising £425 and motor expenses £57.

Exercise 5.6 Accounts with expense accruals

The following trial balance and additional information relates to Jas Patel's business for the year ended 31 March 19X9.

	(£)	(£)
Sales		98 652
Purchases	45 632	
Stock at 1 April 19X8	14 537	
Electricity	4 196	
Motor expenses	1 420	
Wages	13 000	
Rent	3 000	
Drawings	16 000	
Motor vehicle	9 005	
Debtors	5 883	
Creditors		2 965
Discount allowed	540	
Bank		1 365
Capital at 1 April 19X8		10 231
	113 213	113 213

■ Stock at 31 March 19X9 has been valued at £11 126.
■ Electricity for the three months to 31 March 19X9 is estimated to have cost £1 125 but an invoice has not yet been received from the power company.
■ An invoice has not been received for a motor repair on 28 March which was anticipated to cost £150.

Task

Prepare for Jas Patel a trading and profit and loss account and balance sheet for the year ended 31 March 19X9.

Prepayments

A prepayment adjustment is made in recognition that the accounting records currently overstate the cost of resources consumed. The dual aspect is to reduce cost and to increase assets on the basis that the business has paid for resources that it has not consumed at the balance sheet date.

The prepayment adjustment is affected by carrying forward a debit balance to the next trading period and balancing the expense account with a reduced transfer to the profit and loss account.

In the illustration on the next page, insurance is paid at the end of one year to provide cover for the following year.

The debit balance that remains on the expense account is incorporated in the balance sheet as a current asset with the heading 'prepayment'.

Ledger account: Insurance							
Debit				**Credit**			
Date	Narrative	Ref.	Value £	Date	Narrative	Ref.	Value £
1/1/X8	Balance b/f		1 000	31/12/X8	Profit and loss		1 000
31/12/X8	Bank		1 100	31/12/X8	Balance c/f		1 100
			2 100				2 100
1/1/X9	Balance b/f		1 100				

Illustration – Balance sheet extract

Current assets	(£)
Stocks	4 000
Debtors	2 000
Prepayments	1 100
Cash at bank and on hand	100
	7 200

Where a number of prepayments have been made it is acceptable to consolidate them as one figure on the balance sheet. However, make sure that accompanying workings show the make up of the balance sheet total.

Exercise 5.7 Prepayments

Jane Prior has reached the end of her first year of trading. Various expenses relating to the next financial year have been prepaid as at 31 December 19X8.

Jane Prior's unadjusted trial balance as at 31 December 19X8.

	Debit (£)	Credit (£)
Sales		34 810
Purchases	12 890	
Rent	5 000	
Rates	500	
Motor maintenance	400	
Motor vehicle	9 250	
Bank and cash on hand	1 370	
Trade debtors and creditors	2 660	1 860
Capital as at 1 January 19X8		1 350
Drawings	5 950	
	38 020	38 020

- Stock at 31 December 19X8 was valued at £2 350.
- Rent – Jane has signed a five year lease for £4 000 per annum payable a quarter in advance.
- Rates – Jane pays business rates of £400 per annum. She has paid for the full year 1 April 19X8 to 31 March 19X9.
- Motor vehicle maintenance – When Jane purchased her car on 1 January 19X8 she also signed a two-year maintenance contract entailing a one-off payment of £400.

Since the preparation of the trial balance the ledger account for rent has been updated (see the next page).

The trial balance figure of £5 000 has been split into two parts with expenditure amounting to £1 000 being deferred and carried over to 19X9 as a prepayment. The charge to the profit and loss account has been reduced correspondingly to reflect the rent actually relating to 19X8. The balance on the rent account should be shown in the balance sheet as a prepayment under current assets together with other items that have been prepaid.

Ledger account: Rent

Debit				Credit			
Date	Narrative	Ref.	Value £	Date	Narrative	Ref.	Value £
1/1/X8	Bank		5 000	31/12/X8	Profit and loss		4 000
				31/12/X8	Balance c/f		1 000
			5 000				5 000
1/1/X9	Balance b/f		1 000				

Tasks

1 *Prepare and balance off the remainder of Jane's expense accounts that require a prepayment adjustment.*
2 *Prepare for Jane Prior a trading and profit and loss account for the year ended 31 December 19X8 and a balance sheet at that date.*

Exercise 5.8 Prepayments

Prepare the trading and profit and loss account and balance sheet for Casper Weinstock for the year ended 31 December 19X8 from the information below:

Trial balance

	Debit (£)	Credit (£)
Sales		98 426
Purchases	65 854	
Debtors	6 324	
Creditors		3 417
Fixed assets	22 568	
Bank	2 367	
Rent	6 250	
Insurance	1 000	
Rates	1 200	
Sundry expenses	325	
Capital at 1 January 19X8		13 389
Stock at 1 January 19X8	6 544	
Drawings	2 800	
	115 232	115 232

- Stock at 31/12/X8 has been valued at £7 654.
- The rent agreement is for £5 000 per annum.
- Insurance of £500 has been paid for the following financial year.
- Property rates of £1 000 have been paid for the year to 31 March 19X9.

Depreciation

A charge against profits for depreciation spreads the cost of a fixed asset over the periods that benefit from its use. It arises through the need to satisfy the accrual concept and a formal definition of terms is provided in SSAP 12, Accounting for Depreciation.

- *Depreciation* is the measure of the wearing out, consumption or other reduction in the useful economic life of a fixed asset, whether arising from use, effluxion of time or obsolescence through technological or market changes.
- The *useful economic life* of an asset is the period over which the present owner will derive economic benefits from its use.
- *Residual value* is the net realisable value of the asset at the end of its useful economic life, i.e. disposal proceeds less selling costs.

Another important term is *net book value* which is the cost of an asset less the amount it has been depreciated to date.

Net book value = original cost
– accumulated depreciation to date.

The accounting standard does not prescribe the method nor the economic life to be used in the depreciation of an asset. These are decisions best made in the light of the relevant circumstances.

Depreciation is charged as an expense in the profit and loss account and the asset's value in the balance sheet is reduced. The double entry is:

- Debit profit and loss account
- Credit provision for depreciation account (balance sheet account)

Methods for calculating depreciation

There are numerous methods that can be used for calculating depreciation, the most common being the straight line method and the reducing balance method.

Using the **straight line method**, the estimated depletion in the asset's value is spread evenly over its estimated economic life:

The depreciation charge per year

$$= \frac{\text{Cost} - \text{residual value}}{\text{Estimated life in years}}$$

For example, a motor vehicle costing £10 500 with an estimated life of 3 years and a residual value of £1 500 would be depreciated as follows:

Depreciation charge per year

$$= \frac{£10\,500 - £1\,500}{3}$$

$$= £3\,000 \text{ per year}$$

Note: The straight line method may be referred to in terms of the asset's estimated life or as a certain percentage of cost. For example, to depreciate the asset evenly over 10 years is the same as to depreciate at 10 per cent on cost.

The **reducing balance method** does not depreciate assets evenly over their useful economic life, but instead charges more depreciation in the early years of an asset's life. The method is appropriate where the relative benefits of owning the asset reduce as the asset ages. This may be due to obsolescence (e.g. computers) or increased maintenance costs in subsequent years. It is calculated by applying a percentage rate to the asset's net book value (i.e. cost less depreciation to date).

Depreciation per year = net book value × depreciation rate

Illustration – The two depreciation methods

The depreciation of a £120 000 item of equipment over 4 years, to leave a residual value of £7 500 at the end of that period, can be achieved by either the straight line or reducing balance methods.

Straight line method:

	Year 1 (£)	Year 2 (£)	Year 3 (£)	Year 4 (£)
Annual depreciation charge	28 125	28 125	28 125	28 125
Original cost	120 000	120 000	120 000	120 000
Accumulated depreciation	28 125	56 250	84 375	112 500
Net book value	91 875	63 750	35 625	7 500

Reducing balance method using a depreciation rate of 50 per cent:

	Year 1 (£)	Year 2 (£)	Year 3 (£)	Year 4 (£)
Annual depreciation charge	60 000	30 000	15 000	7 500
Original cost	120 000	120 000	120 000	120 000
Accumulated depreciation	60 000	90 000	105 000	112 500
Net book value	60 000	30 000	15 000	7 500

At the end of year 4 the net book value using both methods is identical. However, the reducing balance method has resulted in a higher charge to the profit and loss account in the first two years but lesser amounts in subsequent years.

Classification of capital expenditure

Capital expenditure relates to items that will give economic benefit for more than one accounting period. Firms usually operate a capital expenditure policy that requires all but the smallest of capital items to be accounted for as fixed assets (small items such as desk calculators are usually written off directly to the profit and loss account).

The correct classification of expenditure is important. Revenue expenditure (such as a repair cost) that is capitalised and recorded as a fixed asset would be in breach of the accounting concepts of prudence and the accrual concept for matching costs with revenue. To defer items of no continuing value would directly enhance current profits at the expense of those for future periods.

Generally, all expenditure relating to the acquisition and installation of a fixed asset can be included as being part of the cost of the asset. Hence delivery charges, legal fees and installation expenses can be included. Expenditure that increases the economic value of a fixed asset is also capital expenditure. This includes accessories for machines and building alterations.

Expenditure required to operate and maintain fixed assets is revenue expenditure. Hence the cost of repairs, redecoration and maintenance agreements cannot be treated as a fixed asset cost. However, expenditure incurred to improve the condition of newly acquired assets can be treated as capital expenditure.

Illustration

Speedyproof Ltd is a printing firm supplying packaging samples to the food industry. The following expenditure was incurred in the acquisition of a new printing press:

Date	Description	(£)
1/4/X1	Printing press	20 000
1/4/X1	Installation	2 000
1/4/X1	Maintenance agreement for a year	1 000
1/4/X1	Delivery	600
		23 600

- Plant and equipment is depreciated at 10 per cent on cost with no residual value assumed.
- Assets owned for part of a year are depreciated on a pro-rata basis.
- On 31 March 19X5 the printing press was sold for £10 000.

The accounting treatment of the expenditure is to be explained.

Solution

The cost of the printing press to be capitalised is £22 600 (£20 000 + £2 000 + £600). The maintenance expenditure of £1 000 should be written off to the profit and loss account as an expense.

The annual depreciation charge for the press

$$= \frac{£22\,500}{10 \text{ years}} = £2250$$

The depreciation charge each year until the press was sold would have been:

Year	Part of year	Depreciation charge (£)
19X1	9 months	1 695
19X2	12 months	2 260
19X3	12 months	2 260
19X4	12 months	2 260
19X5	3 months	565
Total		9 040

When the press was sold in 19X5 the sale proceeds were compared to the net book value of the asset and a profit or loss on disposal calculated. Speedyproof's loss on disposal has been calculated using a ledger account and this would be transferred to the profit and loss account as an expense for 19X5.

Disposal account								
Debit				**Credit**				
Date	Narrative	Ref.	Value £	Date	Narrative	Ref.	Value £
31/3/X5	Cost		22 600	31/3/X5	Depreciation		9 040
				31/3/X5	Bank		10 000
				31/3/X5	Loss		3 560
			22 600				22 600

Exercise 5.9 Capital expenditure and depreciation

Speedyproof also had the following items of expenditure during 19X1:

Date	Description	(£)
1/7/X1	Building work at their leasehold premises	
	Redecorations	2 000
	Mezzanine floor for additional storage	1 000
	Repair brickwork	500
		3 500
1/10/X1	Motor vehicle for sales person	
	Basic car	12 000
	Alloy wheels	400
	One year's maintenance contract	100
	Road tax	150
		12 650

For these assets Speedyproof uses the following depreciation policies:

- Expenditure relating to buildings is depreciated over the remaining life of the lease that is due to expire on 30 June 19X9. No residual value is assumed.
- Motor vehicles are depreciated straight line over four years with no residual value assumed.
- Assets owned for part of a year are depreciated on a pro-rata basis.

Disposal of assets:
- On 30 June 19X4 the motor vehicle was sold for £3 000.

Tasks

1 *Identify the capital items of expenditure.*
2 *For both assets calculate each year's depreciation charge.*
3 *Calculate the profit or loss on the disposal of the motor vehicle.*

Depreciation and final accounts

Most businesses maintain separate ledger accounts for the cost and accumulated depreciation of fixed assets and so the trial balance will include both debit and credit balances in respect of each type of asset.

For examination purposes the trial balance is usually prepared before the depreciation charge for the current year has been made. When depreciation has been calculated it should be debited as an expense to the profit and loss account. The dual aspect will be for the credit balance on the accumulated depreciation account to be increased correspondingly. The asset is then stated in the balance sheet at its net book value.

Illustration – Straight line

The following trial balance has been extracted from the books of Jesse Jones as at 31 December 19X9.

	Debit (£)	Credit (£)
Motor vehicles	20 000	
Furniture and fittings	10 000	
Motor – accumulated depreciation		10 000
Furniture – accumulated depreciation		2 500
Sales and purchases	60 000	100 000
Stock at 1/1/X9	15 000	
Motor running expenses	2 000	
Rent	4 000	
Bank	3 000	
Creditors		1 000
Capital		4 700
Disposal account		800
Drawings	5 000	
	119 000	119 000

1 Stock at 31 December 19X9 was valued at £10 000.
2 Motor vehicles are depreciated over 4 years with no residual value assumed. Furniture is depreciated by 10 per cent of cost each year. Assets are not depreciated in the year of disposal.
3 During the year an item of furniture was sold for £800 and the proceeds have been credited to a disposal account. The asset had cost £2 000 during 19X4.

Prepare for Jesse Jones his trading and profit and loss account and balance sheet for the year ended 31 December 19X9.

Solution

Depreciation of the motor vehicle for 19X9	$= \dfrac{£20\,000}{4 \text{ years}}$	$= £5\,000$
Depreciation of the furniture for 19X9	$= 10\% \times (£10\,000 - £2\,000)$	$= £800$
Accumulated depreciation on asset sold	$= 5 \text{ years} \times 10\% \times £2\,000$	$= £1\,000$
Net book value of asset sold	$= £2\,000 - £1\,000$	$= £1\,000$
Loss on sale of asset	$= £800 - £1\,000$	$= £200$
Cost of remaining furniture	$= £10\,000 - £2\,000$	$= £8\,000$
Depreciation of remaining furniture	$= £2\,500 + £800 - £1\,000$	$= £2\,300$
Accumulated depreciation of motors	$= £10\,000 + £5\,000$	$= £15\,000$

Jesse Jones

Trading and profit and loss account
for the period ended 31 December 19X9

	(£)	(£)
Sales		100 000
Opening stock	15 000	
Purchases	60 000	
	75 000	
Less closing stock	10 000	
Cost of sales		65 000
Gross profit		35 000
Less expenses:		
Depreciation – motor	5 000	
Depreciation – furniture	800	
Loss on disposal of furniture	200	
Rent	4 000	
Motor running expenses	2 000	12 000
Net profit		23 000

Jesse Jones

Balance sheet
for the period ended 31 December 19X9

	Cost (£)	Depreciation (£)	(£)
Fixed assets:			
Furniture	8 000	2 300	5 700
Motor vehicles	20 000	15 000	5 000
	28 000	17 300	10 700
Current assets:			
Stocks		10 000	
Bank and cash on hand		3 000	
		13 000	
Current liabilities:			
Creditors		1 000	
Net current assets			12 000
			22 700
Capital brought forward			4 700
Profit for the period		23 000	
Drawings		5 000	18 000
Capital carried forward			22 700

Exercise 5.10 Depreciation

The following trial balance and additional information relates to Roger Symons' business for the year ended 31 March 19X9.

	(£)	(£)
Motor vehicles cost	24 560	
Motor vehicle depreciation		12 322
Equipment cost	12 580	
Equipment depreciation		5 981
Stock at 1 April 19X8	6 558	
Sales		122 956
Purchases	65 417	
Expenses	32 855	
Debtors	12 593	
Creditors		3 244
Bank	9 125	
Capital		37 233
Drawings	17 500	
Carriage in	548	
	181 736	181 736

- Stock at 31 March 19X9 has been valued at £7 881.
- Depreciation rates based on cost are 10 per cent for equipment and 25 per cent for motor vehicles.

Task

Prepare for Roger Symons a trading and profit and loss account and balance sheet for the year ended 31 March 19X9.

Exercise 5.11 Accounts with depreciation

The following trial balance and additional information relates to Mandy Booth's business for the year ended 31 March 19X9.

	(£)	(£)
Plant and equipment cost	15 240	
Plant and equipment depreciation		4 530
Motor cost	19 440	
Motor depreciation		9 670
Stock at 1 April 19X8	1 221	
Sales		49 740
Purchases	31 810	
Expenses	5 542	
Debtors	2 369	
Creditors		1 117
Bank		1 463
Capital		14 102
Drawings	5 000	
	80 622	80 622

- Stock at 31 March 19X9 has been valued at £3 449.
- Depreciation rates based on net book value are 20 per cent for equipment and 30 per cent for motor vehicles.

Task

Prepare for Mandy Booth a trading and profit and loss account and balance sheet for the year ended 31 March 19X9.

Exercise 5.12 Accounts with depreciation and fixed asset disposal

The following trial balance and additional information relates to Henry Vliestra's business for the year ended 30 June 19X9.

	(£)	(£)
Plant and equipment cost	15 600	
Plant and equipment depreciation		8 400
Motor cost	8 840	
Motor depreciation		3 680
Stock at 1 July 19X8	5 843	
Sales		86 347
Purchases	36 810	
Expenses	21 398	
Debtors	5 322	
Creditors		2 194
Bank	2 369	
Capital		6 561
Motor disposal account		1 000
Drawings	12 000	
	108 182	108 182

- Stock at 30 June 19X9 has been valued at £2 445.
- Depreciation rates based on cost are 10 per cent for equipment and 25 per cent for motor vehicles. Assets are depreciated from the year of purchase to the year prior to disposal.
- During the year Henry sold a motor vehicle for £1 000 which had cost him £4 000 during 19X6/X7. No entries have been made in respect of this transaction apart from the posting of sale proceeds to a motor disposal account.

Task

Prepare for Henry Vliestra a trading and profit and loss account and balance sheet for the year ended 30 June 19X9.

Exercise 5.13 Accounts with depreciation and fixed asset disposal

The following trial balance and additional information relates to Joseph Leamoth's business for the year ended 31 December 19X9.

	(£)	(£)
Equipment cost and depreciation	23 344	16 840
Stock at 1 January 19X9	18 543	
Sales		91 347
Purchases	53 996	
Expenses	23 665	
Debtors / creditors	5 399	1 656
Bank	811	
Capital		27 615
Disposal account		3 300
Drawings	15 000	
	140 758	140 758

- Stock at 31 December 19X9 has been valued at £2 445.
- Equipment is depreciated over 8 years straight line with no charge in the year of disposal.
- During the year Joseph sold equipment for £3 300 which had cost him £8 800 during 19X5. The only entry in respect of this transaction has been the posting of the proceeds to a disposal account.

Task

Prepare for Joseph Leamoth a trading and profit and loss account and balance sheet for the year ended 31 December 19X9.

Bad and doubtful debts

Apart from retail trade, most sales are on a credit basis so there is always the risk of the customer defaulting on the trade debt. This may be because the customer:

- wilfully flouts the terms of trade
- questions the ability of the supplier to substantiate its claim in court
- has insufficient cash to settle the debt in full
- has been declared bankrupt.

The business has to consider the cost of pursuing payment against the likelihood of eventual success. There may come a time when the debt has to be considered irrecoverable and at that point this needs to be reflected in the accounting records.

When a debt is considered irrecoverable the book keeping entries are:

- Debit   bad debt account
- Credit   debtors control account (and also the customer's account on the sales ledger)

Bad debts are treated as an administration expense to be written off in the profit and loss account.

To satisfy the accounting concepts of prudence and accrual, there may be a need to recognise that there is a chance of non-payment before the debt is finally considered irrecoverable. The problem of waiting until a debt is proven to be irrecoverable is that it may distort the relative performance of different accounting periods. The debt may be retained on the customer's account in the hope that it might be collected in the future and so when the debt is eventually written off it may be in a different accounting period from the time of sale. There is therefore a need to make an adjustment in the accounts for this timing discrepancy.

Although problems may be known about specific debts, it is often difficult and time consuming to assess accurately the recoverability of all debts. In such circumstances it is usual practice, on the basis of past experience, to consider a proportion of debts outstanding as non-paying. This allowance for future debt write-offs is called a **provision for bad and doubtful debts**. The provision is created with the journal entries:

- Debit   bad debts account (to be transferred to the profit and loss account)
- Credit   provision for bad and doubtful debts (a balance sheet account)

Although the provision has a credit balance it is included under current assets in the balance sheet as it relates specifically to debtors. Here is an illustration:

Current assets	(£)	(£)
Stocks		10 000
Debtors	20 000	
Provision for bad debts @ 5 per cent	1 000	19 000
Prepayments		1 000
Cash at bank and on hand		1 000
		31 000

The provision remains unchanged as a balance from one year to the next unless further adjustments are made via the bad debts account. Using the figures above, if in the next year debtors increase to £2 400 and the provision was to be kept at 5 per cent of debtors, then the provision will have to be increased by £20 (debit bad debts account, credit bad and doubtful debts provision). Conversely, if debtors fall, then a proportion of the provision is released (debit bad and doubtful debt provision, credit bad debts account).

The balance on the bad debts account is charged as an expense to the profit and loss account. Therefore the charge for bad debts will be the sum of the debts actually written off plus or minus the period's movement in the bad and doubtful debt provision.

Illustration – Bad debt provision

Martin Spicer extracted the following balances from his books on 31 December 19X9.

	Debit (£)	Credit (£)
Bank	5 600	
Debtors	50 000	
Provision for bad and doubtful debts		2 000
Bad debts	200	

1 Stocks were valued at £19 100.
2 He estimates that bad debts are 5 per cent of debtors.

■ Prepare the journal entry required to affect the change to the bad debt provision.
■ Prepare the current assets section of Martin's balance sheet at the 31 December 19X9.
■ State the amount to be charged to the profit and loss account in respect of bad debts.

Solution

Journal	Debit (£)	Credit (£)
Bad debts (£2 500 – £2 000)	500	
Provision for bad and doubtful debts		500

Balance sheet extract:

Current assets	(£)	(£)
Stocks		19 100
Debtors	50 000	
Provision for bad debts @ 5 per cent	(2 500)	47 500
Cash at bank and on hand		5 600
		72 200

The amount to be charged to the profit and loss account in respect of bad debts is £700 (£200 + £500).

Exercise 5.14 Bad and doubtful debts

Hannah Garton extracted the following balances from her books on 31 December 19X9.

	Debit (£)	Credit (£)
Bank	2 000	
Debtors	50 000	
Provision for bad and doubtful debts		1 000
Bad debts	550	

■ Stocks were valued at £9 300.
■ Hannah considers it very unlikely one debt for £2 000 will be paid. In addition, 4 per cent of the remainder should also be covered by the bad debt provision.

Task

1 *Prepare the journal entry required to affect the change to the bad debt provision.*
2 *Prepare the current assets section of Hannah's balance sheet as at 31 December 19X9.*
3 *State the amount to be charged to the profit and loss account in respect of bad debts.*

Exercise 5.15 Bad debts

The following trial balance has been extracted from the books of Daljit Mistry as at 30 June 19X9.

	Debit (£)	Credit (£)
Sales & purchases	9 860	23 400
Bad debts	209	
Provision for bad debts		30
Stock at 1/7/X8	687	
Rent	3 000	
Bank	2 871	
Fixed assets	4 500	
Debtors / Creditors	650	592
Capital		5 755
Drawings	8 000	
	29 777	29 777

■ Stock at 30 June 19X9 was valued at £485.
■ The provision for bad debts should be stated at 8 per cent of debtors.

Task

Prepare for Daljit Mistry a trading and profit and loss account and balance sheet for the year ended 30 June 19X9.

Exercise 5.16   Bad debts

The following trial balance and additional information relates to Rosie Cassals' business for the year ended 31 March 19X9.

	(£)	(£)
Sales		31 774
Purchases	11 296	
Stock at 1 April 19X8	654	
Wages	2 530	
Rent	4 000	
Drawings	6 000	
Motor vehicle	5 600	
Debtors	3 300	
Creditors		424
Bad debts	150	
Bank	2 930	
Capital at 1 April 19X8		4 162
Bad debt provision		100
	36 460	36 460

- Stock at 31 March 19X9 has been valued at £926.
- Rosie has decided her bad debt provision should equate to 5 per cent of the debtors balance.

Task

Prepare for Rosie Cassals a trading and profit and loss account and balance sheet for the year ended 31 March 19X9.

Exercise 5.17   Bad debts

The following trial balance and additional information relates to David Tanner's business for the year ended 31 March 19X9.

	(£)	(£)
Sales		57 930
Purchases	27 864	
Stock at 1 April 19X8	2 369	
Wages	2 650	
Rent	6 000	
Drawings	8 000	
Equipment	7 640	
Debtors	6 925	
Creditors		1 983
Bad debts	135	
Bank	905	
Capital at 1 April 19X8		2 425
Bad and doubtful debt provision		150
	62 488	62 488

- Stock at 31 March 19X9 has been valued at £1 968.
- A bad and doubtful debt provision is required to cover a specific seven month old debt of £350. In addition, a general provision is required to cover 4 per cent of the remaining debts.

Task

Prepare for David Tanner a trading and profit and loss account and balance sheet for the year ended 31 March 19X9.

Exercise 5.18 Accounts with adjustments for accruals, prepayments and depreciation

The following trial balance and additional information relates to Pat McClusky's business for the year ended 31 March 19X9.

	(£)	(£)
Motor vehicles cost	65 868	
Motor vehicle depreciation		23 420
Furniture, fixtures and fittings cost	45 650	
Furniture, fixtures and fittings depreciation		21 830
Stock at 1 April 19X8	23 822	
Sales		232 855
Purchases	130 241	
Expenses	58 694	
Debtors	23 411	
Creditors		18 844
Bank	6 543	
Capital		79 580
Drawings	21 600	
Carriage in	700	
	376 529	376 529

- Stock at 31 March 19X9 has been valued at £27 881.
- Depreciation rates based on cost are 10 per cent for furniture, fixtures and fittings and 25 per cent for motor vehicles.
- The trial balance must be adjusted for an expense accrual for £1,985 and an expense prepayment for £300.

Task

Prepare for Pat McClusky a trading and profit and loss account and balance sheet for the year ended 31 March 19X9.

Exercise 5.19 Accounts with adjustments for accruals, prepayments, depreciation and bad debts

The following trial balance and additional information relates to Judith Pearson's business for the year ended 31 March 19X9.

	(£)	(£)
Furniture, fixtures and fittings cost	24 400	
Furniture, fixtures and fittings depreciation		22 200
Stock at 1 April 19X8	2 664	
Sales		53 746
Purchases	21 889	
Wages	13 950	
Rent	7 500	
Debtors	2 650	
Creditors		1 398
Bank		556
Capital		53
Drawings	5 000	
Bad debt provision		100
	78 053	78 053

- Stock at 31 March 19X9 has been valued at £1 987.
- Depreciation is calculated at 25 per cent of fixed asset cost.
- Wages of £180 are to be accrued as due for payment.
- Rent has been paid up to 30 June 19X9.
- The bad debt provision is to be adjusted to equal 4 per cent of debtors.

Task

Prepare for Judith Pearson a trading and profit and loss account and balance sheet for the year ended 31 March 19X9.

Exercise 5.20 Accounts with adjustments for accruals, prepayments, depreciation and bad debts

The following trial balance and additional information relates to Peter Nelson's business for the year ended 31 March 19X9.

	(£)	(£)
Plant and equipment cost	84 630	
Plant and equipment depreciation		27 655
Stock at 1 April 19X8	2 180	
Sales		246 978
Purchases	93 458	
Wages	41 239	
Rent	12 500	
Carriage in	454	
Debtors	24 680	
Creditors		21 506
Bank		1 547
Capital		4 242
Other expenses	19 454	
Drawings	24 500	
Bad debt provision		1 167
	303 095	303 095

- Stock at 31 March 19X9 has been valued at £4 110.
- Depreciation is calculated on a 30 per cent reducing balance basis from the year of purchase. However, it is not charged on assets that are sold during the year.
- A piece of equipment has been sold for £900 and the proceeds have been credited in error to the plant and equipment cost account. The asset had cost £6 500 during 19X6/X7.
- Other expenses of £1 080 are to be accrued as due for payment.
- The rent agreement is for £10 000 per annum.
- The bad debt provision is to be adjusted to equal 4 per cent of debtors.

Task

Prepare for Peter Nelson a trading and profit and loss account and balance sheet for the year ended 31 March 19X9.

Exercise 5.21 Accounts with adjustments for accruals, prepayments, fixed assets and bad debts

The following trial balance and additional information relates to Sandy Paisley's business for the year ended 31 December 19X9.

	(£)	(£)
Bank		5 205
Stock at 1 January 19X9	44 870	
Carriage in	540	
Purchases	157 654	
Discount allowed	1 240	
Discount received		954
Sales		296 325
Rent	10 000	
Motor expenses	8 904	
Telephone	4 211	
Office expenses	2 631	
Bad debts	246	
Wages and salaries	35 868	
Equipment cost	32 860	
Equipment depreciation		14 870
Motor cost	25 792	
Motor depreciation		13 445
Motor disposal account		1 000
Debtors	6 870	
Provision for bad debts		200
Trade creditors		2 677
Capital		7 510
Loan – 5 year @ 10%		10 000
Interest	500	
Drawings	20 000	
	352 186	352 186

- Stock at 31 December 19X9 has been valued at £43 588.
- Depreciation is calculated from the month of purchase to the month of asset disposal inclusive. Motor vehicles are depreciated straight line over 4 years and equipment straight line over 10 years.
- On 1 July 19X9 equipment costing £4 580 was purchased.
- On 30 September 19X9 a motor vehicle that had cost £9 200 on 1 October 19X6 was sold. The sale proceeds have been credited to a motor disposal account but no other entries have been made in respect of the transaction.
- Telephone charges of £550 are to be accrued as due for payment.
- The second half year's interest charge on the loan has not been paid.
- The rent agreement requires the £8 000 p.a. rental to be paid quarterly in advance.
- A bad debt provision is required for a specific debt of £150 and for 5 per cent of the remaining debtor balance.

Task

Prepare for Sandy Paisley a trading and profit and loss account and balance sheet for the year ended 31 December 19X9.

Summary

This chapter has explained the preparation of the trading and profit and loss and balance sheet for sole traders. The trial balance, which is constructed from the business's nominal ledger balances, is adjusted to ensure that the financial reports comply with fundamental accounting concepts.

Accounting adjustment:	Accounting concept	
	Prudence	Accrual
Accruals	■	■
Prepayments		■
Depreciation		■
Doubtful debts	■	■

Further reading

R. J. Bull, David A. Harvey and Lindsey M. Lindley, *Accounting in Business,* 6th edition, Butterworth, 1990.

D. Cox, *Success in Bookkeeping and Accounts,* John Murray, 1989.

Paul Gee, *Spicer and Pegler's Bookkeeping and Accounts,* 23rd edition, Butterworth, 1996.

Richard Giles, *A Complete Course in Business Accounting,* Stanley Thornes, 1996.

Margaret Nicholson, *Accounting Skills,* Macmillan, 1989.

Geoffrey Whitehead, *Bookkeeping,* 4th edition, Butterworth Heinemann, 1993.

Frank Wood and Allan Sangster, *Business Accounting 1,* 7th edition, Pitman Publishing, 1996.

6 Company accounts

On completion of this chapter students should be able to:

- identify and illustrate the structure of the main financial statements
- identify and explain the differing requirements of limited companies and sole traders
- prepare profit and loss accounts and balance sheets from the given data incorporating appropriate adjustments.

Accounts for limited companies are prepared on a similar basis as those for a sole trader (see Chapter 5). However, because the company is recognised as a separate legal entity from its owners, there are important differences in the appropriation of profit and in the firm's capital structure.

Share capital

The capital of a company is split into shares that are recorded at a **nominal value**. For example, a company with 10 000 shares issued at a nominal value of £0.50 has a share capital of £5 000 which is disclosed in the capital section of the balance sheet. The difference between the issue price paid by the shareholder and the nominal value is called the **share premium**.

If shareholders paid the company £0.75 for each share then the premium would be £0.25 per share and £2 500 in total.

Capital structures compared:

Sole trader	£	Company	£
Capital (paid in)	7 500	Share capital	5 000
		Share premium account	2 500
			7 500

As a company establishes a trading record and grows with the accumulation of retained profits, its shares' intrinsic value will increase. Should the company need to raise more cash it should be able to find buyers prepared to pay increasingly higher premiums, otherwise the original investors will not want their ownership to be diluted by the issue of more shares.

The share capital and share premium accounts only reflect the cash actually received by the business. Where the ownership of shares subsequently changes hands, cash is passed between the buyer and seller of the shares, not involving the company itself.

The **authorised share capital** is the maximum number of shares that can be issued and is specified in the company's memorandum of association at the time the company is formed. The restriction on the number of shares that can be issued can only be amended by the existing shareholders voting to increase the company's authorised share capital. The amount of authorised share capital says nothing about the actual financial resources used by the company. The amount of money received by the company corresponds with the shares issued and paid for by the shareholders. The shares may be described as **issued and fully paid** or **issued and partly paid**, whichever the case may be.

The share capital may be divided into a number of share classes depending on the rights attached to each type of share. The main share categories of ordinary shares and preference shares have been described in Chapter 1. The balance sheet should provide an analysis of the company's share capital if there is more than one class of share.

Reserves

Shareholders are, generally, not able to withdraw their capital from the business as a direct result of the limited liability that they enjoy. This in contrast to a sole trader who has no restrictions on withdrawals, because the sole trader is liable for the debts of the business whatever the financial position of the business.

Without restrictions, the shareholders of a failing company could withdraw assets from the business and leave nothing to pay the company's creditors. The companies acts ensure that shareholders can only receive payments in the form of a dividend from distributable reserves. Capital can only be returned after special procedures have ensured there are sufficient funds to pay the creditors.

Distributable reserves are realised profits less realised losses, as normally included in the profit and loss account (i.e. profits are realised when reasonably certain, and losses are realised as soon as they are known). Because of the need to distinguish between those reserves that are available for dividends and those that are not, it is necessary for accumulated profits to be kept separate from capital items. Distributable reserves are often called **revenue reserves**. Reserves that cannot be distributed are called **capital reserves**. The share premium account is an example of a capital reserve.

The main revenue reserve is clearly the accumulated balance on the profit and loss account, which represents the company's retained profits. But to give other stakeholders confidence in the funding of the business, the directors may decide to transfer some of the profit and loss account balance into a **general reserve**. The directors are communicating their intention not to use those funds for dividends. However, the procedure is a voluntary one and

is cosmetic only. It does not change the fact that the general reserve was created out of distributable profits and so is a revenue reserve that could be used for dividends.

Many companies prepare accounts on an historical cost basis as modified by the revaluation of land and buildings. The purpose of this is to show the true market value of company assets. For assets revalued upwards, land and buildings are debited (increased) and this results in a credit that increases shareholders' funds. However, the surplus on revaluation is not a realised profit and so cannot be treated as income in the profit and loss account. The surplus is credited instead to a **revaluation reserve** which is a capital reserve.

Reserves are detailed after share capital in the balance sheet, running from capital reserves to revenue reserves. For example:

	(£)
Capital and reserves	
Ordinary share capital	50 000
Preference share capital	20 000
Share premium account	60 000
Revaluation reserve	30 000
General reserve	50 000
Profit and loss account	25 000
	235 000

Profit appropriation

Because of the need to maintain a running balance of distributable reserves, a profit appropriation account is added to the bottom of the profit and loss account.

The first portion of the company's profits goes in **corporation tax** to the Inland Revenue. Corporation tax is calculated on taxable profits which are not necessarily the same as accounting profits. The main difference is usually in the treatment of fixed assets. Accounting profits will have been charged depreciation, based on the company's accounting policies, whereas taxable profits are reduced by capital allowances that are calculated on the same basis for all companies. Corporation tax is computed when the accounts are prepared but is not paid until up to 9 months after the accounting year end. It follows that the corporation tax for the current year becomes a current liability in the balance sheet.

The next profit appropriation is the **dividends** payable to the company's shareholders. Dividends paid during the year are called **interim dividends** and those dividends that are being proposed by the directors at the year end are called **final dividends**. Final dividends require the ratification of the shareholders, usually at the company's annual general meeting. Because final dividends have not been paid at the year end, they are a current liability in the balance sheet.

Some of the balance on the profit and loss account may also be appropriated to change the capital structure of the company (an example being the transfer to a general reserve as described above).

Illustration of an appropriation account

	(£)	(£)
Profit before taxation		21 200
Taxation		7 100
Profit after taxation		14 100
Dividends – paid	3 000	
– proposed	6 000	9 000
Retained profit for the year		5 100
Transfer to general reserve		–4 000
Retained profit brought forward		18 900
Retained profit carried forward		20 000

Bonus share issues

Bonus shares are shares issued to shareholders without money being paid for them. The accounting entries are:

- debit   a reserve
- credit   share capital

On the face of it, a free issue of shares looks to be advantageous to shareholders but the benefits are more subtle than they first appear.

For example, Splits plc, which has net assets (and hence capital) of £50 000, makes annual profits of £20 000 and has an issued share capital of 10 000 shares. The company directors, with shareholder approval, have decided to issue 10 000 bonus shares to shareholders in equal proportion to their current holdings.

The values relating to shares before and after the bonus issue are:

	Pre-issue (£)	Post-issue (£)
Net assets	50 000	50 000
Profit	20 000	20 000
Number of shares in issue	10 000	20 000
Net assets per share	5.00	2.50
Earning per share	2.00	1.00

Because the underlying business has not changed in value, twice as many shares means (theoretically at least) half as much value per share. Each shareholder is left with the same value of shares in total – it is just that each holding is divided into a greater number of shares.

So the question is, why do companies make bonus share issues? In fact they may want to do so for two reasons:

1 Companies that have grown significantly may command a high share price that undermines the shares' marketability. A bonus issue can be used to deflate the market price and increase marketability. This is of benefit to existing shareholders if the resulting new share price is slightly higher than the theoretical new price. For example, if Split's share price was £20.00 prior to the bonus issue, then a 1 for 1 bonus issue should theoretically lead to a new share price of £10.00. But shareholder value will have been increased by 1 per cent if the post issue price became £10.10.

2 A bonus issue can be used to change the capital structure of the business. The capital section of a company's balance sheet is of interest to creditors and shareholders. It informs the user of the accounts how much of the company's capital can be distributed in the form of dividends. A bonus issue converts a reserve into share capital, so if that reserve is a revenue reserve, then the company is restricting the size of future dividends. This device can be used to reassure creditors by increasing the capital base that cannot be used for dividends.

Exercise 6.1 Changes to capital structure

The abbreviated balance sheet of Fluid Ltd for the year ended 31 December 19X5 was as follows:

	£'000
Net assets	1 000
Ordinary share capital @ 50p	200
Share premium account	200
Revaluation reserve	100
General reserve	100
Profit and loss account	400
	1 000

During the next three years the following changes occurred:

1 Fluid issued 100 000 shares for £2 each on 1 January 19X6.
2 In 19X6 the company made after-tax profits of £112 500. A final dividend of 12.5p per share was proposed and £30 000 was transferred to the general reserve.
3 On 1 January 19X7 a bonus issue to capitalise part of the profit and loss account was made. Four shares were issued for every ten shares held.
4 In 19X7 the company made after-tax profits of £290 000 out of which a final dividend of 20p per share was paid.
5 On 1 January 19X8 fixed assets were revalued from £400 000 to £600 000.
6 On 2 January 19X8 the whole of the general reserve was converted to capital with the issue of bonus shares.
7 In 19X8 the company made after-tax profits of £344 000 out of which a final dividend of 15p per share was paid.

Task

Prepare an abbreviated balance sheet in columnar form after each of the above items has been recorded (the approach is illustrated below with the first two set of figures).

Part solution:

	0 £'000	1 £'000	2 £'000
Net assets	1 000	1 200	1 250
Ordinary share capital @ 50p	200	250	250
Share premium account	200	350	350
Revaluation reserve	100	100	100
General reserve	100	100	130
Profit and loss account	400	400	420
	1 000	1 200	1 250

Exercise 6.2 Changes to capital structure

The abbreviated balance sheets of Flow Ltd have been prepared after a change in the company's capital structure.

		1	2	3	4	5
	£'000	£'000	£'000	£'000	£'000	£'000
Net assets	300	350	450	550	700	700
Ordinary share capital @ 25p	100	100	150	150	150	300
Share premium account	50	50	100	100	100	100
Revaluation reserve					100	100
General reserve				50	50	50
Profit and loss account	150	200	200	250	300	150
	300	350	450	550	700	700

Task

Explain what has occurred between the preparation of each balance sheet. Where shares have been issued, state the number of shares and their issue price.

Loan stock

Debentures were described in Chapter 1 as long-term loan stock issued under the company's common seal. They often carry a fixed rate of interest with a specified date of redemption.

Where a company has debenture stock it may be that interest is outstanding at the year end and this must be accrued for and shown under current liabilities.

Illustration

A company has the following balances on its 30 June 19X7 year end trial balance.

	(£)	(£)
Debentures @ 10% due 19X9		50 000
Debenture interest paid	2 500	

Assuming that there had been no issues or redemptions of debentures during the year, the annual interest charge should be £5 000. The £2 500 in the trial balance represents interest paid, presumably at the half year. A further £2 500 requires accruing.

The accounts will therefore have the following lines in respect of debentures:

	(£)
Profit and loss account	
Debenture interest	5 000
Balance sheet	
Current liabilities	
Debenture interest	2 500
Long-term liabilities	
Debentures @ 10% 19X9	50 000

Preparation of company accounts

The following example will be used to illustrate the preparation of company accounts.

Illustration

The following trial balance has been extracted from the books of Keating Limited at 31 December 19X9.

	(£)	(£)
Purchases	123 854	
Sales		298 410
Staff wages and salaries	26 428	
Rent	12 000	
Motor expenses	23 964	
Post, stationery and telephone	5 783	
Directors' salaries	36 400	
Dividends paid	5 000	
Share capital		100 000
Profit and loss account		56 847
Motor vehicles	42 872	
Furniture fixtures and fittings	166 640	
Motor vehicle depreciation		24 870
Furniture fixtures and fittings depreciation		29 871
Debtors	37 940	
Creditors		18 644
Stock at 1/1/X9	29 872	
Bank	66 389	
Debentures @ 10% interest		50 000
Debenture interest paid	2 500	
Provision for doubtful debts		1 000
	579 642	579 642

- The company has an authorised share capital of 600 000 ordinary shares of 25p each.
- Stock at 31 December 19X9 was valued at £38 876.
- Corporation tax for the year has been computed as £10 740.
- The directors are proposing a final dividend of 5p a share.
- The provision for doubtful debts is to be adjusted to 5 per cent of debtors.
- Depreciation policy requires depreciation to be calculated on a straight line basis, 25 per cent for motor vehicles and 10 per cent for furniture fixtures and fittings.
- Motor expenses of £500 are to be accrued as due.

Prepare for Keating Limited a trading and profit and loss account for the year ended 31 December 19X9 and a balance sheet at that date.

Solution

The adjustments unique to the company's accounts are:

1 Debenture interest that requires matching against 19X9's profits is £5 000 (£50 000 × 10%). As £2 500 has already been paid, an accrual is required to charge an additional £2 500 against profits and to recognise this as a liability to debenture holders (debit profit and loss, credit expenses accruals).

2 Corporation tax of £10 740 is to be appropriated from the current year's profits and needs to be recognised as a current liability (debit profit and loss, credit corporation tax payable).

3 The final dividend needs to be included in the accounts. To determine the total amount being proposed it is first necessary to establish the number of shares that rank for a dividend. From the trial balance it is known that issued share capital has a nominal share value of £100 000. From the first note it is also known that each share has a nominal value of 25p, therefore there must be 400 000 shares in issue. At 5p per share, the final dividend proposed is worth a total £20 000. This is an appropriation of the current year's profits that should be recognised as a current liability (debit profit and loss, credit dividends payable).

Keating Limited
Trading and profit and loss account
for the year ended 31 December 19X9

	(£)	(£)
Sales		298 410
Opening stock	29 872	
Purchases	123 854	
	153 726	
Less closing stock	38 876	
Cost of sales		114 850
Gross profit		183 560
Less expenses:		
Rent	12 000	
Wages	26 428	
Motor expenses	24 464	
Post	5 783	
Directors' salaries	36 400	
Depreciation – motor	10 718	
Depreciation – FFF	16 664	
Bad debts	897	133 354
Profit before interest		50 206
Interest		5 000
Profit before tax		45 206
Tax		10 740
Profit after tax		34 466
Dividends – paid	5 000	
– proposed	20 000	25 000
Retained profit for the year		9 466
Retained profit at 1 January 19X9		56 847
Retained profit at 31 December 19X9		66 313

Keating Limited
Balance sheet
as at 31 December 19X9

	(£)	(£)	(£)
Fixed assets	Cost	Depreciation	
Furniture fixtures and fittings	166 640	46 535	120 105
Motor	42 872	35 588	7 284
	209 512	82 123	127 389
Current assets			
Stocks		38 876	
Debtors	37 940		
Bad and doubtful debt provision	−1 897	36 043	
Bank		66 389	
		141 308	
Current liabilities			
Creditors		18 644	
Accruals (motor £500, interest £2500)		3 000	
Tax payable		10 740	
Dividend payable		20 000	
		52 384	
Net current assets			88 924
Total assets less current liabilities			216 313
Long term liabilities			
Debentures @ 10 per cent			50 000
			166 313
Capital and reserves			
Share capital			100 000
Profit and loss account			66 313
			166 313

Exercise 6.3 Basic company accounts

Risdene Ltd is a trading company that requires its accounts to be prepared from the information below in respect of its financial year ended 31 December 19X8.

Trial balance	Debit £'000s	Credit £'000s
Stock 1 January 19X8	25	
Trade debtors / creditors	125	85
Purchases	1 100	
Sales		1 950
Directors remuneration	90	
Other wages and salaries	385	
Other operating expenses	75	
Bank	20	
Debentures (10%, redemption 2008)		100
Share capital		300
Dividend paid	50	
Fixed assets	690	
Profit and loss account		125
	2 560	2 560

- The company's authorised share capital is 1 000 000 shares at £0.50 nominal value.
- Closing stock has been valued at £125 000
- The directors are proposing a final dividend of 10 pence per share.
- The corporation tax charge for 19X8 is estimated to be £90 000.

Task

Prepare the company's trading and profit and loss account for the year ended 31 December 19X8 and a balance sheet at that date.

Exercise 6.4 Basic company accounts

Union Ltd is a trading company that requires its accounts to be prepared from the information below in respect of its financial year ended 31 March 19X9.

	Debit £'000s	Credit £'000s
Stock 1 April 19X8	520	
Trade debtors / creditors	682	358
Purchases	8 500	
Sales		14 320
Directors' remuneration	250	
Other wages and salaries	790	
Other operating expenses	3 256	
Bank	274	
Debentures (8%, redemption 2003)	1 000	
Share capital		2 000
Dividend paid	100	
Fixed assets	3 680	
Profit and loss account		374
	18 052	18 052

- The company's authorised share capital is 4 000 000 shares at £1.00 nominal value.
- Closing stock has been valued at £525 000
- The directors are proposing a final dividend of 20 pence per share.
- The corporation tax charge for the year is estimated to be £349 000.

Task

Prepare the company's trading and profit and loss account for the year ended 31 March 19X9 and a balance sheet at that date.

Exercise 6.5 Company accounts

The following trial balance has been extracted from the books of Howard Limited.

	(£)	(£)
Debenture interest	2 400	
Creditors		23 870
Stock at 1/1/X9	15 250	
Bank	26 936	
Debentures @ 12% interest		40 000
Staff wages and salaries	36 977	
Electricity	1 840	
Repairs and renewals	5 710	
Post, stationery and telephone	2 893	
Directors' salaries	35 000	
Purchases	170 274	
Sales		282 456
Debtors	51 550	
Share capital		80 000
Profit and loss account		32 174
Equipment cost	44 660	
Leased property	100 000	
Equipment depreciation		14 990
Property depreciation		20 000
	493 490	493 490

- The company has an authorised share capital of 100 000 ordinary shares of £1 each.
- Stock at 31 December 19X9 was valued at £19 840.
- Corporation tax for the year has been computed as £2 200.
- At the company's annual general meeting the directors are to propose the payment of a final dividend of 6p a share.
- Depreciation policy requires depreciation to be calculated on a straight line basis, 20 per cent for equipment and 10 per cent for leased property.
- Charges in respect of repairs £600 and electricity £250 are to be accrued as due.
- A bad debt provision equal to 2 per cent of debtors is to be created.

Task

Prepare for Howard Ltd a trading and profit and loss account for the year ended 31 December 19X9 and a balance sheet at that date.

Exercise 6.6 Company accounts with analysis of reserves

The following trial balance has been extracted from the books of Fiztron Limited.

	(£)	(£)
Debenture interest	1 500	
Creditors		23 574
Stock at 1/1/X9	25 890	
Bank	66 841	
Debentures @ 15% interest		20 000
Staff wages and salaries	123 420	
Other operating expenses	85 460	
Purchases	341 870	
Sales		600 085
Debtors	44 740	
Share premium account		20 000
Revaluation reserve		40 000
Share capital		200 000
Profit and loss account		35 822
General reserve		10 000
Land cost	80 000	
Buildings cost and depreciation	120 000	25 000
Equipment cost and depreciation	156 000	71 240
	1 045 721	1 045 721

- The company has an authorised share capital of 600 000 ordinary shares of 50p each.
- Stock at 31 December 19X9 was valued at £29 540.
- Corporation tax for the year has been computed as £6 445.
- At the company's annual general meeting the directors are to propose the payment of a final dividend of 2p a share.
- Depreciation policy requires depreciation to be calculated on a straight line basis, 4 per cent for buildings and 10 per cent for equipment. Land is not depreciated.
- The directors have decided to transfer a further £10 000 from the profit and loss account to the general reserve.

Task

Prepare for Fiztron Ltd a trading and profit and loss account for the year ended 31 December 19X9 and a balance sheet at that date.

Summary

Company accounts differ from those of a sole trader because the firm is recognised as a separate legal entity from its owners. The profit and loss appropriation account shows how profit has been divided between corporation tax, dividends and retained profits. The capital section of the balance sheet distinguishes between capital reserves and those reserves that are distributable.

Further reading

R. J. Bull, David A. Harvey and Lindsey M. Lindley, *Accounting in Business*, 6th edition, Butterworth, 1990.

Paul Gee, *Spicer and Pegler's Bookkeeping and Accounts*, 23rd edition, Butterworth, 1996.

Richard Giles, *A Complete Course in Business Accounting*, Stanley Thornes, 1996.

Frank Wood and Allan Sangster, *Business Accounting 1*, 7th edition, Pitman Publishing, 1996.

On completion of this chapter students should be able to:

- identify and illustrate the structure of the main financial statements
- identify and explain the differing requirements of a range of organisations
- prepare financial statements from the given data incorporating appropriate adjustments.

The nature of a business influences the format of its financial statements. The main categories of business for accounting purposes are trading, manufacturing and service.

Trading businesses

Trading businesses comprise the wholesale and retail sectors. All of the accounts illustrated in Chapters 5 and 6 have been for trading businesses (i.e. they buy goods for resale). The main financial reports comprise the trading account and profit and loss account and the balance sheet.

Manufacturing businesses

Manufacturing businesses make finished goods from the raw materials they purchase. Where more than one firm is involved in the production process of a final product, the finished goods from one business may be the raw materials for another. For example, steel sheet is a finished product of British Steel but it is the raw material from which washing machines and other consumer durables are made.

There will generally be three categories of stock held by the business:

1 *raw materials* – the goods purchased by the business
2 *work in progress (WIP)* – goods that have been partly manufactured
3 *finished goods* – goods that have been fully manufactured.

The balance sheet will therefore include amounts for each type of stock as part of current assets; and to comply with the accruals concept, the profit statement will also have to account for changes in the levels of raw material and WIP, just as the trading account includes an adjustment for changes in stock ready for sale.

Cost structure of a manufacturing business

(See also Chapter 12.)

A manufacturing business incurs conversion costs in addition to the cost of raw materials purchased.

Direct costs can be attributed to specific products and so they vary with the level of production. The total of all direct costs is called prime cost.

Direct materials are the raw materials purchased from suppliers. To calculate the amount of stock used a calculation is performed which is similar to that applied to finished stock in the trading account:

		(£)
	Opening stock of raw materials	22 500
Add	Purchases of raw materials	157 500
		180 000
Less	Closing stock of raw materials	25 000
=	Direct materials	155 000

Direct wages are paid to employees who are directly involved in the manufacture of the business's products. **Direct expenses** relate to services supplied by other businesses that again can be attributed to specific products. They include work sub-contracted out (such as specialist machining) and royalties paid to use a patented product or production process.

All costs associated with the production process that cannot be attributed to specific products are classified as **factory overheads**. These include apportionments of general business expenses such as site rent and rates, in addition to factory items like production supervision and machine maintenance that cannot be attributed to specific products.

Total production cost = prime cost + factory overhead.

Total production cost includes costs to complete items in WIP at the start of the accounting period and also to start manufacture of items that remain in WIP at the end of the period. An adjustment is made to find the production cost of completed units because the trading account is solely concerned with finished goods that are in a saleable state.

	(£)
Total production cost	10 000
Add: Opening WIP	1 500
Less: Closing WIP	−2 000
Cost of completed units transferred to the trading account	9 500

The manufacturing account that accumulates all production costs is reported with the trading and profit and loss account and as a combined financial report they are given the title **manufacturing, trading and profit and loss account**.

Basic format

Rowley Engineering Ltd
Manufacturing, trading and profit and loss account
for the year ended 31 December 19X9

	£'000	£'000
Opening stock of raw materials	100	
Add purchases of raw materials	1 000	
	1 100	
Less closing stock of raw materials	200	
Direct materials		900
Direct labour		900
Direct expenses		100
Prime cost		1 900
Factory overheads		
Management and supervision	250	
Indirect wages	150	
Rent	100	
Power	100	
Depreciation of equipment	100	700
Total production cost		2 600
Add: Opening WIP		200
Less: Closing WIP		100
Cost of completed units transferred to the trading account		2 700
Sales		5 000
Opening stock of finished goods	300	
Add Production cost transfer	2 700	
	3 000	
Less Closing stock of finished goods	200	
Cost of sales		2 800
Gross profit		2 200
Less expenses:		
Administration costs	500	
Selling and distribution costs	700	1 200
Net profit		1 000

The trading and profit and loss account sections of the profit statement are similar to those for a trading business, the only difference being that the transfer from the manufacturing account replaces the normal purchases figure. Where a business manufactures and purchases finished goods, the trading account will include amounts for the factory transfer and for purchases of finished goods.

The balance sheet of a manufacturing business will be similar to that of a trading business. The only exception will be the analysis of stocks under current assets. For Johnson Pressings Ltd, the current assets section is:

Current assets:	£'000	£'000
Stocks		
Raw materials	200	
Work in progress	100	
Finished goods	200	500
Debtors		600
Bank and cash		100
Total		1 200

Exercise 7.1 Basic manufacturing account

Thorn Co. Ltd is a manufacturing company that has just completed its fourth year of trading.

The company's trial balance at 31 December 19X4 is:

	(£)	(£)
Raw material stock – 1 January X4	10 123	
WIP – 1 January X4	4 560	
Finished goods stock – 1 January X4	8 000	
Sales		345 500
Purchases	59 823	
Direct wages	32 560	
Distribution overheads	55 000	
Factory overheads	64 890	
Administration expenses	95 000	
Fixed assets	80 000	
Debtors	57 984	
Bank	5 250	
Share capital		50 000
Profit and loss account		63 800
Creditors		13 890
	473 190	473 190

Closing stock valuations: raw materials £15 987, work in progress £5 969 and finished goods stock £12 500.

Task

Prepare a manufacturing and trading and profit and loss account for the year ended 31 December 19X4 and a balance sheet at that date.

Exercise 7.2 Basic manufacturing account

Blinko manufactures glass washers for the leisure industry. The firm's trial balance at 31 December 19X2 was:

	(£)	(£)
Raw material stock – 1 January X2	2 325	
WIP – 1 January X2	6 120	
Finished goods stock – 1 January X2	9 200	
Sales		242 700
Purchases	67 158	
Direct wages	42 670	
Factory overheads	23 961	
Administration expenses	20 000	
Fixed assets	76 000	
Debtors	19 250	
Capital at 1 January X2		27 250
Bank	16 180	
Creditors		12 914
	282 864	282 864

Closing stocks were valued on 31 December 19X2 at: raw materials £5 827, work in progress £5 607 and finished goods stock £11 500.

Task

Prepare a manufacturing and trading and profit and loss account for the year ended 31 December 19X2 and a balance sheet at that date.

Apportionment of overheads

With a separate account for the production function, there will be a need to divide shared costs between the different functions of the business. For example, property costs are often apportioned because different parts of the business premises are occupied by different departments. A proxy measure of resource usage is used as a basis for cost apportionment.

Illustration

A business incurs property rent of £50 000 per annum for a 2 000 square metre industrial unit. The annual rental is to be apportioned to the business functions on the basis of area used. The factory occupies 1 200 sq. m, distribution 500 sq. m and administration 300 sq. m.

	Sq. m	%	Annual rent (£)
Factory	1 200	60.0	30 000
Distribution	500	25.0	12 500
Administration	300	15.0	7 500
	2 000	100.0	50 000

(Questions will usually provide the apportionment percentages, however for more details concerning the apportionment of overheads see Chapter 12.)

Exercise 7.3 Manufacturing account with apportionment of overheads

Kevin Snape, a sole trader and manufacturer of children's toys, requires the preparation of a manufacturing, trading and profit and loss account for the year to 31 December 19X9 together with a balance sheet at that date. His trial balance for the year to 31/12/X9 was:

Debit (£)	Credit (£)	
Purchases / Sales	43 410	144 850
Direct wages	28 652	
Overheads	42 440	
Raw materials 1/1/X9	5 263	
W I P 1/1/X9	6 411	
Finished goods 1/1/X9	9 883	
Debtors/creditors	3 560	2 296
Bank	14 382	
Plant and machinery – cost / depreciation	19 864	5 997
Motor vehicles – cost / depreciation	12 000	4 000
Capital at 1/1/X9		40 722
Drawings	12 000	
	197 865	197 865

- Stock valuations at 31 December 19X9 were: raw materials £4 850, WIP £8 241 and finished goods £9 543.
- Depreciation has already been charged and is included in overheads.
- Overhead costs are to be apportioned 60 per cent to the factory, 20 per cent to distribution and 20 per cent to administration.

Exercise 7.4 Preparation for assessment

Moonpress Mouldings Limited, a manufacturer of plastic mouldings, requires the preparation of a manufacturing, trading and profit and loss account for the year to 31 December 19X9 together with a balance sheet at that date.

Trial balance for the year to 31/12/X9

	Debit (£)	Credit (£)
Sales		950 000
Purchases	315 500	
Direct wages	205 400	
Indirect factory salaries and wages	51 400	
Administration salaries	65 230	
Distribution wages and salaries	45 900	
Electricity	19 120	
Postage, stationery and telephone	25 450	
Motor expenses	40 230	
Raw materials 1/1/X9	31 330	
W I P 1/1/X9	10 580	
Finished goods 1/1/X9	49 870	
Debtors/creditors	92 460	64 310
Bank	11 330	
Rent	52 500	
Plant and machinery	315 470	99 820
Motor vehicles	41 000	25 690
Returns	460	980
Repairs and maintenance	7 100	
Provision for bad debts		1 500
Share capital – £1 shares		100 000
Profit and loss account		138 030
	1 380 330	1 380 330

- Stock valuations at 31 December 19X9 were: raw materials £19 850, WIP £13 640 and finished goods £42 780.
- Depreciation policy: plant and machinery 10 per cent on cost, motor vehicles 20 per cent on cost.
- The debtors' accounts have been reviewed and it has been decided to write off immediately £1 900 of debt to the profit and loss account. The provision for doubtful debts is to be restated at 2 per cent of the remaining debtors.
- Costs to be accrued: repairs £400, electricity £1 870, telephone £2 050.
- A final dividend of 3p per share is proposed by the directors.

- Corporation tax of £18 000 is to be provided for.
- The rent agreement is for £42 000 per annum.
- Costs are to be apportioned to the company's departments in the following proportions:

	Factory	Distribution	Administration
Motor vehicles	40%	40%	20%
Rent	70%	20%	10%
Repairs and maintenance	75%	10%	15%
Electricity	80%	10%	10%

Service businesses

Service businesses include firms such as professional partnerships (e.g. lawyers and accountants), office cleaning businesses and staff agencies. What tends to differentiate these businesses from manufacturing and retail firms is that they do not provide tangible goods to any great extent, although they may use consumable materials such as cleaning materials, stationery, etc. Because there is no movement in stock balances there is no need for a trading account, only a profit and loss account and balance sheet.

Basic format

Phoenix Accountancy Services
Profit and loss account
For the year ended 31 December 19X9

	(£)	(£)
Sales		100 000
Less expenses:		
Salaries and wages	50 000	
Office costs	8 000	
Travel	10 000	68 000
Net profit		32 000

However, where costs can be attributed to the services being charged to customers, then these costs can be classified as cost of sales, which enables gross profit to be calculated; for example, the wages paid to office cleaners. This analysis provides useful management information and is a requirement for published company accounts.

The balance sheet for a service business is similar to that for other businesses, the exception being that there are no stocks to be reported under current assets.

Exercise 7.5 Non-trading sole trader

The following trial balance at 31 December 19X9 has been extracted from the books of Avril Cleaning Services, an office cleaning firm.

	(£)	(£)
Office expenses	200	
Wages	15 810	
Motor vehicle – cost and depreciation	5 660	1 415
Equipment – cost and depreciation	7 131	2 377
Sales		29 855
Debtors	2 100	
Bank	1 915	
Drawings	4 500	
Capital at 1/1/X9		4 278
Telephone	225	
Cleaning materials used	384	
	37 925	37 925

- Depreciation is calculated on a straight line basis over 4 years for the motor vehicle and over 3 years for the equipment.
- Accruals are to be made in respect of the following costs: office expenses £160 and wages of £325.

Task

Prepare for Avril Cleaning Services a profit and loss account for the year ended 31 December 19X9 and a balance sheet at that date.

Exercise 7.6 Non-trading limited company

The following trial balance at 31 March 19X9 has been extracted from the books of Business Training Solutions Ltd.

	(£)	(£)
Rent	15 000	
Electricity	650	
Stationery & post	1 255	
Salaries – directors and staff	36 870	
Equipment – cost and depreciation	38 970	13 540
Sales		87 964
Debtors / creditors	4 665	656
Bank	24 974	
Dividends paid	5 000	
Share capital		10 000
Profit and loss account		15 224
	127 384	127 384

- Authorised share capital consists of 30 000 50p ordinary shares.
- Corporation Tax of £7 000 is to be provided for.
- Depreciation of equipment is calculated on a 20 per cent reducing balance basis.
- Accruals are to be made in respect of the following costs: electricity £300 and staff bonuses £4 000.
- The rent agreement provides for annual charge of £12 000.
- The directors have decided to propose a final dividend of 25p per share.

Task

Prepare for Business Training Solutions Ltd a profit and loss account for the year ended 31 March 19X9 and a balance sheet at that date.

Summary

The format and content of business accounts should reflect the nature of the business. To summarise the requirements for different business sectors:

Further reading

R. J. Bull, David A. Harvey and Lindsey M. Lindley, *Accounting in Business,* 6th edition, Butterworth, 1990.

Paul Gee, *Spicer and Pegler's Bookkeeping and Accounts,* 23rd edition, Butterworth, 1996.

Richard Giles, *A Complete Course in Business Accounting,* Stanley Thornes, 1996.

Frank Wood and Allan Sangster, *Business Accounting 1,* 7th edition, Pitman Publishing, 1996.

Business sector:	Service business	Trading firm	Manufacturing firm
Profit statement	Profit and loss account	Trading and profit and loss account	Manufacturing, trading and profit and loss account
Statement of net worth	Balance sheet	Balance sheet including stocks	Balance sheet including an analysis of stocks

8 Partnership accounts

On completion of this chapter students should be able to:

- apply appropriate techniques to meet the changing needs of partnerships.

Partnerships, like sole traders, have no separate legal identity from that of their owners. The structure of accounts for partnerships is similar although not identical to that for sole traders. A partnership is a business formed by two or more people, so it is necessary to show how profits are shared and how ownership is divided between the partners.

Sharing of profits

Partners should have agreed when entering into the partnership how profits would be shared. The arrangement should have been recorded in a written partnership agreement together with other conditions such as number of hours to be worked, holiday entitlement and procedures in the event of the partnership being dissolved.

Profit sharing schemes should reflect the time, skills and capital that each partner is bringing to the business. Typically profits are shared in three ways:

- salary
- interest on capital invested
- sharing of any remaining profit or loss.

The agreement may also require the partners to pay interest where drawings are made prior to the year end.

The accounting schedule that shows the sharing of profits is called the 'profit appropriation account'.

Illustration

Smith and Jones are in partnership sharing profits 75 per cent and 25 per cent respectively. The partnership agreement provides for interest on capital of 10 per cent and salaries of £10000 each. Interest on drawings is also to be paid at 10 per cent per annum. Smith has paid in capital of £20000 and Jones £10000. Profits for the year just ended amounted to £38000. The partners have made drawings in the middle of the year, with Smith taking £15000 and Jones £12000.

Prepare the partnership's profit appropriation account.

Solution

	(£)	(£)
Net profit		38 150
Profit appropriation account		
Add interest on drawings		
Smith (£15 000 × 10 per cent × $\frac{6}{12}$)	750	
Jones (£12 000 × 10 per cent × $\frac{6}{12}$)	600	
		1 350
		39 500
Partners' salaries		
Smith	10 000	
Jones	10 000	20 000
Interest on capital		
Smith (£20 000 × 10 per cent)	2 000	
Jones (£10 000 × 10 per cent)	1 000	3 000
Share of profits		
Smith (75 per cent)	12 375	
Jones (25 per cent)	4 125	16 500
		39 500

Note the interest on drawings has been charged on the second six months of the year only.

Exercise 8.1 Profit appropriation account

Jennifer Ladds and Bertie Boyes are in business providing a mobile catering service for special occasions. Last year they made a net profit of £18 000.

Task

Prepare their appropriation account for the year using the following information:

Salary	Jennifer	£5 000
	Bertie	£4 000
Drawings	Jennifer (middle of the year)	£9 000
	Bertie (start of the year)	£7 000
Capital	Jennifer	£2 000
	Bertie	£1 000
Share of profits	Jennifer	60 per cent
	Bertie	40 per cent
	Interest on drawings	5 per cent
	Interest on capital	20 per cent

Capital accounts and current accounts

The capital of a sole trader is usually represented by a single capital account that is updated with new capital being introduced, profits for the accounting period and the owner's drawings. The same principles apply to the capital of a partnership although greater control may be required to ensure a minimum level of capital is left in the business.

It is essential that all businesses have sufficient financial resources to survive. For a partnership this may require some safeguards to ensure partners do not withdraw more capital than is good for the business. It is usual, therefore, to identify a fixed amount of capital that each partner should contribute to the funding of the business and to agree that this capital is not available for subsequent drawings. The principle is that drawings should come from profits and not from capital.

To help control the level of drawings and hence the permanent capital of the partnership, two types of owners' accounts are created: capital accounts and current accounts.

Capital accounts – represent the amount that partners have contributed as permanent finance.

Current accounts – monitor partners' entitlement to profit and their drawings from it.

Illustration

In the Smith and Jones partnership, the partners started the year with a current account balance of £3 000 and £2 000 respectively. The capital section of the partnership's balance sheet is required.

Smith and Jones – Balance sheet extract

	(£)	(£)	(£)
	Smith	Jones	
Capital accounts	20 000	10 000	30 000
Current accounts			
Balance brought forward	3 000	2 000	
Salary	10 000	10 000	
Interest on capital	2 000	1 000	
Share of profits	12 375	4 125	
	27 375	17 125	
Less drawings	−15 000	−12 000	
Less interest on drawings	−750	−600	
	11 625	4 525	16 150
			46 150

Exercise 8.2 Profit appropriation and capital and current accounts

Norman Black and Tracy Blue are in partnership producing fashionable socks. Tracy does most of the work but she needed Norman's money to set up the business. During last year they made £48 000 net profit. The following information has been made available:

Tracy's salary		£10 000
Interest to be paid on drawings		10 per cent
Interest to be paid on capital provided		20 per cent
Profits to be shared 50/50		
Capital accounts:	Norman Black	£25 000
	Tracy Blue	£ 5 000
Drawings:	Norman Black (mid year)	£25 000
	Tracy Blue (mid year)	£25 000
Current accounts b/f	Norman Black	£ 5 000
	Tracy Blue	£ 2 000

Tasks

Prepare:

1 *the appropriation account for Black and Blue, and*
2 *an extract of the balance sheet showing the balances on the partners' capital and current accounts.*

Partnership Act 1890

Where there is no partnership agreement, the provisions of the *Partnership Act 1890* apply to the sharing of profits. Unless an agreement expresses the contrary:

1 profits and losses are shared equally between the partners
2 no partner is entitled to a salary
3 partners are not entitled to interest on their capital

4 no interest is chargeable on partner's drawings
5 where a partner has contributed more capital than was agreed, the excess is considered to be a loan which will attract interest at 5 per cent per annum.

It follows that an agreement is essential if these provisions are not to apply.

When preparing accounts it is important to distinguish between the profits earned by partners and the remuneration paid to employees. Salaries paid to employees are an expense to be deducted before arriving at a net profit for the business, whereas salaries of partners are an appropriation of profit.

Exercise 8.3 Appropriation of profit

Sunday, Patel and Foley have traded in partnership for a number of years, selling car parts and accessories to small garages and the general public. The partnership agreement stipulates that Sunday will receive a salary of £15 000 per annum, that interest on capital is to be at 10 per cent per annum and any remaining profit or loss is to be shared equally between the partners.

A trial balance has been prepared from their accounting records for the year ended 31 December 19X8.

	(£)	(£)
Capital accounts		
Sunday		55 000
Patel		35 000
Foley		35 000
Current accounts		
Sunday		14 536
Patel		12 165
Foley		10 230
Bank	5 689	
Trade debtors	16 745	
Trade creditors		17 932
Stock at 1/1/X8	32 764	
Sales		337 841
Wages	53 647	
Drawings		
Sunday	25 800	
Patel	16 800	
Foley	18 540	
Purchases	165 840	
Shop expenses	14 368	
Land	50 000	
Buildings	150 000	
Mortgage		105 423
Mortgage interest	8 121	
Motor vehicles	54 820	
Motor vehicles expenses	9 993	
	623 127	623 127

Notes:

1 *Stock at 31 December 19X8 was valued at £65 103.*
2 *Depreciation is charged on a reducing balance basis: buildings at 2 per cent and motor vehicles 25 per cent.*
3 *A provision of £1 205 is to be created for a debt that is unlikely to be recovered.*

Tasks

Prepare a trading and profit and loss accounts for the year ended 31 December 19X8 and a balance sheet at that date.

Exercise 8.4 Appropriation of profit

Cheung, Collier and Cristal are in partnership selling computer equipment and software. The partnership agreement states that each partner will receive a salary of £12 000 per annum and that remaining profits will be shared 40 per cent to Cheung and 30 per cent to each of the other partners.

A trial balance has been prepared from their accounting records for the year ended 30 June 19X9.

	(£)	(£)
Capital accounts		
Cheung		17 852
Collier		15 961
Cristal		12 400
Bank	7 354	
Debtors	2 456	
Creditors		3 650
Stock at 1/7/X8	8 245	
Sales		160 740
Drawings		
Cheung	19 632	
Collier	17 980	
Cristal	20 830	
Purchases	95 120	
Shop expenses	2 627	
Rent	6 250	
Motor vehicles	26 840	
Motor vehicle depreciation		8 620
Computer equipment – for demonstration and design work	12 860	
Computer equipment depreciation		4 692
Motor vehicles expenses	3 721	
	223 915	223 915

Notes:

1 *Stock at 30 June 19X9 was valued at £25 103.*
2 *The partners do not operate separate capital and current accounts.*
3 *Depreciation is charged on a straight line basis: motor vehicles 25 per cent, computer equipment 50 per cent. All of the computer equipment was purchased in the past 2 years.*
4 *Rent has been prepaid to 30 September 19X9.*

Tasks

Prepare a trading and profit and loss accounts for the year ended 30 June 19X9 and a balance sheet at that date.

Partnership changes

The accounts of a partnership will be affected by the following changes:

1 partners may decide to change their profit sharing arrangements
2 a new partner may be admitted
3 a partner may retire.

The admission of a new partner, or the retirement or death of an existing partner, means in legal terms the end of one partnership and the start of a new one.

The capital account of a retiring partner will be deleted with the consideration agreed, e.g. debit capital, credit bank. The capital account of a new partner will be credited with the value of assets introduced to the partnership, e.g. debit bank, debit motor vehicles and credit capital account.

Whatever the reason for a partnership change, it is a time when the true value of the business's assets and liabilities will be reassessed. It must be remembered that the values attached to items in the balance sheet are the result of accounting convention and are not necessarily a true reflection of their market value.

Revaluation of assets

To reflect the true value of each partner's interests in the business it is necessary to update the partners' capital accounts with the agreed valuations of the business's assets. The revaluation adjustments are affected via a revaluation account.

	Debit	Credit
Fixed assets		
If an asset's value is greater than its cost	asset cost account	revaluation
If an asset's value is less than its cost	revaluation account	asset cost
Accumulated depreciation (the account balance is deleted on revaluation)	accumulated depreciation	revaluation account
Other assets		
If asset value is less than amount in accounts	revaluation account	asset

In some cases liabilities are revalued. If liabilities are greater than stated in the accounts, it is necessary to debit the revaluation account and credit the respective liability account.

The surplus or deficit arising on the revaluation is shared between the old partners in their normal profit sharing ratios.

Illustration

Major, Minor and Minnow have been in partnership for a number of years and the time has come for Major to retire from the business. Profits are shared in the proportions: Major 50 per cent, Minor 30 per cent and Minnow 20 per cent. The partnership's balance sheet at the time of the change was as follows:

Major, Minor and Minnow Balance sheet at date of change	(£)	(£)	(£)
Fixed assets	*Cost*	*Depreciation*	
Land and buildings	50 000	10 000	40 000
Plant	20 000	10 000	10 000
	70 000	20 000	50 000
Current assets			
Stocks		5 500	
Debtors		3 000	
Bank		24 500	
		33 000	
Current liabilities		4 000	
Net current assets			29 000
Net assets			79 000
Capital accounts			
Major			33 000
Minor			26 000
Minnow			20 000
			79 000

The partners agreed that the assets should be revalued to the following amounts:

- Land and buildings £60 000 (to market value)
- Plant £9 000 (to market value)
- Stocks £5 000 (to mark down some slow moving stock)
- Debtors £2 800 (to reflect a doubtful debt of £200)

It has been decided that Major will leave half his capital in the business in the form of a loan that will be repaid in two years time. The remainder of his capital account will be settled in cash.

The ledger accounts

Capital accounts

	Major (£)	Minor (£)	Minnow (£)		Major (£)	Minor (£)	Minnow (£)
Loan	21 075			Brought forward	33 000	26 000	20 000
Bank	21 075			Revaluation	9 150	5 490	3 660
Carried forward		31 490	23 660				
	42 150	31 490	23 660		42 150	31 490	23 660

Revaluation account

	(£)		(£)
Plant cost	11 000	L&B cost	10 000
Stock	500	L&B depn	10 000
Debtors	200	Plant depn	10 000
Major	9 150		
Minor	5 490		
Minnow	3 660		
	30 000		30 000

The partnership's balance sheet immediately after Major retired:

Major, Minor and Minnow

Balance sheet after change	(£)	(£)	(£)
Fixed assets	Cost	Depreciation	
Land and buildings	60 000	0	60 000
Plant	9 000	0	9 000
	69 000	0	69 000
Current assets			
Stocks		5 000	
Debtors		2 800	
Bank		3 425	
		11 225	
Current liabilities		4 000	
Net current assets			7 225
			76 225
Long-term liabilities – Major's loan			21 075
Net assets			55 150
Capital accounts			
Minor			31 490
Minnow			23 660
			55 150

Exercise 8.5 Asset revaluation

Portillo and Lilley have been in partnership for four years sharing profits in the ratios 3 to 2 respectively. At the start of year 5 they wish to admit Redwood as a partner. The new profit sharing ratios will be Portillo 4, Lilley 3 and Redwood 2.

Portillo and Lilley

Summary balance sheet as at the end of year 4	(£)	(£)	(£)
Fixed assets			
Land and buildings			90 000
Plant			70 000
			160 000
Current assets			
Stocks		29 000	
Debtors		24 000	
Cash		3 000	
Total current assets			56 000
Total net assets			216 000

	Portillo	Lilley	
Capital accounts:	144 000	72 000	216 000

As part of the new agreement, it has been decided that property will be revalued to £125 000 and plant to £68 000. A subsequent review of debtors has taken account of Redwood's concerns over one or two of the older balances and it is agreed that a £3 000 provision for doubtful debts should be created.

On being admitted as a partner at the start of year 5, Redwood paid £50 000 into the partnership's bank account as his agreed capital contribution.

Tasks

1 *Prepare a revaluation account and partnership capital accounts to record the changes agreed.*
2 *Prepare the opening balance sheet for the new partnership after all the transactions have been recorded.*

Goodwill

In many cases, the revaluation of tangible assets fails to value a business fully. In establishing the business, valuable trading relationships and competitive advantages will have been developed, and these will be of great benefit for future trading periods. The premium assigned to this benefit is called **goodwill**. Partners that are retiring will require some compensation for leaving their share of this goodwill to the remaining partners. Similarly, new partners buying into the business will be required to pay for the goodwill from which they will subsequently benefit.

The valuation of goodwill is subjective, although the respective parties may agree to quantify it by some predetermined formula. It is not unusual for it to be agreed that goodwill represents a multiple or a proportion of annual profits.

Illustration

Green and Brown agree to admit Grey as a partner. The terms of admission require him to pay for goodwill in addition to a proportion of the business's net assets. Goodwill is to be valued at 75 per cent of average profits of the last three years. Profits have been £57 000, £40 000 and £47 000.

The original partners shared profits in the proportions Green 60 per cent and Brown 40 per cent, and their capital balances were £40 000 and £20 000 respectively.

After admitting Grey, profits would be shared Green 50 per cent, Brown 35 per cent and Grey 15 per cent. Grey would bring into the business a motor vehicle valued at £5000 and cash of £25000.

Solution

Average profits are £48000 so goodwill is therefore valued at £36000.

When adjusting the partners' capital accounts for goodwill, it is necessary to compare their new share of goodwill with their old share.

	Original share in goodwill (£)	New share in goodwill (£)	Posting to capital account (£)
Green	21600	18000	3600 credit
Brown	14400	12600	1800 credit
Grey		5400	5400 debit
	36000	36000	

The original partners, who are in effect selling a share of the goodwill to Grey, will require their capital accounts to be increased to compensate for their lost share of future profits. Grey's capital balance will be correspondingly reduced to reflect his purchase of the goodwill.

Capital accounts

	Green (£)	Brown (£)	Grey (£)		Green (£)	Brown (£)	Grey (£)
Goodwill			5400	Brought forward	40000	20000	
Carried forward	43600	21800	24600	Bank			25000
				Motor vehicle			5000
				Goodwill	3600	1800	
	43600	21800	30000		43600	21800	30000

An alternative approach includes goodwill in the accounts as an intangible fixed asset. The goodwill balance is created by recognising the partners who created it and crediting their capital accounts accordingly. The above example dealt with in this way would result in the following ledger accounts:

Capital accounts

	Green (£)	Brown (£)	Grey (£)		Green (£)	Brown (£)	Grey (£)
Carried forward	61600	34400	24600	Brought forward	40000	20000	
				Bank			25000
				Motor vehicle			5000
				Goodwill	21600	14400	
	61600	34400	30000		61600	34400	30000

Goodwill

	(£)		(£)
Green	21600	Carried forward	36000
Brown	14400		
	36000		36000

The net assets of the balance sheet are increased by £36000 and the capital accounts by a similar amount.

In situations where it is not clear how goodwill should be accounted for, it is generally considered preferable not to record goodwill in the accounts.

Exercise 8.6 Goodwill

Weinberg and King have successfully traded as political lobbyists sharing profits equally. At the start of their third year of trading they have agreed that Hurd will join the firm. He will contribute £20000 in capital and the new profit sharing ratios will be Weinberg 4, King 3 and Hurd 3.

The partnership's balance sheet at the end of year 2:

Weinberg and King
Summary balance sheet as at the end of year 2

	(£)	(£)	(£)
Total net assets			30000
	Weinberg	King	
Capital accounts	15000	15000	30000

It is agreed that the goodwill of the partnership that Hurd will be buying into is worth £30000.

Tasks

Prepare appropriate ledger accounts and a summary balance sheet at the start of year 3 for the new partnership, assuming goodwill is:

1 *to be valued as an asset in the accounts*
2 *not to be held as an asset in the accounts.*

Exercise 8.7 Goodwill

Schumacher, Hill and Mansell have been in partnership for five years producing components for the motor racing industry. Profits have been shared equally but at the end of year 5 Mansell decides to leave after a disagreement concerning profit sharing. The goodwill of the partnership is valued at £3 000 but is not to be recorded in the accounts. Mansell receives consideration in the form of net assets from the business.

Schumacher, Hill and Mansell

Summary balance sheet as at the end of year 5

	(£)	(£)	(£)	(£)
Total net assets				180 000
	Schumacher	Hill	Mansell	
Capital accounts	60 000	60 000	60 000	180 000

Task

Prepare the partners' capital accounts and a summary balance sheet at the start of the new partnership.

Exercise 8.8 New partner with revaluations and goodwill

Welsh, Wild and Adder are in partnership sharing profits equally. At the end of year 3 it is agreed that Shines will join the partnership, contributing £30 000 in cash and a motor vehicle valued at £8 000. The new profit sharing arrangement is to be Welsh 4, Wild 4, Adder 5 and Shines 3.

The balance sheet immediately before the change:

Welsh, Wild and Adder
Balance sheet as at the end of year 3

	(£)	(£)	(£)
Fixed assets	*Cost*	*Depreciation*	
Property	160 000	40 000	120 000
Furniture, fixtures & fittings	32 000	7 000	25 000
Motor vehicles	50 000	20 000	30 000
	242 000	67 000	175 000

Current assets		
Stocks	2 000	
Debtors	45 000	
Bank	5 000	
	52 000	
Current liabilities	12 500	
		39 500
		214 500
Capital		
Welsh		71 500
Wild		71 500
Adder		71 500
		214 500

It has been agreed that the following asset revaluations will be made on the admittance of Shines:

- property   £140 000
- fixtures and fittings £22 000
- motor   £25 000
- debtors   £42 000

The partnership has built up a valuable customer bank and the goodwill arising from this is to be valued at £48 000. A goodwill account is not to be opened.

Tasks

Prepare:

1 *the revaluation and capital accounts necessary to record the above items*
2 *a balance sheet of the new partnership at the start of year four.*

Exercise 8.9 Partner retiring with revaluations and goodwill

Blair, Brown and Scargill have had arguments regarding the direction of their business partnership and Scargill has decided to leave to set up his own firm. Year 10 of their partnership has just been completed with profits shared Blair 3, Brown 1 and Scargill 1.

Blair Brown and Scargill

Balance sheet as at the end of year 10	(£)	(£)	(£)
Fixed assets	Cost	Depreciation	
Property	68 000	7 000	61 000
Furniture, fixtures & fittings	23 000	16 500	6 500
Motor vehicles	29 500	10 500	19 000
	120 500	34 000	86 500
Current assets			
Stocks		25 700	
Debtors		44 600	
Bank		500	
		70 800	
Current liabilities		22 300	
			48 500
			135 000
Capital			
Blair			81 000
Brown			27 000
Scargill			27 000
			135 000

The following asset valuations have been agreed:

Property	£90 000
Furniture fixtures & fittings	£9 000
Motor vehicles	£18 000
Goodwill	£70 000
Stocks	£24 000
Debtors	£43 800

Scargill is to take assets out of the business with the following valuations on them: furniture £1 600, motor vehicle £3 600 and stock £1 400. The remainder of his capital is to be transferred to a loan account to be repaid in two years' time.

Goodwill is not to be recorded as an asset in the partnerships books. After the changes Blair and Brown are to share profits in the proportions Blair 80 per cent and Brown 20 per cent.

Tasks

Prepare:

1 *a revaluation account and partners' capital accounts to record the transactions agreed*
2 *a balance sheet of the new partnership at the start of year eleven.*

Summary

The accounts of a partnership are differentiated from those of a sole trader by a profit appropriation account and by a balance sheet that contains a detailed breakdown of each partner's interest in the firm.

Profit sharing will be subject to the Partnership Act 1890 unless a partnership agreement has been created that overrides its provisions.

Partnership changes include changes to profit sharing ratios, new partners joining and existing partners retiring. Depending on the agreements reached there may be a need to account for asset revaluations and goodwill.

Further reading

R. J. Bull, David A. Harvey and Lindsey M. Lindley, *Accounting in Business*, 6th edition, Butterworth, 1990.
Paul Gee, *Spicer and Pegler's Bookkeeping and Accounts*, 23rd edition, Butterworth, 1996.
Richard Giles, *A Complete Course in Business Accounting*, Stanley Thornes, 1996.
Frank Wood and Allan Sangster, *Business Accounting 1*, 7th edition, Pitman Publishing, 1996.

9 Incomplete records

On completion of this chapter students should be able to:

- prepare financial statements from incomplete record situations.

Accountants are sometimes confronted with the problem of preparing accounting statements from incomplete information. Difficulty may be experienced in obtaining full records in respect of:

- sales
- payments to suppliers or employees
- owners' drawings from the business
- the value of assets or liabilities at a point in time – e.g. value of stock at the time of theft or damage.

Several techniques can be used to fill the information gaps.

Statement of affairs

The capital of a business at a point in time can be determined by finding the value of net assets.

If the value of net assets is known at the start and end of an accounting period, then the change in value will equal the net change in owners' capital. This may be the only way of determining business profits if there are insufficient records to construct a profit and loss account.

Illustration

Balance sheets	Year 2 (£)	Year 1 (£)
Fixed assets	10 000	8 000
Current assets	5 000	6 000
Current liabilities	3 000	3 500
Net current assets	2 000	2 500
Total net assets	12 000	10 500

Using the accounting equation (capital = assets – liabilities) the capital brought forward into year 2 was £10 500 and the capital carried forward is £12 000. The net assets of a business change when the owners put more capital into the business; when the business makes a profit or a loss in a period; and when the owners draw money out of the business. If it is known that no further capital was introduced into the business and drawings were £3 000, then profit for year 2 can be derived:

	Year 2
	(£)
Capital brought forward	10 500
Profit (balancing item)	4 500
Drawings	(3 000)
Capital carried forward	12 000

Exercise 9.1 Statement of affairs

Calculate the profit made by I. Lostum, who has lost all records of transactions made in year 2.

List of balances	Year 2	Year 1
	(£)	(£)
Fixed assets	67 000	37 500
Cost accruals	2 000	1 500
Stocks	5 000	4 800
Trade creditors	2 500	4 000
Trade debtors	900	800
Bank and cash	1 700	650
Prepayments	200	300

During the year Lostum is estimated to have received drawings of £3 900.

Exercise 9.2 Statement of affairs

Calculate the profit made by Paperless, a business that has lost all records for year 2.

List of balances	Year 2	Year 1
	(£)	(£)
Prepayments	100	50
Fixed assets – cost	18 000	7 800
Fixed assets – depreciation	4 500	2 000
Cost accruals	800	400
Stocks	1 560	1 320
Trade creditors	2 500	4 000
Bank and cash	1 700	650
Trade debtors	900	800

During the year, the partners of Paperless contributed a further £20 000 in capital to the business. According to the partners' personal bank accounts, drawings for the year totalled £6 500.

Mark-up and margin

A valuable tool to piece together the trading account of a business is the mathematical relationship between the cost of goods sold and the sales value.

Mark-up – profit is expressed as a percentage of cost, e.g. an item costing £8 which is sold with a mark-up of 25 per cent will be priced at £8 + 25 per cent × £8 = £10.

Margin – profit is expressed as a percentage of sales, e.g. an item selling for £10 with a 20 per cent margin results in a profit of £2 and therefore must have cost £8.

These two measures can be valuable for calculating missing information where the relationship between sales and costs is constant. To apply the technique, remember that for mark-up, cost = 100 per cent; and for margin, sales = 100 per cent.

	(£)	Mark-up	Margin
Sales	10	125 per cent	100 per cent
Cost of sales	8	100 per cent	80 per cent
Gross profit	2	25 per cent	20 per cent

Illustration – Using margin

A business has recorded the following items for the year just ended: sales £6 400, opening stock £500, closing stock £1 000 and profit margin 25 per cent. The records concerning purchases are incomplete and so they are to be derived from the information available.

At this stage it may be helpful to arrange the data that is available in the familiar format of a trading account.

	(£)	(£)
Sales		6 400
Opening stock	500	
Purchases	not known	
Closing stock	1 000	
Cost of sales		
Gross profit – 25 per cent margin		

As profit is 25 per cent of sales then cost of sales must be 75 per cent of sales, i.e. £4 800. The sub-total of opening stock and purchases must therefore be £5 800. Hence purchases can be derived as £5 300. The completed trading account looks like this:

	(£)	(£)
Sales		6 400
Opening stock	500	
Purchases (balancing item)	5 300	
	5 800	
Closing stock	1 000	
Cost of sales		4 800
Gross profit – 25 per cent margin		1 600

Exercise 9.3   Margin

Find the value of purchases from these details: sales £4 400, opening stock £700, closing stock £1 000 and profit margin 50 per cent.

Illustration – Using mark-up

A business has recorded the following items for the year just ended: sales £22 400, opening stock £5 200, closing stock £1 900 and mark-up of 40 per cent. The records concerning purchases are incomplete and so they are to be derived from the information available.

Arranging the data in the format of a trading account:

	(£)	(£)
Sales		22 400
Opening stock	5 200	
Purchases	not known	
Closing stock	1 900	
Cost of sales		
Gross profit – 40 per cent mark-up		

As profit is 40 per cent of cost, sales must be 140 per cent of cost. Cost of sales must therefore be £22 400 × 100/140 = £16 000. The sub-total of opening stock and purchases is then £17 900. Hence purchases can be derived as £12 700. The completed trading account looks like this:

	(£)	(£)
Sales		22 400
Opening stock	5 200	
Purchases	12 700	
	17 900	
Closing stock	1 900	
Cost of sales		16 000
Gross profit		6 400

Exercise 9.4   Mark-up

Find the value of purchases from: sales £9 200, opening stock £200, closing stock £900 and mark-up of 60 per cent.

Exercise 9.5   Mark-up and margin

Determine the unknown value in each of the following problems.

1   *Find sales from: purchases £3 400, opening stock £700, closing stock £1 000 and profit margin 22.5 per cent.*
2   *Find opening stock from: purchases £23 100, sales £32 625, closing stock £6 270 and mark-up 45 per cent.*
3   *Find closing stock from: purchases £13 460, sales £22 000 opening stock £4 120 and profit margin 35 per cent.*
4   *Find purchases from: sales £8 100, opening stock £600, closing stock £950, goods taken for own use £500 and profit margin 50 per cent.*
5   *Find sales from: purchases £3 260, opening stock £850, closing stock £590, goods taken for own use £20 and profit margin 30 per cent.*

Exercise 9.6   Applying mark-up

Lawson Enterprises has an accounting year end on 31 March. Unfortunately the stock was not counted until 7 April, after several transactions had been made. The stock take provided a stock valuation of £3 560. During the seven days up to 7 April the stores received goods costing £1 410 and issued goods with a sales value of £4 620. Calculate the value of stock at 31 March if the business calculates selling prices on a 65 per cent cost plus basis.

Exercise 9.7   Applying margin

Royston & Plank suffered a fire in their warehouse on 15 October which resulted in stock being destroyed. A stock take after the fire showed that stock costing £2 540 was still in a saleable condition. Since the last stock valuation of £6 740 on 30 September, the business has made sales of £46 500 and purchases of £30 740. Calculate the value of the stock destroyed based on the firm's pricing policy of 30 per cent profit margin.

Working control accounts

Where transaction records are insufficient to prepare detailed ledger accounts, it may still be possible to construct working control accounts that simulate the ledger accounts. Unknown items may be derived from figures required to balance the working control accounts.

Illustration

It is necessary to determine the amounts paid to creditors despite not having a record of payments. The following balances have been ascertained:

	(£)
Opening stock	12 000
Closing stock	14 000
Creditors brought forward	5 000
Creditors carried forward	9 000
Sales for the year	48 000

The business prices sales on a 50 per cent mark-up on cost.

Working control accounts can be prepared with the balances provided:

Stock

Detail	Debit (£)	Detail	Credit (£)
Balance b/f	12 000	Cost of sales	
Purchases		Balance c/f	14 000

Creditors

Detail	Debit (£)	Detail	Credit (£)
Bank		Balance b/f	5 000
Balance c/f	9 000	Purchases	

Using 'mark-up' it can be deduced that cost of sales was £32 000 (£48 000 × 100\150). Balancing off the stock account gives a total of £46 000 on the credit side. Therefore to balance the account, purchases must have been £34 000. Purchases are then credited to creditors giving a credit total of £39 000 on the creditors account. Hence payments to creditors can be derived as being £30 000. The completed working control accounts:

Stock

Detail	Debit (£)	Detail	Credit (£)
Balance b/f	12 000	Cost of sales	32 000
Purchases	34 000	Balance c/f	14 000
	46 000		46 000

Creditors

Detail	Debit (£)	Detail	Credit (£)
Bank	30 000	Balance b/f	5 000
Balance c/f	9 000	Purchases	34 000
	39 000		39 000

Working control accounts can be used for all items including bank, fixed assets and expenses. Working control accounts are not ledger accounts in the true sense, because as their name implies they are merely workings to solve a problem. There is no requirement to prepare an account for all items but they are useful for expense accounts where adjustments for accruals and prepayments are required.

Exercise 9.8   Working control accounts

The following balances have been ascertained:

	£
Opening stock	19 000
Closing stock	17 000
Creditors brought forward	6 500
Creditors carried forward	9 000
Payments to creditors	65 500

The business prices sales with a 30 per cent profit margin.

Using working control accounts for stock and creditors, determine the value of sales for the year.

Exercise 9.9   Working control accounts

It has been ascertained that the only bank transactions made by a business relate to receipts from debtors, payments to creditors and drawings made by the business partners.

	£
Opening stock	4 500
Closing stock	5 750
Creditors brought forward	2 000
Creditors carried forward	3 500
Debtors brought forward	8 500
Debtors carried forward	6 500
Bank brought forward	1 900
Bank carried forward	1 650
Payments to creditors	23 250

Sales are calculated with a 100 per cent mark-up on cost.

Tasks

1 *Prepare working ledger accounts for stocks, creditors, debtors and bank.*
2 *Find the amount paid in respect of drawings.*

Exercise 9.10   Working control accounts

It has been ascertained that the only bank transactions made by a business relate to customers' receipts, payments to creditors and drawings made by the business partners.

	£
Opening stock	520
Closing stock	790
Creditors brought forward	1 500
Creditors carried forward	1 960
Debtors brought forward	1 320
Debtors carried forward	1 840
Bank balance brought forward	3 950
Bank overdraft carried forward	48
Cash received from debtors	23 500
Cash sales	3 200

Sales are calculated with a 60 per cent profit margin.

Tasks

1 *Prepare working ledger accounts for stocks, creditors, debtors and bank.*
2 *Find the amount paid in respect of drawings.*

Exercise 9.11   Working control accounts

A retailer sells for cash only and takes drawings direct from the cash till. Unfortunately no records are kept of either sales or drawings.

The following is a summary of bank transactions made:

	£
Payments to suppliers	29 500
Cash paid in	35 400
Rent paid	6 000

The following payments out of the cash till have been verified:

	£
Wages	7 800
Expenses	990

Balances for the year are as follows:

	£
Opening stock	1 980
Closing stock	3 260
Creditors brought forward	650
Creditors carried forward	430
Bank brought forward	2 100
Bank carried forward	450
Cash brought forward	250
Cash carried forward	460

Sales are set at 180 per cent of cost.

Task

Calculate the retailer's sales and drawings for the year.

Preparing final accounts

For the preparation of a full set of accounts it is useful to identify the information that is missing and to have an outline plan of how the items can be deduced. The use of working control accounts makes the logical path more obvious.

Exercise 9.12 Accounts from incomplete records

PaperFree is run by upholsterer and interior designer Paul Wild. Keeping accounting records has not been Paul's priority but the time has come to prepare accounts for his second year of trading.

Customers are charged on a 70 per cent profit margin basis. They pay on delivery by either cheque or cash although no sales invoices or records of work done have been maintained.

Paul takes drawings out of the cash till before banking his takings. No record exists of these amounts although he does have details of cash payments to suppliers amounting to £450.

An analysis of bank statements and cheque stubs has enabled the following summary of bank transactions to be prepared:

Transactions	Detail	£
Receipts	Cash and cheques paid in	27 600
Payments	Rent	6 000
	Suppliers	7 100
	Expenses	3 650
	Workbench and tools	4 900

The following balances at the start and end of the year have been ascertained:

	Start (£)	End (£)
Bank balance	1 200	7 150
Cash balance	100	50
Creditors	1 900	4 750
Stock	2 600	3 100
Fixed assets (at written down value)	11 100	12 000

Notes:

- Fixed assets are depreciated by 25 per cent per annum using the reducing balance method.
- The rent agreement is for £4 000 per annum.

Tasks

Prepare:

1 *working control accounts for bank, cash, fixed assets, creditors and stock*
2 *a trading and profit and loss account for the year*
3 *a balance sheet.*

Exercise 9.13 Accounts from incomplete records

The partnership of Swindle and Mistri has come to the end of its first year of trading but complete accounting records have not been maintained.

The firm supplies mechanical components for machine repair and maintenance work with a 30 per cent mark-up on cost. The partners each paid £25 000 into the business as capital and they share profits equally.

The following balances have been verified at the end of the year:

	End (£)
Cash balance	450
Creditors	15 250
Stock	4 950
Debtors	24 500

Drawings have been taken out of the cash till: Mistri always takes £200 a week but Swindle withdraws irregular amounts and has not kept a proper record. Swindle has confirmed, though, that he drew £2 000 from the bank. Payments of £550 have also been made out of the cash till for motor expenses.

Fixed assets are to be depreciated at 20 per cent on cost. Rent has been paid for the first quarter of year 2 and electricity usage of £500 needs to be accrued as due.

Bank transactions	Detail	(£)
Receipts	Cash and cheques paid in	149 100
	Mistri – capital	25 000
	Swindle – capital	25 000
Payments	Rent	(5 000)
	Suppliers	(139 700)
	Utilities	(2 700)
	Fixed assets	(20 000)
	Motor expenses	(3 300)
	Swindle – drawings	(2 000)

Tasks

Prepare for the partnership:

1 *a trading and profit and loss account for the year*
2 *a balance sheet with capital and current account balances for each partner.*

Summary

The preparation of final accounts from incomplete records can be aided by the three techniques described in this chapter:

1 statement of affairs – to establish total net assets and hence capital at a point in time.
2 mark-up and margin – to make use of fixed relationships between sales and costs
3 working control accounts – to derive unknown items using the principles of double entry book-keeping.

Further reading

R. J. Bull, David A. Harvey and Lindsey M. Lindley, *Accounting in Business*, 6th edition, Butterworth, 1990.
Paul Gee, *Spicer and Pegler's Bookkeeping and Accounts*, 23rd edition, Butterworth, 1996.
Richard Giles, *A Complete Course in Business Accounting*, Stanley Thornes, 1996.
Frank Wood and Allan Sangster, *Business Accounting 1*, 7th edition, Pitman Publishing, 1996.

10 Published accounts for companies

On completion of this chapter students should be able to:

- prepare financial statements for individual limited companies

- evaluate the requirements of a range of accounting standards.

The regulatory framework described in Chapter 3 has important implications for the preparation of published accounts for companies. The annual report for a company must include: directors' report, auditors' report, profit and loss account, statement of total gains and losses, balance sheet, cash flow statement and notes to the accounts.

The companies acts and the Accounting Standards Board (ASB) prescribe the information which must be disclosed in the accounts of a limited company and the manner in which it must be presented. Although more than one format is allowed by the *Companies Act 1985*, the most popular is 'format 1' for both the profit and loss account and the balance sheet. The statement of gains and losses is specified by FRS (Financial Reporting Standard) 3 and the cash flow statement is governed by FRS 1. FRS 3 also has important implications for the format of the profit and loss account in a quest by the ASB to provide users of accounts with better information on which to interpret the financial performance of a company. Both the companies acts and the ASB influence the content of the notes to the accounts.

The profit and loss account

The *Companies Act 1985* specifies standard headings that must be used when preparing the profit and loss account. As the format specified by the Act is one that must be applied to a whole range of companies, the headings are necessarily of a general nature.

Profit and loss account – Outline of format 1

	Notes	Year X2 (£'000)	Year X1 (£'000)
Turnover	1	500	400
Cost of sales	2	(250)	(200)
Gross profit or loss		250	200
Distribution costs	2	(100)	(80)
Administration expenses	2	(100)	(100)
Other operating income		50	50
Operating profit		100	70
Income from other fixed asset investments		5	4
Other interest receivable and similar income		5	1
Interest payable and similar charges	5	(20)	(30)
Profit before tax on ordinary activities		90	45
Tax on profit or loss on ordinary activities		(30)	(15)
Profit or loss on ordinary activities after taxation		60	30
Dividends		(30)	(20)
Retained profit for the year		30	10
Retained profit brought forward		250	240
Retained profit carried forward		280	250

For comparative purposes the previous year's results are shown against those for the current profit. The Companies Act also requires an analysis of certain items and these are disclosed in **notes to the accounts.** These are numbered with a note reference number on the face of the profit and loss account.

The minimum information required on the face of the profit and loss account includes:

- the profit (or loss) before tax on ordinary activities and
- dividends paid and proposed, and
- transfer to or from reserves.

Other headings not included on the face of the profit and loss account must be disclosed in the notes to the accounts.

The following profit and loss account for the fashion retailer Oasis plc illustrates the use of format 1.

Oasis plc
Profit and loss account
for the year to 27 January 1996

	Note	1996 £'000s	1996 £'000s	1995 £'000
Turnover	1		60 910	47 104
Cost of sales			(28 167)	(21 723)
Gross profit or loss			32 743	25 381
Distribution costs			(18 796)	(13 825)
Administration expenses				
exceptional flotation costs		(1 345)		0
other administrative expenses		(4 154)	(5 499)	(3 218)
Other operating income			543	214
Operating profit	2		8 991	8 552
Interest receivable and similar income			906	718
Interest payable and similar charges	3		(30)	(43)
Profit on ordinary activities before taxation			9 867	9 227
Tax on profit or loss on ordinary activities	5		(3 811)	(3 182)
Profit after taxation			6 056	6 045
Dividend	6		(1 799)	(2 002)
Retained profit			4 257	4 043

Oasis has used the basic format with an analysis of administration costs as required by FRS 3 (explained later in the chapter). Note that where there are nil values for a standard heading it should be omitted.

Illustration

The following data relating to Ketron Ltd has been extracted from the company's trial balance for the year ended 31 December 19X9.

	(£'000)	(£'000)
Purchases	1 205	
Sales		2 955
Carriage out	115	
Utilities	165	
Salaries	458	
Opening stock	236	
Delivery vehicle expenses	59	
Depreciation – delivery vehicles	123	
Depreciation – FF&F	45	
Loss on sale of delivery vehicle	10	
Bad debts	19	
Interest paid on bank overdraft	23	
Interest paid on debenture redeemable 19Y9	25	
Dividend paid	25	
Audit	30	
Goodwill – amortisation	10	
Retained profit brought forward		363
Advertising and promotion	34	

Notes:

1 Closing stock has been valued at £259 000.
2 The directors are proposing a final dividend of £50 000.
3 The corporation tax charge for the year is £160 000.
4 Salaries are to be apportioned 50/50 between expense headings distribution and administration.
5 Depreciation of furniture, fixtures and fittings is to be charged to administration expenses.

Prepare the company's profit and loss account in a form suitable for publication.

Solution

It is important to use a methodical approach for analysing items between the standard headings. The first step is to analyse operating costs and expenses into cost of sales, distribution and administration.

	Cost of sales (£'000)	Distribution (£'000)	Administration (£'000)
Purchases	1 205		
Carriage out		115	
Utilities			165
Salaries		229	229
Opening stock	236		
Delivery vehicle expenses		59	
Depreciation – delivery vehicles		123	
Depreciation – FF&F			45
Loss on sale of delivery vehicle		10	
Bad debts			19
Audit			30
Goodwill – amortisation			10
Advertising and promotion		34	
Closing stock	−259		
Total	1 182	570	498

The allocation of items, particularly between distribution and administration, is a matter of judgement. Some items that can cause problems include:

Item	Allocate to:
Bad debts	Administration – the accounts department is responsible for credit control.
Goodwill amortisation	Administration
Research and development	Cost of sales

The profit and loss account can now be prepared.

Ketron Ltd
Profit and loss account for the year ended 31 December 19X9

	£'000
Turnover	2 955
Cost of sales	1 182
Gross profit or loss	1 773
Distribution costs	570
Administration expenses	498
Operating profit	705
Interest payable and similar charges	48
Profit before tax on ordinary activities	657
Tax on profit or loss on ordinary activities	160
Profit or loss on ordinary activities after taxation	497
Dividends	75
Retained profit for the year	422
Retained profit brought forward	363
Retained profit carried forward	785

Exercise 10.1 Profit and loss account

The following balances relating to LookInn Ltd have been extracted from the company's records for the year ended 31 December 19X9.

	(£'000)	(£'000)
Purchases	551	
Sales		1 510
Carriage in	30	
Salaries	325	
Opening stock	542	
Delivery vehicle expenses	147	
Depreciation – delivery vehicles	52	
Depreciation – FF&F	48	
Bad debts	15	
Interest paid on bank loan	12	
Dividend paid	25	
Audit	10	
Rent	40	
Sundry administrative expenses	68	
Retained profit brought forward		410
Advertising and promotion	41	

Notes:

1 Closing stock has been valued at £470 000.
2 The directors are proposing a final dividend of £25 000.
3 The corporation tax charge for the year is £20 000.
4 Salaries are to be apportioned 60/40 between expense headings distribution and administration.

5 *Depreciation of furniture, fixtures and fittings is to be charged to administration expenses.*

6 *Rent is to be apportioned £30 000 to distribution and £10 000 to administration.*

Task

Prepare the company's profit and loss account for the year ended 31 December 19X9 in a form suitable for publication.

Balance sheet

The *Companies Act 1985* format 1 for the balance sheet uses an item prefix system to show how items are to be disclosed.

Items prefixed with letters (A, B, C, etc.) and Roman numerals (I, II, III, etc.) must be shown on the face of the balance sheet. Descriptions of items prefixed in this way cannot be altered although they can be omitted if there is no value for either year.

Items prefixed with Arabic numbers (1, 2, 3, etc.) may be analysed in the notes to the accounts if it improves the presentation of the balance sheet. Item descriptions can be altered to improve understanding in the context of a particular company.

Balance sheet – Format 1

	(£'000)	(£'000)	(£'000)
A CALLED UP SHARE CAPITAL NOT PAID			100
B FIXED ASSETS			
I Intangible assets			
1 Development costs	100		
2 Concessions, patents, licences, trade marks, etc.	100		
3 Goodwill	100		
4 Payments on account	100		
		400	
II Tangible assets			
1 Land and buildings	100		
2 Plant and machinery	100		
3 Fixtures, fittings, tools and equipment	100		
4 Payments on account	100		
		400	
III Investments (details required)		100	
			900

C CURRENT ASSETS			
I Stocks			
1 Raw materials	100		
2 Work in progress	100		
3 Finished goods and goods for resale	100		
4 Payments on account	100		
	400		
II Debtors			
1 Trade debtors	100		
2 Amounts owed by group undertakings	100		
3 Amounts owed by associated undertakings	100		
4 Other debtors	100		
5 Called up share capital not paid	100		
6 Prepayments and accrued income	100		
	600		
III Investments			
1 Shares in group undertakings	100		
2 Own shares	100		
3 Other investments	100		
	300		
IV Cash at bank and in hand	100		
(Total of C)		1 400	
D PREPAYMENTS AND ACCRUED INCOME		100	
(Total of C + D)		1 500	
E CREDITORS: AMOUNTS FALLING DUE WITHIN ONE YEAR			
1 Debenture loans	100		
2 Bank loans and overdrafts	100		
3 Payments received on account	100		
4 Trade creditors	100		
5 Bills of exchange payable	100		
6 Amounts owed to group undertakings	100		
7 Amounts owed to associated undertakings	100		
8 Other creditors including taxation and social security	100		
9 Accruals and deferred income	100		
		(900)	
F NET CURRENT ASSETS (LIABILITIES)			600
G TOTAL ASSETS LESS CURRENT LIABILITIES			1 600
H CREDITORS: AMOUNTS FALLING DUE AFTER MORE THAN ONE YEAR			
1–9 same detail as under E above			(100)
I PROVISIONS FOR LIABILITIES AND CHARGES			
1 Pensions and similar obligations	100		
2 Taxation, including deferred taxation	100		
3 Other provisions	100		
			(300)
J ACCRUALS AND DEFERRED INCOME			(100)
			1 100
K CAPITAL AND RESERVES			
I Called up share capital			100
II Share premium account			100
III Revaluation reserve			100

IV Other reserves

1 Capital redemption reserve	100	
2 Reserve for own shares	100	
3 Reserves provided for by the articles of association	100	
		300
V Profit and loss account		500
		1100

The format appears complex, but it groups items into the familiar categories of fixed assets, current assets, current liabilities and long-term liabilities. However, note that current liabilities are labelled **creditors: amounts due within one year** and long-term liabilities are called **creditors: amounts falling due after more than one year.**

Some sections of the format are optional. Prepayments and accrued income can be disclosed under section D but most companies show them as a sub-heading of debtors under item 6. Accruals and deferred income may be disclosed under section J but again many companies choose to show them as a sub-heading of creditors under item 9, section E or H as appropriate.

Other rules include:

■ Figures for the previous year are shown for comparative purposes in further columns to the right of those for the current year.
■ The letters and numbers for each line do not have to be shown.
■ Brackets ( ) may be used to show liabilities as a deduction from assets if this improves presentation.

In addition to the detail required by format 1, it is necessary to analyse 'other creditors including taxation and social security'.

■ the amount payable in respect of corporation tax
■ other taxation balances such as PAYE and social security deductions
■ dividends payable and
■ other creditors.

Illustration – A published balance sheet

Oasis plc
Balance sheet as at 27 January 1996

	Note	1996 (£'000)	1995 (£'000)
Fixed assets			
Tangible assets	8	9742	7022
Current assets			
Stocks	8	5153	4699
Investments	10	391	483
Debtors	11	2778	2311
Cash at bank		7698	4889

	Note		
		16020	12382
Creditors: amounts falling due within one year	12	9805	7861
Net current assets		6215	4521
Total assets less current liabilities		15957	11543
Creditors: amounts falling due after more than one year	13	275	228
Provisions for liabilities and charges	14	288	178
		15394	11137
Capital and reserves			
Share capital	15	5246	1166
Share premium account	16	0	472
Profit and loss account	16	10148	9499
		15394	11137

Note that Oasis aggregates figures for certain items and so it is necessary for further detail in notes to the accounts to conform with the standard format (these are considered later).

Illustration – Balance sheet

The following data relating to Ketron Ltd has been extracted from the company's trial balance for the year ended 31 December 19X9.

	(£'000)	(£'000)
Trade creditors		237
VAT		45
Accruals		53
Debtors	441	
Provision for bad debts		5
Delivery vehicles – net book value	482	
Furniture, fixtures and fittings – net book value	598	
Bank overdraft		205
Debentures redeemable in 19Y9		180
Goodwill – net book value	90	
Share capital (authorised 200000 shares @ £1)		150

Notes:

1 *Closing stock has been valued at £259000.*
2 *The directors are proposing a final dividend of £50000.*
3 *The corporation tax charge for the year is £160000.*
4 *Trade creditors include £25000 that is due for payment in two years time.*

Prepare the company's balance sheet as at 31 December 19X9 in published account format together with supporting notes for creditors.

Solution

Ketron Ltd

Balance sheet as at 31 December 19X9

	(£'000)	(£'000)
Fixed assets		
Intangible assets		90
Tangible assets (482 + 598)		1 080
		1 170
Current assets		
Stocks	259	
Debtors (441 – 5)	436	
	695	
Creditors: amounts falling due within one year (see note)	725	
Net current liabilities		(30)
Total assets less current liabilities		1 140
Creditors: amounts falling due after more than one year		205
		935
Capital and reserves		
Share capital		150
Profit and loss account		785
		935

Notes to the accounts

Creditors due within one year

	(£'000)
Bank overdraft	205
Trade creditors	212
Other creditors including taxation and social security	255
Accruals	53
	725

Analysis of other creditors

	(£'000)
Corporation tax	160
Dividends	50
Other creditors	45
	255

Creditors due after more than one year

	(£'000)
Debentures due 19X9	180
Trade creditors	25
	205

Exercise 10.2   Format 1 balance sheet

The following data relating to LookInn Ltd has been extracted from the company's trial balance for the year ended 31 December 19X9.

	(£'000)	(£'000)
Trade creditors		51
Bank loan (due 1.6.19Y0)		50
Accruals		15
Debtors	172	
Provision for bad debts		10
Delivery vehicles – net book value	36	
Furniture, fixtures and fittings – net book value	124	
Bank balance	58	
Debentures redeemable in 19Y5		150
Share capital		100

Notes:

1   *Closing stock has been valued at £470 000.*
2   *The directors are proposing a final dividend of £25 000.*
3   *The corporation tax charge for the year is £20 000.*
4   *Trade creditors include £12 000 that is due for payment in fifteen months' time.*

Task

Prepare the company's balance sheet as at 31 December 19X9 in published account format together with supporting notes for creditors.

Notes to the accounts

The profit and loss account and balance sheet are required to be supported by **notes to the accounts** which provide greater information for various items.

The basis on which material items have been accounted for should be disclosed in an **accounting policies note**. Policies that are commonly disclosed:

■ *Turnover* – The basis on which sales are valued and assumed to be realised. This is usually the invoiced amount exclusive of VAT.
■ *Fixed asset investments* – The basis for valuation in the balance sheet; for example, are they at original cost or are they revalued to market prices.
■ *Depreciation* – The rate and method used for each class of fixed asset.
■ *Stocks* – Usually a confirmation that accounting

standard requirements are being followed by stating that stocks are valued at the lower of cost or net realisable value.

- *Research and development (R&D)* – Stating whether R&D expenditure is written off to the profit and loss account as incurred or if it is capitalised in the balance sheet.

Profit and loss account notes

Certain costs charged in arriving at **operating profit** should be disclosed.

- Audit fee
- Hire charges, including operating lease rentals, distinguishing between payments for plant and machinery and those relating to the renting of land and buildings
- Depreciation charged for the year
- In respect of research and development: expenditure written off in the period and amount of previous expenditure amortised this period
- Exceptional items (see FRS 3 later in the chapter)
- Staff costs including directors' emoluments (the requirements are described in Chapter 3).

Illustration

Oasis plc (from their accounts for the year ended 27 January 1996)
Operating profit is after charging the following amounts:

	(£'000)
Staff costs including directors:	
Wages and salaries	7 901
Social security costs	668
Pension costs	56
Depreciation of tangible fixed assets	2 011
Loss on disposal of tangible fixed assets	50
Auditors' remuneration	
Auditing	22
Flotation costs	256
Other services	10
Operating lease rentals – property	4 738
– machinery	58

A note in respect of **interest payable** should distinguish the amounts in respect of: (i) bank loans and overdrafts and other loans that fall due for repayment within five years; and (ii) all other loans.

The **taxation** charge should be supported by a note stating the basis of computation, including the tax rate used.

An analysis of **dividends** is required, distinguishing for each class of shares between interim dividends paid and final dividends proposed.

Illustration

Oasis (from their accounts for the year ended 27 January 1996)

Note 6 – Dividend

	1996 (£'000)
Interim dividend paid	52
Final dividend proposed	1 747
	1 799

Balance sheet notes

Like the profit and loss account, the balance sheet is supported by notes to explain some items in more detail.

In particular, where items have been summarised on the face of the balance sheet, the detail of the Arabic numbered items should be given in the notes. This often applies to stocks and creditors that have been aggregated for presentation purposes.

Fixed asset schedule

A fixed asset schedule is required to show the values for cost and depreciation for each category of fixed asset, together with details of movements during the year. The following example is typical of the layout used.

Oasis plc

Note 8 – Tangible fixed assets

	Short leases Leasehold property (£'000)	Fixtures and fittings (£'000)	Total (£'000)
Cost			
At 29 January 1995	1 904	7 463	9 367
Additions	606	4 196	4 802
Disposals	(2)	(131)	(133)
At 27 January 1996	2 508	11 528	14 036
Depreciation			
At 29 January 1995	197	2 148	2 345
Charge for the period	176	1 835	2 011
Disposals	(2)	(60)	(62)
At 27 January 1996	371	3 923	4 294
Net book value			
At 27 January 1996	2 137	7 605	9 742
At 29 January 1995	1 707	5 315	7 022

Where there are **revaluations** of assets during a period, then an additional line will be required in both the cost and depreciation sections. At the time of revaluation, the cost section will be adjusted to the revalued amount and the accumulated depreciation will be cleared to nil.

The accounting entries are:

debit/ credit   Fixed asset cost
debit   Fixed asset accumulated depreciation
credit   Revaluation reserve

After an asset has been revalued, SSAP 12 (see page 145) requires subsequent depreciation calculations to be based on the revalued amount.

Illustration

Buildings with an original cost of £350 000 and accumulated depreciation of £50 000 are revalued at the start of 19X8 to £450 000. Depreciation on buildings is charged at 2 per cent per annum. The buildings section of the fixed asset schedule at 31 December 19X8:

	Buildings (£'000)
Cost	
At 1 January X8	350
Revaluation	100
At 31 December X8	450
Depreciation	
At 1 January X8	50
Charge for the period	9
Revaluation	(50)
At 31 December X8	9
Net book value	
At 31 December X8	441
At 31 December X7	300

Exercise 10.3   Fixed asset schedule

The fixed assets of Solidarity Ltd at 1 January 19X8 were as follows:

	Cost (£)	Depreciation (£)
Land	200 000	
Buildings	500 000	50 000
Plant	250 000	120 000
Motor vehicles	57 000	24 000
Total	1 007 000	194 000

1   During the year, Solidarity purchased plant for £40 000 and motor vehicles for £24 000.
2   A motor vehicle was disposed of on 10/10/X8 for £3 000. It was originally purchased on 1/7/X6 for £10 000.
3   On 1/1/X8 the company's properties were valued by independent advisors. Land was valued at £250 000 and buildings at £600 000. The directors have decided to include these valuations in the company's accounts.
4   The company's depreciation policy requires the following rates to be applied to assets from the year of acquisition to the year prior to disposal: buildings straight line at 2 per cent on cost or if revalued on the revaluation, plant 10 per cent on cost and motor vehicles 40 per cent on reducing balance.

Task

Prepare a fixed asset schedule for Solidarity as at 31 December 19X8.

Exercise 10.4   Fixed asset schedule

The following balances have been extracted from Pear Ltd's trial balance at 31 March 19X9.

	Cost (£)	Depreciation (£)
Land	300 000	
Buildings	400 000	30 000
Plant	854 000	265 000
Motor vehicles	98 000	45 000
Total	1 652 000	340 000

1   On 1 April 19X8 the company purchased plant for £50 000 and motor vehicles for £18 000.
2   Land and buildings were independently valued on 1/4/X8 at £900 000 (buildings £450 000). The directors have decided that these values should be included in the accounts.
3   On 30/9/X8, £3 000 was received for the disposal of some plant that had been purchased on 1 April 19X6 for £12 000. The proceeds have been credited to the plant cost account and no other entries have been made in respect of the transaction.
4   Depreciation for the year to 31/3/X9 has not yet been entered in the books. Depreciation is provided on a straight line basis assuming residual values of 10 per cent of cost. Rates are 4 per cent for buildings, 10 per cent for plant and 25 per cent for motor vehicles. Depreciation is calculated from the month of purchase to the month of disposal inclusive.

Task

Prepare Pear's fixed asset schedule for the year to 31 March 19X9.

Net current assets

Where more than one category of **stocks** has been summarised on the face of the balance sheet, the notes should provide the detail as required by the Companies Act format, i.e. balances for raw material, work in progress, finished goods and payments on account.

Illustration

Oasis

Note 9 – Stocks	1996 (£'000)
Raw materials	761
Goods for resale	4 392
	5 153

In addition to the detail required by the standard format, it is also necessary to highlight **debtors** due after more than one year. This will be shown in a note unless the amount is so material that understanding of the accounts would be enhanced by disclosure on the face of the balance sheet.

Illustration of format 1 disclosure for debtors

Oasis

Note 11 – Debtors	1996 (£'000)
Trade debtors	905
Other debtors	516
Prepayments	1 357
	2 778

(Oasis did not have any debtors due after more than one year.)

Notes for **creditor** balances were considered earlier in the chapter to provide the detail required by format 1. In the illustration from Oasis below, the additional information concerning other creditors has been included in the main note.

Oasis

Note 12 – Creditors: amounts falling due within one year	1996 (£'000)
Trade creditors	1 347
Other creditors	490
Corporation tax	3 835
Other taxation and social security	1 571
Dividend	1 747
Accruals and deferred income	815
	9 805

Oasis

Note 13 – Creditors: amounts falling due after more than one year	1996 (£'000)
Deferred income	275
	275

Capital and reserves

The **share capital** of the company must be analysed by class of share. The amount of authorised share capital should also be disclosed.

Oasis

Note 15 – Share capital	1996 (£'000)
Authorised	
69 942 900 ordinary shares of 10p	6 994
Issued and fully paid	
52 457 175 ordinary shares of 10p	5 246

Where share capital has been issued during the accounting period, the following details must be given: the reason for the issue, the class of share allotted, the aggregate nominal value and the consideration received.

In the case of Oasis, share capital increased by £4 080 000 during the year due to a bonus issue. The shares were created by the appropriation of reserves as shown in the statement of reserves in the next section.

Statement of reserves

Where there has been any movement on reserve accounts during the year, a reserve note is required. The note should state the balance on each reserve at the beginning and end of the year, and provide a description of transfers to and from the reserves during the year.

Typical movements:

- Retained profit for the year
- Share issue involving a share premium

- Bonus issue where reserves are converted to shares
- Revaluation of fixed assets involving a revaluation reserve
- Transfer from the profit and loss account to a general reserve.

Oasis

Note 16 – Reserves

	Share premium account (£'000)	Profit and loss account (£'000)
At 29 January 1995	472	9 467
Prior year adjustment	0	32
	472	9 499
Bonus share issue	(472)	(3 608)
Profit for the year		4 257
At 27 January 1996	0	10 148

Exercise 10.5   Published accounts with notes

Celia Fashions Ltd is a manufacturer of high quality evening wear. The following data relates to its accounting year ended 30 June 19X8.

Trial balance at 30 June 19X8	(£ '000)	(£'000)
Debentures 8 per cent 19Y5		450
Land and buildings – (land cost £500 000)	1 500	200
Plant – cost/depreciation	740	325
Motor vehicles – cost/depreciation	164	63
Sales		2 350
Purchases	637	
Trade debtors and creditors	246	105
Wages and salaries	870	
Utilities	80	
Debenture interest paid	18	
Bank	52	
Raw materials 1/7/X7	89	
Finished goods 1/7/X7	264	
Factory repairs and maintenance	42	

Administrative expenses	65	
Share capital @ 25p nominal value		430
Profit and loss account		953
Dividends paid	86	
Bad debts	23	
	4 876	4 876

Notes:
1 *Closing stocks: raw materials £81 000 and finished goods £232 000.*
2 *Wages and salaries are to be analysed: factory 60 per cent, distribution 20 per cent and administration 20 per cent.*
3 *Utility costs are to be apportioned £50 000 to the factory, £20 000 to distribution and £10 000 to administration.*
4 *The company's land and buildings were valued on 30 June 19X8 and the directors have decided to incorporate these valuations into the accounts. Land was valued at £700 000 and the buildings £1 100 000.*
5 *Depreciation rates based on cost are 2 per cent for buildings, 10 per cent for plant and 25 per cent for motor vehicles.*
6 *Buildings and plant depreciation charges are allocated to the factory, the motor vehicles are all in respect of delivery vans and salespeople's cars.*
7 *The directors propose a final dividend of 10p per share.*
8 *The tax charge is computed as £124 000.*
9 *The directors also wish to transfer £500 000 to a general reserve from the profit and loss account.*

Task

Prepare for Celia Fashions Ltd a profit and loss account and balance sheet for the year ended 30 June 19X8, together with notes in respect of:

- fixed assets
- stocks
- creditors
- reserves.

Accounting standards

Accounting standards issued by the Accounting Standards Board place additional reporting requirements on businesses and also provide guidance on how certain items should be accounted for.

The standards that affect the vast majority of companies are:

Reference	Subject
SSAP 2	Disclosure of accounting policies
SSAP 9	Stocks and long-term contracts
SSAP 12	Accounting for depreciation
SSAP 13	Accounting for research and development
SSAP 17	Accounting for post balance sheet events
SSAP 18	Accounting for contingencies
FRS 1	Cash flow statements
FRS 3	Reporting financial performance

SSAPs 2 and 9 are described in Chapter 3, SSAP 12 is considered in Chapter 5 and FRS 1 is the subject of the next chapter. The main provisions of the other standards are explained in this section.

Research and development – SSAP 13

SSAP 13 is concerned with the accounting treatment of expenditure relating to the research and development (R&D) of new or improved products and production processes.

The accounting treatment of R&D expenditure brings two accounting concepts into conflict. The accrual concept requires expenditure incurred for some future benefit to be deferred so that the cost can be matched against the future revenues that it has helped to create. The prudence concept requires costs that relate to uncertain future revenues to be written off immediately. SSAP 13 provides guidance in deciding which concept should have priority depending on the circumstances.

The accounting standard defines three broad categories of R&D expenditure.

> *'Pure research is experimental or theoretical work undertaken primarily to acquire new scientific or technical knowledge for its own sake rather than directed towards any specific aim or application. Applied research is original or critical investigation undertaken in order to gain new scientific or technical knowledge and directed towards a specific practical aim or objective. Development work uses scientific or technical knowledge in order to produce new or substantially improved materials, devices, products or services, to install new processes or systems prior to the commencement of commercial production or commercial applications, or to improving substantially those already produced or installed.' (SSAP 13)*

SSAP 13 requires pure and applied research to be charged directly to the profit and loss account as incurred. It also gives precedence to the prudence concept when accounting for development expenditure. Development expenditure must also be charged as incurred unless *all* of the following conditions are satisfied:

1. there is a clearly defined project
2. the related expenditure is separately identifiable
3. the project is technically feasible and commercially viable
4. future revenues must exceed the sum of costs deferred and costs still to be incurred
5. adequate resources must be available to enable the project to be completed.

Development costs include the direct costs of labour, materials and expenses charged to the project. In addition, overheads incurred in running the development facility can also be capitalised by absorbing them on an appropriate basis, probably on a direct labour hour basis. Where development costs are deferred, they will be treated as an intangible fixed asset.

Where R&D work is being sold as a service to a specific customer, the costs incurred will be accounted for under SSAP 9 as a work in progress balance. The balance sheet valuation will be the lower of cost or net realisable value just like any other stock for resale.

Fixed assets used by the R&D function should be accounted for under SSAP 12 with all other tangible fixed assets.

In the same way that the costs of tangible fixed assets are depreciated over their economic lives, capitalised R&D expenditure should be **amortised** over its economic life. An appropriate amortisation method should reflect the length of time and pattern of benefits forecast to accrue. Different bases can be categorised as either being time based or volume based.

Illustration

The cost of developing a new product during year 19X5 was £90 000. This has been deferred in accordance with SSAP 13. Sales of the new product over the next four years are forecast to be: £500 000, £900 000, £700 000 and £150 000.

On a time-based method an amortisation rate of 25 per cent would be appropriate for an asset with a four-year life. This would produce an amortisation charge of £22 500 per annum. However, a volume-based approach would better reflect the pattern of benefits being forecast for this project. Development expenditure of £90 000 is forecast to result in total revenues of £2 250 000. Allocating development expenditure on the basis of each year's revenue would give amortisation charges of £20 000, £36 000, £28 000 and £6 000.

The accounting standard requires details concerning deferred development expenditure to be disclosed in a note similar to the one described earlier for tangible fixed assets. Movements to both cost and amortisation balances should be disclosed. Using the figures from the above illustration, the relevant note for each year would appear as follows:

Development costs	19X5 (£)	19X6 (£)	19X7 (£)	19X8 (£)	19X9 (£)
Cost					
At the beginning of the year	0	90 000	90 000	90 000	90 000
Additions	90 000	0	0	0	0
At the end of the year	90 000	90 000	90 000	90 000	90 000
Amortisation					
At the beginning of the year	0	0	20 000	56 000	84 000
Charge for the year	0	20 000	36 000	28 000	6 000
At the end of the year	0	20 000	56 000	84 000	90 000
Net book value					
At the end of the year	90 000	70 000	34 000	6 000	0
At the beginning of the year	0	90 000	70 000	34 000	6 000

Exercise 10.6   Research and development

Green PLC has incurred expenditure on the following research and development projects.

1   Investigation into the chemical reaction of various materials, £75 000.
2   Development of a new screen for the next range of micro computers, £3 050 000 – competition means sales are uncertain although the managing director is optimistic.
3   Investigation to see how various materials insulate electricity flows, £150 000.
4   The keyboard on the existing range of computers has been refined at a cost of £100 000, its recent market launch is anticipated to increase gross profits by £500 000.
5   A machine has been developed for £50 000 to substantially speed up the process of product testing.
6   The research director is enthusiastic about a new electronic switch which was a by-product of work on a new disk drive. He is uncertain how it will be used but it is a major breakthrough in that type of technology.

The company's accounting policy in respect of R&D expenditure is to write off the cost of all research and development work to the profit and loss account in the year in which it is incurred, except for development expenditure that satisfies the deferral conditions of SSAP 13.

Tasks

1   *Identify which items should be charged directly against revenue in the profit and loss account and which items may be capitalised.*
2   *For those items capitalised, where will they appear in the balance sheet, and on what basis should they be amortised?*

Accounting for post balance sheet events – SSAP 17

Events occurring after the balance sheet date should be included in the accounts if they enhance understanding of the business's financial position at the year end. SSAP 17 considers those events that occur between the year end and the date that the accounts are approved by the directors.

Financial year	Period during which accounts are prepared
	Post balance sheet event

The standard identifies two types of post balance sheet events. **Adjusting events** are events which provide additional evidence relating to conditions existing at the balance sheet date. If the amounts concerned are material they should be included in the year's financial statements. **Non-adjusting events** are events which arise after the balance sheet date and concern conditions which did not exist at that time. However, non-adjusting events may need to be explained in a note to the accounts if their value is so significant that otherwise the accounts would be misleading. The nature of the event should be described, and an estimate of its financial effect should be given if possible.

Examples of possible adjusting events include: information concerning the net realisable value of stocks at the year end; discovery that a debtor not covered by a bad debt provision was insolvent at the year end; the confirmation of items that were uncertain at the year end, such as the amounts receivable for an insurance claim that was being negotiated at the year end.

Exercise 10.7   Post balance sheet events

The financial statements of Dryden Ltd for the year ended 30 June 19X7 have not yet been approved by the directors. Sales for the year totalled £23 million with a net profit of £2 million. The following events have occurred since the date of the balance sheet.

1 Due to a decision on 14 June 19X7 to change the company's product range, stock valued at £350 000 on 30 June 19X7 was sold on 10 July 19X7 for £50 000.
2 Hardy Ltd, a company that owed Dryden Ltd £7 000 at 30 June 19X7, went into liquidation on 16 July 19X7. Indications are that creditors will receive 50p for every £1 owed.
3 On 23 July 19X7 the company secured a major contract worth £15 million in sales revenue over the next three years.
4 The company's premises were damaged on 15 August 19X7 by a terrorist bomb planted on a nearby railway line. Uninsured losses amounted to £500 000.

Task

Explain how each of the four events should be treated in the financial statements for the year ended 30 June 19X7.

Accounting for contingencies – SSAP 18

A contingency is defined by SSAP 18 as 'a condition which exists at the balance sheet date, where the outcome will be confirmed only on the occurrence or non-occurrence of one or more uncertain future events'.

Examples include unresolved legal disputes and continuing obligations under product warranties.

The preparer of business accounts can take one of three options when accounting for contingencies: include them in the accounts at a realistic valuation; exclude them from the financial statements but disclose them in a note to the accounts; or ignore them completely.

The overriding requirement is for the accounts to give a 'true and fair view' of the financial position of the company, having particular regard to the prudence concept. It is prudent not to include contingent gains in the accounts and to accrue for contingent losses if they are probable. The accounting treatment of contingencies can be summarised as follows:

Event is:	Contingent gain	Contingent loss
Probable	Note to the accounts	Accrue in the accounts
Possible	Ignore	Note to the accounts
Remote	Ignore	Ignore

Where contingencies are to be disclosed in a note, SSAP 18 states that the following should be given: 'the nature of the contingency; the reasons for the uncertainty; and a prudent estimate of the financial effect of the contingency, or if this is not possible a statement that an estimate cannot be practically made'.

Exercise 10.8 SSAPs 17 and 18

Aftercare Ltd specialises in the maintenance of computer systems. During the year ended 31 December 19X8 the draft accounts show that the hardware division made profits of £80 000 on turnover of £460 000; the software division made £120 000 on turnover of £350 000.

At a meeting on 10 March 19X9 between the finance director and the firm's auditors, the following matters were considered:

1 A software upgrade sold on 16 December for £10 000 was returned on 5 January 19X9 after the customer found that it failed to meet the performance promised. The materials would be re-boxed for a future sale.
2 The company is being sued for unfair dismissal by an ex-service director. He was fired at the office party on 22 December after arguments with fellow directors. It was uncertain whether his £50 000 claim for loss of earnings would have to be paid.
3 On 5 February the directors decided to withdraw from the market for the maintenance of mainframe computers. Related stock costing £40 000 would have to be sold off for £20 000. Three quarters of this stock was on hand at the year end.
4 On 10 February 19X9 a customer's network failed, causing £5 000 worth of damage to computer hardware. The customer had taken out an Aftercare's comprehensive service agreement that covered this type of incident.
5 On 12 February 19X9 the company signed a new service agreement with Redding plc worth £100 000 p.a. Aftercare's sales director had been in talks on and off with Redding for six months.
6 On 20 February 19X9 the company made an out of court settlement for infringement of a site software licence. The £10 000 settlement was more than matched by a £20 000 provision included in the 19X8 accounts.
7 A new software utility designed in-house and sold to twenty clients before the year end was found to have several coding defects. Two clients had already reported problems and had insisted on a full refund of the £500 sales price.

Task

Describe the accounting treatment required for each item having regard to the requirements of SSAPs 17 and 18.

Reporting financial performance – FRS 3

FRS 3 has had a major effect on the format and content of the profit and loss account. It has made some important additions to the standard formats required by the *Companies Act 1985*.

The standard helps users of accounts to understand a company's underlying performance despite significant changes to the structure of the business and the existence of abnormalities in its financial performance. Greater information concerning the composition of reported profit figures helps interpretation of past performance and should also facilitate a more informed view of the business's future performance.

The standard:

1 requires an analysis of results to show the effect of business acquisitions and the discontinuation of operations
2 provides guidance on the treatment and disclosure of abnormal items
3 requires additional financial reports: statement of total gains and losses, note of historical cost profits and losses and a reconciliation of movements in the shareholders' funds.

Continuing operations, acquisitions and discontinued operations

Continuing operations are business activities that are continuing at the date of the accounts; **acquisitions** are purchases of other businesses that have occurred during the current accounting period; and **discontinued operations** are those activities sold or terminated during the current accounting period.

Turnover and operating profit must be analysed on the face of the profit and loss account between continuing and discontinued operations. Acquisitions should be shown as a component of continuing operations. Other items included in operating profit also require analysing but the analysis may be shown in a separate note to the accounts.

Basic format	(£'000)	(£'000)
Turnover		
Continuing operations		350
Acquisitions		100
		450
Discontinued operations		50
		500
Cost of sales		(250)
Gross profit or loss		250
Distribution costs		(100)
Administration expenses		(100)
Other operating income		50
Operating profit		
Continuing operations	90	
Acquisitions	8	
	98	
Discontinued operations	2	
		100
Interest payable and similar charges		(10)
Profit before tax on ordinary activities		90
Tax on profit or loss on ordinary activities		(30)
Profit or loss on ordinary activities after taxation		60
Dividends		(30)
Retained profit for the year		30

Note to the accounts

	Continuing (£'000)	Discontinued (£'000)	Total (£'000)
Cost of sales	(220)	(30)	(250)
Distribution costs	(90)	(10)	(100)
Administration expenses	(92)	(8)	(100)
Other operating income	50	0	50

Continuing operations include the following amounts relating to acquisitions: cost of sales £50 000, distribution £22 000 and administration £20 000.

Exercise 10.9 Profit and loss format – discontinued operations

Kettering Molecular Ltd achieved the following results for the year ended 31 December 19X9:

	(£'000)
Turnover	810
Cost of sales	513
Gross profit	297
Distribution costs	57
Administration expenses	40
Other operating income	2
Operating profit	202
Interest receivable	3
Profit on ordinary activities before taxation	205

Included in these figures are the results of its Simulation Division, a part of the business disposed of on 1 October 19X9. Its results were: turnover £110 000, gross profit £45 000, distribution costs £35 000 and administration expenses £13 000.

Task

Prepare a profit and loss account with a relevant note providing an analysis of results as required by FRS 3.

Exercise 10.10 Discontinued and acquired operations

Rochester Pharmaceuticals PLC achieved the following results for the year ended 31 December 19X9:

	(£m)
Turnover	580
Cost of sales	260
Gross profit	320
Distribution costs	110
Administration expenses	105
Other operating income	5
Operating profit	110
Interest payable	10
Profit on ordinary activities before taxation	100

Included in these figures are the results of AB Chem Ltd, a business acquired on 1 July 19X9. Its results were: turnover £23m, gross profit £13m, distribution costs £5m and administration expenses £3m.

Also included are the results of FlawChem, a business discontinued on 30 September 19X9. Its results for the nine months were: turnover £51m, gross profit £27m, distribution costs £18m, administration expenses £7m.

Tasks

1 *Prepare the profit and loss account for Rochester Pharmaceuticals with a supporting note in accordance with the requirements of FRS 3.*
2 *For users of Rochester's accounts, comment on the value of the information required by FRS 3.*

Abnormal items

Before the introduction of FRS 3 it had become normal practice for businesses to distinguish between profits relating to so-called normal trading activities and those of an extraordinary nature. Extraordinary items were reported on separate lines below profit after tax on the profit and loss account. Problems arose in the judgement of what was extraordinary as it was widely accepted that companies would try to classify as extraordinary any large item that adversely affected results.

To ensure consistent reporting, FRS 3 has clarified the meaning of the following terms:

Ordinary activities are any activities related to the company's business. These include changes in the company's environment, whether due to political, regulatory, economic or geographical influences. Items are considered ordinary even if they are infrequent or unusual in nature. **Extraordinary items** are material items that possess a high degree of abnormality, fall outside of ordinary activities and are not expected to recur.

As the definition for ordinary activities is so all-encompassing, extraordinary items should now be very rare. The profit and loss line 'profit on ordinary activities' will therefore include all items that should pass through the profit and loss account.

However FRS 3 does recognise that financial statements would be more meaningful if **exceptional items** were highlighted.

Exceptional items are material items, whilst falling within ordinary activities, that need to be disclosed because their size or incidence would otherwise distort a true and fair view of the business's performance.

Guidance is given on how exceptional items should be disclosed:

1   The standard identifies three items that will always be considered as exceptional provided they are material in value. They should be disclosed on the face of the profit and loss account after operating profit but before interest. These items are:

- the profit or loss on the termination of a business activity,
- the cost of a fundamental restructuring of the business, and
- the profits or losses on the disposal of fixed assets.

2   Other exceptional items should be included under their normal profit and loss account headings, e.g. distribution, and then highlighted in the note 'Operating profit is stated after charging'. If it is necessary to give more prominence to an exceptional item, it must be shown on the face of the profit and loss account as a constituent part of its usual profit and loss heading (for example, the analysis of administration expenses for Oasis shown at the beginning of the chapter).

Illustration

A company has experienced the following costs:

- a loss on the sale of a fixed asset – £30 000 (included in distribution costs)
- cost of legal action to protect a product patent – £30 000 (included in administration costs)
- a bad debt of £100 000 (included in administration costs)
- auditors' remuneration £5 000
- depreciation of tangible fixed assets £10 000.

Its results are:

	(£'000)	(£'000)
Turnover		600
Cost of sales		(250)
Gross profit or loss		350
Distribution costs		(130)
Administration expenses		(200)
Operating profit		20
Interest payable and similar charges		(10)
Profit before tax on ordinary activities		10

Solution

The loss on the sale of a fixed asset requires disclosure after operating profit on the face of the profit and loss account. The legal action could be considered an exceptional item that should be disclosed in a note to the accounts. The bad debt is of such magnitude that it should

be disclosed on the face of the profit and loss account. The audit and depreciation charges are not exceptional items but they do require disclosure as part of operating profit.

Profit and loss account	(£'000)	(£'000)
Turnover		600
Cost of sales		(250)
Gross profit or loss		350
Distribution costs		(100)
Administration expenses		
Bad debt		(100)
Other administrative expenses		(100)
Operating profit		50
Loss on sale of fixed asset		(30)
Profit on ordinary activities before interest		20
Interest payable and similar charges		(10)
Profit before tax on ordinary activities		10

Note to the accounts

Operating profit is stated after charging:

	£'000
Depreciation of fixed assets	10
Auditors remuneration	5
Exceptional item: legal fees	30

FRS 3 also identifies certain items as **prior year adjustments.** They should be adjusted for directly against accumulated retained profits without going through the current year's profit and loss account. Prior year adjustments can only be made for significant changes to accounting policy or where fundamental errors have been found in results previously reported.

Exercise 10.11   Exceptional items

Cawley Manufacturing Ltd has experienced abnormal items although these have not been highlighted in its draft profit and loss account.

Profit and loss account for the year ended 30 June 19X9	(£'000)
Turnover	1 210
Cost of sales	610
Gross profit	600
Distribution costs	280
Administration expenses	340
Operating profit	(20)
Interest receivable	10
Profit on ordinary activities before taxation	(10)

All operations are continuing.

Included in the results are the following items:

- Profit on disposal of fixed assets of £35 000 has been credited to distribution costs.
- Bad debts of £60 000 have been charged to administration expenses.
- A redundancy payment of £10 000 was made to a sales manager.
- The firm lost a legal case concerning patent rights and as a result suffered costs and compensation payments amounting to £80 000 which have been included in administration costs.

Task

Prepare the company's profit and loss account with notes in accordance with FRS 3 insofar as the information allows.

Exercise 10.12 Exceptional items

A company with profits of £700 000 on turnover of £5 000 000 has the following items included in its accounts. For each item identify where and how they should be disclosed.

- This year for the first time the company had secured work from the Ministry of Defence which the sales manager described as 'an extraordinary achievement'. The contract was for £100 000 and provided £40 000 operating profit.
- A large customer has been declared bankrupt and this has resulted in a bad debt write off of £300 000.
- Due to the sale of part of the company activities, the head office functions had to be reorganised at a cost of £200 000.
- The disposal of fixed assets relating to continuing activities produced a profit of £400 000.

Figure 10.1 How to account for exceptional items

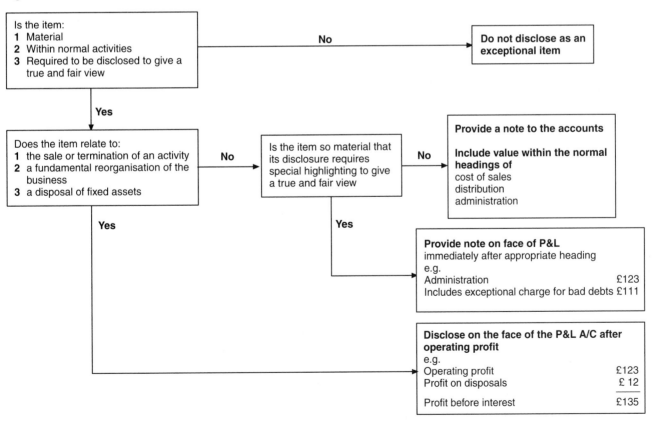

Exercise 10.13   Published accounts

F Marcos plc is an international trading company based in London. The following trial balance has been extracted from the company's records for the year ending 31 December 19X8.

	(£ '000)	(£'000)
Land buildings	1 500	400
Plant	900	350
Motor vehicles	300	120
Sales		4 650
Purchases	2 356	
Trade debtors and creditors	290	135
Employee costs – distribution	431	
– administration	205	
Heat and light	60	
Motor expenses	56	
Telephone	84	
Bad debts	223	
Interest	40	
Hire of plant	50	
Stock	154	
Bank		125
Fixed asset disposal account		31
Sundry expenses	78	
Share capital (£1 shares)		200
Debentures @ 10 per cent 19Y9		200
Share premium account		300
Profit and loss account		216
	6 727	6 727

Notes:

1 *Stock at 31 December 19X8 has been valued at £175 000.*
2 *The employee cost figures comprise gross salaries of £520 000, national insurance £51 000 and pension contributions of £65 000. Directors' emoluments included in these figures were:*

	Gross (£)	Pension costs (£)
Chairman and chief executive	60 000	10 000
Finance director	50 000	5 000
Sales and marketing director	45 000	5 000
Non executive director	5 000	0

3 *On 1 January 19X8 the land and buildings were revalued to £1 500 000. Included in this figure was £500 000 for land originally costing £400 000.*
4 *During the year, new plant was purchased for £100 000 and two motor vans originally costing £24 000 in 19X6 were sold for £11 000. In addition, plant in Italy costing £50 000 and depreciated by £20 000 was disposed of for £20 000. Withdrawal from this market was prompted by an operating loss of £30 000 on sales of £300 000 up to 30 September 19X8.*

5 *It is company policy to depreciate assets on a straight line basis – buildings at 2 per cent, plant at 10 per cent and motor vehicles at 25 per cent. Assets are depreciated in full in the year of purchase but are not depreciated in the year of disposal.*
6 *On 3 January 19X9, an inspection of stock highlighted a product line purchased in September 19X8 for £23 000 that had not been sold due to market changes. The items had a normal sales value of £40 000 but discounts of up to 60 per cent would have to be offered to move the stock.*
7 *Year end adjustments are required in respect of the following: debenture interest for the 6 months to 31 December will be paid on 5 January 19X9; the audit fee has been agreed at £12 000; corporation tax of £100 000 is to be provided for; and the directors are proposing a final dividend of 50p per share.*
8 *Of the bad debt charge, £201 000 relates to the failure of the company's distributor in the Philippines.*

Task

Prepare the company's annual accounts for the year to 31 December 19X8, in a form suitable for publication insofar as the information allows.

Exercise 10.14   Published accounts

Freshwinds plc is a manufacturing business quoted on a stock exchange. The company's management have ambitious plans for growth. In addition to in-house product development, on 5 July 19X8 they acquired valuable contracts sold off by the liquidator of a failed competitor, Badbreeze Ltd. The acquisition was made for the value of associated working capital.

Trial balance at 31 December 19X8	(£ '000)	(£'000)
Land and buildings – (buildings cost £1 600 000)	2 100	205
Plant – cost / depreciation	2 510	450
Sales		7 695
Purchases	2 650	
Trade debtors and creditors	1 155	605
Wages and salaries	2 165	
Power	240	
Telephone	125	
Interest paid	70	
Bank overdraft		917
Raw materials 1/1/X8	258	
Work in progress 1/1/X8	453	
Finished goods 1/1/X8	375	
Repairs and maintenance	80	
Sundry expenses	335	
Share capital @ 50p		1 200
Profit and loss account		1 814
Dividends paid	60	
Research and development capitalised/ amortised	352	65
Bad debts	23	
	12 951	12 951

Notes:

1 *Closing stocks: raw materials £268 000, work in progress £684 000 and finished goods £195 000.*

2 *Wages and salaries are to be analysed: cost of sales £1 295 000, distribution £505 000 and administration £365 000. Sundry costs, telephone and power are to be analysed: cost of sales 70 per cent, distribution 20 per cent and administration 10 per cent. All repairs and maintenance relate to the factory.*

3 *The following costs included in cost of sales relate to research and development expenditure:*

Project	Description	Salaries £	Materials £
R125	To develop a new table fan. A working prototype has been received enthusiastically by the sales team and one retailer has already placed an order worth £100 000 giving a 50 per cent gross margin.	28 000	6 000
R126	A small fan assembly commissioned by a computer manufacturer. Costs will be reimbursed at the end of development work.	36 000	8 000
R127	New age table fan. The project is approaching the prototype stage for testing on consumer panels.	9 000	1 000

4 *Research and development projects recover associated overheads at 50 per cent of salary costs.*

5 *A competitor is taking legal action against Freshwinds for infringement of a product patent. The company's legal advisors believe the company has a 50 per cent chance of losing the case but the possible compensation payment is difficult to estimate.*

6 *The activities acquired from Badbreeze ltd contributed: sales £226 000 and gross profit £122 000 and incurred the firm in distribution costs of £24 000 and administration costs of £15 000.*

7 *Company policy requires depreciation and amortisation rates of 2 per cent on cost for buildings and 10 per cent on cost for plant and development costs.*

8 *The directors propose a final dividend of 10p per share. The tax charge is computed as £225 000.*

Task

Prepare Freshwinds' profit and loss account and balance sheet for 19X8, having regard to relevant legislation and accounting standards. Notes to accounts are required insofar as the information allows.

Summary

Regulatory pressures ensure that all companies publish accounts in standard formats with minimum disclosure requirements for certain items. To disclose more than the minimum required may place a business at a competitive disadvantage, because once the accounts are published they are in the public domain. It is therefore important for preparers of accounts to be fully aware of company reporting requirements. This awareness has to be clearly demonstrated by students in published accounts assessments with a clear distinction between the reporting requirements (in the form of financial statements and notes to the accounts) and explanations to the assessor as to how figures were calculated (workings).

Further reading

Geoff Black, *Student's Guide to Accounting and Financial Reporting Standards, 1996/7*, DP Publications, 1996.

David Chopping and Len Skerratt, *Apply GAAP 1996/7*, Accountancy Books, 1996.

Richard Giles, *A Complete Course in Business Accounting*, Stanley Thornes, 1996.

Peter Walton, *Corporate Reports: Their Interpretation and Use in Business*, 2nd edition, Stanley Thornes, 1994.

Frank Wood and Allan Sangster, *Business Accounting 2*, 7th edition, Pitman Publishing, 1996.

11 Cash flow statements

O n completion of this chapter students should be able to:

■ prepare cash flow statements from given data incorporating appropriate adjustments.

The cash flow statement is a primary financial statement that complements the profit and loss account and balance sheet. The Financial Reporting Standard for Cash Flow Statements (FRS 1) applies to all companies other than those classified as 'small' by the Companies Act. The cash flow statement describes the flows of financial resources during an accounting period and redresses a weakness of the balance sheet, which only describes financial resources at one point in time. Essentially the statement is concerned with identifying where cash came from, and went to, during the accounting period.

Using the concept of double entry, a change in cash can be explained by looking at the changes to the other balance sheet balances.

	19X9 £'000s	19X8 £'000s	Change £'000s
Fixed assets	150	125	+25
Current assets			
Stocks	25	22	+3
Debtors	30	35	−5
Cash	5	15	−10
	60	72	
Current liabilities	20	25	−5
Net current assets	40	47	
Total net assets	190	172	
Capital and reserves			
Share capital	110	100	+10
Profit and loss account	80	72	+8
	190	172	

The retained profit for the year can be reconciled to the change in cash.

Item	£'000s £	Explanation
Retained profit for the year	+8	The difference between the two P & L account balances
Increase in stocks	−3	An increase in stocks uses cash
Decrease in debtors	+5	Customers paid more than the current period's sales.
Decrease in creditors	−5	More cash was paid to suppliers than the period's purchases.
Increase in fixed assets	−25	An outflow of cash
Share issue	+10	An inflow of cash
Decrease in cash	−10	This reconciles with the balance sheet change in cash

This simple statement is not of course a true statement of cash flows because some items are affected by bookkeeping entries in addition to cash flows, i.e. retained profits and fixed assets. However, the principle of being able to explain the changes in cash by changes in other balances underpins the construction of the cash flow statement. The cash flow statement is in many ways a rearrangement of figures found in the profit and loss account and balance sheet, and in this respect the cash flow statement provides little information that a financial analyst would not have been able to determine anyway.

The cash flow statement categorises cash transactions to help the user appreciate the nature of cash flows – for example, whether a decrease in the cash balance has been caused by the underlying business operations; because of investment for the future; or because the company has repaid a loan. They each have different implications for the future of the company.

The basic format

	£'000
Cash from operating activities	1 000
Returns on investments and servicing of finance	−200
Taxation	−250
Investing activities	−150
Net cash inflow before financing	400
Financing	50
Increase in cash and cash equivalents	450

Operating cash

The first line of the cash flow statement is the cash generated from operating activities. This can be derived by two approaches, depending on the information that is available.

The **direct method** requires payments relating to operations to be deducted from amounts received from customers. The following example is taken from Marks and Spencer plc.

Marks and Spencer plc
Extract from cash flow statement
for the year ended 31 March 1996

	£ million
Cash received from customers	7 046.0
Cash payments to suppliers	−4 741.9
Cash paid to and on behalf of employees	−928.4
Other cash payments	−566.9
Net cash flow from operating activities	808.8

The analysis for the direct method appears as a section at the top of the cash flow statement.

Whilst this method is easy to understand, most companies have decided to use the **indirect method** because it is often easiest to prepare in practice. Operating cash is calculated from operating profit by reversing out the adjustments made to conform with the accruals concept. The advantage of this method is that operating cash can be derived from figures in the profit and loss account and balance sheet without the need for further analysis of financial transactions.

Illustration

Extract from the accounts of Princedale plc for the year ended 31 December 1995:

Reconciliation of operating profit to net cash inflow from operating activities	1995
	£000
Operating profit	2 977
Depreciation charge	1 036
Profit on sale of tangible assets	(61)
Decrease in stocks	203
Increase in debtors	(679)
Increase in creditors	(1 551)
Net cash inflow from operating activities	1 925

It is important to consider why each of these adjustments has been made:

1. Depreciation is a cost in the profit and loss account, but is not an outflow of money so should be added back to profit.
2. Profit on the sale of a fixed asset represents the difference between the sale proceeds of an asset and its net book value (original cost less accumulated depreciation). The cash flow resulting from this transaction is the sale proceeds, which is considered further down the cash flow statement under 'investing activities'. Thus an accounting profit (or loss) is a bookkeeping item that needs to be subtracted from (or added to) profit.
3. Accounting for the change in stock levels reverses the adjustment made to purchases in the trading account. Where there has been a decrease in stocks, there will have been a positive effect on the cash balance with less funds tied up in stocks.
4. A change in the level of debtors is caused by a difference between the amount of credit sales and the amount of money received from customers during the year. If debtors increase, then the cash received from debtors must have been less than the value of credit sales included in the profit and loss account. The increase in debtors therefore needs to be deducted

from profit to reflect the effect on cash.

5 An increase in creditors shows that the cash paid to creditors must have been less than the value of credit purchases charged to the profit and loss account. An increase in creditors is therefore good for the bank balance and so needs to be added to profit to reflect the effect on cash.

The adjustments for working capital items 3, 4 and 5 would clearly have been the other way round if stocks had increased and debtors and creditors had decreased. To summarise the working capital adjustments to reconcile operating profit to operating cash:

	Increase	Decrease
Stock	Subtract	Add
Debtors	Subtract	Add
Creditors	Add	Subtract

Exercise 11.1 Reconciliation of operating profit to operating cash

During 19X9, Dasher Ltd generated an operating profit of £450 000 after a depreciation charge of £190 000. The following working capital balances have been extracted from the company's balance sheet:

	19X9 £'000	19X8 £'000
Current assets		
Stocks	52	65
Debtors	71	49
Bank	22	30
	145	144
Creditors due within one year:		
Trade creditors	35	45
Net current assets	110	99

Task

Reconcile operating profit to operating cash.

Returns on investment and servicing of finance

This section of the cash flow statement is concerned with the receipt and payment of interest and dividends. Returns on investments include interest received on deposits and loans, and dividends received from investment in the shares of other companies. Servicing of finance includes interest payments on debt finance and dividends paid to the company's shareholders.

The charges or credits made to the profit and loss account in respect of dividends and interest do not necessarily equate to amounts of cash actually paid or received. It is necessary to isolate cash flows from the adjustments made to satisfy the accruals concept. Adjustments are often necessary because finance items are generally paid in arrears. For example, dividends paid will comprise the previous year's final dividend plus the current year's interim dividend. To reconcile items in the profit and loss account and cash flow statement see table below:

Profit and loss account		Cash flow		Amount outstanding at the start of the year		Amount outstanding at the end of the year
Interest receivable	=	Interest received	−	interest receivable B/F	+	interest receivable c/f
Interest payable	=	Interest paid	−	interest payable B/F	+	interest payable c/f
Dividends receivable	=	Dividends received	−	dividends receivable B/F	+	dividends receivable c/f
Dividends payable	=	Dividends paid	−	dividends proposed B/F	+	dividends proposed c/f

Items that are receivable will be disclosed as debtors in the balance sheet and those that are payable will be disclosed as creditors due within one year. If there are no payable or receivable balances in the balance sheet then clearly the cash flows equate to the profit and loss account amounts.

Illustration

The following figures have been extracted from the 19X2 accounts of a company:

Balance sheet	19X2 (£)	19X1 (£)
Creditors		
Interest payable	0	600
Dividend proposed	1 400	1 200

Profit and loss account	19X2 (£)
Interest	1 200
Dividends	2 200

Calculate the value of the cash flows relating to interest and dividends payable.

Solution
Working control accounts provide a methodical approach to this type of problem.

The first step is to insert the profit and loss account and balance sheet figures that have been provided. The actual cash paid will be the balancing item.

Interest payable

	(£)		(£)
Bank	1 800	Balance B/F	600
Balance C/F	0	Profit and loss	1 200
	1 800		1 800

The £1 800 paid is the item required to balance the accounts.

For dividends payable:

	(£)		(£)
Bank	2 000	Balance B/F	1 200
Balance C/F	1 400	Profit and loss	2 200
	3 400		3 400

Again the bank entry is the balancing item.

Exercise 11.2 Returns on investment and servicing of finance

The following figures have been extracted from a company's 19X2 accounts:

Balance sheet	19X2 (£)	19X1 (£)
Creditors		
Dividend proposed	13 500	12 000
Interest payable	1 500	1 500

Profit and loss account	19X2 (£)
Interest	3 000
Dividends	22 500

Task

Calculate the payments for interest and dividends during 19X2.

The same principles can be applied to interest and dividends receivable, but remember that ledger accounts for receivable items will have debit brought-forward balances and will be credited with cash receipts.

Taxation

The taxation line of the cash flow statement relates to corporation tax only. Other creditor balances in respect of PAYE and VAT are included in the operating cash figure.

Mainstream corporation tax is paid up to nine months after the respective year end, hence the amount paid in the current year will relate to last year's tax creditor. However, the actual amount paid may differ slightly because the tax creditor is created before the tax computations are finalised with the Inland Revenue. The approach used to isolate interest paid can be applied to find the tax actually paid.

Profit and loss tax charge = tax paid − tax creditor B/F + tax creditor c/f.

Illustration

The following figures have been extracted from a company's set of accounts for year 19X2:

Balance sheet	19X2 (£)	19X1 (£)
Creditors Tax payable	1 000	1 500

Profit and loss account	19X2 (£)
Tax charge	950

Calculate the value of the cash flows relating to interest, tax and dividends.

Solution

Corporation tax	(£)		(£)
Bank	1 450	Balance B/F	1 500
Balance c/f	1 000	Profit and loss	950
	2 450		2 450

Again the bank entry is the balancing item.

Exercise 11.3 Taxation

The following figures have been extracted from a company's 19X2 accounts:

Balance sheet	19X2 (£)	19X1 (£)
Creditors Tax payable	11 500	9 700

Profit and loss account	19X2 (£)
Tax payable	11 000

Task

Calculate the tax paid during 19X2.

Investing activities

The cash flow statement section 'investing activities' discloses the cash flows relating to the purchase and sale of fixed assets. Unless it is clear that some of the debtor and creditor balances relate to capital items, it may be assumed that all additions and disposals have been transacted for cash.

Fixed assets in the balance sheet will be stated net of the following movements during the year:

- *Add acquisition of new assets* – an outflow of cash
- *Less net book value of disposals* – an accounting movement
- *Less depreciation* – an accounting movement.

Where a cash flow statement is to be constructed without the aid of a detailed fixed asset schedule, working control accounts can again be used.

Illustration

A business has the following end-of-year balances relating to motor vehicles.

Motor vehicles

	19X2 (£)	19X1 (£)
Cost	21 000	15 000
Depreciation	9 000	6 000
Net book value	12 000	9 000

The profit and loss account includes a depreciation charge of £5 000 and a profit on disposal of motor vehicles of £1 000. Related disposal proceeds were £4 000.

Identify the cash flows relating to motor vehicles.

Solution

An effective approach is to prepare ledger accounts for motor vehicle cost, depreciation and disposal. First insert all the information that is given and then deduce the other transaction values to balance the ledger accounts.

Motor vehicle cost

	(£)		(£)
B/F	15 000	Disposal (2)	5 000
Purchases (3)	11 000	C/F	21 000
	26 000		26 000

Motor vehicle accumulated provision for depreciation

	(£)		(£)
Disposal (1)	2 000	B/F	6 000
C/F	9 000	Charge	5 000
	11 000		11 000

Motor vehicle disposal account

	(£)		(£)
Cost (2)	5 000	Bank	4 000
Profit	1 000	Depreciation (1)	2 000
	6 000		6 000

To balance the accounts

1   The depreciation account had only one missing entry relating to the depreciation on the fixed asset disposal. This provided the disposal account with accumulated depreciation of £2 000.
2   The disposal account was balanced on the assumption that the cost of the asset disposed of must have been £5 000.
3   This provided a balancing figure on the motor cost account for purchases of £11 000.

The relevant cash flows are the disposal proceeds of £4 000 (an inflow) and asset purchases of £11 000 (an outflow).

Exercise 11.4   Investing activities

A business has the following end-of-year balances relating to computer equipment.

	Year 1 (£)	Year 2 (£)
Cost	4 500	7 000
Depreciation	1 200	2 800
Net book value	3 300	4 200

The profit and loss account includes a depreciation charge of £2 300 and a loss on disposal of computer equipment of £200. Computer sale proceeds were £700.

Task

Identify the cash flows relating to computer equipment.

Financing balances

In the balance sheet, share capital and loan stock will be stated net of the following movements:

■ New finance that has resulted in an inflow of cash – e.g. a share issue or a new loan
■ Less repayment of finance – e.g. redemption of debentures or the repayment of a loan

Illustration

During 19X2 a business has issued new shares and has also redeemed at par ordinary shares with a nominal value of £500. Calculate the proceeds of the new share issue using the following year-end balances:

	19X2 (£)	19X1 (£)
Share capital	6 000	5 000
Share premium account	4 000	2 000

Solution

The share capital has increased by £3 000 (£10 000 – £7 000). This is after £500 has been paid out for the redemption of existing shares, so the value of the new issue must have been £3 500.

This problem could have been solved using working ledger accounts. Whichever method is used, it is important that workings clearly show how cash flows have been calculated.

Cash and cash equivalents

A cash equivalent is defined as an item that had a maturity period of no more than three months at the time it arose. They are therefore either highly liquid assets that will soon be converted back to cash or debt that requires repayment in the near future.

The definition is important because it has implications on how financial items are disclosed. A government bond purchased with four months to maturity would be disclosed under 'investing activities', whereas a two-month bond would be treated as a cash equivalent. A bank loan for six months is a financing item, whereas a bank loan repayable in one month's time is a cash equivalent.

Preparation of the cash flow statement

Once the constituent sections have been calculated, it is possible to prepare the cash flow statement.

Pro forma
Cash flow statement
for the year ended 31 December 19X2

	£'000	£'000
Net cash inflow from operating activities		1 000
Returns on investments and servicing of finance		
Interest received	10	
Interest paid	−100	
Dividends received	20	
Dividends paid	−130	
Net cash outflow from returns on investments and servicing of finance		−200
Taxation		−250
Investing activities		
Payments to acquire intangible fixed assets	−15	
Payments to acquire tangible fixed assets	−145	
Receipts from sales of tangible fixed assets	10	
Net cash outflow from investing activities		−150
Net cash inflow before financing		400
Financing		
Issue of ordinary share capital (net of issue expenses)	200	
Issue of debenture stock	100	
Redemption of preference shares	−250	
Net cash inflow from financing		50
Increase in cash and cash equivalents		450

Notes to the cash flow statement

The cash flow statement should be accompanied by certain notes to the accounts.

The **reconciliation of operating profit to net cash inflow from operating activities** used by the indirect method to arrive at operating cash must be disclosed as a note to the published accounts.

In addition, the following notes are required to show how the cash statement reconciles to certain balance sheet accounts.

An **analysis of change in cash and cash equivalents** shows the movement in summary form of cash and cash equivalents.

	19X2 £'000
Balance at 1 January 19X2	(90)
Net cash in flow	450
Balance at 31 December 19X2	360

An **analysis of balances of cash and cash equivalents** shows the constituent parts of cash and cash equivalents as they are disclosed in the balance sheet and how they have moved during the year.

	19X2 £'000s	19X1 £'000s	Change in year £'000s
Cash at bank and on hand	230	0	230
Overdrafts and short term loans	0	(190)	190
Investments	130	100	30
	360	(90)	450

An **analysis of changes in financing during the year** reconciles the financing section of the cash flow statement to the relevant balances in the balance sheets.

	Ordinary share capital £'000	Preference share capital £'000	Debentures £'000
Balance at 1 January 19X2	900	400	500
Net cash in flow	200	−250	100
Balance at 31 December 19X2	1 100	150	600

Illustration

Spendthrift Limited has undergone a year of significant expansion, leaving the company with additional debt and a reduced bank balance. The following information has been provided for the company's year ending 30 June 19X9:

Spendthrift Limited
Balance sheet
for the year ended 31 June 19X9

	19X9 £'000s	19X8 £'000s
Fixed assets:		
Leasehold property	800	500
Equipment	400	300
	1 200	800
Current assets:		
Stocks	280	250
Debtors	110	140
Bank	0	60
	390	450
Creditors payable within one year:		
Bank overdraft	64	0
Creditors	120	110
Proposed dividends	48	40
Taxation	25	20
	257	170
Net current assets:	133	280
Total assets less current liabilities	1 333	1 080
Creditors due after more than one year		
Debentures	700	450
Net assets	633	630
Capital and reserves:		
Ordinary share capital – 50p shares	400	400
Profit and loss account	233	230
	633	630

Extract from the profit and loss account	19X9 £'000s
Operating profit	145
Interest payable	(30)
Profit before tax	115
Taxation	(24)
Profit after tax	91
Dividends	(88)
Retained profit for the year	3

Notes:
1 Depreciation is charged on the net book value of assets at the start of the year. Rates are 10 per cent for leasehold property and 20 per cent for equipment.
2 There were no fixed asset disposals during the year.

3 In addition to paying the proposed dividend and tax relating to the year ended 30 June 19X8, the company paid an interim dividend of 5p a share.

Prepare a cash flow statement together with supporting notes consistent with the requirements of FRS 1 for the year ended 30 June 19X9.

Solution
Workings

- Depreciation: the depreciation charge included in the accounts for the leasehold property is £500 000 × 10 per cent = £50 000, and for equipment £300 000 × 20 per cent = £60 000.
- Purchases of leasehold property were therefore £800 000 – £500 000 + £50 000 = £350 000 and purchases of equipment were £400 000 – £300 000 + £60 000 = £160 000. Alternatively workings can take the form of working ledger accounts:

Leasehold property account – at net book value

	£'000		£'000
B/F	500	Depreciation	50
Additions	350	C/F	800
	850		850

Equipment – at net book value

	£'000		£'000
B/F	300	Depreciation	60
Additions	160	C/F	400
	460		460

- There are no balance sheet entries for interest payable or interest receivable so the cash flow figures will equate to those in the profit and loss account.
- Dividends paid comprise those in current liabilities for last year plus this year's interim dividends. The current year's proposed dividends are not a cash flow.

Dividends

	£'000		£'000
Bank	80	Balance B/F	40
Balance C/F	48	Profit and loss	88
	128		128

- Because the current year's tax charge is not mirrored exactly by a corresponding creditor in the balance sheet, the amount paid in respect of the previous year's charge could not have been the same as the £20 000 provided for at 30 June 19X8.

Corporation tax

	£'000		£'000
Bank	19	Balance B/F	20
Balance C/F	25	Profit and loss	24
	44		44

In fact the amount paid was £1 000 less, giving a cash outflow of £19 000 for the year.

■ The only change in finance was the increase in debentures of £250 000 (£700 000 – £450 000).

Note to the accounts

Reconciliation of operating cash flows to operating profit

	19X9 £'000s
Operating profit	145
Add depreciation charged – lease	50
– equipment	60
Less increase in stocks	(30)
Add decrease in debtors	30
Add increase in creditors	10
Operating cash	265

The cash flow statement can now be prepared:

Spendthrift Limited
Cash flow statement
for the year ended 30 June 19X9

	£'000s	£'000s
Net cash inflow from operating activities		265
Returns on investments and servicing of finance		
Interest paid	(30)	
Dividends paid	(80)	
Net returns on investments and servicing of finance		(110)
Taxation		(19)
Investing activities		
Acquisition of tangible fixed assets		(510)
Net cash inflow before financing		(374)
Financing activities		
Debenture issue		250
Increase in cash and cash equivalents		(124)

Analysis of change in cash and cash equivalents:

	19X9 £'000
Balance at 1 July 19X8	60
Net cash in flow	(124)
Balance at 30 June 19X9	(64)

Analysis of balances of cash and cash equivalents as shown in the balance sheet:

	19X9	19X8	Change in year
Cash at bank	0	60	(60)
Bank overdraft	(64)	0	(64)
	(64)	60	(124)

Analysis of changes in financing during the year:

	Debentures £'000
Balance at 1 July 19X8	450
Net cash in flow	250
Balance at 30 June 19X9	700

An evaluation of the cash flow statement confirms that the significant investment in fixed assets has been financed by an increase in net debt. Operating cash flow was adequate to cover finance and tax charges, although there is probably little scope to increase borrowings further without first increasing owner's capital. This may be achieved by a share issue or the retention of future profits.

Exercise 11.5 Cash flow statement and notes

The balance sheet together with other information relating to Droplets Limited is provided on the next page.

Droplets Limited
Balance sheet
for the year ended 31 December 19X9

	19X9 £'000s	19X8 £'000s
Fixed assets:		
Cost	345	301
Depreciation	179	141
	166	160
Current assets:		
Stocks	68	44
Debtors	75	61
Bank	35	48
	178	153
Current liabilities:		
Creditors	6	4
Proposed dividends	20	10
Taxation	22	5
	48	19
Net current assets:	130	134
Total assets less current liabilities	296	294
Long term liabilities – debentures	0	80
Net assets	296	214
Capital and reserves		
Ordinary share capital	200	150
Profit and loss account	96	64
	296	214

Extract from the profit and loss account

	19X9 £'000s
Operating profit	78
Profit on sale of fixed asset	10
	88
Interest paid	5
Profit before tax	83
Taxation	21
Profit after tax	62
Dividend	30
Retained profit for the year	32

- Operating profit is after charging £66 000 depreciation.
- Purchases of fixed assets amounted to £81 000 during the year.

Task

Prepare a cash flow statement for the year ended 31 December 19X9 together with supporting notes consistent with the requirements of FRS 1.

Exercise 11.6   Cash flow statement and notes

From the following information in respect of Royston plc, prepare the cash flow statement together with accompanying notes for 19X2 as required by FRS 1.

Balance sheet
at 30 June 19X2

	19X9 (£)	19X9 (£)	19X8 (£)	19X8 (£)
Fixed assets				
Land and buildings		292 000		240 000
Plant and machinery		236 000		180 000
		528 000		420 000
Current assets				
Stocks	46 900		55 000	
Debtors	78 200		65 000	
Bank	4 600		19 500	
	129 700		139 500	
Creditors due within one year				
Creditors	27 500		32 300	
Corporation tax	24 000		25 000	
Dividends	18 000		24 000	
Debentures	0		50 000	
	69 500		131 300	
Net current assets		60 200		8 200
		588 200		428 200
Creditors due after one year				
Debentures		175 000		150 000
Net assets		413 200		278 200
Capital and reserves				
Ordinary shares		125 000		100 000
Share premium account		84 870		50 000
Revaluation account		60 000		–
Profit and loss account		143 330		128 200
		413 200		278 200

Profit and loss account
for the year ended 30 June 19X2 (£)

Sales	654 250
Operating profit	89 630
Interest payable	20 000
Profit before tax	69 630
Taxation	24 500
Profit for the year	45 130
Dividends	30 000
Retained profit for the year	15 130

Operating profit is stated after charging:

- Depreciation charge: buildings £8 000 and plant £24 000.
- Audit fee £7 500.

No disposals of fixed assets occurred during the year and the only fixed asset purchases related to plant.

Exercise 11.7 Cash flow statement and notes

From the following information in respect of Ready To Go plc, prepare a cash flow statement together with accompanying notes for 19X2 as required by FRS 1.

Balance sheet
at 30 June 19X2

	19X2		19X1	
	£'000s	£'000s	£'000s	£'000s
Fixed assets				
Land and buildings		589		920
Plant and machinery		781		875
		1 370		1 795
Current assets				
Stocks	389		463	
Debtors	921		871	
Bank	841		0	
	2 151		1 334	
Creditors due within one year				
Creditors	435		410	
Corporation tax	88		85	
Dividends	50		60	
Overdraft	0		145	
	573		700	
Net current assets		1 578		634
		2 948		2 429
Creditors due after one year				
Debentures		900		836
Net assets		2 048		1 593

Capital and reserves

Ordinary shares	400	300
Share premium account	300	200
Revaluation account	200	100
Profit and loss account	1 148	993
	2 048	1 593

Profit and loss account
for the year ended 30 June 19X2 £'000

Sales	1 874
Operating profit	300
Disposal of fixed assets	115
Profit before interest	415
Interest payable	95
Profit before tax	320
Taxation	90
Profit for the year	230
Dividends	75
Retained profit for the year	155

- Operating profit is stated after charging depreciation: buildings £31 000 and plant £110 000.
- The exceptional item relates to the disposal of property having a net book value of £400 000.

Summary

The cash flow statement reports on financial performance without adjustments to comply with the accrual concept and so is considered more factual than the profit and loss account. The cash flow statement focuses attention on the company's:

- ability to generate cash from operating activities
- financial adaptability in managing (i) its sources of finance and (ii) its investing activities
- investment to maintain or increase operating capacity.

Further reading

Richard Giles, *A Complete Course in Business Accounting*, Stanley Thornes, 1996.

Frank Wood and Allan Sangster, *Business Accounting 2*, 7th edition, Pitman Publishing, 1996.

On completion of this chapter students should be able to:

- identify and evaluate costs arising from business activity
- review mechanisms to record and analyse costs
- prepare reports to meet defined management needs and appraise findings.

Financial accounting's primary purpose is to report on financial performance for monitoring the managers' stewardship of the business. However, financial measures such as profit and cash flow tend to take a holistic view of business operations, with little direct reference to operational, non-financial measures that are likely to be more relevant to management's day-to-day decision making. Financial accounting also concentrates on historical data with little help to determine its relevance for the future.

Managers want to know how much it costs to use a machine for a specific batch of materials; its annual cost has little direct relevance to day-to-day operations. In addition, increased competition creates continual pressure for management to reduce costs, but cost reduction strategies require cost information to establish financial benefits before changes can be made in product or process design.

To satisfy management's needs, a branch of accountancy known as management accounting has developed. It concentrates on the micro aspects of the business, looking at the incidence of cost in relation to business activity. Management accounting is orientated to the future and uses appropriate historical data concerning cost behaviour to help with future projections. Business strategies are evaluated as part of the decision making process and not just in retrospect.

The Chartered Institute of Management Accountants (CIMA) is the main UK professional body concerned with management accounting. Unlike financial accountancy, which has to conform to legal regulations, management accounting is developed to meet the changing needs of individual businesses. However, management accounting does have a theoretical base, and CIMA has provided definitions of certain terms. These will be quoted where relevant.

This chapter is concerned primarily with the measurement of cost and is a foundation for techniques examined later for the management responsibilities of decision making, planning and control.

Analysis of costs

One reason that organisations calculate the cost of business activities is to determine the cost of providing the customer with a final product or service. In this context businesses are using a knowledge of costs together with a knowledge of revenues to determine whether or not something that is planned will reap the rewards desired.

Costs can be categorised into three types: **labour** costs are the payments to the business's employees; **materials** are the physical goods consumed in making a supply to a customer; and **expenses** are the costs of all the other resources consumed, e.g. rent and the services of other businesses.

Cost is measured in terms of the money that has to be used to buy a particular resource. However, relating the incidence of costs to a business's product is not always easy. Business operations that make a multitude of products often share factory facilities and so the problem arises as to how to divide common costs between the products.

Generally a cost can be identified with one of two cost concepts:

Cost units are a measure of a firm's output. These cost units are defined by CIMA as: 'a quantitative unit of product or service in relation to which costs are ascertained'. The unit of measure is decided by the nature of a firm's output. It may be an object like a computer, a specified service such as cleaning the windows of a building, or in standard units of measure such as the number of passenger miles on an aircraft. Total unit cost is product cost and can be a basis for setting sales prices.

Cost centres are part of the organisation structure of the business. Costs are related to the department or section of the organisation that incurs them. CIMA defines a cost centre as: 'a location, function or items of equipment in respect of which costs may be ascertained and related to cost units for control purposes'.

An appropriate level of analysis will depend upon the circumstances. For a printing firm that uses printing presses costing £1m each, it may be decided that each machine is to be a cost centre. In this way the total cost of running each press can be ascertained including costs for operating, maintenance and depreciation.

The purpose of the costing exercise is to determine the cost of a cost unit, therefore all costs should be allocated to cost units whenever possible. Only when costs cannot be attributed to a specific product are they to be charged to a cost centre – for example, take two costs incurred in a workshop of a garage, the wages of a mechanic working on customers' cars and the cost of electricity used for powering workshop tools and lighting. The wages of the mechanic can be identified with cost units provided a record is kept of how time has been spent, e.g. by each repair or service job, but it is not practical to record the electricity attributable to specific jobs. This cost should be allocated to the cost of running the workshop (i.e. it is a cost centre cost).

Exercise 12.1 Cost units and cost centres

Identify appropriate cost units and cost centres for the following organisations:

- Next – the clothes retailer
- Mirror Group – the newspaper publisher
- Wimpey – the house builder.

Direct costs

Costs that can be attributed and recorded against a specific cost unit are known as **direct costs.**

Direct labour (or direct wages) is the term used to describe payments to workers who make products or provide services. An engineering firm will incur direct wages paid to machine operators and an office cleaning firm will pay direct wages to its cleaners. **Direct material** is the cost of material used to make specific products or services. The engineering firm may require materials in the form of base metals and ready made components, the cleaning firm will require chemicals and materials for specific cleaning contracts. **Direct expenses** are other costs incurred specifically for the final product or service. These include royalty payments that are based on unit volumes and the cost of sub-contractors directly working on cost units.

The total of direct costs is called **prime cost.**

Indirect costs

Costs that are not direct costs are classified as **indirect costs.** They either cannot be attributed to specific cost units (such as property rent) or it is impractical to do so (e.g. the electricity of the garage workshop).

Indirect labour relates to wages and salaries paid to employees while they are not making a cost unit. This category includes office staff for management, administration and distribution, but also includes the cost of many factory workers including maintenance engineers and stores personnel. **Indirect materials** are items that are too low in value to have recording systems to relate them to specific products, e.g. lubricating materials, rags for cleaning down machines and small nuts and bolts. **Indirect expenses** encompass a wide range of costs including property rents, power, stationery and depreciation of fixed assets.

Indirect costs are often called **overheads.**

Analysis of product cost

When presenting product cost information it is normal practice to identify direct costs with a sub-total for prime cost. Indirect costs are split between overheads for the factory and expenses for the distribution and administration functions of the business.

Illustration – Cost analysis schedule

Category	Cost heading	£
Direct costs	Direct materials	1 500
	Direct labour	1 000
	Direct expenses	500
	Prime cost (total of all direct costs)	3 000
Indirect costs	Manufacturing overhead	2 000
	Total manufacturing cost (stock valuation)	5 000
	Selling and distribution costs	3 000
	Administration costs	1 000
	Total product cost	9 000
Profit		1 000
Sales value		10 000

Exercise 12.2   Analysis of cost

International Dynamo Ltd manufactures two types of dynamos for push-cycles: the 'Ultra' and the 'Standard'. Production details for the month of March:

1   Direct factory workers earn £1 000 per month, 11 work on the Ultra and 20 on the Standard.
2   Direct material costs were £8 000 for the Ultra and £10 000 for the Standard.
3   An invoice for £1 500 was received from Speciality Machining Ltd for work done on the Ultra model.
4   A royalty fee of £1 on each Ultra is payable to Sam Wright, designer of the Ultra.
5   Production quantities for March were 1 000 Ultras and 6 000 Standards.

Tasks

1   *Prepare a table analysing total prime cost by model.*
2   *Calculate the prime cost per unit for each model.*

Exercise 12.3   Analysis of cost

John Wesley Ltd incurred the following costs during 19X9 in the manufacture of woollen socks:

Cost	(£)	Cost	(£)
Machine operators	70 000	Rent for factory	9 000
Accountant's salary	18 000	Delivery to shops	4 000
Wool	9 000	Postage	1 000
Maintenance of machines	3 000	Managing Director	25 000
Salesman's car expenses	4 000	Advertising	3 000
Bank interest	1 000	Salesman's salary	12 000
Heating for the factory	2 000	Office clerks	20 000
Motifs (sowed onto socks)	1 000	Factory Manager	18 000

Tasks

1   *Analyse the costs into direct and indirect categories and prepare a total cost analysis schedule.*
2   *If the firm manufactured 200 000 identical pairs of socks during 19X9, what was the prime cost and total cost per pair of socks?*
3   *If the firm had instead made 50 000 scarves and 100 000 pairs of socks, what are the problems in calculating the cost of the individual products?*

Valuation of materials

Prices rarely remain stable and identical stock items may be purchased at different prices depending on underlying inflation and prevailing market conditions. The problem arises of how to value stock issues and stock balances. For example, two consignments of the same item of stock are received, one for 10 items at £10 each and the other for 10 items at £11 each. If 15 items are issued from stores how should the £210 total cost be split between materials used and materials remaining in stock?

Regulatory influences dictate that stock should be valued at historical cost (i.e. what the materials cost the business) or net realisable value if that is lower (market value less further costs before sale). Several methods have been devised to deal with the problem.

Using **first-in first-out (FIFO)**, the oldest stock is assumed to be issued first and the purchase price of these items is used to cost stores issues. The most recently purchased stock (often at higher prices) is assumed to be remaining in stores. The method is based on what the business paid for the stock and so satisfies legal requirements. **Last in first out (LIFO)** requires that the latest stock received is costed out first. This method is based on historical cost but is not favoured by either SSAP 9 or the tax authorities (for it lowers reported profits). An alternative approach is to calculate an **average cost (AVCO)** per unit for each stock item every time there is a new receipt of stock. The calculation is on a weighted average basis. As part of a cost control system, some organisations set a **standard cost** for stock items. This is used to record all stock receipts and issues with any difference between standard and actual cost being transferred to separate cost variance accounts (see Chapter 17 for more details). Standard cost is acceptable for financial accounts provided it is a reasonable approximation of historical cost.

Exercise 12.4   Stock valuation

A garage stocks car alarms that sell for £70 each. There were 5 alarms in stock at the beginning of week 1, which had cost £42 each. Deliveries of further alarms are made each week and their details, together with numbers of alarms sold, are as follows:

Week no	Alarms bought Number	Cost each £	Number of alarms sold
1	10	40.00	7
2	5	45.00	6
3	5	44.00	6
4	5	45.00	7

Stock cards have been prepared for weeks 1 and 2 using FIFO, LIFO and weighted average cost.

Stores record card – FIFO

Code	12a
Desc.	Alarm

Date	Receipt			Issue			Balance		
Week no.	Number	Unit Price	Amount	Number	Unit Price	Amount	Number	Unit Price	Amount
0							5	42.00	210.00
1	10	40.00	400.00				5 10	42.00 40.00	610.00
1				5 2	42.00 40.00	290.00	8	40.00	320.00
2	5	45.00	225.00				8 5	40.00 45.00	545.00
2				6	40.00	240.00	2 5	40.00 45.00	305.00

Stores record card – LIFO

Code 12a Desc. Alarm										
Date	Receipt			Issue			Balance			
Week no.	Number	Unit Price	Amount	Number	Unit Price	Amount	Number	Unit Price	Amount	
0							5	42.00	210.00	
1	10	40.00	400.00				5 10	42.00 40.00	610.00	
1				7	40.00	280.00	5 3	42.00 40.00	330.00	
2	5	45.00	225.00				5 3 5	42.00 40.00 45.00	555.00	
2				5 1	45.00 40.00	265.00	5 2	42.00 40.00	290.00	

Stores record card – Weighted average cost

Code 12a Desc. Alarm										
Date	Receipt			Issue			Balance			
Week no.	Number	Unit Price	Amount	Number	Unit Price	Amount	Number	Unit Price	Amount	
0							5	42.00	210.00	
1	10	40.00	400.00				15	40.67	610.00	
1				7	40.67	284.67	8	40.67	325.33	
2	5	45.00	225.00				13	42.33	550.33	
2				6	42.33	254.00	7	42.33	296.33	

Each method allocates £1 280 (£210 + £1 070) between cost of goods issued and the value of closing stock at the end of week 4. For accounts drawn up at the end of week 4, the cost of goods sold will be offset against sales revenue in the business's trading account, and the stock carried forward will be the stock valuation in the balance sheet.

Tasks

1 *Complete the stock record cards for weeks 3 and 4.*

2 *Complete the following table from the stock record cards:*

| | FIFO | LIFO | AVCO |
	£	£	£
Stock brought forward	210.00	210.00	210.00
Stock purchased	1 070.00	1 070.00	1 070.00
Stock available for use	1 280.00	1 280.00	1 280.00
Cost of goods sold			
Stock carried forward			
	1 280.00	1 280.00	1 280.00

3 *Calculate the gross profit for the four-week period for each method.*
4 *Which stock valuation method provides the highest profits under conditions of i) rising prices and ii) falling prices.*

Exercise 12.5   Stock valuation

Costly Castings produce castings for the automobile industry. The following receipts and issues were recorded for the month of April:

Week	Number of castings produced	Cost per casting (£)	Number of castings sold
1	23	120	12
2	22	135	21
3	18	125	20
4	25	141	30

There were no castings in stock at the start of week 1.

Tasks

Calculate using FIFO, LIFO and AVCO:

1 *the cost of castings sold each week and*
2 *the value of stock at the end of each week.*

Exercise 12.6   Stock valuation

Vibrant Dyes produce colouring dyes for the clothing industry. The liquid containers are stored and distributed in large plastic crates. The following receipts and issues were recorded for the month of October:

Week	Number of crates produced	Cost per crate (£)	Number of crates sold
1	20	240	18
2	14	245	18
3	15	250	12
4	24	254	20

There were just 5 crates in stock at the start of October, arising from a period when costs were stable at £250 per crate.

Tasks

Calculate using FIFO, LIFO and AVCO:

1 *the cost of crates sold each week and*
2 *the value of stock at the end of each week.*

Labour remuneration systems

The remuneration of employees can be calculated in various ways. The system used should be appropriate to the circumstances and should motivate employees towards management objectives. Essentially, different schemes either provide remuneration based on time served or on some measure of performance. An employee's pay may wholly or partly consist of:

- a fixed salary
- a wage based on the number of hours worked including overtime premiums where appropriate
- attendance allowances where the worker may be called out to work
- allowances for dangerous or inconvenient work
- commissions based on the amount of business generated
- piece work rates based on the amount of work completed
- bonuses based on performance.

Exercise 12.7   Time rate

Joanne is an hourly paid employee. Her standard hourly rate is £5.50. If she works over 35 hours a week, overtime is paid at time and a half.

Tasks

What is her weekly gross pay if:

1 *she works 31 hours*
2 *she works 35 hours*
3 *she works 40 hours*
4 *she works 43 hours.*

Exercise 12.8 Piecework

Paul is paid on a piecework basis. For each unit of product 'Alpha' he makes he earns £4.50, and for each product 'Beta' he earns £1.25.

Tasks

What is his weekly gross pay if:

1 *he makes 36 product Beta*
2 *he makes 20 product Alpha and 41 product Beta*
3 *he makes 17 product Alpha and 29 product Beta.*

Exercise 12.9 Commission

Jason works as a second-hand car salesman. He earns a basic salary of £15 000 p.a. plus a commission based on the value of sales he achieves each month. He earns no commission on the first £3 000 of sales each month, but thereafter he earns a commission of 3 per cent on sales value.

Tasks

What is his monthly gross pay if:

1 *in January he sells cars for £6 000*
2 *in February he sells cars for £7 500*
3 *in March he sells cars for £2 800*
4 *in April he sells cars for £3 500.*

Exercise 12.10 Bonuses

Audrey, a tea packer, can increase her £3.60 basic hourly rate if she packs more than the standard number of tea boxes per hour. The standard time allocated to fill and seal one tea box is 20 seconds. Her bonus is calculated weekly on one half of the time she saves at her standard hourly rate.

Tasks

What is her weekly gross pay if:

1 *she works 40 hours and packs 7 000 boxes*
2 *she works 35 hours and packs 6 900 boxes*
3 *she works 45 hours and packs 8 900 boxes*
4 *she works 38 hours and packs 6 850 boxes.*

Labour costing

Wages and salaries may relate to direct or indirect labour. For those employees that are involved in direct work there needs to be a system that enables wages to be charged to cost units. Indirect workers can be identified with the cost centres they work in and costed accordingly.

The first step in the costing system for direct workers is the recording of time against a cost unit, either using a time sheet or by electronic means such as on a mobile key pad. Cost units are often referred to by a job, batch or process number.

Illustration

Dennington Estates Management Ltd provide a landscaping and garden maintenance service, primarily to commercial customers. Jobs are either annual agreements for maintenance or one-off jobs for ground clearance or landscape changes. In both cases costs are accumulated on a computerised job costing system with a job number for each separate agreement. Job numbers consist of five digits commencing with a J and followed by four numbers. When the gardeners are not working on customers' jobs they work in the tree nursery (cost centre T001) or materials warehouse (cost code W001).

The time sheet in Figure 12.1 is one of several for week 43.

Figure 12.1 Timesheet

Name R Jordie	Time sheet			Week number 43
Day	Description	Code	Hours	Amount £
Monday	S Smith	J1574	8	40
Tuesday	S Smith	J1574	4	20
Tuesday	Nursery	T001	4	20
Wednesday	Cawley	J1579	7	35
Wednesday	Nursery	T001	1	5
Thursday	Fleming	J1576	3	15
Thursday	Denning	J1511	3	15
Thursday	Warehouse	W001	2	10
Friday	Lessing	J1497	2	10
Friday	Isologic	J1580	4	20
Total			38	190

Signed: Authorised:

The gardener completes the fields for description of work, job number and number of hours worked and signs the time sheet at the end of the week. The manager responsible authorises the time sheet before forwarding it to the accounts department. The accounts department calculates the employee's pay and then allocates the total wages paid to the jobs worked on. The amounts calculated for each line on the time sheet are then transferred to a cost record for each job and cost centre.

Overheads

Overheads are indirect costs that cannot be directly related to specific products or services delivered to customers. However, in addition to any commercial reasons, according to the Companies Act 1985 and SSAP 9, stock valuation should include a reasonable proportion of production overhead. The inclusion of overheads in product costs is called **absorption costing** and is often a three-stage process.

1 Overhead costs need to be shared out to the various cost centres on a fair basis. Where costs are known to have been incurred by a specific department, e.g. the wages of its indirect workers, then they should be *allocated* accordingly. If there are costs that cannot be allocated to individual cost centres, e.g. rent that is paid for the whole business, then they should be shared out as fairly as possible. This process is called *cost apportionment*.
2 Some costs will relate to service departments that are not directly involved in the production process, although they may provide services to the production departments. Examples include departments for personnel management, stores, plant maintenance, canteen and production planning. Service department costs are then shared out to their internal customers in proportion to the amount of service they provide to each. This process is called *secondary apportionment*.
3 Having allocated or apportioned all production overheads to the production departments, these costs need to be included in the total costs of the products made. The process of including overheads in product costs is called *overhead absorption*.

Apportionment

The Chartered Institute of Management Accountants (CIMA) defines apportionment as 'the division of costs among two or more cost centres in proportion to the estimated benefits received, using a proxy, e.g. square feet.'

Proxy measures of benefits received include: number of employees, labour hours, floor area (e.g. m^2), machine hours and maintenance hours.

Illustration

A factory consisting of three production lines incurs rent of £30 000 p.a. This could reasonably be apportioned in proportion to the square metres occupied by each department. It has been determined that shop A occupies 400 m^2, Shop B 1 000 m^2 and Shop C 600 m^2.

	Basis of apportionment	A	B	C	Total
Floor area m^2		400	1 000	600	2 000
per cent of floor area		20	50	30	100
Rent (£)	Floor area	6 000	15 000	9 000	30 000

Figure 12.2 Bases for apportionment

Nature of cost	Possible bases of apportionment
Building services	
Building depreciation	Area occupied
Building insurance	Area occupied
Building repairs	Area occupied
Rent and rates	Area occupied
Lighting and heating	Area occupied
Personnel services (e.g. canteen, training, welfare, recruitment, etc.)	Nos. of personnel
Materials services	
Central stores	Average stock balance
Materials insurance	Average stock balance
Materials handling	Number of stores requisitions
Equipment services	
Electric power	Power rating of machines
Machine depreciation	Value of machinery
Machine insurance	Value of machinery
Repairs and maintenance	Value of machinery or machine hours
Production services	
Management and planning	Nos. of personnel

Exercise 12.11 Apportionment

Apportion the following costs of Accra Ltd over its various cost centres for the month of December 19X9.

Rent	£20 000
Electricity	£ 5 000
Machine insurance	£ 2 000
Christmas party	£ 1 000
Canteen subsidy	£ 2 500
Oil and rag	£ 500

	Welding section	Drilling section	Assembly department	Paint shop
Number of workers	10	5	7	3
Area of factory (m²)	300	100	500	200
Value of machines £	20 000	50 000	5 000	25 000
Machine kW ('000s)	10	70	10	10

Exercise 12.12 Allocation and apportionment

Calculate the total production overhead for each department of Treelyn Ltd from the following information for March 19X9:

Rent	£3 000	
Power	£5 000	
Fork lift	£ 500	(60% shop A, 40% shop B)
Machine insurance	£1 000	
Depreciation of machines	£2 000	
Training	£ 500	

	Indirect Materials £	Indirect labour £
Shop A	2 000	10 000
Shop B	1 000	20 000
Shop C	500	20 000
Shop D	5 000	

	Shop A	Shop B	Shop C	Shop D
Area – m²	500	200	300	200
Number of workers	12	6	7	5
Value of machines (£)	50 000	100 000	50 000	5 000
Machine hours	12 000	12 000	10 000	2 000

Apportionment of service department costs

The apportionment of service department costs uses the same technique as the apportionment of shared costs. First find an appropriate proxy measure of demand for the department's services. For example, the apportionment of a factory store could be based on the number of stores requisitions each department made.

Illustration

A works canteen costs £120 000 in a year to subsidise. The canteen is to be apportioned to three production

departments on the basis of the number of employees in each.

Basis of apportionment	A	B	C	Canteen	Total
Number of employees	15	24	21		60
per cent of employees	25	40	35		
	(£)	(£)	(£)	(£)	(£)
Department costs	123 000	581 000	451 000	120 000	1 275 000
Secondary apportionment	30 000	48 000	42 000	–120 000	0
Production overheads	153 000	629 000	493 000	0	1 275 000

Note that the apportionment of cost does not change the total cost incurred. The process just takes the cost from one department and spreads it over those departments that use its service.

Complications can arise when departments provide services to other service departments. In this case the general rule is to apportion the *servicing* department's costs before those of the *serviced* department.

Situations may be encountered where there are *reciprocal services*. This is where two or more service departments work for one another as well as for productive departments. This is a circular problem that can be solved in one of three ways:

1 *Elimination method* – eliminate service departments from further apportionments once they have been apportioned.
2 *Continuous allotment method* – continue apportioning further amounts between servicing departments until the values become insignificant.
3 *Simultaneous equations* – e.g. if the stores are to receive 15 per cent of maintenance charges and maintenance 5 per cent of stores then:

Total stores cost after apportionment = Stores departmental costs + 15 per cent of total maintenance costs

Total maintenance costs after apportionment = Maintenance departmental costs + 5 per cent of total stores costs

Bearing in mind that apportionment is by its very nature a fairly rough tool, the elimination method is adequate for most situations and is easier to use.

Exercise 12.13 Allocation and apportionment

The Victoria Hotel is a medium-sized provincial hotel, appealing mainly to the business traveller. It has 60 rooms charged at a flat rate of £40 a night throughout the week excluding breakfast. The manager is reviewing the hotel's financial results for the year to 31 December 19X8 when room utilisation was running at 60 per cent.

	Rooms and reception (£)	Restaurant (£)	Bar (£)	Kitchen (£)	Management and administration (£)	Total (£)
Income						
Room let	438 000					438 000
Food		160 000	37 500			197 500
Drinks		66 000	159 000			225 000
Total	438 000	226 000	196 500			860 500
Expenditure						
Wages – permanent	60 000	15 000	15 000	37 500	63 000	190 500
Wages – casual	27 000	40 000	34 000			101 000
Food				52 500		52 500
Drinks			75 000			75 000
Rent and property related					270 000	270 000
Other	35 000	5 000	5 000	5 250	51 075	101 325
Total	122 000	60 000	129 000	95 250	384 075	790 325
Profit	316 000	166 000	67 500	−95 250	−384 075	70 175
Floor area – m²	1 500	250	250	125	125	2 250

Drinks are priced with a 200 per cent mark-up on cost and food is priced at a 200 per cent mark-up in the bar and 300 per cent in the restaurant.

Tasks

The manager is concerned that the information is not presented in a format that allows him to determine the relative profitability of each area of the business. Rearrange the data with all costs allocated to the three profit centres: rooms, restaurant and public bar.

1 *Reallocate the costs for food and drinks.*
2 *Apportion the property costs on the basis of floor area.*

3 *Apportion the cost of the kitchen to the restaurant and bar in proportion to food cost.*
4 *Apportion management costs to the profit centres in proportion to total sales.*
5 *What does the new format convey regarding the profitability of each profit centre?*

Absorption of overheads into product cost

CIMA defines absorption of overhead as 'the charging of overheads to cost units by means of rates separately calculated for each cost centre. In most cases the rates are pre-determined.'

The method of absorption should as far as possible accurately reflect the work load each product places upon the production facilities. There are six widely recognised bases of absorption – all attempt to recover the cost centre (department) overhead over the products passing through in a prescribed period. This is achieved with an overhead absorption rate (OAR) applied to some measure of production activity.

As the CIMA definition makes clear, overhead absorption rates are pre-determined. That is to say, at the start of an accounting period, budgeted costs are compared with some measure of production activity. This gives a standard overhead absorption rate per unit of activity that is used until the next budget review. These standard rates will be used to cost products so variances in actual expenditure or actual activity levels will result in overhead under or over absorption. This is then written off to the trading account. Of course the aim is to minimise

overhead under or over absorption as it indicates that individual product costs recorded are not actual costs.

Overhead absorption method:	Calculation:
Direct labour hour rate =	$\dfrac{\text{Cost centre overheads}}{\text{Direct labour hours}}$
Direct wages rate =	$\dfrac{\text{Cost centre overheads}}{\text{Direct wages}}$
Direct materials rate =	$\dfrac{\text{Cost centre overheads}}{\text{Direct material cost}}$
Prime cost rate =	$\dfrac{\text{Cost centre overheads}}{\text{Prime cost}}$
Machine hours rate =	$\dfrac{\text{Cost centre overheads}}{\text{Machine hours}}$
Unit cost rate =	$\dfrac{\text{Cost centre overheads}}{\text{Number of units produced}}$

Illustration

Reeves Manufacturing Co. operates a machine shop that is budgeted to incur the following costs during 19X8. Overheads are recovered on a direct labour hour basis.

	Machine shop (£)
Direct costs	
Materials	400 000
Labour – 50 000 hours @ £6	300 000
Overheads	
Allocated costs	
Indirect materials	30 000
Indirect labour	170 000
Apportioned costs	
Property and utility costs	220 000
Secondary apportionment	
Stores	80 000
Total overhead	500 000
Budgeted labour hours	50 000
Overhead absorption rate per hour (£500 000/50 000 hours)	£10

With this information it is now possible to cost a product provided its direct costs and number of direct labour hours are known.

Illustration

Reeves Manufacturing Co receives a customer's order that requires £20 000 of material and 2 000 direct labour hours. The total production cost of the order is therefore:

	(£)
Direct costs	
Materials	20 000
Labour – 2 000 hours @ £6	12 000
Overhead – 2 000 hours @ £10	20 000
Total factory cost	52 000

Although absorption costing can be criticised for being a rather crude method for arriving at product cost it is relatively simple to use and is an effective method for recovering overheads with a cost plus pricing policy.

In most cases absorption rates based on labour hours, labour cost and machine hours are the most accurate OARs as they are based on some measure of business activity. It is difficult to think of a situation where the value of direct material has a significant effect on factory overheads. Generally, labour intensive operations should be based on a labour base and capital intensive operations on machine hours.

Exercise 12.14 Overhead absorption rates

Calculate six different overhead absorption rates for the Milling Shop based on the following information for March:

Labour hours	1 200
Direct wages	£6 000
Direct materials	£7 500
Machine hours	1 000
Nos. of units produced	250
Total overheads	£9 000

Exercise 12.15 Overhead absorption rates

Calculate six different overhead absorption rates for the Drilling Shop based on the following information for June:

Labour hours	15 000
Direct wages	£90 000
Direct materials	£60 000
Machine hours	18 000
Nos. of units produced	20 000
Total overheads	£75 000

Exercise 12.16 Absorption costing and product pricing

Prince Electronics assembles micro-computers from bought-in components. It has three departments through which a computer has to pass before it is a completed. Most of the work is labour intensive, although the test department makes considerable use of expensive test equipment. Production information for September:

	Assembly	Test	Packaging
Direct materials £	90 000	0	5 000
Production overhead £	25 000	15 000	7 500
Direct wages £	50 000	5 000	7 500
Machine hours	500	1 400	150

Two models of computers were produced:

		Z1	Z2
Number produced		300	200
Material cost each		£150	£250
Direct wages	Assembly	£90	£115
	Test	£8	£13
	Packaging	£15	£15
Machine hours	Assembly	1.0	1.0
	Test	2.0	4.0
	Packaging	0.3	0.3

Tasks

1 Calculate overhead recovery rates for each department based on: (i) direct wages and (ii) machine hours.
2 Calculate total production cost for the Z1 and Z2 using: (i) all OARs based on direct wages; (ii) all OARs based on machine hours; and (iii) if different, your preferred combination of bases.

Allocation, allotment and apportionment

It is important that a methodical approach is used to solve overhead apportionment/absorption problems. The following case study illustrates the use of an *overhead analysis sheet*.

Illustration

ABC Ltd manufactures electrical components. Its production function is organised into three departments: mouldings, wiring and assembly; and two service departments: canteen and stores.

The following data are budgeted for each department for the month of April:

	Moulding	Wiring	Assembly	Canteen	Stores
Number of direct workers	14	23	10		
Number of indirect workers	2	5	2	4	6
Indirect wages	£2 500	£15 000	£3 000	£2 900	£6 000
Floor area – m²	100	300	200	100	100
Number of stores requisitions	300	800	700	0	0
Power usage – units	900	800	200	200	100

Expenses budgeted for April

	Costs £
Rent	4 800
Electricity	1 100

Direct workers are employed for 160 hours per month and paid at £8 per hour. Overhead is recovered on a direct labour hour basis. Customers' orders are priced with a 50 per cent mark up on factory cost.

Job number 98124 is a customer's order that is estimated to require £2 500 of material and manufacturing times of 200 hours in moulding, 300 hours in wiring and 150 hours in assembly.

What is the selling price to be quoted to the customer for job number 98124?

Solution

The layout, shown in Figure 12.3, using an Overhead Analysis Sheet ensures a methodical approach to the problem.

Job number 98124

	(£)
Direct material	2 500
Direct labour – 650 hours @ £8	5 200
Overheads:	
Moulding – 200 hours @ £3	600
Wiring – 300 hours @ £6	1 800
Assembly – 150 hours @ £5	750
Total cost	10 850
Mark up @ 50 per cent	5 425
Selling price	16 275

Exercise 12.17 Allocation, apportionment and absorption

Remring Ltd is an engineering company producing products to customers' specifications. Its production function is organised into three departments: fabrication,

Figure 12.3 Overhead Analysis Sheet

		Production depts			Service depts		
Cost head	Method of apportionment	Moulding (£)	Wiring (£)	Assembly (£)	Canteen (£)	Stores (£)	Total
Allocated items Indirect wages		3 570	15 000	3 180	2 900	6 190	30 840
Apportioned items Rent Electricity	Floor area Power used	600 450	1 800 400	1 200 100	600 100	600 50	4 800 1 100
Secondary apportionment Canteen Stores	Employee nos. Requisitions	840 1 200	1 680 3 200	720 2 800	−3 600 0	360 −7 200	0 0
Total overhead		6 660	22 080	8 000	0	0	36 740
Number of direct labour hours Overhead absorption rate		2 220 £3.00	3 680 £6.00	1 600 £5.00			

drilling and assembly; and two service departments: plant maintenance and production control. The plant maintenance department repairs and maintains the production department's machines. The production control department prepares production plans for customers' jobs and uses these to monitor and control the flow of work through the factory.

The following data is budgeted for each department for the month of May:

	Fabrication	Drilling	Assembly	Maintenance	Production control
Number of workers	12	9	6	2	2
Direct wages	£22 000	£16 000	£2 085		
Indirect wages	£2 355	£2 760	£2 085	£3 000	£3 125
Floor area – m²	200	100	200	50	50
Number of customer jobs	25	20	35		
Number of machines	6	12	2		

Expenses budgeted for April

Costs	(£)
Rent	9 300
Factory management	7 750

Overhead is recovered on a direct wage basis. Customers' orders are priced with an 80 per cent mark up on cost.

Task

Job number A984 is a customers' order that is estimated to require £3 100 of material and direct wages of £900 in fabrication, £600 in drilling and £200 in assembly.

What is the selling price to be quoted to the customer for job number A984?

Exercise 12.18 Review questions

1 What is the distinction between direct and indirect cost?
2 Describe two methods for valuing stock issues that are in accordance with the requirements of SSAP 9.
3 What is the meaning of the following terms: allocation, apportionment and absorption?
4 What is the difference between total product cost and stock valuation as required by SSAP 9?

Exercise 12.19 Cost measurement

Clone-it Ltd assembles personal computers from components purchased from other firms. The following bill of materials lists the components required to make one PC.

Description	Number
Casing	1
Mother board	1
Hard disk	1
Floppy disk drive	2
Processing chips	1
Wiring	2 m
Cable	2
Keyboard	1
Monitor	1
Output ports	3

The components are ordered from suppliers in the following batch sizes

Description	Number	Total order value £
Casing	100	1 000
Mother board	200	8 000
Hard disk	50	7 500
Floppy disk drive	200	6 000
Processing chips	300	6 000
Wiring	200 m	50
Cable	250	200
Keyboard	50	1 500
Monitor	50	3 500
Output ports	150	3 000

Employees working in the assembly department earn £8 an hour and take 6 hours to assemble and test one computer. Employees working in the packaging department take one hour to pack one computer and earn £5 an hour. Management and clerical staff cost £8 000 per month.

Other costs include heat and light of £2 400 per quarter, telephone £500 per month and distribution costs of £50 per PC.

The business uses premises that cost £192 000 depreciated over 40 years and equipment that cost £30 000 depreciated over 5 years.

The production and sales volume for June was 500 computers.

Tasks

Required for the month of June:

1 *Identify, with explanations, which costs are direct costs and which are indirect.*
2 *Calculate total costs for Clone-it Ltd for the month of June analysed between direct and indirect costs.*
3 *Calculate the total cost of one PC for June.*

4 *The business has capacity to produce 600 computers per month. If the business could secure orders for a further 100 computers during July what would the total extra cost be? How much are the marginal costs for each additional PC? Explain why the marginal cost is different to the total cost of one PC calculated in (3) above.*

Summary

Costs are identified with two cost concepts – cost units and cost centres – and are categorised under the headings of materials, labour and expenses. Systems for materials costing have to account for changing price levels and calculations based on FIFO, AVCO and preset standards are widely used. Indirect expenses are classified as overheads relating to specific cost centres. Where costs cannot be accurately allocated to cost centres, they are apportioned using a proxy measure of demand. Once all costs are recorded against either cost units (product costs) or cost centres, the costs relating to cost centres are absorbed into product costs using a proxy measure of production activity, such as labour or machine hours. In this way, all factory costs of a manufacturing business can be related to products produced. The same techniques can be applied to service businesses, although a cost unit might be defined in terms of time, e.g. accountancy services are usually measured and charged by the hour.

Further reading

Management Accounting, published monthly by the Chartered Institute of Management Accountants.

Leslie Chadwick, *Management Accounting*, Routledge, 1993.

David Crowther, *Managing Accounting for Business*, Stanley Thornes, 1996.

Colin Drury, *Management Accounting Handbook*, Butterworth Heinemann, 1996.

Colin Drury, *Management and Cost Accounting*, 4th edition, International Thompson Business Press, 1996.

T. Lucey, *Management Accounting*, 4th edition, DP Publications, 1996.

13 Handling costing data

On completion of this chapter students should be able to:

- understand statistical techniques used to collect costing information
- use statistical techniques to describe and present cost data
- use statistical measures to summarise cost data.

A medium sized business can generate millions of items of cost data during the course of a year. The activities of employees, the use of materials and all indirect costs are recorded against cost units or cost centres.

Costing systems have traditionally been designed to provide stock valuation figures for financial reporting purposes. However, statistical techniques can also transform the mass of cost data into valuable information for management decision making.

Statistical techniques can be used routinely to provide regular management reports, or can be used in an ad hoc manner to satisfy a particular need.

Collection of data

Where businesses operate a formalised costing system, cost data are routinely collected and recorded and these cost records are a valuable source of data for further analysis and management reporting.

For some exercises it may be practical to analyse the whole set of data, but this can be too time consuming. As a minimum, it will be necessary to collect a sample of data that is sufficient to come to an informed conclusion.

Sampling

Sampling arises from the need to understand certain features or attributes of a set of data. For example, to find an average value or to establish a trend in a set of cost centre costs. The whole set of data that is being investigated is called the **population** and a selection taken from it is a **sample**. The sampling objective is to select a number of items of data that are representative of the population. For a sample to be representative of the whole population a sampling technique must be used to ensure all items in the population have equal chance of being selected.

The individual items chosen by the sampling technique are known as **sampling units**; and a **sampling frame** is a list of all the units in a population as far as they can be ascertained. Where job costs are being investigated over the past year, a sampling unit would be an individual job and the sampling frame would be the list of all those jobs completed during the year. If the sampling frame is incomplete or inaccurate, then so will be the sample that is drawn from it.

Figure 13.1 Relationship between sampling frame, sample and sample units

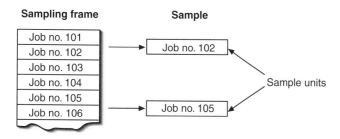

The accuracy of the sample in estimating the attributes of the population will also depend upon:

- the size of the sample (the larger the sample, the greater the probability that it is representative of the population)
- the sampling method used
- the range of values in the population (the greater the variability of the population, the more difficult it will be to construct a representative sample).

A number of sampling methods have been developed to address the problems of obtaining a representative sample in different circumstances.

Simple random sampling

Simple random sampling is a straightforward approach and is the preferred method where the whole population can be included in the sample frame. As its name implies, a data number is assigned to each sample unit and random numbers are then generated to choose the sample. Each item in the population has an equal chance of being selected for the sample.

Random numbers can be taken from random number tables (Appendix II) or can be generated on a spreadsheet using the =RND( ) function (Microsoft Excel).

Numbers are chosen from the random number table by reference to the highest data entity number.

Illustration

During a month there were 450 incidences of direct workers recording 'idle time' on their time sheets. An investigation to find reasons for this unproductive labour cost is to be based on a sample of 50 bookings. Each of the 450 occurrences is assigned a number and a random number table (Appendix II) is to be used to select the sample.

Starting at a random point in the table, it is possible to work along the rows or down the columns to select data entity numbers. Taking as a starting point the sixth column of four digits, the first numbers are as follows:

Table		Use	
92	47	924	7
38	83	388	3
09	57	095	7
44	97	449	7
23	57	235	7

The population of labour bookings has three digits (450) so taking the first 3 digits from 92 47 gives 924. This is too high a number so is ignored. The first four bookings to be taken from the sampling frame have numbers 388, 95, 449 and 235. When the bottom of the column is reached it is necessary to start at the top of the table again using the next 3 unused digits, in this case 780. The procedure is continued until the 50 numbers have been obtained.

Stratified sampling

One criticism of simple random sampling is that it may not accurately reflect the weighting of different groups within the population. *Stratified sampling* ensures that the different groups are properly represented and allows the random selection of items within each group.

Many businesses that manufacture complex engineering products monitor the cost of materials by constructing their own index of material costs. Materials used may fall into distinct groups whose costs are subject to different market conditions. Groups could be steel, wiring, mechanical components, electrical components, computer chips, paints and packaging materials. Once each group has been weighted according to their latest total purchase value, individual items within each stock group can be selected using random numbers (indices are considered later in the chapter).

As stratified sampling is used for large populations where there are distinct groups of items, it can result in valuable information about each group in the population. For example, for a particular year, it may be found that packaging costs are up 20 per cent and computer chips are down 50 per cent.

Systematic sampling

Systematic sampling can be used where the sample must be a certain percentage of the population, even if the population size is unknown at the outset. It is often used for quality control checks, with items chosen at regular intervals having taken the first item on a random basis. For example, if it is decided that 1 per cent of items are to be checked and the first item chosen was the 46th item, subsequent items would be the 146th, 246th, 346th and so on.

It is important that the interval between selections does not coincide with a regular pattern in the data set. For example, a quality check sample based on an interval of 100 may not be appropriate for a business that also produces 100 items a day. The result will be that the sample is taken at the same time every day, when in fact quality of work may not be uniform throughout the day.

Although bias can be introduced into systematic sampling if the sampling frame is not truly random and the sample interval is inappropriate, in its basic form it is a random method where individual items have an equal chance of selection. However, there may be circumstances where items should not be given equal weighting in the selection process.

When handling costing data, the value of individual items may differ significantly and it may be desirable to introduce bias into the selection process to give greater weighting to large value items.

For example, inventory control checks on physical stock balances should give emphasis to high value items. This can be achieved by listing items with their total cost value and this is accumulated for all items in the sampling frame. Items are selected either using fixed sample intervals or random numbers which are generated up to the total value of the stock held.

Illustration

Stock number	Description	Number	Unit price	Total value (£)	Accumulated value (£)
Brought forward					501 250.27
1254x	Flange	50	.15	7.50	501 257.77
1255x	BT Assembly	400	7.50	3000.00	504 257.77
1256x	Rotary arm	800	1.25	1000.00	505 257.77
Total stock value					505 257.77

If random number 502 520 was generated, stock number 1255x would be one of those items chosen for the inventory check.

Quota sampling

The sampling methods described so far have resulted in the random selection of items. In the case of *quota sampling*, items are not pre-selected but are chosen by the person collecting the data. The only stipulation is that there should be a fixed quota, either in total or for known groups in the population. For example, when investigating reasons for job cost overruns, it may be decided that 10 jobs should be reviewed in each of three production departments. The method introduces bias in the sampling process as matters of convenience may decide the selection of specific jobs. Despite this, the method is widely used in practice because it is simple and it minimises the time spent on investigative exercises.

Exercise 13.1   Random number table

To ensure material usage is being properly controlled, it has been decided to obtain a sample of 30 stock issue notes to check authorisation signatures. The total number of stock issues during the period under review was 695 and each stock issue note has been referenced from 1 to 695 accordingly. Using a random number table (see Appendix II), identify the 30 issue notes to be investigated.

Exercise 13.2   Sampling

Diverse Engineering Ltd works as a sub-contractor for the manufacture of mechanical components. The firm has experienced a wide range of gross margin percentages on individual jobs which the factory director suspects is due to poor price estimating on work passing through the machine shop. Over the past year the business has completed 250 jobs with the following numbers for each factory department: 157 machining, 203 fabrication work, 98 assembly of supplied components. It is estimated that it will take 10 minutes to investigate the details of individual jobs and so analysis is to be based on a sample of 40 jobs completed during the year.

Tasks

1 *Describe how each of the sampling methods could be used by Diverse Engineering.*
2 *Evaluate the advantages and disadvantages of each method for this particular exercise.*

Exercise 13.3   Sampling

Costly Castings Ltd is appraising the possible purchase of a new machine which may reduce the time spent on a machining operation. The operation has been performed approximately 2 000 times during the past two years. As part of the appraisal process, the management accountant requires the average time of the operation using existing machinery. It has been decided that the best source of information will be the time sheets of the eight direct workers who do periodically use the machine.

Task

Recommend, with reasons, a sampling method that would be suitable to ascertain the average time for the machining operation.

Sampling error

A precise measure of a data set can only be achieved by undertaking a *census* of the whole population. Samples are inaccurate for what they leave out of the analysis, so it follows that the bigger the sample, the more accurate the analysis. Sampling error can occur where:

■ the sampling frame is incomplete – for example records are excluded because it would be inconvenient and time consuming to visit a distant location
■ there is subjective choice in which items will be sampled
■ the sample is not strictly adhered to – for example where costing records are missing
■ the sample frame for systematic sampling is not randomly organised.

Despite these problems samples are widely used to estimate population characteristics such as mean and standard deviation. It is therefore important to recognise that even when you are using a sampling method that results in true random selection, there will always be the potential for error. The calculation of the sample mean will only be an approximation of the population mean.

Sample theory is explored in more detail in Chapter 18.

Presentation of data

How data are presented largely determines the effectiveness of the data handling exercise. The recipient of the information has to understand it before he or she can act upon it. The use of summary tables and graphical presentations can be a valuable part of the communication process.

A **variable** is a piece of data that has been measured or observed, e.g. the unit cost of products or labour wage rates. A **data set** is a list of the variables that have been collected. It may be the whole population of variables or a sample from that population.

A variable may be either **qualitative** in the sense that the label given to the variable is not numerically significant, e.g. cars categorised according to colour. Or the variable may be **quantitative** as it is expressed in numerical terms, such as production batches being grouped by their size, e.g. batches of 100, 200 and 300.

Quantitative data can be further analysed into whether they are continuous or discrete. **Continuous data** are characterised by many possible values, where the incidence of any one value will be correspondingly low. For example, the amount of time taken to do a task can be measured down to minutes and seconds.

Discrete data have distinct values that are not sub-divided with intermediate values. Examples are the number of tasks needed to complete a job or the number of doors on a car. Discrete data are often characterised by whole numbers but not necessarily so, for example, standard hourly pay rates of £3.65, £4.50 and £5.80 are discrete items against which the numbers of workers can be recorded. In this example it is not possible for workers to earn £3.80 per hour.

Where a variable occurs a number of times, its frequency can be summarised and presented in a frequency table. The frequency table is suitable for qualitative and discrete quantitative data.

Illustration

Sample of factory batch sizes

300 100 500 200 100 400 300 300 100 400

100 100 200 300 100 300 300 400 300 200

300 100 500 400 300 300 200 100 200 300

A frequency table is prepared after tallying the frequency of each batch size.

Batch size	Frequency	Cumulative frequency
100	8	8
200	5	13
300	11	24
400	4	28
500	2	30
	30	

The cumulative frequency is useful to demonstrate the number of frequencies falling in a range of variables. For example, 80 per cent (24/30) of batches do not exceed 300 items.

Where there are large numbers of variables, presentation may be improved if frequencies are grouped into classes. This technique is particularly appropriate for continuous quantitative data or where the number of discrete values is too great to provide a clear summary of the data. The resulting table is called a **grouped frequency table**.

The following data describe the time taken to inspect a sample of 30 stock deliveries received by a factory.

Minutes

4.5	8.7	6.7	10.6	13.8	5.0	11.8	7.0	12.0	10.1
11.2	18	15.2	10.1	7.0	9.1	12.3	8.4	13.8	13.2
16.4	7.3	13.0	12.4	22.2	10	5.4	8.1	10.9	14.4

A frequency table of the data would be as follows.

Inspections in minutes	Frequency	Cumulative frequency
5–7	7	7
8–10	7	14
11–13	9	23
14–16	5	28
17–19	1	29
20–22	1	30
	30	

The number and size of each class is a matter of judgement, but between 5 and 12 classes can show trends without losing the benefits of summarised data.

For further analysis it is important to understand the boundaries of each class of data. Taking the 8–10 minute class from the frequency table above:

Figure 13.2 Class boundaries

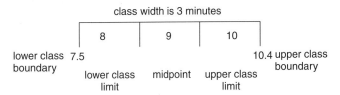

It is particularly important to define class boundaries clearly where there are continuous data as the boundaries are often not the same as the specified class limits. In the illustration in Figure 13.2 values ending in 0.5 of a minute are rounded up into the next class.

The cumulative frequency step polygon provides a graphical presentation of the cumulative frequencies taken from a frequency table (Figure 13.3).

Figure 13.3 Cumulative frequency graph

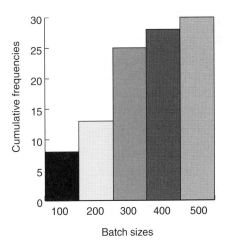

The steps of the graph in Figure 13.3 reflect the discrete values of the variables.

The **ogive** is a cumulative frequency polygon for grouped data. The cumulative frequencies are plotted against the upper boundary of each class. The logic here is that any readings up to the upper class boundary of each class will be included in the frequencies for that class. The points plotted on the graph are joined with straight lines.

The median of a set of data can easily be read from a cumulative frequency curve by reading from the mid frequency on the vertical axis (Figure 13.4).

Bar charts are an easily understood medium that can be used to good effect in business. Bar charts are drawn against a horizontal axis describing the variables, and a vertical axis showing value. The height of each bar corresponds to the frequency for each variable. In general, bar charts are used with qualitative and discrete

Figure 13.4 Cumulative frequency graph – ogive

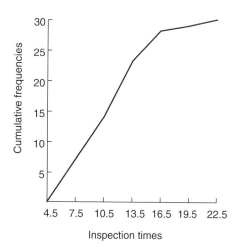

Batch size	Frequency	Degrees
100	8	96
200	5	60
300	11	132
400	4	48
500	2	24
	30	360

The number of degrees is calculated by comparing the frequency for each class with the total frequencies recorded:

$$\text{Degrees} = \frac{\text{Frequency of item}}{\text{Total number of frequencies}} \times 360 \text{ degrees}$$

For example, the degrees for batch size of 100:

$$= \frac{8}{30} \times 360 \text{ degrees} = 96 \text{ degrees}$$

Using a protractor the pie chart can now be drawn.

quantitative variables. However, classes of continuous data can be presented, provided the labels make clear that the horizontal axis is not a continuous scale. For the discrete data example in Figure 13.5, even if the batch sizes had increased by irregular amounts (say 100, 250 and 500 items) it would still have been acceptable to space the bars equally as the batch sizes are labels only. To show the discrete nature of the data, each bar is separated by a space.

Figure 13.6 Pie chart for batch sizes

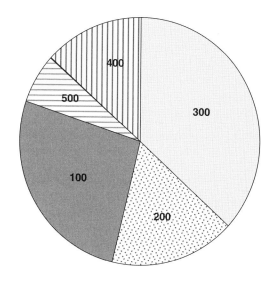

Figure 13.5 Bar chart for batch sizes

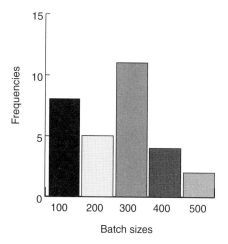

The **pie chart** is an alternative to a bar chart for the presentation of discrete data or groups of continuous data. The area of each segment of the pie is in proportion to the values or frequencies of each class of data.

To prepare a pie chart the first step is to divide the 360 degrees of the pie according to the relative size of each variable in the data set. Take the example of batch sizes:

Whilst **histograms** and simple bar charts look similar, there are important differences. Bar charts are generally used for discrete data, whereas histograms are used for continuous data.

Using the frequency data relating to inspection times the histogram in Figure 13.7 can be constructed.

The horizontal axis of a histogram is a numeric scale corresponding to the range of item values. Hence in the example in Figure 13.7, each bar represents a group of inspection times. The bars are drawn without spaces between them because the upper class boundary of one

Figure 13.7   Histogram

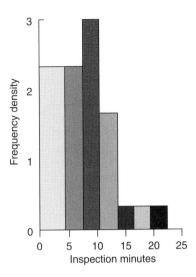

group is immediately followed by the lower class boundary of the adjacent group. The vertical axis is a scale of frequency density calculated by dividing the frequency by the class width. Its value has no meaning other than to show the relative frequency of different classes of data.

Another important feature of a histogram is that the area of the bars is in proportion to the frequencies of each class of data. Where the bars are of equal width, clearly the height of the bar is then proportional to the class frequency. But for ranges of data where few items are recorded, it may be appropriate to increase the class widths.

In the example of inspection times, there was only one item in each class over 16 minutes. The last two classes could be joined together making a class width of 6 minutes against the normal width of 3 minutes.

Inspections in minutes	Frequency	Class width – minutes	Frequency density
5–7	7	3	2.33
8–10	7	3	2.33
11–13	9	3	3.00
14–16	5	3	1.66
17–22	2	6	0.33
	30		

To group together classes for a bar chart would result in a bar being equivalent to the combined height of the individual classes. But a histogram retains the relative frequencies of the data. The height of the bar covering the class 17–22 should be no higher than the average height of the two classes it replaces. Each of the two previous classes had a density of one reading for a three minute class, i.e. 0.33. In relating area of the bars to frequency, the two

readings in the new class 17–22 also correspond to a frequency density of 0.33. After having grouped two classes the resulting graph will have the same profile as the previous graph.

Of course, some detail would have been lost if the widened classes covered ranges with differing frequency densities. The grouping of data is a matter of judgement, but generally groups should cover wider ranges where there are relatively few items recorded.

The **stem and leaf diagram** is an alternative method for presentation where the volume of data is not great and where the values are comprised of just two significant figures.

Illustration

22	56	48	39	11	18	45	52	35	21
36	19	44	29	22	43	27	37	28	30

The value of each item is split into two, the first digit being the stem and the second the leaf.

				Nos.
Stem	1	1 8 9	Leaves	3
	2	2 1 9 2 7 8		6
	3	9 5 6 7 0		5
	4	8 5 4 3		4
	5	6 2		2
				20

The optional summation of leaves on the right hand side ensures that all the items have been recorded.

It can help analysis if the diagram is re-drawn with the leaves in numerical order.

				Nos.
Stem	1	1 8 9	Leaves	3
	2	1 2 2 7 8 9		6
	3	0 5 6 7 9		5
	4	3 4 5 8		4
	5	2 6		2
				20

Although perhaps not so pleasing on the eye as a bar chart, the stem and leaf diagram does not lose the detail of the data set.

Exercise 13.4   Stem and leaf

1   Prepare a stem and leaf diagram from the following set of costs:

£2.30 £5.80 £6.50 £5.40 £1.50 £4.60 £8.70 £5.10 £3.80 £4.60
£3.10 £5.70 £6.90 £7.50 £6.40 £7.60 £5.70 £4.30 £3.20 £4.20

2   Comment on the usefulness of the diagram compared to the original data set.

Exercise 13.5 Histogram and ogive

1 Prepare a histogram and an ogive from the following set of costs:

£6.21 £10.80 £14.40 £7.40 £14.80 £13.81 £11.40 £9.52 £14.95 £10.52
£8.25 £11.65 £13.65 £9.85 £10.46 £14.98 £11.65 £8.84 £7.42 £9.89
£10.23 £11.66 £12.85 £12.82 £10.46 £11.64 £9.78 £11.82 £13.23 £12.81

2 Evaluate the distribution of costs.

Methods for summarising a data set

There are various mathematical measures that can be used to summarise the characteristics of a set of data.

Centrality

The central point in a set of data is identified by an average figure. There are three methods of calculating an average: the mean, median and mode.

Each method will be demonstrated with the following data:

2   6   4   3   5   6   3   4   3   2

The **median** is the middle value in the data set. It is necessary to first sort the items by order of value:

2   2   3   3   3   4   4   5   6   6

As this is a data set with an even number of items there are two middle items so it is necessary to take a simple average of the two values:

$$= \frac{3 + 4}{2} = 3.5$$

The **mode** is the value that occurs most frequently. In this example the value 3 is the mode. Where there are two values that occur most frequently then the distribution is said to be bimodal.

The **median** and mode are easy to calculate and exclude extreme values in the distribution that may distort the identification of a typical value.

The **mean** is calculated by adding all the values together and dividing by the number of items.

$$= \frac{2 + 6 + 4 + 3 + 5 + 6 + 3 + 4 + 3 + 2}{10} = 3.8.$$

Where the data are grouped

$$\text{the mean} = \frac{\Sigma fx}{\Sigma f}$$

where f = frequencies, x = mid-point of each class

Illustration

Inspections in minutes	Frequency	Mid point	Frequency × mid point
5–7	7	6.0	42.0
8–10	7	9.0	63.0
11–13	9	12.0	108.0
14–16	5	15.0	75.0
17–22	2	19.5	39.0
	30		327.0

$$\text{Mean} = \frac{327}{30} = 10.9 \text{ minutes}$$

Unlike the median and mode the mean considers all items in the data set to find a central point. This fact, however, also leads to the mean's disadvantage as it tends to be influenced by extreme values in the data set. Perhaps most importantly though, the mean can be used with other mathematical techniques to interpret data further. The median and mode tend to have a limited application other than being averages that are simple to understand.

Dispersion

Whilst the average of a data set gives a central value, additional measures are required to determine how values are spread around this central point.

Consider the following distributions

Group A	15	16	18	20	21
Group B	5	10	17	25	33

Both groups have a mean of 18, but the distribution in group A is much less dispersed than in group B.

One measure of dispersion is to take the difference between the highest and lowest values in the data set:

Range = highest value – lowest value

For group A the range is 5 and for group B it is 28.

Although simple in concept, the range does provide a measure of dispersion that is easily understood and is a valuable addition to the knowledge about the central value.

The disadvantage of the range is that it considers extreme values only and does not describe how the items are spread within the range. The following two distributions have the same range but clearly the values in Machine Shop A are more concentrated around a central point than in Machine Shop B.

Machine Shop A

Scale – minutes	11	12	13	14	15	16	17	18	19	20

Readings

Machine Shop B

Scale – minutes	11	12	13	14	15	16	17	18	19	20

Readings

The **standard deviation** is a measure of dispersal that considers individual values and is calculated with reference to the mean of the data set, i.e. how close individual values are to the central value.

It is the positive square root of the variance where the variance is calculated:

$$\text{Population variance } \sigma^2 = \frac{\Sigma\,(x - \mu)^2}{n}$$

σ^2 = variance
σ = standard deviation
x = individual values
μ = mean of the data set
n = number of items

Illustration

A factory has processed 10 identical stock orders that have taken the following number of hours to complete:

8   7   9   5   8   5   7   7   8   6

Find the standard deviation measured in hours.

Solution

The mean value is 7 (70/10).

Readings	Reading – mean $(x - \mu)$	Difference^2 $(x - \mu)^2$
8	1	1
7	0	0
9	2	4
5	–2	4
8	1	1
5	–2	4
7	0	0
7	0	0
8	1	1
6	–1	1
Total	0	16

$$\text{Population variance } \sigma^2 = \frac{\Sigma\,(x - \mu)^2}{n}$$

$$= \frac{16 \text{ hours}^2}{10} \qquad = 1.6 \text{ hours}^2$$

$$\text{Standard deviation} = \sqrt{1.6 \text{ hours}^2} = 1.26 \text{ hours}$$

The distribution can be summarised as having an average of 7 hours and a standard deviation around this point of 1.26 hours.

Where sample data are being analysed, it is possible to estimate the standard deviation of the population using a similar but not identical calculation as for the population as a whole. The denominator n is replaced with $(n - 1)$.

Illustration

If the data relating to ten stock orders above were a sample of items taken from a larger population, then the standard deviation would be calculated as:

$$\text{Sample variance } s^2 = \frac{\Sigma\,(x - \mu)^2}{n - 1}$$

$$= \frac{16}{9} \qquad = 1.78 \text{ hours}^2$$

$$\text{Standard deviation} = \sqrt{1.78} = 1.33 \text{ hours}$$

The standard deviation of the sample is an *estimate* of the standard deviation of the whole population. It is slightly larger than if the data set represented the whole population.

The **standard deviation of a grouped frequency distribution** uses the mid-point and the frequency of each group:

$$\text{Population variance } \sigma^2 = \frac{\Sigma f(x - \mu)^2}{\Sigma f}$$

Where f = number of frequencies

Illustration

For 40 factory employees, find the mean and standard deviation of time lost through machine breakdowns during the last month.

Time lost in minutes	Nos. of employees	Mid point	$(x - \mu)$	$(x - \mu)^2$	$f(x - \mu)^2$
0–19.9	12	9.95	–27	729	8 748
20–39.9	12	29.95	–7	49	588
40–59.9	8	49.95	13	169	1352
60–79.9	6	69.95	33	1 089	6534
80–99.9	2	89.95	53	2 809	5 618
	40				22 840

$$\text{Mean} = \frac{\Sigma fx}{\Sigma f} = \frac{(12 \times 9.95) + (12 \times 29.95) + (8 \times 49.95) + (6 \times 69.95) + (2 \times 89.95)}{40}$$

$$= \frac{1478}{40} = 36.95 \text{ minutes}$$

$$\text{Variance } \sigma^2 = \frac{\Sigma (x - \mu)^2}{\Sigma f}$$

$$= \frac{22840}{40} = 571 \text{ minutes}^2$$

Standard deviation $= \sqrt{571 \text{ minutes}^2} = 23.9$ minutes

The formula is modified where the data relates to a sample. As with the change for discrete data, the denominator becomes $\Sigma f - 1$. In the above example, the variance would be 585.6 minutes^2 and the standard deviation 24.2 minutes.

Relative dispersion

To aid interpretation it is often useful to consider the relative dispersion between data sets. All that is required is to compare the standard deviation to the mean to obtain what is called the coefficient of variation.

$$\text{Coefficient of variation} = \frac{\text{standard deviation}}{\text{mean}} \times 100\%$$

Illustration

From the illustration of ten factory orders, there is a mean of 7 hours and a standard deviation of 1.26 hours.

The coefficient of variation $= \dfrac{1.26}{7.0} \times 100\% = 18\%$

A low coefficient of variation signifies that items are grouped around the central point. Where the figures are used to estimate future values, a low coefficient gives greater confidence that the mean is typical of past values.

Skewness

A distribution may be symmetrical or it may have more frequencies at one end of its range than the other.

For distributions displaying marked skew characteristics, it is more appropriate to use the median as the centre point of the range of values. The median is not influenced by extreme values that are included in the calculation for the mean.

The degree of skewness can be calculated using:

$$\text{Pearson coefficient of skewness} = \frac{3 \text{ (mean} - \text{median)}}{\text{standard deviation}}$$

The nearer the result is to zero, the more symmetrical are the data. In addition, the formula indicates the direction of skew, e.g. a positive result indicates positive skew.

Figure 13.8   Skewness

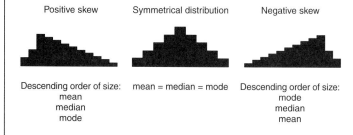

Positive skew	Symmetrical distribution	Negative skew
Descending order of size: mean median mode	mean = median = mode	Descending order of size: mode median mean

Illustration

The example earlier concerning time lost due to breakdowns had most of its readings in the first two groupings with a tail off in the next three groups. This indicates a positive skew which can be checked by calculation.

Time lost in minutes	No. of employees	Cumulative nos.
0–19.9	12	12
20–39.9	12	24
40–59.9	8	32
60–79.9	6	38
80–99.9	2	40
	40	

The mean and standard deviation have already been calculated as 36.95 minutes and 23.9 minutes respectively.

The median is the middle value so corresponds to the mean of the 20th and 21st employees. The median is therefore assumed to lie 8.5/12ths through the 20–39.9 minute group. Therefore:

$$\text{Median} = 19.9 \text{ (representing first 12 employees)} + \frac{8.5}{12.0}$$

$$\times (39.9 - 19.9)$$

$$= 34.1 \text{ minutes}$$

$$\text{Pearson coefficient of skewness} = \frac{3 \times (36.95 - 34.1)}{23.9}$$

$$= 0.35$$

This confirms the distribution has a positive skew. The relative size of the skew can be appreciated better by comparing skew factors of different distributions.

Exercise 13.6 Analysing and presenting data

The following is a sample of labour costs to repair machines that have broken down:

£5.20 £5.60 £5.75 £5.43 £4.90 £5.25 £6.05 £5.40 £5.50 £5.62
£5.35 £5.56 £5.45 £5.46 £5.71 £5.37 £5.95 £5.49 £5.68 £5.28
£5.43 £5.87 £5.27 £6.02 £5.38 £5.32 £5.64 £5.54 £5.59 £5.70

Tasks

1 *Prepare a grouped frequency table with between 7 and 9 cost groups.*
2 *Draw a histogram and cumulative frequency polygon.*
3 *Calculate the mean and standard deviation from the frequency table.*
4 *Calculate the coefficient of skewness. Comment on the result.*

Exercise 13.7 Analysing and presenting data

Rentawash Ltd rents washing machines through its network of high street shops. As part of its rental agreement, the cost of all services and repairs not caused by improper use are suffered by the company. In previous years the mean cost of a callout to a faulty washing machine has remained steady at around £35 for materials and labour. Costs of individual repairs have been distributed symmetrically around this mean with a standard deviation of £4.

The company's cost accountant is now concerned about the costs incurred in respect of a new model, the SF102. An earlier investigation has satisfied him that the actual number of callouts in relation to the number of machines is not unusual.

The following sample of callout costs in respect of the SF102 has been selected:

£32 £42 £39 £33 £57 £34 £35 £37 £32 £36
£39 £35 £38 £36 £37 £60 £36 £34 £33 £36
£36 £42 £40 £35 £33 £37 £35 £38 £51 £32

Tasks

For the sample of callout costs in respect of the SF102:

1 *construct a frequency table*
2 *calculate the mean, mode and median*
3 *draw a bar chart*
4 *calculate the standard deviation*
5 *calculate the coefficient of skewness*
6 *write a report to the cost accountant making reference to the results of the above tasks which should be attached as appendices.*

Index numbers

To provide a measure of how values change over time, it is sometimes necessary to construct an index. The most well known index is the Retail Price Index. It measures general price inflation in the economy and is used by the government and other organisations to change people's entitlement to such things as wages and pensions. How an index is constructed is particularly important as this will determine whether it accurately reflects the values it is measuring.

The principle is to compare the value of items against a **base value** determined for a **base period**. It is a matter of convenience which base period should be used, providing accurate and comparable values can be obtained.

Illustration

An office cleaning company has decided to construct an index of hourly wage costs. It uses 31 December 19X3 as its base period.

31 December of:	19X3	19X4	19X5	19X6	19X7	19X8
Hourly rate £	2.72	2.80	2.85	2.98	3.20	3.50
Wage cost index	100.0	102.9	104.8	109.6	117.6	128.7

For each year the index is calculated, the current hourly rate is compared to the base value and multiplied by 100. So for 19X6, $(£2.98/£2.72) \times 100 = 109.6$.

It is easy to interpret each value of the index in relation to the base period. Wages in 19X4 were 2.9 per cent higher than in 19X3 and wages in 19X7 were 17.6 per cent higher. To determine the change between years other than the base year, take the change in the index and compare this with the earlier index number.

For example, to determine the wage increase in percentage terms during 19X8:

$$= \frac{(128.7 - 117.6)}{117.6} \times 100 \text{ per cent} = 9.4 \text{ per cent.}$$

Exercise 13.8 Constructing an index

A printing business wishes to construct an index of paper costs. The cost of a standard roll of paper over the past ten years has been:

	X0	X1	X2	X3	X4	X5	X6	X7	X8	X9
Cost	£123	£125	£127	£131	£135	£138	£142	£148	£153	£155

Tasks

1 *Calculate the index for each year using X0 as the base period.*
2 *What has been the percentage increase in costs between X4 and X9?*

Composition of the index

Just as the Retail Price Index (RPI) is comprised of many items to reflect the spending patterns of typical consumers, indices used in the costing context will be made up of numerous items, perhaps running into thousands. The index has to represent the relative importance of the different items it is monitoring. For example, for a house builder, the cost of bricks will be far more important than the cost of nails. It therefore becomes necessary to weight items according to their relative value.

The change in cost levels can either be due to a change in price or a change in the mix of items purchased. If the emphasis is on monitoring price changes, then it is important that the method isolates the change in total value caused by price movements from changes in quantities.

The **Laspeyre price index** weights all prices according to quantities used in the base period.

The index is calculated $= \dfrac{\Sigma p_n q_o}{\Sigma p_o q_o}$

where p = price
  q = quantity
  n = in current period
  o = in base period

The **Paasche price index** weights prices according to current period usage, and this requires all past values of the index to be recalculated. This method may be difficult to implement where current quantities are not yet available.

The index is calculated $= \dfrac{\Sigma p_n q_n}{\Sigma p_o q_n}$

Illustration

FabSteel Ltd, a steel fabricator, incurs just two direct costs, the cost of labour and the cost of steel sheet. All products require a similar mix of labour and materials and so for pricing purposes the management have decided that price lists can be updated more conveniently using an index based on prime cost. Using 19X3 as the base period, the relative weighting of the two input costs are to be decided by reference to the total quantities used in that year.

31 December of:	19X3 (£)	19X4 (£)	19X5 (£)	19X6 (£)	19X7 (£)	19X8 (£)
Hourly rate	5.50	5.90	6.25	6.50	6.80	7.15
Steel sheet /square metre	2.25	2.30	2.29	2.38	2.45	2.49
Total hours	85 000	87 000	88 000	91 000	92 000	91 000
Total steel square metres	122 000	135 000	145 000	163 000	181 000	185 000

Each year's material and labour cost prices are weighted using 19X3 quantities:

31 December of:	19X3 (£)	19X4 (£)	19X5 (£)	19X6 (£)	19X7 (£)	19X8 (£)
Hours in base period	85 000	85 000	85 000	85 000	85 000	85 000
Metres of steel in base period	122 000	122 000	122 000	122 000	122 000	122 000

Base quantities × period rate:						
Labour	467 500	501 500	531 250	552 500	578 000	607 750
Steel sheet	274 500	280 600	279 380	290 360	298 900	303 780
Cost of 19X3 resources used	742 000	782 100	810 630	842 860	876 900	911 530

The total prime cost index can now be calculated with 19X3 equal to 100.

31 December of:	19X3 (£)	19X4 (£)	19X5 (£)	19X6 (£)	19X7 (£)	19X8 (£)
Prime cost index	100.0	105.4	109.2	113.6	118.2	122.8

Exercise 13.9 Paasche price index

1 Rework the index for FabSteel Ltd using the Paasche method for constructing a price index.
2 Evaluate the differences between the two indices.

Sample weighting by category

Where an index represents a population of hundreds or possibly thousands of items, then by necessity the index will be based on a sample of items. To monitor the change to as large a proportion of costs as possible, there will be a need to bias sampling to large value items. For a price index of stock materials, this could be achieved by using a systematic sampling technique, or perhaps by simply choosing the 100 items with the highest annual purchase value.

However, for a materials price index it is important that the index reflects the nature of stock categories and the unique market conditions affecting individual categories. Consider the following items taken from the stock records of an engineering company involved in the manufacture of products containing mechanical and electronic components.

	Annual purchases (£)
Steel bar	200 000
Circuit board C34	40 000
Circuit board C35	40 000
Circuit board C36	40 000
Circuit board C37	40 000
Circuit board C38	40 000

If it were decided that all items with purchases of over £100 000 would comprise the materials cost index, then clearly the steel bar would be included and all of the circuit boards would be excluded. The problem is that taken together, the circuit boards have a combined purchases figure identical to the steel bar. Whole categories of stock that may have their own unique cost pressures may be excluded because they are made up of a large number of different items.

The problem can be overcome by first identifying categories of items that should be represented by the index. The value of each category can then be given a weighting which will be represented by items taken from that category. In the example above, if the circuit board category were represented by just one of the boards, it would carry the same weighting as the steel bar.

An index must remain relevant to current circumstances, just as the RPI is updated annually to reflect current spending patterns. This either requires the Paasche method to be used, or for the base period to be regularly reviewed in the case of the Laspeyre method.

Exercise 13.10   Index with weighted categories

1   Construct a retail price index for a household, using a sample of ten to fifteen items that are weighted according to the value of the category they represent.
2   Update the index on a monthly basis.

Exercise 13.11   Wage rate index

A charity providing care in the community for elderly people charges its clients a standard hourly rate for services such as cleaning, shopping and gardening. The charge was £2.20 per hour during 19X8, up from £2.10 in 19X7 – irrespective of whether the work was undertaken by a volunteer or a paid worker. Unfortunately 19X8 saw the charity make a loss on care activities, having broken even in 19X7 and despite having set the composite charge-out rate after agreeing wage rates for the year.

Tasks

1   *Calculate a composite wage rate index that could be used to monitor the charge-out rate in future. The base period for the index is to be 19X4, and the weightings are to be based on the hours for 19X8, including the unpaid volunteers' work.*
2   *Evaluate the data handled and advise the charity's Management Committee on the process they must go through when setting charge-out rates in future.*
3   *What implications does this have for maintaining a meaningful wage rate index?*

	19X4	19X5	19X6	19X7	19X8
Volunteers' hours	5 200	6 300	7 350	7 580	6 950
Paid shopping					
Hours	800	900	1 000	950	1 000
Hourly rate	£2.00	£2.05	£2.10	£3.00	£3.10
Paid cleaning					
Hours	7 500	7 700	7 200	6 400	6 800
Hourly rate	£3.20	£3.30	£3.50	£4.00	£4.20
Gardening					
Hours	1 900	2 500	2 400	2 900	3 050
Hourly rate	£2.50	£2.60	£2.70	£3.10	£3.20

Summary

Using basic statistical tools to handle and present costing information is a vital part of cost management. Handling costing data involves the following:

Collection of data using:

- simple random sampling
- stratified sampling
- systematic sampling.

Presentation of data using:

- frequency tables
- stem and leaf diagrams
- bar and pie charts
- histograms
- frequency polygons
- ogives.

Measures to summarise data:

- centrality – using the averages of mean, mode and median
- dispersion – using range and standard deviation
- skew
- index numbers.

Further reading

Audrey Curnock, *Quantitative Methods for Business*, Stanley Thornes, 1995.

K. Hoye and R. Ingram, *Statistics for Business*, Butterworth Heinemann, 1991.

T. Lucey, *Quantitative Techniques*, 5th edition, DP Publications, 1996.

Clare Morris, *Quantitative Approaches in Business Studies*, 4th edition, Pitman, 1996.

Frank Owen and Ron Jones, *Statistics*, 4th edition, Pitman, 1994.

Mik Wisniewski, *Foundation Quantitative Methods for Business*, Pitman, 1996.

14 Costing systems

On completion of this chapter students should be able to:

- identify and illustrate the appropriate systems and techniques for specific business situations
- record costs, prepare reports and interpret findings based on given data.

The application of the cost measurement principles described in Chapter 12 requires systems that are appropriate to the nature of the business.

The systems described in this chapter relate to the following situations:

- individual job production
- batch production
- process technologies
- long-term contracts.

The main issue that the recording system has to address is work in progress (WIP). At any point in time there will be work that has been started but not yet finished. Each system is concerned with the recording of costs as they are incurred during the WIP stage and then determining what happens to the costs as products are completed. Costs of completed products and services are either cost of sales if they relate directly to a customer's order, or represent the cost of stock if transferred for future use to the business's stockroom.

Consider a relatively simple situation of a furniture manufacturer incurring the usual costs of labour, materials and expenses. During a particular week, 10 tables and 20 wardrobes were completed and a further 4 tables and 5 wardrobes were started but not completed. How can the unit costs of completed furniture and the cost of WIP be determined?

A system is required that records costs against separately identifiable items of work. If a number of identical items are manufactured in small batches, then costs can be accumulated for each batch. At a point in time, batches will be either completed or will be remaining in WIP. Unit costs of completed items can be calculated by dividing the batch total cost by the number of items made. The cost of unfinished work can easily be identified and be classified as WIP.

For complex situations, such as for process industries or long-term building projects, the division of costs between completed work and WIP is particularly difficult. This is because the resources that have been input are lost for physical identification purposes in the production process.

The problem that each system is trying to address can be expressed in diagrammatic form (Figure 14.1).

Figure 14.1 Data flow for a costing system

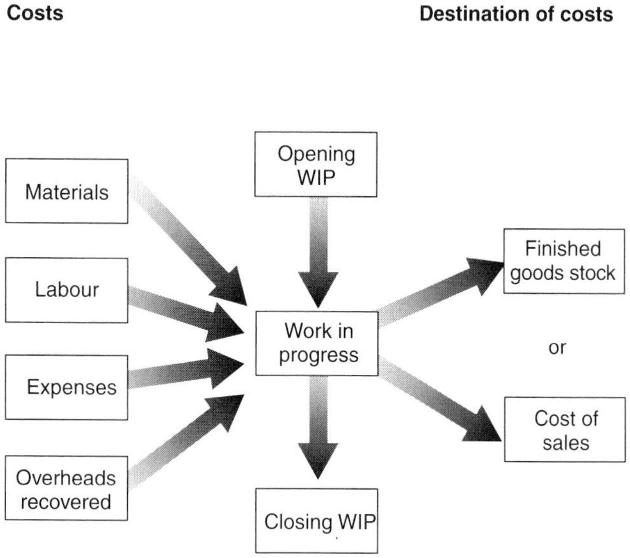

Costs   **Destination of costs**

Job costing

Job costing is used where goods or services are provided to satisfy specific customer orders. For example, the cost of accountancy services or the cost of cleaning an office block can be accumulated by a unique job number.

Direct costs and overheads recovered are accumulated for individual customers' jobs on a cost record. For a manual costing system the job cost sheet in Figure 14.2 is typical of the format used.

When a job has been completed its cost is transferred (credited) from WIP and if it relates to a customer's order it will be debited to cost of sales. If the job is to manufacture a stock item, the cost will be debited to finished goods stock.

Figure 14.2 Job cost sheet

Job cost sheet						
Job number: 98124						
Sales order: 9874						
Order data: 12 Dec. X8						

Date	Description	Ref.	Material £	Labout £	Overhead £	Traded £	Job total £
23-01	Stores	1158	547.00				547.00
25-01	Time sheets	T5874		124.00	248.00		919.00
26-01	Stores	I168	50.00				969.00
01-02	Time sheets	T5885		150.00	300.00		1419.00
01-02	Journal	SJ421				−1419.00	0.00
			597.00	274.00	548.00	−1419.00	0.00
	Memorandum						
01-02	Sales	S652				1850.00	
	Profit					431.00	

Batch costing

Batch costing is appropriate where batches of similar items are manufactured for stock. The method of accumulating costs for batch costing is very similar to that for job costing. As items manufactured in batches are more likely to be ordered for stock, each item completed will be valued in stock at the total cost for the batch divided by the number of units produced. For example, 200 flanges made for stock at a batch cost of £440 would result in the individual items being received into stock valued at £2.20 each.

Exercise 14.1   Batch costing

Lot Engineering Ltd uses a batch costing system for recording the cost of components that it manufactures. During week 35 the machine shop worked on four batches. Batches 1011 and 1013 were completed during the week. Batches 1012 and 1014 remained in WIP at the end of the week. The machine shop incurred £2 000 of direct labour and £3 000 of apportioned overhead during the week. Overhead is recovered on a direct labour cost basis.

The summarised time sheet details of the direct workers and the cost of direct material issues were as follows:

Batch number	To produce	Direct labour hours	Materials (£)
1011	150 of C101	40	500
1012	200 of T214	50	750
1013	100 of C564	80	400
1014	500 of A489	30	500
		200	2 150

Tasks

1   *Calculate the total and unit cost of finished batches.*
2   *Calculate the cost of work in progress.*

Process costing

Process costing is appropriate where materials are required to flow through one or more standard processes before being transferred to stock. For example, making paint or mass producing food products.

A unique problem of process technologies is that the identity of materials passing through the system is lost. At the end of an accounting period, some materials will have been converted into a finished state, whilst some will remain in the process. The technique of process costing uses the concept of *equivalent units* to separate the cost of completed work from that continuing in WIP.

For each classification of cost added to the process, the units in WIP at the end of the accounting period are assessed for their state of completeness. This enables an average cost for a completed unit to be derived.

Illustration – Closing WIP with equivalent units

The following information relates to the production in week 34 of Protector, a wood preservative.

■ Resources added – 500 kg of materials £3 000 and labour £2 200.
■ Closing WIP – 150 kg which is 60 per cent complete in respect of labour.
■ Transfer to stores – 350 kg of Protector.
■ Overheads are recovered on a 150 per cent of labour cost basis.
■ All materials are introduced at the start of the process.

Solution

The first stage is to establish the equivalent number of completed units in WIP at the end of week 34 and add these to the completed units to find total production in terms of completed units. Labour and overhead costs for WIP are equivalent to 90 completed units (150 kg × 60 per cent).

	Completed units	Equivalent units in c/f	Total equivalent completed units	Total cost (£)	Cost per completed unit (£)	Cost per unit in WIP (£)
Materials	350	150	500	3 000	6.00	6.00
Labour	350	90	440	2 200	5.00	3.00
Overhead	350	90	440	3 300	7.50	4.50
Total				8 500	18.50	13.50

Cost per completed unit

$$= \frac{\text{Total cost}}{\text{Total equivalent completed units}}$$

Cost of each completed unit = £18.50.

Cost for a partly completed unit = Cost per completed unit × completeness per cent

(This is calculated for each cost category.)

From this information it is possible to prepare a process account in the form of a standard ledger account with additional columns to record the number of units being processed.

Process account for week 34 – Protector

Detail	Units	Debit (£)	Detail	Units	Credit (£)
Materials	500 kg	3 000	Completed	350 kg	6 475
Labour		2 200	WIP c/f	150 kg	2 025
Overheads		3 300			
	500 kg	8 500		500 kg	8 500

Exercise 14.2   Closing WIP with equivalent units

The production of the garden chemical Elphi usually involves work in progress at the end of each working week. However, the current week is immediately after the Easter shut-down, and started with no WIP. During the week resources applied to the process consisted of 2 000 kg of raw materials costing £2 000, labour of £4 200 and overheads recovered at 50 per cent on labour cost. All materials are introduced at the start of the process. During the week, 1 400 kg of completed product were transferred to the finished goods store. At the end of the week, work in progress consisted of 600 kg of product considered to be 50 per cent complete for labour and overhead.

Task

Prepare the process account for Elphi from this information.

Opening and closing WIP

In practice most accounting periods will open and close with partly converted materials in the process. The principle of equivalent units is continued but it is important to recognise that the unit costs of one period may not be the same as the next. This may be due to changing input costs or varying efficiency from one period to the next. There are a number of methods for calculating stock valuation when unit costs are changing. Chapter 12 discussed the FIFO and AVCO methods.

The same techniques can be applied to process costing. This section will concentrate on AVCO to value WIP but it is important to appreciate that general principles of stock valuation also apply to inventories in process technologies.

Illustration

The following information relates to the production of hand-dyed fabrics in week 14 by Dyeing Fabrics Ltd.

- Opening work in progress – 10 m of fabric costing £300, 50 per cent complete for labour with a cost of £120 and overhead £60
- Resources added during week 14 – 80 m of fabric £2 580 and labour £2 288.
- Transfers to the finished goods store amounted to 82 m of fabric.
- Closing work in progress consisted of 8 m of fabric which was 50 per cent complete for labour.
- Overheads are recovered on a 50 per cent of labour cost basis.
- All fabric is introduced at the start of the process and all dyes are treated as consumable materials recovered in the overhead absorption rate.

Solution

This solution describes the preparation of the process account for Dyeing Fabrics for week 14, using the average cost method.

As before the first stage is to establish the equivalent number of completed units in WIP at the end of week 14 and add these to the completed units to find total production in terms of completed units.

	Completed units	Equivalent units WIP c/f	Total equivalent completed units	Opening WIP cost (£)	Period costs (£)	Total costs (£)	Cost per completed unit	Cost per unit in WIP
Materials	82	8	90	300	2 580	2 880	32.00	32.00
Labour	82	4	86	120	2 288	2 408	28.00	14.00
Overhead	82	4	86	60	1 144	1 204	14.00	7.00
Total				480	6 012	6 492	74.00	53.00

Process account for week 14 – Dying Fabrics

Detail	Units metres	Debit (£)	Detail	Units metres	Credit (£)
WIP B/F	10	480	Completed fabrics	82	6 068
Material added	80	2 580	WIP c/f	8	424
Labour		2 288			
Overhead		1 144			
	90	6 492		90	6 492

Exercise 14.3   Opening and closing WIP

The following information relates to the production in week 15 of hand-dyed fabrics.

- Opening work in progress – 8 m of fabric costing £256, labour 50 per cent complete £112 and

overhead £56.
- Resources added – 90 m of fabric £2 978 and labour £2 612.
- Transfers to the finished goods store amounted to 86 m of fabric.
- Closing work in progress – 12 m of fabric, 40 per cent complete for labour.
- Overheads are recovered on a 50 per cent of labour cost basis.
- All fabric is introduced at the start of the process and all dyes are treated as consumable materials recovered in the overhead absorption rate.

Task

Prepare the process account for Dyeing Fabrics for week 15 using the average cost method.

Process losses

Most production processes will involve some loss of materials input. This may be due to evaporation, spillage or residue lost in the factory plant. A normal level of loss may be inherent in the nature of the process, in which case it will be usual to deduct some material from the costing records and describe this as *normal losses*. If the business routinely receives a salvage or scrap value for this material, then this can be applied to reduce the overall cost of the process. When calculating the average cost of a completed unit, the scrap value is deducted from material costs.

Some losses may occur that are not planned and have arisen due to human error, plant fault or perhaps defects in the materials being input. In these cases the lost quantity and associated cost of equivalent units is transferred from the process account to an expense account called *abnormal losses*. Conversely it may be possible to improve on normal processing efficiency, in which case this gain will be added to costs and credited to an *abnormal gains* account. These adjustments mean that stock held is valued at cost based on normal processing efficiencies and ensures compliance with SSAP 9 in this respect.

Illustration

The colouring process involves converting the proprietary brand Semathen from white powder to green tablet form. At the start of week 19, 25 kg of material were in WIP. These materials have undergone 20 per cent of the conversion process. The cost records showed that work in

progress was valued at £440 for materials, £50 for labour and £60 for overheads.

During week 19, 285 kg of powder costing £4 760 was introduced to the process and £2 500 of labour was used in the conversion process. Overheads are recovered using 120 per cent of labour costs.

Work in progress at the end of week 19 consisted of 10 kg of materials and these were 50 per cent complete in terms of conversion costs.

The process incurs a normal loss of materials equivalent to 1 kg for every 5 kg completed and accepted into finished goods stores. The powder lost in the process has no value and is destroyed by incineration.

Solution

In order to prepare a 'Colouring Process' account for week 19, using the average cost method for valuing work in progress, the first stage is, as usual, to establish the equivalent number of completed units in WIP at the end of week 19 and add these to the completed units to find total production in terms of completed units. The complication with this problem is the normal losses, and at this stage it may be useful to complete the units columns of the process account.

The WIP b/f weighed 25 kg and the materials input in the period amounted to 285 kg, giving a total of 310 kg. Of the total 310 kg in the process, 10 kg remained in WIP at the end of the week. Therefore completed units plus normal loss amounted to 300 kg. Using the normal loss proportion, 250 kg therefore relates to completed units.

	Completed units	Equivalent units equivalent WIP c/f	Total equivalent completed units	Opening WIP cost (£)	Period costs (£)	Total costs (£)	Cost per completed unit	Cost per unit in WIP
Materials	250	10	260	440	4 760	5 200	20.00	20.00
Labour	250	5	255	50	2 500	2 550	10.00	5.00
Overhead	250	5	255	60	3 000	3 060	12.00	6.00
Total				550	10 260	10 810	42.00	31.00

Process account – Colouring

Detail	Units Kg	Debit (£)	Detail	Units Kg	Credit (£)
WIP B/F	25	550	Completed	250	10 500
Material added	285	4 760	Normal losses	50	0
Labour		2 500	WIP c/f	10	310
Overhead		3 000			
	310	10 810		310	10 810

Exercise 14.4 Normal losses

Prepare the process account for Semathen colouring for week 20 from the following data.

- The 10 kg of opening work in progress is valued at £200 for materials, £50 for labour and £60 for overheads.
- During week 20, 250 kg of powder was added to the process at a cost of £3 980. Conversion costs included £2 070 for labour. Overhead continues to be recovered at 120 per cent of labour costs.
- Work in progress at the end of week 20 consisted of 20 kg of material, 60 per cent complete as far as the conversion process was concerned.
- Loss of material in the process was in line with the normal proportion of 1 kg for every 5 kg of product completed.

Task

Prepare a 'Colouring Process' account for week 20, using the average cost method for valuing work in progress.

Exercise 14.5 Normal losses with scrap value

Cottage Industries is a clothing manufacturer specialising in garments made by traditional methods. The following data relates to its weaving process.

Production is measured in kilograms of cloth. A loss of 10 per cent of materials is recognised as each roll is completed. Every 1 kg of waste materials can be disposed of for £1.

At the start of week 2, 20 kilograms of material were partly complete from the previous week and this was valued at £90 for materials, £200 for labour and £135 for overhead.

During week 2 a further 110 kg of materials costing £352 were issued from stores to the weaving process. The wages for the week amounted to £2 425 and overheads apportioned to the process were £513.

At the end of week 2 there were 30 kg of material still in WIP and these were considered 100 per cent complete for materials and overhead, but only 50 per cent complete for labour.

Task

Prepare a 'Weaving Process' account for week 2, using the average cost method for valuing work in progress.

Contract costing

Contract costing is appropriate for large products produced over an extended period of time, such as a ship or civil engineering project.

The accounting system employed for long-term contracts seeks to satisfy the same requirements as those for job and process technologies. However, unlike process costing, there are no regular transfers of finished products; a contract is an ongoing project that continues to accumulate costs.

The problem with long-term contracts is that the work may take several years before completion. If a system was not in place to recognise the value of work completed as the projects progressed, the business's trading results would be very volatile. Some years may see little if any reported turnover, whilst others would report turnover and profits bearing little relationship to work actually done in the period.

There are specific provisions in SSAP 9, Accounting for Stocks and Long Term Contracts, that relate to contract costing. Provided the final result of a project can be forecast with reasonable certainty, it is appropriate to recognise a proportion of the profits of a contract in relation to the amount of work completed. This is an instance of the accruals concept being applied provided the prudence concept is satisfied.

Hence the costs incurred on a contract will either be treated as cost of sales, or as relating to uncompleted work that will be disclosed as WIP in the balance sheet.

The contract account can be prepared as a ledger account with costs debited for:

- direct costs of materials, labour and expenses
- central costs apportioned to the contract
- cost of plant used – which is either charged in the form of a depreciation charge, or the full purchase cost is charged with the current net book value carried down at the end of each period.

The contract account will be credited and the trading account debited with the cost of work completed.

Balances on the contract account at the end of the period will be in respect of:

- prepayments and accruals for costs – prepayments and unused materials are carried forward from the credit side, accruals from the debit side
- cost of work not completed, carried forward as WIP.

Profit is only taken on a contract for work that has been certified as complete and after verifying that the full contract is forecast to make profits in future periods. Where contract losses are being forecast they are recognised immediately by increasing the cost of sales transfer to the trading account.

Illustration of basic principles

Worley Construction have two road construction contracts, at Newton and Wymington. The costs for six months to June 19X8 were:

	Newton (£'000)	Wymington (£'000)
Wages	450	640
Materials issued to the site	350	710
Plant – purchase price	240	570
Sub-contractors	120	290
Head office charges	50	65
Site expenses	65	25
Value of plant at 30 June X8	200	510
Sub-contractors costs not paid	10	20
Materials unused at 30 June X8	25	105
Sales value of stages completed	800	1150
Cost of stages completed	600	800
Contract value	2500	3500
Estimated costs to completion	800	700

This is the end of the first financial period for both contracts, and so no profits have previously been taken in respect of either contract.

The following are required in respect of each contract:

1 a contract account for the six months to June 19X8
2 a forecast of final profit or loss
3 a trading account to 30 June X8.

Solution for Newton

Contract account for Newton

Detail	Debit (£'000)	Detail	Credit (£'000)
Wages	450	Plant c/f NBV at 30 June X8	200
Materials issued to the site	350	Materials c/f at 30 June X8	25
Plant – purchase price	240	Trading a/c – Cost of sales	600
Sub-contractors	120	WIP c/f	460
Head office charges	50		
Site expenses	65		
Sub-contractors c/f	10		
	1285		1285

Before transferring the stated cost of stages completed, it was first necessary to verify that the contract was forecast to continue making profits during the remainder of its life.

At this stage, the contract has incurred costs of £1060000, comprising the £1285000 debited to the contract account less amounts remaining unused – plant and materials £225000. The main decision is therefore how much is to be traded as cost of sales and how much remains as WIP.

SSAP 9 requires that inventories must be valued at the lower of cost and net realisable value. If the cost of WIP is not at least matched by its net realisable value, the excess of cost should be charged to the trading and profit and loss account immediately.

For Newton, WIP would be valued at £460000 if £600000 were transferred to the trading account (£1060000 – £600000). Net realisable value of WIP is remaining sales value £1700000 (£2.5m – £0.8m) less cost to completion, which is forecast to be £800000, giving a net £900000. Therefore WIP cost is lower than realisable value, so the WIP can be valued at £460000.

Another approach is to look at the contract as a whole:

Forecast result to completion	(£'000)
Contract value	2500
Cost incurred to date	−1060
Estimated costs to completion	−800
Final profit	640

The contract is anticipated to produce a total profit of £640000, which is in excess of the profit estimated to have been made on stages completed to date. It is therefore acceptable to trade a profit of £200 000 against sales of £800 000.

Trading account

Detail	Debit (£'000)	Detail	Credit (£'000)
Cost from contract account	600	Sales	800
Profit for year	200		
	800		800

Exercise 14.6   Contract account

Complete the same tasks for the Wymington contract.

Contracts with forecast losses

Where a contract is forecast to make a loss on completion, the total loss is to be recognised in the current period's trading results. This satisfies the prudence concept and it is a requirement stipulated in SSAP 9.

The loss is recognised by increasing the current transfer to the trading account, so that the WIP balance is matched by its net realisable value.

Illustration

Victorian Homes have two house-building projects, and the costs for the 12 months to 31 October 19X8 are:

	Yelden (£'000)	Higham (£'000)
Wages	800	900
Materials issued to the site	1135	2500
Plant – depreciation charged	280	350
Sub-contractors	650	1960
Head office charges	85	205
Site expenses	55	45
Site expenses not paid	15	20
Materials unused at 31 October X8	60	285
Sales value of stages completed	1400	4100
Cost of stages completed	1300	4200
Total estimated sales value	4300	8750
Estimated costs to completion	1500	3305

This is the end of the first financial period for both contracts, so no profit has previously been taken in respect of either contract.

1   Prepare the contract account for Yelden.
2   Forecast the total profit or loss for the project.
3   Prepare a trading account to 31 October for the contract.

Solution

Contract account for Yelden for year to 31 October 19X8

Detail	Debit (£'000)	Detail	Credit (£'000)
Wages	800	Materials c/f	60
Materials issued to the site	1135	Trading a/c – Cost of sales	1560
Plant – depreciation charged	280	WIP c/f	1400
Sub-contractors	650		
Head office charges	85		
Site expenses	55		
Site expenses not paid	15		
	3020		3020

Before using the £1.3 million stated cost of stages completed as the cost of sales figure, it was first necessary to verify that the contract WIP was lower than its net realisable value.

Forecast result to completion	(£'000)
Contract value	4300
Cost incurred to date (£3 020k–£60k)	–2960
Estimated costs to completion	–1500
Final loss	–160

The contract is anticipated to produce a total loss of £160 000 and it is necessary to realise this immediately in the trading account.

Trading account

Detail	Debit (£'000)	Detail	Credit (£'000)
Cost from contract account	1560	Sales	1400
		Loss	160
	1560		1560

The answer can be verified by considering the net realisable value of WIP.

	£'000
Sales to be traded (4 300–1 400)	2900
Estimated costs to completion	–1500
Net realisable value of WIP c/f	–1400

The cost of work in progress is now exactly matched by its net realisable value.

Exercise 14.7   Contract account

Using the data from the Victorian Homes illustration:

1   Prepare the contract account for Higham.
2   Forecast the total profit or loss for the project.
3   Prepare a trading account to 31 October for the contract.

Intermediate periods

Where the contract account is being prepared for an intermediate year, the same principles hold, except of course the account will have opening balances for WIP, plant on site, materials not used, and prepayments.

The only complication arises when forecasting final profitability. In testing to ensure that net realisable value of WIP is at least equal to cost incurred, it is important to consider only the sales value not yet traded rather than the full contract value, as some of the contract value may have been traded in previous periods.

Exercise 14.8 Contract account

Bromswold Construction has just come to the end of the second year of a three-year contract called Canyon Theme Park. Transaction details for the second year ended 31 December 19X8 are as follows:

	Canyon T.P. (£'000)
Work in progress brought forward	5 650
Plant brought forward	900
Raw materials brought forward	370
Unpaid site expenses brought forward	42
Materials purchased	1 560
Labour	1 460
Sub-contractors	3 540
Site expenses	290
New plant purchased	45
Sub-contractors not paid	110
Value of plant at 30 December X8	725
Cumulative sales value of work completed	9 650
Cumulative cost of work completed	8 100
Contract value	16 500
Estimated costs to completion	1 500

In 19X7 Bromswold traded sales of £2 750 000 and costs of £2 400 000 in respect of the contract.

Task

Prepare the contract account and trading account in respect of Canyon Theme Park for the year to 31 December 19X8.

Summary

Costing systems should be appropriate to the nature of the business and must provide a record of costs for measuring profitability of sales and the valuation of stocks. They tend to fall into one of the following four categories:

- job costing
- batch costing
- process costing
- contract costing.

Further reading

Management Accounting, published monthly by the Chartered Institute of Management Accountants.

Leslie Chadwick, *Management Accounting*, Routledge, 1993.

David Crowther, *Managing Accounting for Business*, Stanley Thornes, 1996.

Colin Drury, *Management Accounting Handbook*, Butterworth Heinemann, 1996.

Colin Drury, *Management and Cost Accounting*, 4th edition, International Thompson Business Press, 1996.

T. Lucey, *Management Accounting*, 4th edition, DP Publications, 1996.

15 Costing techniques

On completion of this chapter students should be able to:

- measure and evaluate the impact of changing activity levels on business performance
- record costs, prepare reports and interpret findings based on given data.

Providing a customer with a product or service incurs the business in direct and indirect costs. But how much a product costs is often difficult to determine.

Case study

How much is that sandwich in the window?

Joe's Sand Wedge Bar is renowned for its generous portions. One day, Joe is busy readying his business for the lunch-time rush when his friend Chris arrives. Chris runs a similar sandwich bar on the other side of town, but her morning round of the business park has left her short of stock for lunch time. 'If you have any sandwiches spare I'll take them for cost, if that's alright Joe.'

'OK by me', Joe replies.

The trouble is, Joe does not know how much a sandwich costs him. He reckons bread, butter and filling cost an average 20p a time. What about his time? 10p a sandwich?

'Say 30p each?'

'Great', says Chris, and is gone with a box under her arm before Joe has second thoughts.

Joe muses, 'Is that all it cost me? OK I have the rent but I would have to pay that anyway ... I suppose I've lost

profit if I run out later ... and I certainly wouldn't make a living if I sold to everyone at 30p .... but I charged her for my time and I don't have any work on at the moment ... so what does a sandwich cost me?'

The problem is that there is no comprehensive definition of what product cost is. It is important, however, to use a method of calculation that is appropriate to the situation.

Direct costs (those costs that can be directly attributed to a particular product) present few problems, provided an effective recording system is in place. For example, with a little more thought Joe could easily have ascertained the direct costs of his sandwiches. But indirect costs, such as Joe's rent and the other points he raised, are more difficult to evaluate.

Different costing techniques account for business overheads (indirect costs) in different ways. Chapter 12 introduced the basic principles of cost accounting and showed how overheads could be included in product cost using the technique of absorption costing. This technique is required to produce the information necessary to value stocks in accordance with SSAP 9 for reporting of financial performance. This chapter will introduce two further techniques: marginal costing and activity based costing. These are more relevant for planning and decision making purposes.

Before examining these costing techniques, it is useful to consider how costs behave as business volumes change.

Cost behaviour

The various costs incurred by a business change in different ways as business activity changes.

Fixed costs

Fixed costs remain unchanged with changes in business activity. Typical examples include staff salaries, property rents and interest payable on loans.

Figure 15.1 Fixed costs

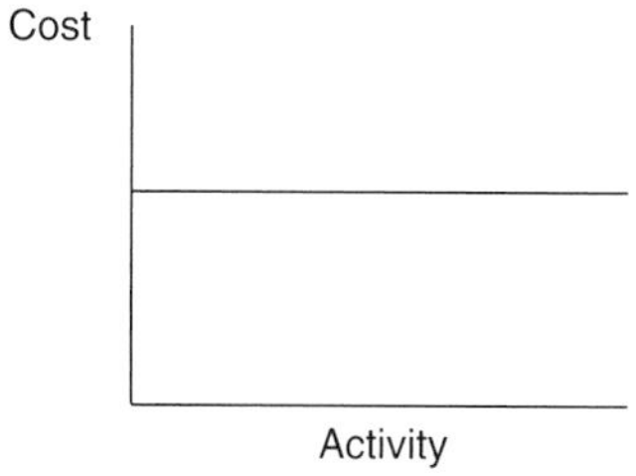

Variable costs

Variable costs change in direct proportion to the level of business activity. Examples include materials used in the manufacture of products, and salespeople's commissions.

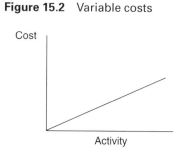

Figure 15.2 Variable costs

Semi-variable costs

Semi-variable costs contain fixed and variable cost elements, e.g. telephone charges include both a line rental, which is fixed cost, and call charges, which are variable.

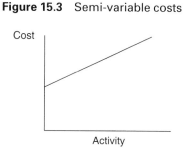

Figure 15.3 Semi-variable costs

Stepped costs

Stepped costs are stable for a range of business volumes but above a certain level of activity they jump to a new level. For example, supervisors become ineffective with wide spans of control and so there comes a point where the recruitment of one extra worker may result in the need for a further supervisor.

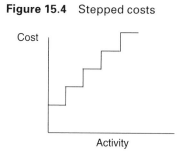

Figure 15.4 Stepped costs

In reality most costs classified as fixed are in fact stepped costs. As activity increases, the current business set-up becomes inadequate for greater capacities and investment in new business premises and operating plant becomes necessary. However, within a particular range of business activity, many costs are fixed at least in the short term.

Care must be taken when classifying costs as fixed or variable.

In the long run all costs are variable as there is always the possibility of discontinuing business activities, and in extreme cases, even the whole business can be closed down.

In the short run most costs are fixed because they become unavoidable, particularly where there is a contractual agreement to incur them. For example, direct workers are only variable costs in the short term if they are paid on a piece-work basis. Where there is a contractual obligation to pay wages on a time-period basis (e.g. an annual salary), wages are a fixed cost in the short term. This is because for many businesses it is often impractical and undesirable to change the size of the work force in line with fluctuations in work load, even when considering periods running into several months. Because of contracts of employment and the time taken to train new workers should activity increase again, most work forces have to be considered fixed for at least several months. Cost analysis will depend on the circumstances, but in the very short term, perhaps only material usage and direct expenses can be considered variable costs.

Another important consideration when classifying items as fixed or variable costs is to clarify the basis on which costs vary. For decision-making purposes, costs are variable if they are affected by the decision to increase or decrease business activity. For example, the cost of electricity for a factory will depend on the power requirement of machines and the number of hours that lighting is required. The power used by machines will vary according to the number of products being produced; the lighting will only vary according to business activity if extra hours of darkness are worked.

Comparing the different classifications of cost

There are two main classifications of cost: one describes whether costs can be attributed to a particular product or not (direct and indirect costs), and the other considers how costs vary with the level of production (fixed and variable costs). The two classifications are clearly closely related:

- Direct costs are generally variable costs.
- Indirect costs will comprise fixed costs but may also include some variable costs.

It is important, however, not to lose sight of the differences between the two types of classification. Variable costs may not be easily attributed to specific products being produced, e.g. electricity charges. Even if each department was separately metered, numerous products may be being worked on in an environment where electricity is being consumed in various ways, including machine power, heating and lighting. It would be difficult and time consuming to relate expenditure on electricity directly to the specific products being produced.

On the other hand, some jobs being worked on may incur a fixed cost that can be related directly to the job. For example, a sub-contractor may insist on a minimum charge for small batches of work.

Total business costs can be calculated using the two classification methods:

$$\text{Total cost} = \text{Direct costs} + \text{Indirect costs.}$$

$$\text{Total cost} = \text{Variable costs} + \text{Fixed costs.}$$

Exercise 15.1 Cost classifications

1 Explain the difference between direct costs and variable costs.
2 Consider the following costs to be incurred next month by a computer assembly plant that is expecting production to increase by 20 per cent to satisfy a surge in demand:
   a piece-work assembly workers
   b vehicle running expenses
   c purchase of visual display units
   d goods received inspectors
   e executive's secretary
   f gardener
   g telephone switchboard operator
   h advertising.

- Classify each cost into fixed, variable and semi-variable costs.
- Classify each cost into direct and indirect.
- Over what time period will each of the fixed costs become variable costs?

Costing techniques

The main costing techniques considered in this chapter are:

- absorption costing
- marginal costing and
- activity based costing.

Absorption costing

The method of including all costs, including fixed costs, in product costs is called **absorption costing.** As described in Chapter 12, there is a need to apportion indirect costs such as rent and rates to production cost centres before calculating overhead absorption rates.

The technique ensures all costs are considered when pricing on a cost plus basis. For external financial reporting purposes, businesses have to use a partial form of absorption costing to value inventories to comply with SSAP 9. Stocks should be valued with a fair proportion of business overheads related to the production function to ensure cost of sales is accurately matched with revenues earned from customers (SSAP 2 'accruals' concept). For financial reporting, distribution and administration expenses must be treated as period costs and charged to the profit and loss account as they are incurred, and so will not be absorbed into stock valuations.

However, some firms do use the total absorption costing technique to price their products so unit costs are calculated outside the formal costing system with elements included for non-manufacturing overheads. Distribution and administration costs are often absorbed as a percentage of factory cost or of sales value.

Illustration

Total Ltd uses the total absorption costing method to price its factory output. The company is budgeting to manufacture and sell 1 000 Red product, 500 Blue product and 2 000 Yellow product. Non-manufacturing overhead for the year is forecast to be £185 000 and this is absorbed as a percentage of factory cost.

Factory costs to comply with SSAP 9 are as follows:

	Red (£)	Blue (£)	Yellow (£)	Total (£)
Direct costs	50 000	40 000	80 000	170 000
Factory indirect costs	40 000	60 000	100 000	200 000
Total factory cost (as per SSAP 9)	90 000	100 000	180 000	370 000

Non-manufacturing overhead absorption rate

$$= \frac{\text{Non-manufacturing overhead}}{\text{Factory cost of output}}$$

$$= \frac{185\,000}{370\,000} = 50\% \text{ of factory cost}$$

Non-manufacturing overhead	45 000	50 000	90 000	185 000
Total product cost	135 000	150 000	270 000	555 000
Cost per unit	£135	£300	£135	

From this example it should be evident that the absorption of non-manufacturing overhead is often on an arbitrary basis. Few of the distribution and administration costs incurred actually vary in line with changes in factory cost or sales value.

Despite the universal use of factory overhead absorption for financial reporting purposes, the technique has serious shortcomings for decision-making purposes, as it does not attempt to explain how costs will change as volumes change. Because some costs are fixed, an additional unit of production will incur less cost than the average unit cost, although this is not always clear to those making decisions.

Exercise 15.2 Absorption costing

Timberworld manufactures quality tables and chairs using traditional manual processes. Production output is measured in terms of dining room suites, of which 30 were made during the month of May. The costs incurred during May were: wood £150 per suite, rent and rates £1 000, power and telephone £650, administration and selling salaries £3 250, motor expenses £600 and direct labour £240 per suite. The business also uses equipment in its workshops that cost £15 000 and is estimated to last ten years.

Tasks

1 *Analyse the costs into direct and indirect costs.*
2 *Calculate total costs for May, and using total absorption costing, calculate the cost of one dining room suite.*
3 *During June the same cost structure applied but 40 dining room suites were made. Calculate total and unit costs for the month.*
4 *Why have different unit costs resulted for May and June?*

Marginal costing

Marginal costing is a valuable tool for decision-making purposes as it considers how costs vary with changes in business activity. Marginal cost is the variable cost of producing a unit at the margin, i.e. the border of current output. It therefore equates to variable elements of cost plus or minus changes to stepped costs if appropriate.

In general:

Marginal cost = variable cost = prime cost + variable overheads and expenses.

An important concept of marginal costing is the **contribution** each unit of production makes towards fixed overheads and business profits (the term 'production' is used here in the context of describing the cost of providing a customer with a good or service):

Contribution = sales price − marginal cost.

For a contribution to be made, the sales price must exceed the marginal cost. Although to make a profit it is necessary that total sales revenues exceeds total costs, an individual sale can be justified provided marginal cost is less than the sales value.

Illustration

Roadrunners & Co. operate a courier service for documents and parcels using small motor vans. The business charges its customers 60p per mile. Fixed costs are £2 000 per month and variable costs amount to 10p per mile. The vehicles travel a fairly consistent 5 000 miles each month, although the business could cope with 8 000 miles a month.

The general manager has been approached by a local company which requires 2 000 miles of courier work each month but is not prepared to pay more than 40p per mile.

Is the new business worth taking on?

	Normal	New – Marginal	Total
Number of miles	5 000	2 000	7 000
	(£)	(£)	(£)
Sales revenue	3 000	800	3 800
Variable cost @ 10p / mile	500	200	700
Contribution	2 500	600	3 100
Fixed costs	2 000	0	2 000
Profit	500	600	1 100

Because the new business incurs no additional fixed overhead, it makes a considerable contribution to fixed overheads and profits (£0.40 − £0.10 = £0.30/mile). In fact profits would more than double by just adding 40 per cent more miles despite prices at 33 per cent below normal levels. There may of course be other considerations to be taken into account before accepting the 40p price. The effect on existing price levels must be considered in case it became known that some customers received preferential rates. In addition, just because the business would make a contribution at 40p does not mean that a better price could not be obtained with more negotiation. As with any other pricing policy, it is important to consider market conditions.

Exercise 15.3 Absorption and marginal costing compared

The Dilton Hotel measures its output in terms of number of guest nights. It provides food and drinks to overnight guests only and has incurred the following costs over the past two trading quarters.

	To June (£)	To September (£)
Food	4 500	6 000
Rent	5 000	5 000
Casual staff	3 600	4 800
Permanent staff	6 000	6 000
Drinks	900	1 200
Laundry	1 350	1 800
Power	2 650	2 650
Depreciation	3 000	3 000

The total number of beds filled each night during the June and September quarters were 900 and 1200 respectively.

Tasks

1 *Using total absorption costing, calculate the average cost per night for one guest during each quarter.*
2 *The hotel is about to launch an off-peak special offer. What is the minimum price that the hotel should charge for a night at the hotel?*
3 *Explain the differences between (1) and (2) above.*

It should be apparent that for decision-making purposes it is important to consider only those costs and benefits that change as a result of making a specific decision, i.e. marginal costs and revenues. It will be a matter of judgement which are **relevant costs** in any given situation.

Illustration

Jill has come to the end of another day selling fruit and vegetables at the local market. She purchased 50 kg of bananas for £20 and has sold 45 kg of bananas at 1kg for £1. The remainder will not keep till next market day. What is the minimum price Jill should charge for the remaining 5 kg of bananas?

The bananas are an example of a **sunk cost** as they have already been incurred. The saying 'don't throw good money after bad' is based on the principle that sunk costs are not relevant to deciding future action. Jill should therefore accept whatever price she can obtain for the bananas.

Exercise 15.4 Relevant costs

A factory extension has been started with £25 000 costs incurred to date and with further costs estimated to be £100 000. Total future benefits from having the larger factory are now thought to be £100 000 less than the £200 000 originally forecasted. If work is terminated, compensation of £20 000 will have to be paid to the builder. State with reasons the recommended course of action.

Costs that will be incurred irrespective of the current decision are **unavoidable costs.** For example, a potential job will result in sales revenue of £80 but will cost £50 in material and £50 in labour paid to a salaried worker who would otherwise be left idle. It would appear that the product would provide a negative contribution of £20 and so should not be accepted. However, the salary is an unavoidable cost and if the job was not accepted the business would have to accept a net cost of £50 anyway. Taking the relevant cost of £50 for materials from revenue of £80 gives a positive contribution of £30. The firm would be £30 better off by accepting the job.

Exercise 15.5 Sunk costs and unavoidable costs

Troy Engineering Ltd has incurred sales and design expenses of £10 000 to secure work from British Aerospace, although the £59 000 contract has not yet been signed. The contract will require £30 000 of direct labour paid on a piece-work basis. Fixed overheads will be absorbed at 50 per cent of direct labour cost. Unfortunately the materials for the contract have mistakenly already been purchased for £30 000, and to return them to the supplier would involve a 20 per cent handling charge. The managing director wants to sign the contract because factory capacity is under utilised, but he has not been able to increase the contract price. Advise the managing director on the relevant costs of accepting the contract.

Opportunity cost is a measure of the benefit forgone by following one course of action rather than another. Opportunity costs are not recorded by the costing system, but they are relevant to decision making.

Illustration

A factory is operating at full capacity generating sales revenues from a single product of £5 000 per week, with variable costs of £2 000 and fixed costs of £2 000. A new product line could be introduced that would require 10 per cent of factory capacity and would generate sales revenues of £1 000 with variable costs of £750.

If the new product replaced 10 per cent of current production, then contribution lost from the original product would be 10 per cent × (£5 000 – £2 000) = £300. This is the opportunity cost of introducing the new

product.

Contribution from the new product would be £1 000 – £750 = £250.

The opportunity cost is greater than the contribution from the new product, so on a purely financial basis the new product should not be launched.

The golden rule is to take decisions that *maximise contribution*. Decision-making situations where the use of marginal costing may be appropriate include:

1 special prices for extra business,
2 dropping an existing product,
3 changing product mix to maximise profit where resources are limited, and
4 whether to make or buy a product.

Exercise 15.6 Special sales price

Sharnham Engineering has budgeted the following figures assuming an 80 per cent utilisation of its factory capacity.

	(£ '000)
Sales (150 000 units)	600
Direct production costs	300
Factory overheads	100
Administration and distribution costs	100
Total costs	500
Net profit	100

Direct production costs and 30 per cent of administration and distribution are variable costs.

A potential customer has offered work that would use the remaining 20 per cent of factory capacity. A firm order is conditional on a sales price of £3.00 per unit.

Tasks

1 *What is the budgeted total cost of each unit?*
2 *Calculate the contribution of additional units sold for £3.00 each.*
3 *Should the firm accept the order? Explain your answer.*
4 *Calculate the net profit assuming the order is accepted.*

Exercise 15.7 Dropping an existing product

Fagin's make a range of products similar to those provided by its competitors. The business has capacity for 500 of each product every month. Unfortunately, resources are dedicated to each type of product and cannot be transferred to alternative uses. Fixed costs are £17 500 per month.

Product	Red (£)	Blue (£)	White (£)	Orange (£)	Purple (£)
Direct materials	5	10	7	20	14
Direct labour	10	15	8	10	6
Prime cost	15	25	15	30	20
Fixed overhead apportioned	5	5	5	10	10
Total unit cost	20	30	20	40	30
Profit on cost @ 20%	4	6	4	8	6
Selling price	24	36	24	48	36

An increase in the number of competitors has led to changes in market prices, and Fagin's can no longer charge prices calculated on a cost plus basis.

Market price – (£)	25	45	20	34	18

Tasks

1 *Calculate Fagin's profit assuming 500 units of each product are sold at the new market prices.*
2 *On what basis could Fagin's maximise its profit?*
3 *What is the maximum profit Fagin's can earn?*

Exercise 15.8 Terminating an operation

The directors of Parts Nationwide Ltd, a machinery components distributor, have been presented with the following information at their recent board meeting:

Profit and loss for year 3	Leeds (£'000)	Birmingham (£'000)	Reading (£'000)	Caerphilly (£'000)
Sales	480	350	250	230
Cost of goods	330	245	180	170
Gross profit	150	105	70	60
Sales costs	40	30	35	20
Local administration	30	20	30	20
Head office allocation	50	35	25	25
Net profit	30	20	(20)	(5)

The results are similar to the previous year's, and there seems little prospect of improvement in the foreseeable future. Unfortunately, sales depend upon maintaining a branch presence, so sales are not transferable to another sales office. Most of the head office costs are fixed, but it is estimated that £40 000 is directly variable on the number of branches head office has to service.

Task

Should the directors terminate activities at Reading and Caerphilly?

Exercise 15.9 Make or buy

Latimer Mouldings calculates its product costs by adding 200 per cent of direct labour to prime cost to cover factory overhead. Budgeted overheads are £80 000 fixed and £60 000 variable.

Stock item RT123 is valued at £30 per unit, including £9 of direct material. The purchasing manager can obtain the same item from a local sub-contracting firm for £25.

Task

Should the firm make or buy the item?

Exercise 15.10 Make or buy

Minnow Computing designs and manufactures most of the items used to assemble its state of the art laptop computers. It is agreed that the next product development should include an updated floppy disk drive to speed up data transfer.

The cost of developing and manufacturing 20 000 of the new drives is as follows:

	Total £
Research and development – 3 000 hours @ internal charge rate £30	90 000
Direct materials	150 000
Direct labour	50 000
Factory overheads	150 000

The 3 000 hours of research and development time could otherwise be contracted out to clients at £50 an hour. Of the factory overhead, 60 per cent comprises fixed costs.

Task

Should Minnow make or buy, assuming comparable disks could be purchased for £19 each?

Limiting factors

There may be situations where there are inadequate resources to satisfy the demand for a firm's products. These resource factors include skilled labour, specialist materials and plant capacity. Where just one factor is limited, the usual marginal costing principles can be used. More complex situations involving more than one limiting factor require linear programming techniques, which are described in Chapter 18.

The objective is to find a product mix that maximises contribution using only the resources available. To maximise contribution, it is necessary to find the products that generate the *largest contribution per unit of the limiting factor*.

Illustration

Greek Times produces and sells just two products, Alpha and Beta. Each month the business can sell 100 units of each product. However, the amount of raw material available is limited to 200 kg, and so full production is not possible. Fixed costs per month amount to £4 000.

	Alpha	Beta
Selling price – (£)	100	100
Direct costs:		
Materials (£)	20	40
Labour (£)	40	20

Material cost £20 per kilogram.

1 Advise on the product mix that will maximise contribution to overheads and profit.
2 Produce a profit statement to show the contribution and net profit from this product mix.

Solution

1 Identify the limiting factor – it is stated that only 200 kg of raw material is available.
2 Calculate the contribution per unit for each product.

	Alpha (£)	Beta (£)
Selling price	100	100
Variable costs	60	60
Contribution	40	40

3 Calculate the contribution per unit of limiting factor and rank the products accordingly.

	Alpha	Beta
Contribution per unit	£40	£40
Number of kilograms used	1kg	2kg
Contribution per kilogram	£40	£20
Rank	1st	2nd

4 Maximise production of the highest ranking products. All Alpha units that can be sold should be produced. The next step is to identify the amount of limiting factor remaining before deciding on the production quantity of the next product. In this case 100 kg of material remaining is sufficient to produce just 50 units of Beta.

	Alpha	Beta
Number of units	100	50
Material used	100kg	100kg
Material remaining	100kg	0

The optimum product mix is therefore 100 Alphas and 50 Betas.

A profit statement can now be produced to show the contribution and net profit expected from this product mix.

Profit statement

	Alpha (£)	Beta (£)	Total (£)
Sales	10 000	5 000	15 000
Direct costs			
Materials	2 000	2 000	4 000
Labour	4 000	1 000	5 000
Contribution	4 000	2 000	6 000
Fixed overheads			4 000
Net profit			2 000

Exercise 15.11 Limiting factor

ColourLabs is planning to produce and sell the following products in the next month:

	Red	Orange	Blue	Green
Selling price £	30	30	30	30
Direct costs:				
Materials £	14	4	10	8
Labour £ @ £4 / hour	6	16	10	12
Number of units planned	200	200	200	200

The number of labour hours available is limited to 1500.

Tasks

1 *Determine the production mix that will maximise contribution.*
2 *Calculate the maximum contribution possible.*

Exercise 15.12 Limiting factor

A clothes manufacturer can sell more products than its factory can produce. The business can hire sufficient workers, but machine capacity is limited to 3 500 hours per month.

Initial plan	Overall (£)	Jacket (£)	Suit (£)	Top (£)
Selling price	40.0	30.0	50.0	10.0
Costs per unit:				
Direct materials	20.0	16.0	20.0	2.0
Direct labour	10.0	10.0	15.0	2.0
Fixed overheads absorbed on labour cost	5.0	5.0	7.5	1.0
	Nos	Nos	Nos	Nos
Machine hours/unit	4	1	3	2
Number of units planned per month	1000	500	200	1000

Task

Calculate the maximum profit possible.

Exercise 15.13 Limiting factor

K. Wood Ltd manufactures household items made of Kauri, a tree indigenous to New Zealand. Supplies of the wood are limited as felling of live Kauri trees is now outlawed, but the business can obtain 40 cubic metres of wood for the current year.

The product range:

	Occasional table	Wooden bowl	Picture frames	Cabinet
Resources required:				
Kauri – cubic metres	0.10	0.01	0.02	0.20
Direct labour hours	5.0	0.80	2.0	7.0
Sundry variable materials £	1.50	0.20	0.50	4.00
Sales information:				
Forecast number of sales p.a.	200	400	300	100
Sales price	£150	£12	£30	£250

Kauri can be obtained for £100 per cubic metre and labour costs £7 per hour.

Task

Calculate the maximum contribution possible.

Break-even point

One of the most important financial targets that businesses must attain if they are not to fail is the level of sales required to pay for all costs. This is called the break-even point. At this point, total sales value equals total cost.

The break-even point can be found by a graphical approach or by calculation using the following equation:

$$\text{The break-even point in sales units} = \frac{\text{Fixed costs}}{\text{Contribution per unit}}$$

Illustration

John Newell is preparing a business plan to present to his bank manager to raise finance for a new restaurant. He believes he can realistically expect 80 customers a week but he wants to show how many customers he needs to attract each week to break even. Fixed costs are estimated to be £480 a week and a typical three-course meal priced at £12 will incur variable costs of £4.

Graphical approach
A table is first prepared of costs and revenues for a number of activity levels (see the next page).

Number of customers	Fixed Cost (£)	Variable Cost (£)	Total Cost (£)	Sales revenue (£)
0	480	0	480	0
25	480	100	580	300
50	480	200	680	600
75	480	300	780	900
100	480	400	880	1 200

A break-even chart is drawn with lines for fixed cost, total cost and total revenue (Figure 15.5).

Figure 15.5 John Newell – break-even chart

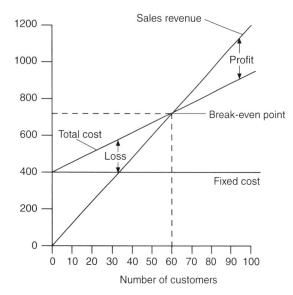

The break-even point is where the sales revenue and total cost lines intersect. The distance between the revenue line and total cost line at other activity levels is a measure of the total profit or loss that could be expected. For example, at 40 customers per week the total cost line is £160 more than the sales revenue line, indicating a loss of that amount.

Calculation method

The contribution per customer, which is sales price less marginal cost, has to be calculated first.

Contribution per customer = sales price – variable cost

$$= £12 - £4 \quad = £8$$

Hence

Break even point $= \dfrac{£480}{£8} = 60$ customers per week.

Sales value at break even = number of customers × sales price

$$= 60 × £12 \quad = £720.$$

A target profit

The same techniques can be used to find the level of activity required to achieve a target level of profit. Using the graphical approach, the number of customers can be calculated by finding the point where the distance between the sales revenue and total cost lines is the desired amount.

To calculate the level of sales needed to attain a target profit:

$$\text{Number of sales units} = \frac{\text{fixed cost} + \text{profit}}{\text{contribution per unit}}$$

John Newell is aiming to make £200 profit each week so his target volume is:

$$\text{Number of sales units} = \frac{£480 + £200}{£8} = 95 \text{ customers per week.}$$

Margin of safety

The margin of safety is a measure of actual or planned sales in relation to the break-even point.

$$\text{Margin of safety} = \frac{\text{Sales} - \text{Break-even sales}}{\text{Break-even sales}} × 100\%$$

It can be measured using sales quantities or sales values.

For John Newall's planned number of customers:

$$\text{Margin of safety} = \frac{80 - 60}{60} × 100\% = 33.3\%$$

A large margin of safety minimises the risk of not being able to cover all costs. A small margin of safety shows that continued profitability is highly sensitive to changes in sales levels, with a risk of making losses if sales were to fall.

Exercise 15.14 Break-even, target profit and margin of safety

Kirsty is planning to set up in business as a mobile car mechanic. Her van and equipment will involve fixed costs of £720 a month. She intends to charge customers an average of £80 for a service, which will cost her £20 in materials. She hopes to service 20 cars a month.

Tasks

1 *Draw a break-even chart based on data for 5, 10, 15 and 20 customers per month.*
2 *Identify the break-even point. How many customers must she attract to cover her costs?*

3 If Kirsty needed to draw £420 a month out of the business on which to live, how many cars must she service?

4 If Kirsty was able to service 20 cars a month, what would be her margin of safety based on (i) cost and (ii) cost plus the amount she needs to pay herself?

5 Confirm your answers to questions (2) and (3) by calculation.

Exercise 15.15 Break-even calculations

Insert the missing figures in the grid:

	Firm A	Firm B	Firm C	Firm D	Firm E	Firm F	Firm G	Firm H	Firm I
Sales quantity	150			600		900			
Selling price £		2		3				8	
Total sales £	1800	6000							5000
Unit variable cost £	6		10		100		7	6	
Total variable cost £				1200	10000	2700			1000
Total contribution £		2000	5000		10000				
Fixed cost £		1000	2500		2000	4900	2100		
Profit £	600				1400	210	150	2000	
Break-even quantity			500				700	800	2500
Margin of safety %			100	0		10			

Exercise 15.16 Break-even and evaluation

CountyBus is a bus operator providing services between small towns in the East Midlands. With many people preferring the convenience of the motor car, this is not a lucrative business to be in. The company must run buses only on routes that are commercially viable, and this is tested in the first instance by identifying the break-even point for a bus route.

The costs for a typical 20-mile route are as follows:

	£
Depreciation of bus	13
Fuel for an empty bus	4
Extra fuel for a full bus	4
Road tax and insurance	2
Wages for bus driver	18
Company administration costs	10
Maintenance	5
	56

A bus ticket is sold for 10p for every mile travelled, so for a passenger travelling the whole 20-mile route a ticket would cost £2.00. Each bus has a capacity for 50 passengers.

Tasks

1 Analyse operating expenditure into fixed and variable costs.

2 Draw a break-even chart for a 20-mile route.

3 How many passengers are needed on average for the bus route to break-even?

4 If 80 per cent of the seats were filled for the whole route, how much profit would be made?

5 Bus companies sell season tickets and also concessionary tickets to students and pensioners that cut the cost of travel. What is the logic behind the price discounting?

Exercise 15.17 Break-even and evaluation

Premier Sound and Ultra Sound both manufacture high quality hi-fi turntables that sell for identical prices.

Premier uses traditional techniques that require manually operated machines and hand-finished wooden surrounds. For its last financial year, the company made £20 000 profit on turnover of £162 000. Operating at 90 per cent of capacity, the 900 turntables it produced and sold were more than enough to cover its fixed costs of £52 000.

Ultra has invested in the latest automated machinery that has capacity for 4 000 turntables. At full capacity the company would make profits of £190 000, but due to disappointing demand the 2 500 sold and produced during the past year resulted in a profit of £25 000 on total sales of £450 000.

Tasks

1 For Premier Sound, calculate the variable cost of a turntable.

2 *For Ultra Sound, calculate the variable cost for each turntable and the company's total fixed costs.*
3 *Calculate the break-even point for each company.*
4 *For each company calculate its margin of safety based on these annual results.*
5 *Evaluate the cost structures of Premier and Ultra, giving consideration to their respective sales potential.*

Marginal costing and absorption costing compared

Despite the relevance of marginal costs to decision making, it is also important to recognise certain weaknesses of the technique. Marginal costing looks at a lower cost base than absorption costing and so encourages the acceptance of work that would otherwise look less favourable. This is valid only if it can be argued that a proposition is a special case that will lead to contribution that would otherwise be lost.

A major advantage of absorption costing is that although it is insensitive to market forces, it ensures that all costs are considered. The use of marginal costs may mislead management into setting selling prices that are insufficient to cover fixed costs. This is an important issue that marginal costing does not address. In practice, accountants will often encourage sales personnel to quote prices based on total cost. This is in the belief that if marginal costs were freely available within the business, selling prices would creep downwards as more and more orders were justified on a marginal costing basis.

Despite these problems, decision making is best undertaken using relevant costs that are founded on the principles of marginal costing.

Activity based costing

Traditional costing methods were designed when direct labour was a significant element of total product cost. New technologies have increased the proportion of indirect costs.

A study by accountancy firm Coopers and Lybrand found that most firms put considerable effort into absorbing direct labour cost into product cost, despite this representing a small proportion of total cost. The accurate allocation of indirect costs had received little attention, despite their significant size for most businesses.

Study findings were as follows:

Cost element	Proportion of manufacturing cost (%)	Proportion of effort to allocate (%)
Material	50	10
Labour	10	75
Indirect	40	15

Using absorption costing, indirect costs are still predominantly recovered on a direct wage basis that leads to incorrect total product cost, and hence is a misleading basis for decision making.

New manufacturing techniques have led to:

- a reduction in labour cost
- an increase in capital costs and other indirect costs
- a work force that is in reality a fixed cost in the short term with the move towards salaried staff.

As overheads have increased, there has been a tendency to accept them as being largely uncontrollable. Cost accounting has had difficulty explaining the usefulness of overheads incurred, and for many firms the control of overheads is confined to simple expenditure variances to budget. As budgets are often set with reference to previous cost levels, this has reinforced the status quo. Even where overheads are overspent to budget, there has sometimes been a tendency to explain variances as inaccuracies in the budget setting process.

In recognising that costs are related to business activity, the principles of a new costing technique were proposed by Cooper and Kaplan in 1987. As a result, activity based costing (ABC) is now being introduced in a whole range of organisations, including manufacturing, service and not-for-profit organisations such as universities and hospitals.

ABC attempts to explain the link between products and their demand for activities that incur costs for the business. The ABC process comprises five main stages:

1 Identify the activities that take place in an organisation.
2 Determine the 'cost driver' for each major activity.
3 Create a cost centre/cost pool for each major activity.
4 Calculate a cost driver rate for each cost pool.
5 Trace the cost of activities to products according to a product's demand for activities (as measured by the cost drivers).

The activities identified will depend upon the nature of the business. For an independent supermarket, the main activities may be to:

- purchase goods
- store goods
- display goods
- process goods – bakery and meat counter
- process sales.

The identification of appropriate cost drivers as a proxy measure of activity is not always easy. Traditional approaches to product costing have often assumed production quantity to be the true indication of business activity. On this basis, overhead is charged to products in direct proportion to the number of items being produced or the number of hours worked. This is unlikely to be an accurate description of how costs are actually incurred. The time taken by workers to familiarise themselves with a new product and to set up machinery for a new production run will be the same for a batch of 10 as it is for a batch of 100. Traditional cost systems tend to overstate the cost of high-volume orders, and understate the cost of low-volume orders.

It is necessary to look at the cause of a cost and how it varies. For example, the cost spent on production control may depend far more on the number of jobs flowing through the factory and the number of production departments they go through than on the absolute size of each job.

Many activities are subject to several cost drivers, e.g. delivery vehicles incur cost depending on how long the journey is, how large the lorry is, how many customers have to be visited, etc.

Specimen cost drivers

Activities	Cost drivers
Maintenance	Number of machines, area of buildings
Stores	Number of stores issues, number of stores receipts
Engineering support	Number of engineering changes, number of products
Credit control	Number of customers, number of invoices
Goods in inspection	Number of suppliers, number of purchase orders
Quality audit	Volume of production
Training	Staff turnover, number of changes to work practices
Purchase ledger accounting	Number of suppliers, number of invoices
Wages dept	Number of employees, number of different pay rates
Personnel	Number of employees, number of welfare initiatives
Customer services	Number of orders, number of quality defects
Boxing and shipping	Volume of production, number of products

For each activity it is necessary to identify the appropriate **cost pool**. A cost pool may be equivalent to a traditional cost centre. Obviously the more cost centres are created, the greater is the degree of accuracy in identifying costs to

cost drivers. For example, an accounts department will have separate sections for wages, purchase ledger and credit control. Looking at the chart above, it will be found that each section is subject to a different cost driver. It is easier to calculate the respective cost driver rates if the individual sections are recognised as separate cost centres. For departments that are subject to more than one cost driver, it may be necessary for staff to record their time against activity codes.

As departments interact with one another in the processing of business transactions, it will not be uncommon to find different departments subject to the same cost drivers. For example, in placing a purchase order with a supplier, costs may be incurred in the originating department, the purchase department, goods inwards, stores and the accounts department. All may share the number of purchase orders processed as a cost driver.

Exercise 15.18 Cost drivers

Consider two businesses that produce fruit pies:

Company A produces 20 000 identical pies for one retail chain.

Company B produces 20 000 pies of various types and sizes. The maximum delivery to each of the independent delicatessens it supplies is 50 pies. The maximum production run is for 100 items.

Tasks

1 *Suggest the main activities for a pie maker.*
2 *How might costs vary between the two companies described?*
3 *What are the possible cost drivers?*

Cost driver rates are calculated from the value of cost pools and the cost driver volume.

$$\text{Cost driver rate} = \frac{\text{Cost pool}}{\text{Cost driver volume}}$$

Illustration

The cost of running a firm's warehouse is £80 000 per annum, and during that period it satisfies 50 000 stores requisitions from the factory. It has been decided that the number of stores issue notes is an appropriate cost driver.

$$\text{Cost per stores requisition} = \frac{£80000}{50000} = £1.60$$

The costs allocated to **product cost** are based on the number of cost drivers attributed to the product.

Product cost from each cost pool = Number of transactions $\times$ Cost driver rate.

In the example of warehousing costs, if product Alpha had required 15 stores requisitions whilst it was being produced:

Stores cost for product Alpha = 15 $\times$ £1.60 = £24

The sum of all charges from cost pools gives the total indirect cost allocated to products.

The process of ABC identifies resources *demanded* by a particular activity, but it is important to recognise the distinction between the demand for resources and changes in actual expenditure. For example, the number of check-out workers required at a supermarket could reasonably be said to be driven by the number of customers per hour. If management wanted to ascertain the increased level of staffing required to coincide with a special low price promotion, there may be more activity and hence more demand for check-out resources, but costs will only change if further workers are actually employed. So although ABC results in an average cost driver rate, actual expenditure is more likely to move in steps as and when there is a perceived need to change the level of resources used.

Cost driver rates will be influenced in a similar way with the inclusion of long-term variable overheads in the cost pool. For example, the cost of a purchasing manager can be allocated to the purchasing cost pool for which an appropriate cost driver may be the number of purchase orders placed. The cost per purchase order will therefore include part of the purchasing manager's salary. Hence a cost driver rate is not a marginal cost.

Although ABC displays some similarities to absorption costing in that it is an overhead inclusive cost as opposed to a short-term variable cost, it is important to appreciate that the technique works on the concept that nearly all costs are variable in the long run. It distinguishes between the following three categories of overhead.

Short-term variable costs are traditionally classified as indirect costs, although they are variable in the short term. Electricity charges used to power machinery is an example that should be allocated to the products using a cost driver based on production volumes, such as machine hours.

Long-term variable costs are those costs that are recognised to vary only over the long term with business activity. This category includes the vast majority of indirect costs and should be traced to products using a transaction-based cost driver. Support services will make up a large part of the costs and will include maintenance,

welfare, administration and distribution, none of which experience costs that vary directly with the volume of production. For example, the cost of running the factory stores, because most of the costs are indirect salaries, will change gradually with changes in the volume of stock movements. The number of stores issue notes is an example of a transaction-based cost driver that would be appropriate for this cost pool.

Fixed costs are recognised by ABC as costs that will not change with levels of activity. This should be a small category. Most costs that have traditionally been considered fixed do vary even if very slowly. Take the cost of the company audit or the salary of the managing director; it is difficult to see either remaining unchanged after a fundamental change in activity. Fixed costs should not be allocated to products, but should remain as a final deduction before calculating business profit.

One of the greatest benefits of activity based costing is the understanding it provides that activity causes cost. Whilst indirect costs may not change in the short term, they do over the long term. This has led to a new branch of management theory called Activity Based Management. By concentrating on reducing activity for any given level of output, it should result in reduced costs. ABC concentrates effort on the improvement of business processes rather than pursuing the decreasing returns of labour efficiency exercises. By highlighting the reasons for indirect costs there is the possibility of controlling them rather than accepting them as fixed.

Illustration – Activity based costing

ABC Engineering Ltd manufactures three products that are very similar but do have cosmetic differences. Products A, B and C are produced in batch sizes of 1 000 units, 100 units and 10 units respectively.

Product	Nos. of units produced	Direct labour cost (£)	Direct material (£)	Total machine hours	Number of production runs	Number of stores requisitions
A	10 000	20 000	20 000	5 000	10	20
B	10 000	20 000	20 000	5 000	100	200
C	10 000	20 000	20 000	5 000	1 000	2 000
	60 000	60 000	15 000	1 110	2 220

Long-term variable overheads

	Cost driver	£
Material handling costs	Stores requisitions	22 200
Production planning, set up and supervision	Production runs	166 500
Machine depreciation and maintenance	Machine hours	75 000
		263 700

1 Calculate the unit cost of each product assuming factory overhead is absorbed on a direct labour cost basis.
2 Calculate the unit cost of each product using activity based costing.

Solution

1 Overhead absorption rate $= \dfrac{£263700}{£60000}$

$= £4.395$ per £1 of direct wages.

	A (£)	B (£)	C (£)	Total (£)
Prime cost	40 000	40 000	40 000	120 000
Overhead absorbed – direct wages × £4.395	87 900	87 900	87 900	263 700
	127 900	127 900	127 900	383 700
Number of units	10 000	10 000	10 000	30 000
Cost per unit based absorption costing	£12.79	£12.79	£12.79	

2 Activity based costing

Cost driver rates:

Materials handling $= \dfrac{£22200}{2220} = £10$ per stores requisition.

Set up, etc. $= \dfrac{£166500}{1110} = £150$ per production run.

Machine costs $= \dfrac{£75000}{15000} = £5$ per machine hour.

	A (£)	B (£)	C (£)	Total (£)
Prime cost	40 000	40 000	40 000	120 000
Long-term variable overhead				
Material handling costs	200	2 000	20 000	22 200
Production planning, set up and supervision	1 500	15 000	150 000	166 500
Machine depreciation and maintenance	25 000	25 000	25 000	75 000
Total overhead	26 700	42 000	195 000	263 700
Total cost	66 700	82 000	235 000	383 700
Number of units	10 000	10 000	10 000	
Cost per unit	£6.67	£8.20	£23.5	

Unit costs vary greatly between the two costing methods. Traditional absorption costing results in identical unit costs for all three products, whereas ABC has differentiated between products on the basis of their demand for support services. ABC has recognised that it costs less to produce in large batches than in smaller ones.

Exercise 15.19 Activity based costing for a manufacturing business

DEF Engineering Ltd makes three products, the D, E and F. The data for each product is as follows:

Product	Nos. of units produced	Direct labour cost (£)	Direct material (£)	Total machine hours	Number of production runs	Number of stores requisitions
D	2 000	9 920	20 000	10 000	100	20
E	5 000	75 500	90 000	5 000	50	50
F	6 000	53 500	72 000	12 000	500	1 000
		138 920	182 000	27 000	650	1 070

Long-term variable overheads

	Cost driver	(£)
Sales, distribution and customer services	Number of customers	48 150
Production planning, set up and supervision	Production runs	71 500
Machine depreciation and maintenance	Machine hours	54 000
		173 650

Tasks

1 *Calculate the unit cost of each product assuming factory overhead is absorbed on a direct labour cost basis.*
2 *Calculate the unit cost of each product using activity based costing.*
3 *Evaluate the results of the two methods.*

Exercise 15.20 Activity based costing – cost of suppliers

The costs of various departments associated with the purchase of goods and services from other businesses have been analysed as follows:

Department	Activity based on		
	Annual cost (£)	Number of suppliers (%)	Other 'cost drivers' (%)
Purchasing department	100 000	20	80
Goods received	50 000	15	85
Stores and inventory control	150 000	10	90
Purchase ledger	80 000	40	60
Internal audit	60 000	25	75

The business used 400 different suppliers last year.

A cost efficiency exercise to rationalise the supplier base has cut the number of suppliers to 250.

Tasks

1 Suggest reasons why the number of suppliers might be a 'cost driver' for each of the departments above.
2 Based on the figures provided, what annual cost savings might be achieved?
3 Explain why the annual savings might be higher or lower than this calculation suggests.

Exercise 15.21   Activity based costing – cost of customers

A business is investigating the costs incurred by those departments that are involved in obtaining and processing sales orders. The business sold 12 200 items last year at a fixed selling price of £500 after production costs of £300.

Department	Activity based on		
	Annual cost (£)	Number of customers (%)	Other cost drivers (%)
Sales department	478 000	50	50
Customer service	180 000	40	60
Distribution	300 000	50	50
Stores and despatch	200 000	35	65
Sales ledger	80 000	60	40
General management	300 000	10	90

The business has 3 000 customers, many only requiring one or two units a year. Business from large customers is being lost to competitors who offer substantial discounts for larger orders.

An analysis of sales for the last year revealed the following:

Units	Number of customers	Total number of units
1	500	500
2	700	1 400
3	600	1 800
5	700	3 500
10	500	5 000
Total	3 000	12 200

Tasks

1 Why might the number of customers be a cost driver for each of the departments listed?
2 Suggest one other cost driver for each department.
3 Calculate the total of all cost pools associated with the number of customers cost driver.
4 Calculate for each level of sales, the contribution to profit and other overheads (after deducting costs relating to the number of customers cost driver) that each customer provides.
5 Assuming the same analysis of sales for next year with sales turnover budgeted at £6.1 million, design a pricing scheme for each level of business so that each unit sold provides the same contribution to other overheads and profits.

Exercise 15.22   Activity based costing – service industry

The manager of the BlueSky travel agency is reviewing the financial performance of the business for the past year. The agency earns a standard 10 per cent commission on all holidays booked.

	£
Sales commissions	200 000
Staff salaries	140 000
Property related costs	30 000
Communication and administration costs	20 000
Total costs	190 000
Profit	10 000

Analysis of time spent by BlueSky's travel advisors:

Activity	(%)
Holiday booking and associated paperwork	10
Laying out brochures and organising the shop window	10
Giving general advice to potential customers	40
Training and researching	20
Idle	20
	100

Experience shows that during periods when staff are busy giving advice and price quotes, actual holidays booked are correspondingly high. Although idle time looks high, the manager considers this unavoidable to ensure proper service during busier times. In fact the staff have been complaining about the amount of work they have to put into researching some of the more obscure holiday plans.

Tasks

1   The following cost drivers have been identified:
      Number of holiday products offered.
      Number of holidays booked.
    Which cost driver is appropriate to each of the activities identified above?
2   Calculate the value of staff salaries to be allocated to each activity cost pool (absorb idle time into the other categories).
3   The agency deals with a wide range of holidays:

	Number of different holidays offered or researched	Number of holidays booked	Sales value for the year (£)
Package holiday to a European resort	50	1 600	140 000
Long haul package	10	120	30 000
Specialist adventure trips	10	120	10 000
Independent traveller – individual itinerary	40	60	10 000
USA fly drive	10	100	10 000

Using cost driver rates based on this information, calculate staff wages to be allocated to each type of holiday.

4   Explain how this ABC information could be used.
5   Explain how the following principles of activity based costing have been satisfied in this case study:
    ■ allocation of costs to cost pools
    ■ identification of cost drivers
    ■ product demand for resources based on cost drivers
    ■ the emphasis on demand for resources rather than direct changes in expenditure levels.

Summary

Three main costing techniques have been explained in this chapter. Absorption costing is a legal requirement for the valuation of stocks and satisfies the financial reporting concept of matching costs with sales revenues. It is therefore the method adopted by most routine product costing systems. Marginal costing and activity based costing tend to be used on an ad hoc basis as management techniques to aid decision making. Marginal costing is appropriate for short-term decision making where the knowledge of cost behaviour can maximise contribution to overheads and profits. Activity based costing is used to help understand long-term cost structures for reviewing business strategy.

Further reading

Management Accounting, published monthly by the Chartered Institute of Management Accountants.

Leslie Chadwick, *Management Accounting*, Routledge, 1993.

David Crowther, *Managing Accounting for Business*, Stanley Thornes, 1996.

Colin Drury, *Management Accounting Handbook*, Butterworth Heinemann, 1996.

Colin Drury, *Management and Cost Accounting*, 4th edition, International Thompson Business Press, 1996.

T. Lucey, *Management Accounting*, 4th edition, DP Publications, 1996.

Sri Srikanthan and Keith Ward, *Management Accounting for Financial Decisions*, Butterworth Heinemann, 1991.

16 Financial planning framework

O n completion of this chapter students should be able to:

- examine and explain the financial planning process
- evaluate the contribution of financial information to the decision-making process.

Long range planning

Financial planning is an integral part of organisational strategy building. The financial plan itself is a set of financial statements that forecast the resource implications of making strategic decisions.

For example, a company whose objective is to become a national supermarket operator may decide to embark on a strategy of smaller company acquisitions. The financial plan for the company will consider the financial resources required and the financial performance that will justify their use.

A financial plan is often based on a model of the business that can be used to test strategic proposals.

For example, a business currently selling 500 units per annum at a price of £100 each is considering a price reduction of 10 per cent that may increase volumes by 15 per cent. What are the financial implications if there is a variable cost of £50 per unit?

		Current (£)		Proposed (£)
Sales	500 × £100	50 000	575 × £90	51 750
Variable cost	500 × £50	25 000	575 × £50	28 750
		25 000		23 000

A planning model may consist of thousands of calculations and underlying assumptions. Many businesses construct the financial plan with the aid of a forecasting model or spreadsheet that can recalculate profit, cash flow and the balance sheet after every change in basic assumptions.

One of the basic concepts of financial planning is that it relates to a fixed time period, whether this is one year or five years. The distance of the planning horizon depends upon the needs of the business and the ability to obtain reliable information about the future. Quantifying resource requirements requires some confidence in underlying assumptions, and so it is important to understand the uncertainties that affect the business.

The biggest uncertainties arise from the external environment in which the business operates and Porter, the management theorist, identifies five forces acting on a firm that affect its future market conditions:

1 threats from new entrants
2 the bargaining power of suppliers
3 the bargaining power of customers
4 the threat from substitute products
5 the extent of competitive pressure.

In addition, the business will operate under the influence of other factors:

■ political – changes in legislation
■ economic – future growth rates and economic cycles
■ social norms – evolving issues that concern the general population, such as the environment
■ technological change.

It is change that makes forecasting so difficult. Most of these external influences will be known with some certainty for the short term, but there must be less confidence over longer periods. Political uncertainty will be heightened at election times. Economic conditions tend to follow cycles of growth and recession. Social attitudes tend to change slowly but the reaction to specific issues can be difficult to judge – for example, the reaction to the BSE scare, or the resistance to town by-passes that cut through unspoilt countryside.

Technological change may render a process or a product obsolete in a very short space of time. For example, in 1990 a considerable amount of artwork for packaging and advertising work was drawn by hand. By 1996, nearly all artwork was produced on computers that enabled images to be transferred in digital form from process to process and from one part of the world to another. Design and printing firms that failed to recognise the need to invest in the required training and physical hardware experienced severe financial problems.

Figure 16.1 External uncertainties and the planning horizon

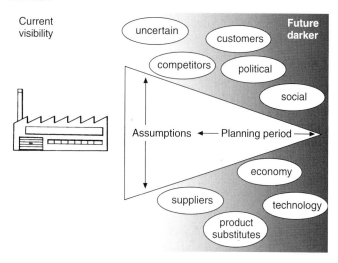

A plan is meaningless if the assumptions on which it is based are inaccurate or poorly evaluated. Although long-term plans will inevitably rely on uncertain assumptions a planning horizon will have to be drawn where reasonable assumptions can no longer be made. This point will vary depending on the type of business.

The financial planning process will highlight the critical uncertainties that need further research or that need to be managed in some way. The construction of a power station is a long-term project which requires a long operating life to pay for itself. The power company's main concerns will be possible changes in electricity demand and in the supply industry itself. Particular concerns will be: demography; technology of products that use electricity; technology for generating electricity, including alternative sources; and political and social attitudes to energy policy. Fortunately most of these factors tend to change fairly slowly, although there has been a big change in attitudes about nuclear power in recent years. Given that the financial evaluation will require perhaps 20 or more years of profitable operation to justify the project, detailed feasibility studies will attempt to quantify items and to measure risk in a systematic fashion. Political risk could perhaps be minimised by reassurances from the government.

Case study

The pubs are a-changing

Public houses must change or gradually die. That is the 1990s message to the pub sector and it is happening at a time when the regulators are dismantling old brewing empires to allow greater competition. But whilst many large operators are sprucing up the Old Red Lion, new operators have also sprung up.

Surrey Free Inns is creating a chain of concept superpubs called the Litton Tree. They are using town centre sites vacated by retailers who have headed for the out-of-town retail parks. The Litton Tree pubs are large and appeal to a wide range of clientele depending on the time of day. During the day they offer food and drink to town centre workers and shoppers, at night the young flock in to the sound of disco music.

A slightly more established newcomer is J D Wetherspoon, which converts well-positioned properties such as old banks into pubs. Another operator, Regent Inns, was floated on the stock exchange in 1993 and is spreading its format fast from its London base into the Midlands and the north of England. Its formula is for large outlets where young singles like to meet and drink.

The trend is for theme pubs and pubs that are family- and female-friendly. The spit and sawdust image is out.

Tasks

1 *What are the main external influences that have caused changes to the pub sector?*
2 *Describe the pubs that are likely to flourish in the early 2000s.*
3 *What strategic initiatives are required by the operators during the rest of the 1990s?*
4 *To construct a long-term financial plan for a pub, what are the main variables that need forecasting?*
5 *What would be an appropriate planning horizon for a pub operator? Explain.*

Whilst long-term planning is required to give strategic direction to the business, it is necessary to prepare plans of shorter duration to satisfy the operational needs of the business.

Most businesses prepare annual budgets that are analysed by month and by cost centre. These provide an immediate target for junior and middle management, and a measure against which actual performance can be monitored and controlled. It is normal practice in many businesses also to prepare a three- or five-year plan in less detail, which is updated annually. This is particularly important where the long-term plan has indicated significant change. Strategic decisions will need to be formulated and financial resource implications will have to be assessed. Although strategic issues should not be addressed only in this annual process, the annual budget encourages an integrated approach to planning for the coming year. Planning is an important part of decision making, and the resulting budget also facilitates subsequent control of the business.

Objectives of long-range planning

1 It should provide an opportunity to examine and state organisational objectives.
2 It should give long-term direction – a process to focus management attention on longer time horizons than current issues. This is particularly important for decisions concerning resource allocation where benefits from capital investment will be repaid over many years.
3 It should provide a framework in which specific short-term budgets (typically one year) can be consistently formulated.
4 It should establish a benchmark of success against

which actual performance can be monitored and controlled.

Disadvantages of planning

1 It is time consuming.
2 It can result in inflexibility and failure to respond to unforeseen changes in position which are not in the plan!

Many businesses attempt to mix the advantages of formal planning (co-ordination, optimisation and control) with a more flexible attitude towards the budget. The plan is frequently reviewed as conditions and needs change, but there is a danger that control is lost as under-performance is built into the next plan update.

Figure 16.2 The planning process

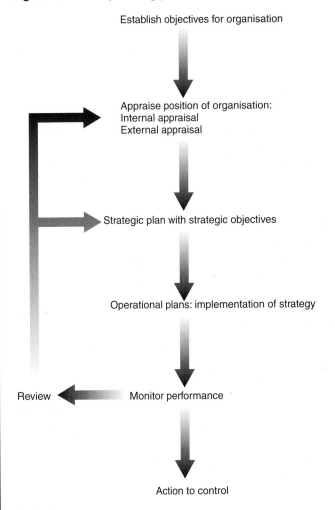

Establish objectives for organisation

Appraise position of organisation:
Internal appraisal
External appraisal

Strategic plan with strategic objectives

Operational plans: implementation of strategy

Monitor performance

Review

Action to control

Objectives

The primary objective of most businesses is to maximise returns to shareholders. This is reinforced by the shareholders' right to appoint the company's directors. It can be argued, though, that financial performance is also consistent with the best interests of other stakeholders. A financially successful company will be secure and be able to raise additional finance for expansion. This is usually in the interests of employees, suppliers and customers in addition to the shareholders.

However, some businesses do have other important stakeholders that affect business objectives. The John Lewis Partnership is primarily concerned for its employees, and so security with adequate salaries will be important.

Position appraisal

An appraisal of the business's current position examines its current performance in the attainment of objectives and assesses where it will be in the future if no action is taken.

For a comprehensive appraisal of the organisation's position, it is useful to have a clear structure for the appraisal process. Numerous techniques have been devised to help provide focus to a position appraisal. These include SWOT analysis, Porter's value chain analysis, the Boston Consulting Group matrix and Gap analysis. Each technique could provide valuable information for building strategies. Emphasis should be placed on future changes and identification of any constraints or limiting factors for which planning may be needed.

Case study

Limiting factors and planning for contraints

Precoat International is a major player in the niche market for prepainted metal sheet used in the construction and consumer durable sectors. The company has unrivalled experience in advising users on the selection and application of precoated materials and a combination of skilled employees and specialist equipment ensure the firm is perceived as a centre of excellence in this specialist area. Compared to painting after the product is assembled, the company's customers benefit from lower costs, enhanced quality, convenience and the avoidance of environmental hazards. Major customers include Candy, Creda, Hoover, Hotpoint and TLG.

When Precoat International wanted to expand its capacity at its plants based in Wales and in Canada, it decided to float its shares on the London Stock

Exchange, raising £1.61m from the issue of new shares. Before committing itself to the expansion it prepared a financial plan based on its confidence about continued growth in the precoated steel market.

Tasks

1 *Capacity of factory plant was a limiting factor in the past but what will be the external influences that constrain growth in the future? As a result of these, what will be the first item to be forecast in any future financial plan/budget?*
2 *If the market for precoated materials slowed down, what additional factors would constrain a strategy of diversification?*

Strategic objectives and strategic plan

Strategic planning provides the catalyst for allocating resources to the various operations of the business. This may lead to the expansion of some operations and the contraction of others. Those operations that provide the best prospects for fulfilling corporate objectives will receive additional investment in terms of management time and financial resources. Operations that show less potential will either be wound down or will be sold off to provide greater resources for other areas.

A programme of expansion is often designed to build upon current operating success and to exploit opportunities that present themselves. The firm may decide to penetrate existing markets to increase market share with price reductions or improvements in the product. It may develop new markets for an existing product or it may develop related products for existing customers.

Diversification into activities currently undertaken by the firm's customers or suppliers is called vertical integration. It may be done on defensive grounds because Porter's five forces appraisal technique has identified threats or weaknesses in the supply chain or in the firm's markets. It may also be done to take advantage of opportunities that provide above-average rates of return to the business. Diversification into unrelated activities could also be made, either to minimise exposure to one industry or because existing activities provide few opportunities to grow.

There may be circumstances where the present industry sector offers promising rewards but the business is not strategically well placed to enjoy them. Perhaps the business needs to be bigger to achieve the economies of scale required to be competitive, or the business may lack the technology or market presence to ensure its success. In these circumstances a merger with another business to redress any inherent weakness may result in a *strategic fit.*

BT and MCI started talks in 1996 to create the telecoms giant Concert. MCI offered access to the US market with potential for faster growth than the UK could offer. BT provided the financial muscle to push for growth far faster than would otherwise have been possible. Together, the merged companies offer the critical mass required to become a global telecoms operator.

A merger or a takeover may be done for the following reasons:

- lack of internal expertise
- an inherent weakness with the current business position
- prohibitive start-up costs
- slow organic growth
- external appraisal shows the need to neutralise a rival company.

Operational plan

The operation plan is a plan of how strategy will be implemented. By its very nature it will be a relatively short-term plan for most businesses and will tend to be quite mechanistic and detailed.

The operational plan is supported with a short-term financial plan, often of one year. It is highly structured with analysis for each cost centre within the organisation's structure. Once some overall assumptions have been laid down by senior management, the preparation of these plans is fairly mechanistic. Annual figures are broken down into time periods – typically of one month (short-term budgets are the subject of Chapter 17).

Monitor, control and review

Financial information is used to monitor and control the business because it has the advantage of quantifying all business factors using just one measure – money. Reasons for money variances can be found from the operating statistics that provide detail and meaning for line managers. Operating statistics should measure in an appropriate way the volume of business throughputs: outputs for a manufacturing firm can be measured in terms of the number of products sold and average price achieved; inputs may include details of material consumed and labour hours used. These statistics can then be compared with assumptions made in the operational plan.

Once reasons for variances from the plan have been established, either a plan of action is required to correct

adverse variances or strategic objectives need to be revised in the light of actual experience.

Strategies for improved financial performance

Accepting that the maximisation of financial returns is the primary business objective, a business must continually grow to provide long-term growth in its share price. As Chapter 2 described, to improve shareholders' wealth the primary measure of management performance is *return on capital employed.* From this measure it is possible to use the following subsidiary ratios to drive specific strategies and operational plans.

Accounting ratio:	Strategic issues
Profitability of sales	pricing cost reduction value enhancement
Utilisation of capital employed	sales growth control of capital employed
Ultimate result: Return on capital employed	expansion contraction

Profitability

The **sales price** directly affects profitability. The setting of prices will generally fall between two extreme positions: prices can be set in relation to product cost, or they can be set in accordance with what the market dictates to achieve a particular marketing objective. Market prices may be accepted passively in the sense that the business charges the 'going rate', or an active approach can be taken to achieve a particular objective. Active strategies include aggressive pricing to increase market share and loss leaders to increase overall sales volume.

Pricing is a valuable marketing tool to differentiate between products and to promote a desired image. Whilst individual products may appear to be making a loss on the prices advocated by marketing specialists, the portfolio of complementary products may achieve the overall financial objective of maximising profit. It is the responsibility of the management accountant to ensure that a price list does achieve financial objectives whilst appreciating the marketing strategies involved.

Although businesses should have a long-term view of pricing policy as part of a profit maximising strategy, marginal costing (Chapter 15) can be particularly valuable in formulating short-term operational plans to ensure contribution to the firm's fixed costs and profits are maximised.

Illustration

The sales director is unhappy with the current selling price of £70 per chair. He has forecast sales volume for a range of selling prices.

Selling price – £		55	60	65	70
Volume – units per month		5 750	5 250	4 500	3 500

Each chair incurs the business in variable costs of £45. Fixed costs are £50 000 per month.

On the basis of this information, at what price should chairs be sold?

Solution

For each alternative it is necessary to identify the total contribution to fixed overheads and profit.

	(£)	(£)	(£)	(£)
At selling price	55	60	65	70
Total sales value	316 250	315 000	292 500	245 000
Variable cost	258 750	236 250	202 500	157 500
Contribution	57 500	78 750	90 000	87 500

The sales price of £65 gives the highest contribution so is the desired price on this information.

Exercise 16.1   Selling price

Jack Caroak forecasts increasing sales volume if he lowers sales price. Volumes above 18 000 units will require an expansion of his premises. Projections of monthly activity:

Selling price – (£)	12	11	10	9
Volume – units	15 000	18 000	22 000	29 000
Factory overheads (£)	30 000	30 000	35 000	35 000

Variable cost is £5 per unit.

Task

On the basis of this information what sales price should Jack be planning for?

In practice exercises such as these are not always easy. The contribution at different prices is directly proportional to the forecast sales volume, which emphasises the value of good research and skilled marketing specialists.

Cost reduction exercises aim to reduce costs by changing product and process design.

Whilst effectiveness is a measure of success at achieving objectives, efficiency can be measured by comparing the inputs and outputs of a process. Cost reduction is an attempt to improve the efficiency of operations without undermining their effectiveness.

Techniques for cost reduction include method study, organisation and methods, variety reduction, value analysis and activity based management.

Method study is a branch of work study that examines the methods used to provide a product or service. The study looks at existing and proposed methods for organising manual tasks, the layout and use of equipment and the scheduling of work through the factory.

Organisation and methods is a similar technique used to improve the efficiency of administrative tasks. Systems of recording and communication are reviewed from an organisation perspective and task benefits are evaluated in the light of resources consumed. This can be a very fruitful area to investigate, bearing in mind the amount of capital and staff employed in administrative functions.

Variety reduction works on the principle that extensive product ranges inevitably increase stock levels of finished goods and component parts. They also require a diversity of skills and knowledge on the part of workers in product design, production and after sales service. The number of products should be reduced if product diversity does not provide a net benefit to the business. The remaining products should have common components wherever possible. Common components can lead to economies of scale with greater automation and bigger batch sizes.

Case study

Saab

When General Motors invested in Saab of Sweden, they reduced operating costs by cutting out many of the thousands of suppliers used. Saab had been using 150 suppliers for car seat components alone. Cost savings were made by sub-contracting to fewer suppliers, who were made more responsible for the finished product.

Without some form of **value analysis** or **value engineering**, products or parts of products may become 'over-engineered'. Value analysis is a process of reviewing the specifications of a product and identifying aspects that attract unnecessary cost. Products should only deliver what the customer is prepared to pay for. In addition, components of a product should be engineered with a common target life span. For example, it is incurring unnecessary cost for a car to have a steering mechanism that will last 20 years when the rest of the car will only last 10 years. A value analysis exercise will look at the product's functions, finish, build quality and its technology.

Case study

Lean enough?

from *The Economist,* 10 February 1996

Remember when Japanese cars were cheap and nasty? ...Car buyers sneered and Detroit chuckled, but not for long.

It is not only that they were economical. They rarely broke down and, unlike Detroit's finest, they did not shed bits as they went along. Moreover, they had plenty of gadgets, such as vanity mirrors with built-in lights or intermittent screen wipers, fitted as standard rather than as expensive options. This recipe earned the Japanese almost a third of the American market and threatened to swamp Europe until import barriers blocked them at 11 per cent.

The forward march of the Japanese car industry has finally been halted....And even at home the Japanese are losing ground to cheap Ford imports in their hitherto impregnable fortress.

The Japanese are responding to these challenges by reversing their earlier formula for success. Goaded by the strong yen, they are ripping out trimmings and selling basic models. Lean production alone is not enough, the argument goes; they need lean machines as well. The aim is to become cheap again, without becoming nasty...

In the first wave of savings, they applied the sort of 'value engineering' techniques perfected by Chrysler in America. This consisted of altering the design of cars so as to simplify manufacture. Together with refinements to their lean production system, these techniques helped Toyota carve $1.5 billion out of its annual costs in 1994.

Now the cost-cutting is entering a more dramatic phase, and for the first time affecting the nature of the products, not just the way they are put together.... Now if you want fancy extras, you have to order them and pay for each separately. Other little things are being changed: Japanese car makers used to paint the parts which most drivers never saw, such as the fuel tank or the drive shaft. Now they are leaving them unpainted. James Harbour, an American productivity expert, argues that by finding ways of stripping out costs without affecting quality or reliability, the Japanese could reduce costs by 40–50 per cent.

Tasks

1 *Identify three reasons why Japanese cars became so popular initially.*
2 *Western car manufacturers responded to the Japanese onslaught with drastic cost cutting through the shedding of expensive workers. Describe the cost cutting measures adopted by Japanese car manufacturers to counter this threat to market share.*
3 *What constraint have the Japanese had to work round when designing their own cost cutting programmes?*
4 *Discuss the likely future developments in the global car market and the implications for financial planning.*

The common thread running through cost reduction techniques is that activity causes costs. This realisation in recent years has lead to **activity based management** based on the activity based costing technique described in Chapter 15. The concept can be extended to review all business activities and to establish appropriate 'cost drivers'. For example, businesses incur additional costs for every supplier they deal with. These costs span from the relatively inexpensive cost of administrating a supplier account on the purchase ledger to expensive review of supplier quality standards and skills training to ensure supplies are reliable and of the correct quality.

Successful cost reduction often requires an appropriate organisational culture. Employees at all levels should be motivated enough to question continuously the net value of the work they do. Without an implanted and accepted efficiency culture, cost cutting can be demoralising as most costs are cut by shedding workers.

Profitability can be influenced by increasing the perceived value of the firm's products in relation to those of its competitors. The concept of **value enhancement** is to increase the value of the product or service to the customer without the firm incurring a corresponding cost increase. This may be achieved by cost reduction programmes that pass savings to the customer, or could be achieved by real increases in product value. A machine that doubles as a washing machine and tumble dryer has added value in that it uses less space for no more money than the products cost individually. Likewise, the value of a laptop computer has been enhanced now that it can be used as a portable photocopier and a communications device for fax, e-mail and multimedia presentations. A car that needs servicing every 12 000 miles has more value than one that requires servicing at 6 000 miles. Of course, value enhancement is often a defensive measure to provide the same specifications as competitors. What is important is that the cost of enhancement is more than matched by increased revenues so that a contribution can be made to fixed overheads and profits.

Sales volume depends on market size and market share. In a growing market, sales volume will increase provided the business can hold on to its market share. In a static or declining market, sales volume can only increase at the expense of competitors.

For most businesses, planning can influence both market size and market share. Market size can be increased by supplying new geographical areas or by targeting different niches in the current area. If the potential for market growth is limited, the business could examine other products that would exploit the firm's competencies.

To an extent the ability to increase market share is linked to the firm's pricing policy. Off-peak pricing or cut-price deals that can provide an extra contribution to fixed overheads and profits are tools that are often used where fixed costs are high and variable costs low. The emphasis for many businesses from airlines to hotels is to ensure that capacity is well used. In addition to the financial ratio sales to capital employed, an important operational measure for these types of businesses is occupancy rate calculated by dividing the number of places filled by the number of places available.

Case study

Macworld

from *The Economist,* 29 June 1996

The world's biggest fast food firm faces cut-price

competitors for every bite of the market. But home or abroad, McDonald's recipe remains the same: open more restaurants, grab more market share.

The company, which has 18 700 McDonald's outlets serving 33m people every day, will open up to 3 200 new restaurants both this year and next. In the first quarter of 1996, like for like sales continued to fall in US restaurants as did operating profit margins. The company acknowledges 'there is more capacity coming on line than there is growth to absorb it'. To boost sales in a mature, slow-growing market, McDonald's has little choice but to build more restaurants – if it passes up a prime site, rivals such as Burger King or Wendy's will grab it.

Rapid growth has hit the firm's quality, service and cleanliness – the three watchwords on which Ray Kroc built the business in the 1950s. However, McDonald's is most vulnerable on price – the principle consideration for many burger eaters. Burger King's recent advertisements chew on a 99 cent Whopper; McDonald's feature a new burger costing more than twice that sum.

MacDonald's battalions have launched counter-attacks on Burger King on three fronts. The first is by cutting operating costs, which have been rising faster than revenues. By simplifying its restaurants, McDonald's has already reduced the average cost of a new one to $1.2m in America, down 25 per cent on six years ago. It has also simplified the menu.

The second tactic is to move upmarket. Last month, in its biggest product launch since the birth of the Big Mac in 1968, the firm unveiled the Arch Delux, a belated assault on the $5 billion a year American market for burgers that come with bacon, lettuce and tomato. The third front is a redoubling of the firm's marketing offensive. Deals include sponsorship of the Olympic games and with Walt Disney to replace Burger King as its fast food marketing partner.

Tasks

1 *How do the firm's organisational strategies link with its financial objective of maximising shareholder value?*
2 *Explain the concept behind McDonald's 'simplification' strategies. Explain some specific operational measures that would be consistent with these strategies.*

Control of capital employed

For a business to increase its return on capital employed it is necessary for it to increase profits and/or reduce capital employed. The control of capital employed is a major responsibility of the business's financial managers. Ultimate responsibility for financial management lies with the finance director. He or she will delegate responsibility to departmental managers, the number and specialisms dependent on the nature and size of the business.

Working capital is the capital tied up in balances concerned with the day-to-day operations of the business. It comprises stocks, debtors and cash, less amounts owed to the business's suppliers. In larger organisations the management of cash and credit transactions is the responsibility of a treasury accountant.

Credit control is about controlling the amounts owed by customers for goods and services they have received on credit. A sale made on credit is a drain on business resources until the debtor pays. Potential customers should be evaluated for their credit worthiness before being allowed a credit account. A credit limit should be imposed that is appropriate having regard to the customer's credit status and potential value to the business.

Once a supply has been made the business should invoice its customers promptly and continually review the state of credit accounts. Exception reports printed daily or weekly can highlight those accounts that have passed their credit limit and/or the normal payment period. The main task of a credit controller is to chase those customers who extend the credit period afforded to them.

Communication methods for credit control will depend on the nature of the industry, who the customer is and the value of the amounts outstanding. It is common for many businesses to use a series of computer-generated letters with messages pitched at varying levels of severity depending on the age of the debt. The telephone has the advantage of immediacy and the potential to develop working relationships with payments staff. But it is also expensive and time consuming for volumes of small debts. One incentive for prompt payment is the offer of settlement discounts. These can ensure earlier receipt of cash but run the risk of customers taking them anyway, or extending normal terms if they miss the discount period.

Although a minimum level of debtors is an ideal attainment, over-strident methods and the early use of legal action can threaten the working relationship between customer and supplier. However, customers who don't pay are worse than no customers at all. A firm but considered approach is best employed, perhaps involving sales personnel in the credit negotiations before relationships become over-strained.

Stocks are often controlled by an inventory controller who is a member of the production or sales function. The effective control of stocks has real financial benefits. Funds tied up in stocks have an opportunity cost in addition to the cost of finance itself. Other costs include handling, storage and the risk of stock damage and obsolescence.

Stocks should therefore be minimised within the context of operational needs. Stock-out situations can be ruinously expensive if this affects the ability to satisfy customer needs. The business should aim for high stock turnover with systematic ordering in line with economic batch quantities. This requires good knowledge of supplier and factory lead times, cost structures and accurate forecasting of future requirements. Purchasing parameters for stock should be reviewed with forecast changes in sales.

Investment in **fixed assets** should be controlled and appraised using one of the appraisal techniques described in the next section. Wherever possible the business should retain the flexibility to react to unforeseen eventualities. To minimise the risk of tying up funds in resources that may be little used, assets could be rented or hired on a short-term basis. If some assets are to be hired and some to be purchased, risk is reduced and flexibility maintained if business funds are tied up in general purpose assets rather than specialist assets.

Capital investment appraisal

Because strategic options have repercussions over many years, it is important that an accounting technique is used that is appropriate to the evaluation of long-term projects.

Business performance is measured by its return on capital employed, so it is entirely consistent to appraise proposed projects on the same basis. It is often called the **accounting rate of return.**

$$\text{Accounting rate of return} = \frac{\text{Average annual profits}}{\text{Average capital employed}} \times 100\%$$

Illustration

Two projects are to be evaluated although only one can be proceeded with because of a shortage of capital. Both projects require immediate cash payments to purchase fixed assets that have lives of 4 years with no residual value. Workings will be demonstrated for project 1.

Project cash flows

Year		Project 1 (£)	Project 2 (£)
0	Cash out flow – fixed assets	−24 000	−20 000
1	Net cash in flow	6 000	4 000
2	Net cash in flow	6 000	6 000
3	Net cash in flow	8 000	8 000
4	Net cash in flow	8 000	10 000

Each project has required an investment in fixed assets which require to be depreciated over 4 years. Depreciation per annum is therefore £6 000 for project 1.

Solution
Annual profits

Year		Project 1 (£)
1	Profit/loss	0
2	Profit	0
3	Profit	2 000
4	Profit	2 000
Total		4 000
Average profit/ annum		1 000

Average capital employed can be calculated by averaging the annual amounts but a simple average is calculated here:

$$\text{Average capital employed} = \frac{\text{Capital at start} + \text{Capital at end}}{2}$$

Project 1

Average capital employed = £12,000

$$\text{Accounting rate of return} = \frac{£1\,000}{£12\,000} \times 100\%.$$

$$= 8.3\%.$$

Exercise 16.2

Calculate the accounting rate of return for project 2.

The project with the highest accounting rate of return is the preferred project. Project rates of return should be compared with the business's cost of capital and the opportunity cost of having to forgo other investment opportunities.

The **payback period** is the amount of time required for a project to repay its initial cost. The calculation is based on cash flows and not on profits.

Taking the earlier illustration, the annual cash flows are first accumulated. The payback period is reached when the cumulative cash flow reaches zero.

Project 1

Year		Annual (£)	Cumulative (£)
0	Cash out flow – fixed assets	−24 000	−24 000
1	Net cash in flow	6 000	−18 000
2	Net cash in flow	6 000	−12 000
3	Net cash in flow	8 000	−4 000
4	Net cash in flow	8 000	4 000

At the end of year 3 there is a cumulative cash outflow of £4 000. However, by the end of year 4 there is a net inflow of £4 000. Therefore the payback period is between 3 and 4 years.

The fraction of year 4 that is required can be calculated as:

$$= \frac{\text{cash inflow required for payback}}{\text{total cash inflow for that year}} \times 12 \text{ months}$$

$$= \frac{£4\,000}{£8\,000} \times 12 \text{ months} = 6 \text{ months}.$$

The payback period is therefore 3 years 6 months.

Exercise 16.3

Calculate the payback period for project 2.

The project with the shortest payback period is to be preferred as longer payback periods increase the risk of unforeseen circumstances arising.

Although the payback period gives some indication of the timing of cash flows it does not consider the pattern within the payback period. Even more importantly, the calculation ignores completely the cash flows after the payback period and so provides no information on the profitability of a project.

Despite these significant shortcomings, the technique is widely used because it is the simplest of the appraisal techniques to calculate and to evaluate. As part of a more sophisticated appraisal system, it is often used as a secondary measure to one of the other techniques.

The main problem with the techniques described so far is that they fail to account fully for the timing of cash flows. Instinctively we all known that £1 in the hand today is worth more than a promised £1 for receipt on some future date. This is because there is a time value of money that allows for:

■ a risk that unforeseen circumstances will prevent receiving the amount anticipated
■ inflation that will lower the real value of money
■ an opportunity cost in sacrificing an alternative use of the money.

The time value of money is often represented by a composite annual percentage rate, e.g. bank deposit rates include amounts to cover the time value of money.

The time value of money is considered by the appraisal technique known as the **discounted rate of return.**

Consider a sum of £100 that is invested in a savings account that returns interest at 10 per cent per annum. Assuming that the interest is left in the account at the end of each year, the savings account balance at the end of each of the next four years will be:

Year	Interest @ 10% pa (£)	End of year (£)
0		100.00
1	10.00	110.00
2	11.00	121.00
3	12.10	133.10
4	13.31	146.41

Using an interest rate of 10 per cent, £100 today is worth £110.00 in one year's time, £121.00 is two years and so on. It can also be said that £110.00 in one year's time is worth £100.00 today and £121.00 in two years' time is also worth £100.00 today. It is also possible to say that £133.10 in three years' time has the same value as £146.41 in four years' time. This can be demonstrated by restating the values in today's money, i.e. they are both worth £100 today invested at 10 per cent p.a.

This provides a valuable tool for valuing cash flows that occur at different times over the life of a business project. By reducing all future cash flows to a common measure, comparisons can be made between projects. The total of all cash flows restated in today's money terms is called the **net present value** (NPV).

The NPV of a future cash flow is found by multiplying it by a discount factor. The size of the factor depends on the discount rate used (cost of capital) and the number of years that it is discounted for. The easiest way of finding a discount factor is to look it up in an NPV table (see Appendix III). For example, cash in four years time discounted at 10 per cent should be multiplied by a factor of 0.6830.

The discount factor can also be calculated. From the table above it is known that £100.00 invested at 10 per cent over 4 years gives a final value of £146.41. The relationship of present value to final value is 146.41/100.0 = 0.6830. Using mathematical notation:

$$\text{NPV discount factor} = \frac{1}{(1 + r)^n}$$

where r = discount rate
          n = number of years

The figures from the earlier illustration will be used again but this time discounted at a rate of 10 per cent p.a.

Year		Cash flow (£)	Discount factor	Present value (£)
0	Cash out flow – fixed assets	–24 000	1.0000	–24 000
1	Net cash in flow	6 000	0.9091	5 455
2	Net cash in flow	6 000	0.8264	4 958
3	Net cash in flow	8 000	0.7513	6 010
4	Net cash in flow	8 000	0.6830	5 464
Net present value				–2 113

Exercise 16.4

Calculate the net present value for project 2 using a discount rate of 10 per cent p.a.

Projects with positive net present values are providing financial returns in excess of the cost of capital. Negative net present values highlight projects that fail to provide adequate financial returns and should be discarded. Where a choice has to be made between projects competing for limited finance, the projects with the highest net present value should be given priority.

It is the cash flows that are relevant to the project that should be discounted. These will include:

Inflows:
■ Sales revenues phased for when they will actually be received.
■ Sale proceeds from the disposal of fixed assets at the project's conclusion.
■ Release of working capital at the end of the project – stocks.
■ Government grants.

Outflows:
■ Investment in fixed assets.
■ Investment in working capital – stocks.
■ Operating costs including material, labour and expenses.
■ Tax payments.

Net present values cannot be calculated directly from accounting profit unless it is clear that accounting profit and cash flows are the same. For most projects the biggest difference between cash flow and profit will be the initial investment. An investment in a fixed asset is an immediate cash outflow but profit figures will include a depreciation charge that spreads its cost over a number of years.

Appraisal by net present values is the most comprehensive technique for project appraisal as it considers:

1 all cash flows to the forecasting horizon
2 the timing of cash flows
3 the cost of capital.

In practice, however, the technique has its disadvantages. In addition to the difficulty of forecasting future cash flows there is the added difficulty of establishing an appropriate discount rate. This is important because the net present value of a cash flow is highly sensitive to the discount rate used.

Discount rate

Investors in the business will require shareholder returns (capital appreciation and dividends) or interest on debt finance. For investment appraisal purposes this is called the **cost of capital.**

Most businesses raise more than one type of finance, for companies these include ordinary shares, preference shares, debentures and bank finance. It therefore becomes necessary to use a weighted average cost of capital (WACC) as a discount factor.

$$\text{Weighted average cost of capital (WACC)} = \frac{\text{Total cost of finance}}{\text{Total capital invested}} \times 100\%.$$

Illustration – Weighted average cost of capital

Middling Ltd is a company financed by 1 000 000 ordinary shares having a nominal value of £1 each. Retained profits in the business amount to £500 000. Advice from a stock broker that specialises in the same industry sector suggests that shareholders do require an annual return of 18 per cent. Middling has also issued debentures worth £500 000 with an annual interest rate of 8 per cent.

Calculate Middling's weighted average cost of capital.

	Cost of capital	Finance provided	Percentage of total finance	Weighted cost
Ordinary shares	18%	£1 500 000	75%	13.5%
Debentures	8%	£ 500 000	25%	2.0%
Total		£2 000 000		15.5%

The discount rate should therefore be based on 15.5 per cent.

It is important that the cost of capital used is appropriate for the project being appraised. A historical weighted average cost of capital should only be used with projects with a normal risk profile and which do not change the gearing ratio of the business. Cash flows for projects with different risk profiles should be discounted with a rate including a risk premium or risk discount. A particularly risky project may require a risk premium adding to the basic cost of capital, say adding 5 per cent on to the 15.5 per cent calculated for the base business. The setting of

the premium is subjective and yet it can alter the net present value calculations significantly.

Businesses that operate formal capital investment appraisal systems will usually have a required rate of return that is consistent with shareholder expectations. This will be a long-term rate that will not be sensitive to short-term changes in interest rates and dividend yields.

Inflation

Changes in the value of money have been a feature of most economies in recent years. Whilst the Western world has experienced relatively stable prices during the 1980s and 1990s, the compound effect of even single-digit **inflation** can influence discounted cash flows significantly.

There are two generally accepted methods for discounting cash flows during periods of changing prices:

1 Cash flows should be measured in money terms and discounted using the nominal cost of capital.
2 Cash flows should be measured in real terms only and should be discounted at the real cost of capital.

Illustration

A business has a cost of capital of 20 per cent which includes a 10 per cent inflation component. The firm's real discount rate is:

$$= \frac{1 + \text{money cost of capital}}{1 + \text{inflation rate}} - 1 = \frac{1.2}{1.10} - 1 = 9.091\%$$

A project has the following net cash flows measured in money terms and in real terms.

Year		In real terms			In money terms		
		Discount factor 9.091%	Cash flow (£)	Present value (£)	Discount factor 20%	Cash flow (£)	Present value (£)
0	Investment	1.0000	−10 000	−10 000	1.0000	−10 000	−10 000
1	Net cash flow	0.9166	5 000	4 583	0.8333	5 500	4 583
2	Net cash flow	0.8401	5 000	4 201	0.6944	6 050	4 201
3	Net cash flow	0.7701	5 000	3 851	0.5787	6 655	3 851
	Net present value			2 635			2 635

In a simple situation such as the one above, both approaches arrive at the same answer. However, differences would occur where individual cash flows are experiencing different inflation rates. For example, costs are to increase at 10 per cent per annum but sales prices will only increase by 5 per cent per annum. In a case such as that the money terms approach will give a more accurate picture.

Exercise 16.5 Accounting rate of return, payback and NPV

Avorcet Ltd is about to replace some of its existing plant. Two machine configurations have been designed by the production engineering department and these have been labelled C1 and C2. Each configuration involves significant capital outlay with cash benefits forecast to flow in over the next 5 years.

Estimated cash flows	C1	C2
£		
Outflow – now	(125 000)	(140 000)
Inflows		
1	30 000	30 000
2	35 000	40 000
3	40 000	50 000
4	40 000	60 000
5	40 000	70 000

The plant has no residual value after 5 years and the company's cost of capital is 15 per cent.

Tasks

1   Calculate for each configuration of plant:
   ■   accounting rate of return
   ■   payback period
   ■   net present value.
2   Analyse the figures you have calculated.

Exercise 16.6 NPV

Borham plc is expanding its distribution network into East Anglia and is considering new premises in Cambridge. According to its sales projections the preferred new premises will be adequate for the next 5 years, at which point new property would have to be sought. The Cambridge property is available for sale at £180 000, or for lease at £18 000 p.a. The company's property advisors suggest that commercial property prices will grow at 2 per cent p.a. for the foreseeable future. Selling and legal costs would amount to 5 per cent of the selling price. The firm's cost of capital is 12 per cent.

Tasks

1   Calculate the net present cost for both buying and leasing the property.
2   Based on this financial information alone, advise Borham on their best course of action.

Exercise 16.7 NPV

Lawton & Co. has been experiencing machine breakdowns in its factory and is considering buying new machinery. The purchase price of the new machinery is £75 000. It will cost a further £6 000 to install and £4 000 will be lost in disruption during the installation and retraining period. Ongoing maintenance costs are estimated at £3 000 p.a. The new machines will help generate contribution to overheads and profit of £40 000 p.a. The machines will have a residual value of £15 000 after 6 years.

If the firm continues with its existing machinery, the cost of repairs and maintenance are estimated to be £8 000 in the next year. These are expected to rise by 25 per cent p.a. thereafter. The machines make products contributing £35 000 per annum to overheads and profits. This figure is likely to decrease after the second year at a compound rate of 10 per cent p.a. as machining errors and disruptions to production increase. The machines will have to be scrapped after 6 years.

The firm's cost of capital is 10 per cent.

Tasks

1   Calculate the net present value of each alternative over the next 6 years.
2   Advise management of their best cause of action.

Exercise 16.8 Complex NPV problem

Universal Cable is in the middle of its cabling program and like other cabling companies is losing customers fast (high churn rate). Of the customers connected at the start of any one year, 40 per cent cancel during the year. All TV customers are also signing up for telephony via the cable for which the company gains extra cash flow of an average £30 per household. But most profits are earned from cable TV.

Universal is currently offering two basic levels of service. For £150 a year, the household can view Sky sports and news channels. Sky movie channels are available for a further £150 a year and 50 per cent of customers choose this service.

Universal has to achieve high contributions on sales to pay for the massive investment in laying cables in the streets. In addition, each customer costs £50 to connect to the cable and a further £20 to disconnect them when they cancel the agreement. These costs are not passed on to the customer.

Market research in a small town about to be cabled shows that if just one level of service (sport and movies together) were offered for £150 per annum, the churn rate might be reduced to 20 per cent. In addition, 25 per cent more households than the currently forecast 5 000 would sign up in the first place.

The company's cost of capital is 15 per cent p.a. and the programme providers are paid 40 per cent of television revenues received.

Tasks

1 *For the small town mentioned, make a 5 year net present value comparison of the existing charging structure to that outlined by market research.*
2 *Evaluate the figures for Universal's management.*

Taxation

The **taxation** of business profits can significantly influence the investment decision. Individuals and partnerships pay income tax, companies pay corporation tax. Taxation complicates matters because it is based on taxable profits not on cash flows. In addition, it is often paid in arrears: up to nine months after the end of an accounting period in the case of a company.

There are a number of reasons why taxable profit is different to the accounting profit, but the main one is the treatment of fixed assets. Accounting profits are stated after charging a depreciation charge based on the business's accounting policies. Taxable profits do not suffer a depreciation charge; instead, they are reduced by capital allowances.

Capital allowances for most assets are calculated on a 25 per cent reducing balance basis. When the asset is disposed of a balancing charge or balancing allowance is made depending on whether a profit or loss has been made against the asset's remaining value.

Illustration

An asset costing £10 000 is used for 3 years before being disposed of for £4 000. Calculate the capital allowances available for this asset based on 25 per cent reducing balance.

	Year 1 (£)	Year 2 (£)	Year 3 (£)
Starting value	10 000	7 500	5 625
Writing down allowance	2 500	1 875	
Balancing allowance			1 625
Written down value at year end	7 500	5 625	
Disposal value			4 000

The total capital allowances would be £2 500 + £1 875 + £1 625 = £6 000. This equates to the total cost incurred by the business over the life of the asset (£10 000 – £4 000).

Once the taxable profit for a period has been established the tax payable is calculated by applying an appropriate tax rate. In recent years UK companies have suffered corporation tax rates in the range of 25–35 per cent depending on the size of the company's profits. For cash flow purposes, tax is assumed to be paid in the year following the relevant accounting period.

Illustration

Lowe Ltd requires an investment appraisal for a new project. The firm's cost of capital is 15 per cent, its corporation tax rate is 25 per cent and capital allowances are calculated at 25 per cent on a reducing balance basis. The project requires an investment in fixed assets of £50 000 and this is forecast to provide accounting profits for 4 years of £10 000 pa. Depreciation has been charged on a straight line basis assuming the assets have no residual value at the end of the four years.

Calculate the project's net present value after allowing for tax payments.

Solution

To calculate the project's capital allowances:

	Year 1 (£)	Year 2 (£)	Year 3 (£)	Year 4 (£)
Starting value	50 000	37 500	28 125	21 094
Writing down allowance @ 25%	12 500	9 375	7 031	
Balancing allowance				21 094
Written down value at year end	37 500	28 125	21 094	0

The project's taxable profit is calculated by adjusting its accounting profit

	Year 1 (£)	Year 2 (£)	Year 3 (£)	Year 4 (£)
Accounting profit	10 000	10 000	10 000	10 000
Add back depreciation	12 500	12 500	12 500	12 500
Less capital allowances	−12 500	−9 375	−7 031	−21 094
Taxable profit	10 000	13 125	15 469	1 406

The tax payments will be delayed one year and so will fall in years 2 to 5.

	Year 1 (£)	Year 2 (£)	Year 3 (£)	Year 4 (£)	Year 5 (£)
Tax @ 25%	0	2,500	3,281	3,867	352

The net present value can now be calculated:

Year		Discount factor 15%	Operating cash flow	Tax payments (£)	Total cash (£)	Present value (£)
0	Cash flow	1.0000	−50 000		−50 000	−50 000
1	Cash flow	0.8696	22 500		22 500	19 566
2	Cash flow	0.7561	22 500	−2 500	20 000	15 122
3	Cash flow	0.6575	22 500	−3 281	18 719	12 608
4	Cash flow	0.5718	22 500	−3 867	18 633	10 654
5	Cash flow	0.4972		−352	−352	−175
Net present value						7 775

Note: NPV is based on cash flows not profit. Operating cash flow was found by adding depreciation back to accounting profit (£10 000 + £12 500).

This simplified description of the tax system does illustrate the main features for investment appraisal purposes.

Exercise 16.9   NPV with taxation

Prudence plc is considering a significant expansion of its production line that will utilise building space freed by the recent introduction of just-in-time processes. The new machinery will cost £1.5m and should generate £0.5m in profits and operating cash inflows in each of the next 4 years. At the end of the 4 years, the machinery will be disposed of for £0.2m. The company's cost of capital is 14 per cent p.a.

The machinery will be accepted by the Inland Revenue for capital allowances, calculated on a 25 per cent reducing balance basis. The company pays corporation tax at 30 per cent.

Task

Based on this information, advise the management of Prudence on whether they should proceed with the expansion.

Exercise 16.10   NPV with taxation

Rush Ltd couriers parcels to anywhere in the European Union. The business requires another ten vans and the directors are considering the relative merits of lease versus buy.

The vans would cost £120 000 in total and would incur maintenance costs of £8 000 p.a. After 3 years the vehicles would be sold for an estimated £25 000. The vehicle distributor has offered an operating lease alternative of £6 000 p.a. for each vehicle, including servicing costs.

The vans would attract capital allowances on a 25 per cent reducing balance basis. The company pays corporation tax at 25 per cent and its cost of capital is 12 per cent p.a.

Task

Based on this information, advise the directors of Rush on whether to buy or lease the required vehicles.

Company valuations

It may be important to value a company for a number of reasons, for example to:

- provide a settlement value where a shareholder of an unquoted company wishes to retire
- provide an appropriate share price at which new shareholders can contribute further capital to the business
- agree a purchase price where the whole business is being bought out by another company.

The valuation of a company is fraught with difficulties and the various techniques that can be used are liable to come up with widely differing results. Business commentators and share tipsters routinely make 'buy' recommendations based on their techniques for share valuations. But for everyone who buys a share at a certain price there is someone else willing to sell. Each have their own perception of what the company is worth and this partly depends on the method used to value the business.

The calculation of the **price earnings** (PE) ratio was described in Chapter 2 and provides a basis for valuing shares quoted on the stock exchange. Companies can command a premium on their price earnings ratios if their growth prospects are better than the industry average.

For a company not listed on the stock exchange, the PE ratios of comparable firms that are quoted can be used as a rough guide to value the business.

Company valuation = Profits attributable to ordinary shareholders × PE ratio

Illustration

An engineering company has established that the PE ratio for quoted companies with similar product ranges and growth prospects is 12. Its recently prepared accounts show the following profit appropriation section:

	£'000
Profit after tax	1 700
Preference share dividends	100
Ordinary share dividends	500
Retained profit	1 100

What is the value of the company's ordinary shares using the industry PE ratio?

Solution

Profits attributable to ordinary shareholders
= £1 700 000 – £100 000 = £1 600 000.

Company valuation = £1 600 000 × 12 = £ 19 200 000

It is debatable whether the share price based on the relatively small number of shares traded each day is a fair valuation of a whole business. It is also difficult to choose a company that is directly comparable in terms of size, risk and growth prospects. Finally, it will also be the case that quoted shares are more valuable than shares in an unquoted company because shareholders will pay a premium for marketability. Aside from these problems, the PE ratio is widely used and is a useful price indicator.

Exercise 16.11 Business valuation

V Shah has a 20 per cent shareholding in a regional supermarket chain that reported profits of £2.1m last year. He wishes to retire from the business and sell his shares to the other shareholders. The company has a reasonably secure share of the local market although growth opportunities are limited due to the competitive nature of the industry. It has been agreed that V Shah's shares should be valued at a 20 per cent discount to the average PE ratio for the food retailing sector.

Tasks

1 *Using a recent copy of the* Financial Times *ascertain a PE ratio that can be used to represent the food retail sector.*
2 *Calculate the value of V Shah's shareholding.*

A business can be valued purely in terms of the **net assets** that it employs. Irrespective of the financial performance of the business, the company may have assets that are under-utilised and worth more to another business than other valuation techniques might imply.

This technique is particularly appropriate if the company's activities are to be terminated and its assets liquidated. In this case, the valuation should reflect the market value of the assets including intangible assets that may not appear in the balance sheet. These may include product or process designs, trading names and market brands.

There is a danger of over-valuing with this technique, especially if the assets are specialised for a particular industry.

Exercise 16.12 Business valuation

The Shepherd's Halt is a grand Georgian building with thirty bedrooms and large gardens. It has been run as an independent hotel for 6 years, the past three of which have been particularly difficult since the small town where it is located was given a by-pass. Last year profits amounted to £25 000. The owners have decided to sell the hotel and they have put it on the market at £600 000, 40 per cent lower than the balance sheet value of the land and buildings alone. To a prospective purchaser who wants to run a hotel before retirement in 10 years' time, Shepherd's Halt looks cheap.

Write a memorandum to the prospective purchaser of Shepherd's Halt with relevant advice on how the hotel could be valued.

Just as an individual project can be valued on the basis of **discounted cash flow**, so can a whole business.

For the individual shareholder in a public company the cash flow receivable is the future dividend stream. A short cut calculation can be used where the dividend is considered to recur to infinity:

$$\text{Share valuation} = \frac{d}{i}$$

where d = dividend per share

i = cost of capital.

For a dividend stream that grows at a constant rate the discounted value of a share can again be computed using a simple equation:

$$\text{Share value} = \frac{d}{(i - g)}$$

where g = growth rate and $i > g$.

Illustration

A share currently pays a dividend of 12p. It is considered probable that dividends will continue growing at 5 per cent compound each year. If an individual's required rate of return is 10 per cent, what is the value of the share?

Solution

$$\text{Share valuation} = \frac{d}{(i = g)} = \frac{£0.12}{(0.10 - 0.05)} = £2.40$$

The same principles can be applied to the valuation of the whole company. However, if a company was totally controlled, the income stream would not depend on the dividend policy of the directors. The cash receivable would be the total cash flow generated by the business. This is likely to fluctuate from year to year depending on

the investment required each year in fixed assets and working capital. The company valuation will equal the NPV of all future budgeted cash flows.

Whilst discounted cash flow is theoretically the more accurate valuation method, the PE ratio and net asset methods are in wide use because of their relative simplicity.

Summary

The ultimate business objective of enhancing shareholder value is a financial objective. Financial performance indicators in the form of accounting ratios can provide a valuable framework to focus strategy on improving financial performance. To improve shareholder wealth the planning process should concentrate on the control of capital employed and on enhancing customer value in relation to cost incurred. The appraisal of long-term activities can be made with the techniques of accounting rate of return, payback and NPV.

The planning process:

■ reduces risk: enhancing knowledge and recognising uncertainty
■ facilitates management of strengths, opportunities, weaknesses and threats
■ encourages co-ordination of the business's processes
■ provides a framework on which to control financial performance.

Further reading

Management Accounting, published monthly by the Chartered Institute of Management Accountants.
Leslie Chadwick, *Management Accounting*, Routledge, 1993.
David Crowther, *Managing Accounting for Business*, Stanley Thornes, 1996.
Colin Drury, *Management Accounting Handbook*, Butterworth Heinemann, 1996.
Colin Drury, *Management and Cost Accounting*, 4th edition, International Thompson Business Press, 1996.
Robert W. Hutchinson, *Corporate Finance: Principles of Investment, Financing and Valuation*, Stanley Thornes, 1995.
T. Lucey, *Management Accounting*, 4th edition, DP Publications, 1996.
Keith Ward, *Strategic Management Accounting*, Butterworth Heinemann, 1992.

17 Information for planning and control

On completion of this chapter students should be able to:

- examine the budgetary planning process and its application to financial planning decisions
- examine and illustrate the use of standard costing systems
- analyse and interpret deviation from planned outcomes.

For businesses to meet their objectives, it is necessary for the individual parts of the organisation to be co-ordinated towards the common purpose. The contribution expected of a department is communicated using a planning document called a budget. Once responsibilities have been assigned, timely reporting of actual performance shows whether the business is on target.

For businesses that are not co-ordinated the consequences can be dire. The production function may make things that the sales function cannot sell, and the purchasing department may be buying materials that the factory will not use.

Formalising short-term operating plans into financial budgets ensures that departments are applying a common set of assumptions that have been approved by senior management. They provide a valuable benchmark against which to measure and judge actual performance, and the analysis of variances gives better insight for future planning. To summarise budgeting objectives:

1 **Co-ordination.** A framework ensures that activities of individuals and departments are consistent with one another. Each departmental budget is co-ordinated and inter-related; for example, the production department's budget is based on the sales budget with adjustment for planned changes in stock balances.
2 **Communication.** Employees at all levels are made aware of the organisation's objectives in terms that are meaningful to their day-to-day work. Performance expectations are stated in terms that are explicit and quantifiable. The process also facilitates an informed message to outside parties. Statements such as 'it is our intention to raise profits by 15 per cent per annum' can be made confidently in the knowledge that they are consistent with underlying planning assumptions.
3 **Motivation.** With real consultation and communication, the targets set for individuals should become a source of motivation. Individual targets can underpin departmental budgets and ensure that there is 'goal congruence' – the aims and objectives of the individual are the same as those of the organisation.
4 **Monitor and control.** Actual performance can be compared with budgeted performance, which provides if necessary a catalyst for remedial action. The reporting process that measures actual performance against budget should save management time by highlighting only significant variances – management by exception. The process need not be viewed

negatively if things are going wrong. Reasons for under-performance may stem from factors outside the individual's control, the highlighting of which should be beneficial for both the individual and the organisation. Variances, whether good or bad, are a valuable starting point in the evaluation of individual and collective performance.

Process of budget setting

The annual and medium-term budget exercise needs to be set in the context of long-term objectives and strategies that have been formulated by the highest level of management. As part of the planning process it is important to recognise constraints on business development. Sales demand is often limited, but other constraints such as lack of skilled workers or machine capacity should be identified.

The administration of the budgeting process is usually the responsibility of the accounts department, although some organisations set up a budget committee to oversee and review budget submissions.

The process of preparing the budget is often governed by a formal budget timetable. The budgeting process is itself an exercise in effective planning if all concerned make a useful contribution. The resulting budget will only meet its objectives if the information and assumptions on which the budget is based have been scrutinised for validity and consistency.

The accounts department is involved at all stages of the budgeting process and an effective accounts team will be providing relevant information and advice to line management and directors as the exercise progresses.

Budget models are often constructed with specialist modelling programs or PC spreadsheets, and can provide decision makers with a valuable 'what-if' tool. The effect of decisions are quickly simulated by a structure of functional inter-relationships. For example, the effect on cash flow and profit of reducing the sales price by 5 per cent and increasing volumes by 10 per cent can be viewed in a matter of seconds, despite the need for perhaps thousands of recalculations in the business model.

Although very mechanistic, budget models formalise the inter-relationship of departments and provide common measures for work flowing through the business.

Figure 17.1   A budget timetable

	BUDGET TIMETABLE	
		For year
		1 April 1999 to 31 March 2000
Date	**Narrative**	**Responsibility**
1/9/98	Board of directors review long-term objectives and strategies and specify short-term goals for the year.	Directors
22/9/98	Budget guidelines and standard forms issued to line managers	Accounts
6/10/98	Actual results to September 1995 are issued to line management with comparisons to current budget and last year's actual results	Accounts
20/10/98	Budget submissions to the management accountant	Line management
27/10/98	First draft of master budget is issued	Accounts
3/11/98	First draft of the budget is reviewed for results and consistency – line managers to justify their submissions	MD and individual directors
6/11/98	New assumptions and guidelines issued to line management	Accounts
10/11/98	Budgets revised and resubmitted	Line management
27/11/98	Second draft of master budget issued	Accounts
24/11/98	Final review of the draft budget	MD and FD
	Final amendments	Accounts
1/12/98	Submission to the board for their approval	FD

MD = Managing Director FD = Financial Director

The budgeting process is aided if the business uses profit or cost centres that accord with individual managers' areas of responsibility. In this way the accounting system can record actual transactions that can be compared with budget. Individual accountability would be enhanced if departmental budgets were broken down to targets for individuals. A simple example would be a total sales budget of £1.2m for a sales area consisting of five sales representatives which results in individual sales targets of £240 000 each.

When setting budget levels, the performance expected must be realistic if the overall plan is to have any value. Budgets based on ideal conditions are unlikely to be attained and so they fail to achieve the main objectives of the exercise. Unattainable budgets will result in the separate activities becoming un-coordinated as one or more departments fail their targets. For example, the sales department may fail to achieve the sales budget, with the result that stocks of goods may remain unsold. In addition, budgets will only be motivating if they are pitched at a reasonably high but attainable level.

The process by which budgets are set can often seem a tortuous one. There are two philosophies to budget setting, marking the extreme situations found in practice. The **top down** approach has top management specifying what the key performance indicators for the business will be, such as sales revenues and profits. This approach is intended to meet shareholder expectations, although it may not result in maximised performance if the business is capable of doing better, or if individuals are not sufficiently motivated to achieve the target set. The **bottom up** approach builds up an organisational budget from the submissions of individual line managers on their view of forecast performance and resource requirements. In effect, the departmental managers are setting their own budgets.

In practice most firms use a mixture of the two approaches. A consensus is reached having regard to the expectations of both senior and line management. Senior management are answerable to the owners of the business for the results achieved, but compromises sometimes have to produce a budget that is judged to be attainable and provides an appropriate balance between short-term and long-term performance.

Budget setting should be based on realistic quantitative evidence of future sales and costs. Many organisations base future predictions solely on past figures with adjustments for forecast growth and inflation rates. Apart from simplicity, the main advantage of this approach is that budgets are based on actual data. The disadvantages are that future conditions may not mirror past ones and any anomalies and inefficiencies of the past will be perpetuated. Ideally every departmental manager should have equally tough but attainable budgets to aim for.

Another approach is **zero based budgeting.** Each department starts with a zero budget and amounts are added as their various activities and resources needed are justified. The aim is to irradicate past anomalies and inefficiencies and to account for future conditions. The problem with this method is that measuring the resources needed has often resulted in reference to past performance which the approach was aimed to replace. In practice, a compromise between the two approaches seems to work best with an activity based approach to the review of costs incurred.

The budgeting process is a routine annual event for many businesses. The process may start in the middle of the financial year with a revision of the current year's budget and with first drafts of the budget for the coming year. To provide a longer term framework within which to budget for the coming year, an outline plan for the next 3 or 5 years is quite common.

It is inevitable that as time passes, trading conditions in the near future become more certain. Together with each month's actual results, many firms undertake a continuous update of the full year profit forecast. This exercise augments rather than replaces the budget. It means that some firms report on a monthly basis the actual figures, the original budget, flexed budget (discussed later), latest forecast and last year's results for comparative purposes.

An essential feature of the budgetary control system is that there should be feedback of actual results, as without information managers cannot act. Typically departmental managers will have regular staff meetings that coincide with the publication of the accounting information. Reasons can be sought for variances from those who have detailed knowledge of activities. An effective system will motivate junior managers to act and if necessary report upwards on their own initiative.

Budget structure

The money values used in the budgets are often underpinned with quantities (units, weights and other measures) to ensure consistency across the various functions. They also provide some relevance to operational activity and so facilitate subsequent monitoring of each function's performance.

Functional or departmental budgets, and budgets for individual balance sheet items, are called **subsidiary budgets.** The term **master budget** is used to describe the budgeted profit and loss account, balance sheet and cash budget. The exact nature of subsidiary budgets will depend on the organisation structure and the operational processes of the business. It is, however, usual for each budget to be analysed by time period, e.g. by week or by month.

Figure 17.2 Structure of profit and loss budget for a manufacturing business

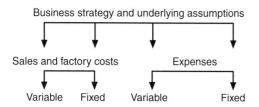

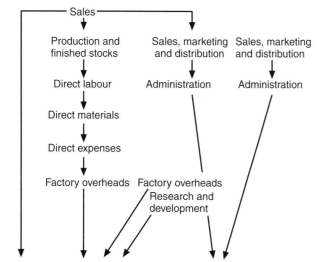

Total sales − Cost of sales = Gross profit − Expenses = Net profit

Illustration – Budget preparation

Adrian Bell trades under the name of 'Shock Alarms' and purchases for resale a home intruder alarm. The alarm, sensors and installation materials cost £50, which Bell plans to resell for £100. The business has 50 alarms in stock on 1 January 19X9 but this needs to be increased to 100 alarms in the first quarter of the year to provide a larger buffer stock. Bell believes sales will be 1 000 alarms during the year, phased over the 4 quarters in the ratio 2, 3, 2, 3. He employs an assistant who will sell 400 of the alarms and he will sell the remainder. His assistant is paid £8 000 pa plus £10 for every alarm he sells. The only other costs the business incurs are the £5 000 pa running costs for the rented industrial unit payable in total at the beginning of the year. All transactions are for cash and Shock Alarms starts 19X9 with £5 000 at the bank.

Prepare relevant subsidiary budgets and the master budget for Shock Alarms for the year ended 31 December 19X9.

Solution

The starting point in the preparation of most budgets will be the **sales budget** as this dictates the level of activity for the rest of the business. The budget is expressed in terms of number of units and sales value.

	Quarter 1	Quarter 2	Quarter 3	Quarter 4	Total
Forecast number of units	200	300	200	300	1 000
Selling price (£)	100	100	100	100	100
Sales turnover (£)	20 000	30 000	20 000	30 000	100 000

To establish the quantity and value of alarms that need to be purchased, the planned change in stock balance has to be considered in addition to anticipated sales. The **stocks and purchases budget** has sections for numbers of units and value. In this example the stock opening and closing balances and stock sales are known, but purchases are not. Purchases must therefore be the balancing item.

In terms of numbers:

Stocks and purchases budget	Quarter 1 Nos.	Quarter 2 Nos.	Quarter 3 Nos.	Quarter 4 Nos.	Total Nos.
Opening stock	50	100	100	100	50
Add purchases (balance)	250	300	200	300	1 050
Less issues (sales)	200	300	200	300	1 000
Closing stock	100	100	100	100	100

Every quarter requires purchases that equal sales except the first quarter when the stock balance is planned to increase.

In value terms:

Stocks and purchases budget	Quarter 1 (£)	Quarter 2 (£)	Quarter 3 (£)	Quarter 4 (£)	Total (£)
Opening stock	2 500	5 000	5 000	5 000	2 500
Add purchases (balance)	12 500	15 000	10 000	15 000	52 500
Less issues (sales)	10 000	15 000	10 000	15 000	50 000
Closing stock	5 000	5 000	5 000	5 000	5 000

Shock Alarms has only one employee but it is still worthwhile preparing a **wages budget** because there is a variable element to his pay. Where there is a variable element of pay based on the level of activity, it makes sense to quantify the variable on which it is paid – in this case the number of alarms sold.

	Quarter 1	Quarter 2	Quarter 3	Quarter 4	Total
Number of sales	80	120	80	120	400
	(£)	(£)	(£)	(£)	(£)
Salary	2 000	2 000	2 000	2 000	8 000
Commission @ £10	800	1 200	800	1 200	4 000
	2 800	3 200	2 800	3 200	12 000

An **expenses budget** is in practice likely to include numerous items, however here there is only one payment in respect of property costs. Conforming to the accruals concept, the annual charge is spread equally over the four quarters.

	Quarter 1	Quarter 2	Quarter 3	Quarter 4	Total
	(£)	(£)	(£)	(£)	(£)
Property costs	1 250	1 250	1 250	1 250	5 000

The figures from the subsidiary budgets can now be used to prepare the master budgets.

Shock Alarms
Budgeted trading and profit and loss account
for the year ended 31 December 19X9

	Quarter 1	Quarter 2	Quarter 3	Quarter 4	Total
	(£)	(£)	(£)	(£)	(£)
Sales	20 000	30 000	20 000	30 000	100 000
Opening stock	2 500	5 000	5 000	5 000	2 500
Purchases	12 500	15 000	10 000	15 000	52 500
	15 000	20 000	15 000	20 000	55 000
Closing stock	5 000	5 000	5 000	5 000	5 000
Cost of sales	10 000	15 000	10 000	15 000	50 000
Gross profit	10 000	15 000	10 000	15 000	50 000
Expenses					
Wages	2 800	3 200	2 800	3 200	12 000
Property costs	1 250	1 250	1 250	1 250	5 000
Total expenses	4 050	4 450	4 050	4 450	17 000
Net profit	5 950	10 550	5 950	10 550	33 000

Shock Alarms
Budgeted balance sheet
for the year ended 31 December 19X9

	Quarter 1	Quarter 2	Quarter 3	Quarter 4	Total
	(£)	(£)	(£)	(£)	(£)
Current assets					
Stocks	5 000	5 000	5 000	5 000	5 000
Prepayment	3 750	2 500	1 250	0	0
Cash at bank	4 700	16 500	23 700	35 500	35 500
	13 450	24 000	29 950	40 500	40 500
Capital B/F	7 500	13 450	24 000	29 950	7 500
Profit added	5 950	10 550	5 950	10 550	33 000
Capital c/f	13 450	24 000	29 950	40 500	40 500

Adrian Bell's capital in the business at the start of 19X9 is represented by the net assets of Shock Alarms at the beginning of the year. Net assets comprised stock of £2 500 and cash £5 000 giving a total of £7 500. It was important not to forget the prepayment in respect of property costs which gradually decreases as the year progresses.

Shock Alarms
Cash budget for the year 19X9

	Quarter 1	Quarter 2	Quarter 3	Quarter 4	Total
	(£)	(£)	(£)	(£)	(£)
Receipts					
Sales	20 000	30 000	20 000	30 000	100 000
Payments					
Purchases	12 500	15 000	10 000	15 000	52 500
Wages	2 800	3 200	2 800	3 200	12 000
Property costs	5 000				5 000
Total payments	20 300	18 200	12 800	18 200	69 500
Receipts – payments	−300	11 800	7 200	11 800	30 500
Balance B/F	5 000	4 700	16 500	23 700	5 000
Balance c/f	4 700	16 500	23 700	35 500	35 500

The cash budget records when cash is received and paid out and so it was important to reflect the actual timing of the property expenditure and not use the figures as charged in the profit and loss account. Remember that the profit and loss account is prepared according to the accruals concept. This means profits may include book entries in respect of accruals, prepayments and depreciation, none of which are cash flows.

Exercise 17.1 Simple budget preparation

Jessica Reed, trading as Dusty Books, wants a financial budget for the year ended 31 December 19X9. She buys books with an average cost of £5 and sells them for an average £8. The shop will start the year 19X9 with 10 000 books in stock, but Reed intends to run down stocks in the first three quarters by 500 books a quarter. She will build the stocks up again to 10 000 books in the fourth quarter. Reed believes she will sell 16 000 books during the year with 7 000 sold in the fourth quarter and the rest spread evenly over the first three quarters. Two part time assistants are employed for a total of £200 a week although this will increase to £300 a week in the fourth quarter. The only other costs the business incurs are the £5 000 pa running costs for the rented shop paid in total at the beginning of the year. All transactions are for cash and Dusty Books will start the year 19X9 with £4 000 in the bank.

Task

Prepare on a quarterly basis the master budget with subsidiary budgets for Dusty Books for 19X9.

Phased payments

Many businesses conduct business on credit terms. They allow customers anything between 7 and 90 days to pay with typical credit periods in the 30–60 day range. Similar credit periods will be expected from suppliers.

In these circumstances there will be a time lag between sales and purchases in the budgeted profit and loss account and the corresponding figures in the cash budget.

As an illustration, a new business that allows 30 days credit to its customers has figures in its sales budget that can be inserted directly into the sales line of its budgeted profit and loss account.

Extract from budgeted profit and loss

	April (£)	May (£)	June (£)	July (£)
Sales	2 000	3 000	4 000	5 000

The cash receipts section of the cash budget can be prepared after taking account of the credit period.

Extract from cash budget

	April (£)	May (£)	June (£)	July (£)
Sales	0	2 000	3 000	4 000

There will be no sales receipts in April and subsequent receipts will equal the previous month's sales. The unpaid sales each month will be shown as a debtor in the budgeted balance sheet.

Extract from budgeted balance sheet

	April (£)	May (£)	June (£)	July (£)
Debtors	2 000	3 000	4 000	5 000

Exercise 17.2 Phased sales

A new business that takes 60 days credit from its suppliers has the following figures that have been taken from its purchases budget.

Extract from the budgeted profit and loss account

	March (£)	April (£)	May (£)	June (£)	July (£)
Sales	1 000	1 500	2 000	3 000	4 000

Task

Prepare the relevant extracts from the master budget to show purchases in the cash budget and creditors in the budgeted balance sheet.

Other payments are frequently timed differently in the budgeted profit and loss account and cash budget as a result of accruals concept being applied in the profit and loss account. Items that are paid in arrears will result in a cost accrual in the budgeted balance sheet and items paid in advance will result in a prepayment.

Exercise 17.3 Accruals and prepayments

Explain the timing of the following items in the cash budget in relation to the budgeted profit and loss account: rent, property rates, electricity, telephone, insurance, gas and car tax.

Exercise 17.4 Timing differences

Waiting Ltd supplies its customers on a 60-day credit basis and takes 30 days' credit from its suppliers. Its fixed assets at the end of March 19X9 had an original cost of £20 000 and accumulated depreciation of £5 000. They are depreciated at 2 per cent straight line every month. The business charges its customers with a 100 per cent mark-up on cost. The cash balance at the end of March 19X9 was £2 000. During February and March 19X9 Waiting Ltd had sales of £5 000 and £6 000 respectively. Purchases of £2 500 were made during March 19X9.

The following subsidiary budgets for the six months to September have been prepared.

	April (£)	May (£)	June (£)	July (£)	August (£)	September (£)
Sales	6 000	6 500	5 000	7 000	7 000	6 000
Indirect expenses	2 000	2 000	2 000	2 500	2 500	2 000

Stocks were £3 000 at the end of March 19X9 and they are to be maintained at a level that is sufficient to supply the next month's budgeted sales. Sales in October 19X9 are forecast to be £7 000.

Task

Prepare for Waiting Ltd a master budget with cash budget for the six months from April 19X9 to September 19X9.

Exercise 17.5 Cash budget

Jack Stanton owns a small building firm, working mainly on house repairs and extensions. He employs four workers, each paid an average £6.00 an hour. They work for a basic 162.5 hour calendar month which equates to 7.5 hours a day. Where necessary he pays overtime at time and a half. Jack estimates that work measured in labour hours for the next twelve months together with related material costs will be:

	July	Aug	Sept	Oct	Nov	Dec	Jan	Feb	Mar	April	May	June
Hours	900	850	900	800	600	300	250	300	400	500	600	800
Materials £	4 000	4 000	4 000	3 500	2 500	1 000	1 000	1 500	2 000	2 500	2 500	4 000

He has agreed the following total number of holidays each month with his workers, including his own.

Holidays	10	10	10	15	5	35	12	5	5	8	5	5

Jack takes £2 000 out of the business each month and works a basic 37.5 hours a week on productive work. Running costs every month amount to £900 for his yard,

and £500 for a van and various items of small plant. Hire of specialist equipment will incur about £1 of charges for every productive labour hour.

Building jobs are quoted at £15 per labour hour plus material cost. There are no partly completed jobs at the end of each month and customers pay in the month following work completion. Jack believes in paying for all costs in the month in which they are incurred. On 30 June X1 there was £250 in the business bank account and customers owed £16 000 for work completed in June X1.

In February Jack plans to purchase a new van for £10 000 and a concrete mixer in May X2 for £1 800.

Tasks

1 *Prepare a twelve-month cash flow forecast for Stanton & Co from 1 July X1 to 30 June X2 (round all figures to whole pounds).*
2 *Comment on the pattern of cash flows for the firm and establish reasons for it.*
3 *Recommend ways in which the cash deficit could be financed assuming similar trading activity in future years.*
4 *How could the firm's cash position be improved without resorting to additional finance?*

Exercise 17.6 Preparation of a business plan

Nick Cotton is about to set up a clothing business called 'CottonWorld' that specialises in imported goods. He has several years' experience in the clothing industry, as a buyer for a large high street retailer and as general manager for a wholesale business importing clothes from the Far East. He believes he could easily achieve £160 000 of sales in year one, £250 000 in year two followed by 30 per cent annual growth thereafter. He requires a business plan for his first year of trading so that he can approach potential investors to add to his £25 000 capital.

Nick intends to import from sources in Taiwan and to sell to retailers in the UK. He already has a letter of intent from one retail outlet to purchase goods valued at £50 000 per annum. Smaller outlets have also expressed interest in the samples he has been displaying in presentations that he is currently doing in his spare time.

Nick estimates his first year's sales (on 100 per cent mark-up) as follows:

Date of supply to customers:	Quarter to 31/3	Quarter to 30/6	Quarter to 30/9	Quarter to 31/12	Total
Sales £	0	40 000	40 000	80 000	160 000

To obtain the price conditions he wanted, he had to agree on payment to his suppliers when goods are about to be shipped to the UK. The lead time between paying for purchases and receiving them through customs in the UK will be three months. Small outlets, comprising half the anticipated sales, will be required to pay at the time of sale. Unfortunately, the larger chains insist on paying in the quarter following delivery.

Nick is committing himself to the following purchases schedule:

Date of shipping:	Quarter to 31/3	Quarter to 30/6	Quarter to 30/9	Quarter to 31/12	Total
Purchases £	40 000	20 000	40 000	40 000	140 000

Other payments include:

	Amount	Period
Warehouse rent and service charges	£5 000	quarterly
Equipment and fittings	£10 000	day one
Carriage to customers	3% of sales	quarterly
Administration wages and expenses	£7 000	quarterly
Motor vehicle	£12 000	day one
Motor vehicle running expenses	£1 000	quarterly
Nick's drawings	£5 000	quarterly

All fixed assets are to be depreciated at 25 per cent per annum.

Tasks

For CottonWorld's first trading year, analysed by quarter, prepare:

1 *a cash budget*
2 *a budgeted trading and profit and loss account*
3 *a balance sheet.*

Limiting factors

One of the objectives of the budgeting exercise is to provide a formal framework on which the various functions of the business can co-ordinate their activities. During budget preparation it will be necessary to ensure that the plans for each of the functions in the organisation are consistent with one another on a period-by-period basis. It will be found that at least one aspect of the business limits the overall volume of business activity. Whilst for most organisations the level of sales will be the limiting factor, for an individual period there may be some other function that proves to be a bottleneck to work flow. Where possible the effects of the limiting factor should be minimised by careful planning. For example, if a manufacturer of non-perishable goods identifies that production cannot keep up with sales during a particular month, it will be necessary to build up stocks during the preceding months.

Illustration

A small textiles firm that manufactures heavy winter pullovers has a production capacity of 150 garments a month and aims to maintain a minimum stock of 100 pullovers at any point in time. Sales of pullovers are forecast to be 50 in September, 100 in October and November and 300 in December. Prepare the production budget to cover the four month period.

Sales will exceed production by 150 garments in December so it is necessary to work back from December to find the nearest month or months that will have sufficient excess capacity to build up stocks in readiness for this peak sales period.

Production budget

	September Nos.	October Nos.	November Nos.	December Nos.
Sock b/f	100	150	200	250
Production	100	150	150	150
Sales	50	100	100	300
Stock c/f	150	200	250	100

To maintain a stock level of 100 garments at the end of December, it is necessary to start the month with 250 pullovers. For November to finish the month with 250 pullovers it must start with 200 and October must start with 150. Only September will operate at less than full capacity, as sales of 50 garments and an increase in stocks of 50 requires production of just 100 pullovers. On the basis of this production budget, the subsidiary budgets of direct labour, direct materials and production overhead would be produced.

Exercise 17.7 Limiting factors

A manufacturer of T-shirts has a production capacity of 5 000 T-shirts a month and aims to maintain a minimum stock of 1 000 T-shirts at any point in time. Sales of T-shirts are forecast to be 2 000 in both March and April, 4 000 in May, 6 000 in June and 8 000 in July. Prepare the production budget to cover the 5 month period. Assume that March starts with 1 000 T-shirts in stock.

Exercise 17.8 Budget with limiting factor

Salts and Aggregates Ltd mixes salt and grit that it buys in bulk and sells in convenient plastic bags. The company's customers include businesses and public organisations that need to keep property access points during icy weather conditions.

Most sales are made during the winter months, but because plant capacity is limited to producing 5 000 bags per month, production has to start some time before sales begin. Sales of 200 kg bags of road grit are forecast to be 2 000 bags in November, 5 000 in December and 10 000 in both January and February. No further sales are envisaged until the following winter. Each bag sells for £2.00.

Sufficient bulk materials and plastic bags must be held in stock to satisfy the coming month's production requirements. Materials (including plastic bags) cost £30 for every 1 000 kg. Both customers and suppliers operate on 30-day credit terms.

Overheads including the lease of the bagging plant amount to £1 000 per month. Direct labour is paid on a piece-work basis of £0.20 per bag.

The company commences September 19X8 with £8 000 in the bank and with £1 200 of materials for which suppliers are still owed.

Task

Prepare for the six month period from 1 September 19X8:

1 *sales forecast*
2 *production and finished goods budget*
3 *purchases and bulk materials budget*
4 *direct labout budget*
5 *overhead budget*
6 *debtors budget*
7 *creditors budget*
8 *budgeted profit and loss account*
9 *budget balance sheet*
10 *cash budget*

Budgets for control purposes

Once constructed, functional budgets provide a basis for subsequent monitoring of actual performance. An important feature of this process is the highlighting of variances to budget. However, the individual manager may or may not be in a position to affect the level of costs incurred. In particular the ability to control costs will depend on the position of the manager in the organisational hierarchy. Some costs may be in the control of one manager but not his or her sub-ordinate. It would be wrong and de-motivating for individuals to be held accountable for costs that they have no control over, so it is not unusual on reports to distinguish between those costs that are controllable and those that are not.

Stores Overhead Report
For July 19X9

	Budget (£)	Actual (£)	Variance (£)
Controllable costs			
Management and supervision	3 500	3 600	100 A
Indirect wages	5 520	5 480	40 F
Fixtures maintenance	200	50	150 F
Total controllable	9 220	9 130	90 F
Uncontrollable costs			
Depreciation	1 600	1 700	100 A
Property cost apportionment	2 950	3 100	150 A
Total uncontrollable costs	4 550	4 800	250 A
Total cost centre overheads	13 770	13 930	160 A

Variances are recorded as being either adverse (A) or favourable (F) depending on whether actual expenditure is more or less than budget respectively. In this example, the departmental manager cannot be held accountable for the overall cost over-run because it has arisen from items for which he has no control.

Exercise 17.9   Controllable costs

Explain, stating assumptions, which of the following costs are controllable by a production design manager.

■ Materials for prototype products.
■ Depreciation of equipment.
■ Hire of specialist test equipment.
■ Wages paid to staff.
■ Apportionment of personnel department costs.

Flexible budgeting

For a budget to have continuing relevance, some cost heads will need adjustment if the original forecasts regarding business activity prove inaccurate. If sales are running over budget there will be cost implications for other departments. For example, if the factory had to produce 20 per cent more production to satisfy booming demand, other things being equal, production costs will increase. Therefore the factory budget needs 'flexing' to reflect a change in underlying assumptions.

Each cost item should be examined to discover its behaviour pattern in relation to changed activity. Particular care should be taken in analysing stepped costs that may vary by more or less than the change in the level of activity.

Illustration

Item	Cost classification	Original budget	Flexed budget
Number of loaves		50 000	55 000
Percentage change			+10%
		(£)	(£)
Direct costs – material and labour	Variable	10 000	11 000
Bakery overheads	Fixed	10 000	10 000
Distribution	Semi-variable 50/50	5 000	5 250
		25 000	26 250

Variable costs such as materials change in proportion to the number of loaves baked. Other costs have at least an element of fixed expenditure unrelated to the level of

activity, so this part is left unchanged. Of the distribution costs originally budgeted, £2 500 is fixed and the variable part is flexed from £2 500 to £2 750, giving £5 250 in total.

Exercise 17.10   Flexible budget

The following budget data for April 19X9 relates to Hayway Electronics Ltd, a manufacturer of car immobilisers.

	Fixed costs included in the budget (£)	Original budget (£)	Actual costs (£)
Direct materials		20 400	21 950
Direct labour		22 950	26 460
Rent	5 000	5 000	5 200
Electricity	500	1 350	1 375
Factory supervision	2 000	2 850	2 750
Administration	2 500	4 200	4 250
Selling and distribution	3 000	9 800	10 550
Total costs		66 550	72 535

The original budget was constructed on the assumption that the business would manufacture and sell 1 700 car immobilisers. Actual performance in fact amounted to 1 900 units and this resulted in some cost heads being overspent against the budget.

Tasks

1 *Prepare a 'flexed' budget for Hayway Electronics based on actual activity levels.*
2 *Prepare a management report highlighting the variances between actual expenditure and the 'flexed' budget.*
3 *Using the figures from Hayway Electronics for illustrative purposes, explain how 'flexed' budgets can be used to control costs.*

Exercise 17.11   Flexible budget

A hotel with 50 beds assumes a 60 per cent occupancy rate when preparing financial budgets. An analysis of fixed and variable costs used for budgetary purposes together with figures for week 30 when occupancy was 70 per cent is listed below:

	Fixed (£)	Variable per guest/week (£)	Actual for week 30 (£)
Sales		210.00	7 350
Costs:			
Rent	2 000		2 000
Power	100	2.00	150
Food	50	40.00	1 650
Laundry and cleaning	100	5.00	250
Reception	200		220
Management and administration	500		550
		(per 10 guests or part thereof)	
Cooks, waiters, etc.	500	50.00	800
Repairs and renewals	350	1.00	150
Other	340		420
Total cost			6 190
Profit			1 160

Tasks

1   *Identify which expense category experiences 'step costs'.*
2   *Prepare a profit statement comparing actual performance with original and flexed budgets.*

Standard costing

Whereas budgets relate to the organisation and its cost/profit centres, standard costing provides supporting analysis on a cost unit basis.

Standard costs are used widely in manufacturing businesses where engineering specifications and factory floor activities are tightly controlled. As part of a total absorption costing system, the standard cost of a product comprises direct labour, direct material, direct expenses and factory overheads. A marginal standard costing system considers variable costs only on a unit basis.

A standard cost card is compiled for each product, detailing standard quantities of material, labour, expenses and overhead absorbed at normal levels of activity.

Standard cost card:

Product: T128a	Standard cost card per unit	Standard rate (£)	Standard cost (£)
Direct materials	2 kg	2.50	5.00
Direct labour	3 hours	6.00	18.00
Overhead absorbed on labour hours	3 hours	2.00	6.00
			29.00

Realistic standards are set with estimates of labour time and material usage needed to manufacture a unit of production in normal batch quantities. These estimates come from an estimating section within a works engineering or work study department.

The purpose of setting standards is to provide a benchmark for actual performance. The difference between a standard cost and an actual cost is called a cost variance. It is described as being adverse or favourable depending on whether actual costs are higher or lower than standard costs.

An important concept for monitoring performance is the **standard hour**. For every piece of work undertaken, it should be possible to express its value in terms of standard hours.

Illustration

The standard time for a worker in the assembly department to assemble a table fan is 15 minutes. A batch of 100 fans have been assembled in 22 hours. What is the time variance on this work?

The value of work done in standard hours is 25 hours (100×0.25 hours). The time taken was 22 hours so there is a favourable time variance of 3 hours.

Exercise 17.12   Standard hours

The standard time for a worker to paint a filing cabinet is 10 minutes. A batch of 250 cabinets have been painted in 45 hours. What is the time variance on this work?

Cost variances are calculated for each element of cost. Variances have either arisen because there is a difference in the amount of the resource used and/or because those resources cost more or less than the standard rate. Therefore it is possible to analyse the total cost variance for each resource into a quantity variance and a price variance.

Total cost element variance	Quantity variance	Price variance
Direct materials total variance	Direct materials usage variance	Direct materials price variance
Direct labour total variance	Direct labour efficiency variance	Direct labour rate variance
Variable overhead total variance	Variable overhead efficiency variance	Variable overhead expenditure variance
Fixed overhead total variance	Fixed overhead volume variance	Fixed overhead expenditure variance

The number and complexity of standards used by a business will depend on the nature of the business and the value placed on the information provided.

Material cost variances

The formulas for calculating the material cost variances are:

Direct material total variance

= (Standard quantity for actual units produced × Standard price) − (Actual units × Actual price)

Direct material usage variance

= Standard price × (Standard quantity for actual units produced − Actual quantity)

Direct material price variance

= Actual quantity × (Standard price − Actual price)

Illustration

Calculate the material variances for total cost, price and usage from the following data.

	Budget	Actual
Number of units produced	8 000	7 000
Kilograms of material – total	20 000	18 200
Cost of materials consumed – total	£32 000	£27 300

Before calculating the variances it is first necessary to identify some of the figures required by the formulas:

Standard quantity for actual units produced $= \dfrac{20\,000 \text{ kg} \times 7\,000}{8\,000} = 17\,500 \text{ kg}$

Standard price per kilogram $= \dfrac{£32\,000}{20\,000} = £1.60$

Actual price per kilogram $= \dfrac{£27\,300}{18\,200} = £1.50$

Direct material cost variance	= (17 500 × 1.60) − (18 200 × 1.50)
	= 28 000 − 27 300 = £700F
Direct material usage variance	= £1.60 (17 500 − 18 200)
	= £1 120A
Direct material price variance	= 18 200 (£1.60 − £1.50)
	= £1 820F

Always check that the sum of the usage and price variance does equal the total cost variance. The calculation of a variance is only the start of the variance analysis exercise. Reasons should be sought for significant variances whether they are adverse or favourable. In this case the total cost variance is the net of two fairly significant cost variances. Actual material usage exceeded standard usage but each kilogram of material cost 10p less than standard price.

Material usage variances may result from work practices that have changed yield or scrap levels or from using materials of different quality. Generally the usage variance is seen as being controllable by the production function. A material price variance may result from using materials of a different quality but is often used to measure the effectiveness of the purchasing function.

Exercise 17.13 Material cost variances

Calculate the material variances for total cost, price and usage from the following data.

	Budget	Actual
Number of units produced	200	210
Kilograms of material	2.5 kg / unit	Total 588 kg
Cost of materials consumed	£4.20 / kg	Total £2 352

Labour cost variances

The formulas for calculating the labour cost variances are:

Direct labour total variance

= (Standard hours for actual units produced × Standard rate) − (Actual hours × Actual rate)

Direct labour efficiency variance

= Standard rate × (Standard hours for actual units produced − Actual hours)

Direct labour rate variance

= Actual hours × (Standard rate − Actual rate)

Illustration

Calculate the labour cost variance, wage rate variance and labour efficiency variance from the following data.

	Budget	Actual
Number of units produced	450	420
Direct labour hours – total	9 000	7 980
Direct wages – total	£54 000	£47 082

Before calculating the variances it is first necessary to identify some of the figures required by the formulas:

Standard hours for actual units produced

$= \dfrac{9\,000}{450}$ hours $\times\,420$ = 8 400 hours

Standard rate per hour

$= \dfrac{£54\,000}{9\,000}$ = £6.00

Actual rate per hour

$= \dfrac{£47\,082}{7\,980}$ = £5.90

Using the cost formulas:

Direct labour total variance

$= (8\,400 \times £6.00) - (7\,980 \times £5.90)$ = £3 318F

Direct labour efficiency variance

$= £6.00 \times (8\,400 - 7\,980)$ = £2 520F

Direct labour rate variance

$= 7\,980 \times (£6.00 - £5.90)$ = £798F

Ensure that the sum of the efficiency and rate variance equals the total cost variance. Actual labour cost was significantly less than that allowed by the standards largely as a result of more production in terms of standard hours than the actual hours used. A slightly reduced labour rate to standard also made a contribution to the overall variance. The difference in labour rate may be due to using different grades of labour than was originally envisaged.

Exercise 17.14   Labour cost variances

Calculate the labour cost variance, wage rate variance and labour efficiency variance from the following data.

	Budget	Actual
Number of units produced	900	800
Direct labour hours	9 hours / unit	8 hours / unit
Direct wages – total	£51 030	£50 560

Variable overhead variances

Variable overheads vary with the number of units produced. The variable overhead variance is therefore the difference between the standard variable overhead for actual production and the actual variable overhead. It represents the variable overhead under or over recovery. It may be calculated in one of two ways:

Variable overhead variance

= (Units produced × Standard variable overhead per unit) – Actual variable overhead

Alternatively, as overhead is often absorbed by some measure of activity other than the number of units (e.g. on labour hours) the following formula may be more appropriate.

Variable overhead variance

= (Standard hours for actual units produced × Variable overhead absorption rate) – Actual variable overhead.

Where overhead is absorbed on a labour hour basis the variable overhead variance can be analysed into efficiency and expenditure components. The overhead efficiency variance is a function of labour efficiency, i.e. actual output in standard hours compared with actual hours used to achieve it. It follows that the variable overhead subsidiary variances provide no additional control information than would be available by analysing the respective labour variances. It merely helps reconcile figures recorded in the costing system. Because of their limited value the variable overhead will not be analysed further in this section.

Illustration – Variable cost variances

Calculate the variable overhead variance from the following data.

	Budget	Actual
Number of units produced	150	160
Direct labour hours	1 050	1 280
Variable overhead	£2.10 / unit	Total £320

Before calculating the variances it is first necessary to identify some of the figures required by the formulas:

Standard hours for actual units produced

$= \dfrac{1\,050 \text{ hours}}{150} \times 160$ = 1 120 hours

Variable overhead absorption rate based on labour hours

$$= \frac{150}{1050} \times \pounds2.10 \qquad = \pounds0.30$$

Variable overhead variance on a standard hour basis

$$= (1\,120 \times \pounds0.30) - (\pounds320) \quad = \pounds16F$$

The same result could be achieved with the calculation based on cost units:

Variable overhead variance on a unit basis

$$= (160 \times \pounds2.10) - \pounds320 \qquad = \pounds16F$$

Exercise 17.15   Variable overhead variances

Calculate the variable overhead variance from the following data. Variable overhead is recovered on direct labour hours.

	Budget	Actual
Number of units produced	80	75
Direct labour hours	1 600	1 425
Variable overhead	Total £4 000	Total £4 275

Fixed overhead variances

Standard costing systems can either be based on total absorption costing or marginal costing principles.

Where a total absorption costing system is used, fixed overheads are absorbed into product cost using a fixed overhead absorption rate or as part of a composite rate which includes both variable and fixed overheads.

The fixed overhead variance

= (Standard hours of actual production × Fixed overhead recovery rate) – Actual fixed overhead

It follows that a fixed overhead variance can be caused by producing either more or less standard hours of production than was budgeted, or if actual expenditure on fixed overhead was different to budget. This results in two subsidiary variances, the fixed overhead volume variance and the fixed overhead expenditure variance respectively.

Favourable volume variances will be experienced when the factory produces more standard hours of production than was budgeted. This can usefully be analysed into an efficiency variance based on labour efficiency, or a capacity variance because the factory had more hours available for production than was budgeted.

The standard total costing method includes all production overhead in product costs and so is consistent with the financial reporting requirements of SSAP 9, Accounting for Stocks and Long Term Contracts.

Where a standard marginal costing system is used, variance analysis is far easier. Fixed overhead is not absorbed into product cost, it is deducted as a total sum from contribution. Hence for profit reconciliation purposes, there is just a fixed overhead expenditure variance.

Fixed overhead expenditure variance

= Budgeted fixed overhead – Actual fixed overhead

The standard marginal costing system and its treatment of fixed overheads is illustrated further with the comprehensive examples at the end of this section on standard costing.

Sales margin variances

To control budgeted profit it is necessary to analyse the contribution provided by sales in addition to costs variances. As cost variances have already analysed differences between budgeted cost and actual cost, sales margin variances are calculated with reference to standard costs. The purpose of sales variance analysis is to identify differences due to variances in selling prices and quantities sold.

Sales margin variance

= Budgeted total margin – (Actual quantity × Actual margin based on standard costs)

Sales volume margin variance

= Standard margin (Actual quantity – Standard quantity)

Sales price margin variance

= Actual quantity(Actual margin based on standard costs – Standard sales margin)

Note: Margin is gross profit in a total absorption costing system and is contribution when using a marginal costing system.

From the following data, calculate the sales margin variances.

	Budget	Actual
Number of units sold	25	20
Sales revenue	£75 000	£56 000
Product cost	£52 500	£44 000
Margin	£22 500	£12 000

Before calculating the variances certain figures need to be determined:

Actual selling price $= \dfrac{£56000}{20} = £2\,800$

Budgeted selling price $= \dfrac{£75000}{25} = £3\,000$

Standard cost $= \dfrac{52500}{25} = £2\,100$

Standard margin $= \dfrac{(£75000 - £52500)}{25} = £900$

Actual margin on standard cost
$= $ Actual selling price $-$ Standard cost
$= £2\,800 - £2\,100 = £700$

Sales margin variance $= £22\,500 - (20 \times £700) = £8\,500A$

Sales volume margin variance $= £900\,(20 - 25) = £4\,500A$

Sales price margin variance $= 20(£700 - £900) = £4\,000A$

The business had budgeted for a total margin of £22 500 but only achieved £12 000. The above calculations show that sales variances accounted for £8 500 of this £10 500 shortfall. The total sales margin variance has been caused by a volume shortfall combined with lower prices.

The remaining £2 000 margin shortfall is due to actual costs being higher than standard costs. This can be demonstrated by flexing the budgeted costs. Standard cost per unit was £2 100 so for 20 units total costs should have been £42 000 as against the £44 000 actually incurred.

Exercise 17.16 Sales variances

From the following data, calculate the sales margin variances.

	Budget	Actual
Number of units sold	500	525
Sales revenue	£70 per unit	Total £39 375
Product cost – total	£30 000	£31 500

Reconciliation of actual profit to budgeted profit

Using a standard marginal costing system, actual profit will differ from budgeted profit because of differences in:

- sales price per unit
- sales volume

- cost per unit (analysed into variances for direct materials, direct labour and variable overhead)
- expenditure on fixed costs.

Using the sales and cost variances illustrated, reasons can be established for the difference between budgeted profit and actual profit.

Illustration

Cornelian Ltd manufactures picture frames with decorative gemstones. The following profit statement relates to the month of June:

	Actual (£)	Budget (£)	Flexed cost budget (£)	Variance (£)
Sales	79 500	70,000		
Costs				
Direct materials	21 465	17 500	18 550	2 915A
Direct wages	16 536	15 000	15 900	636A
Variable overheads	15 264	12 500	13 250	2 014A
Total variable costs	53 265	45 000	47 700	5 565A
Contribution	26 235	25 000		
Fixed overhead	19 080	20 000	20 000	920F
Net profit	7 155	5 000		
Number of frames produced and sold	5 300	5 000	5 300	
Kilograms of material	2 385	2 000	2 120	
Labour hours	2 544	2 500	2 650	

Variable overheads are recovered on a labour hour basis.

1 Calculate all variances to budget as far as the information allows.
2 Use the variances to reconcile actual profit to budgeted profit.

Solution

Sales margin variance
$= £25\,000 - (5\,300 \times £6) = £6\,800\ F$

Sales volume margin variance
$= £5\,(5\,300 - 5\,000) = £1\,500\ F$

Sales price margin variance
$= £5\,300\,(£6 - £5) = £5\,300\ F$

Direct material total variance
$= (2\,120 \times £8.75) - (2\,385 \times £9) = £2\,915A$

Direct material usage variance
$= £8.75\,(2\,120 - 2\,385) = £2\,318.75A$

Direct material price variance
= 2385 × (£8.75 – £9)   = £ 596.25A

Direct labour total variance
= (2650 × £6) – (2544 × £6.50)   = £ 636A

Direct labour efficiency variance
= £6 (2650 – 2544)   = £ 636F

Direct labour rate variance
= 2544 (6 – 6.5)   = £1272A

Variable overhead variance
= (5300 × £2.50) – £15264   = £2014A

Fixed overhead expenditure variance
= £20000 – £19080   = £ 920F

Cornelian
Profit statement
Reconciling actual and budgeted profit

	(£)	(£)
Budgeted profit		5000
Sales margin volume variance	1500.00F	
Sales margin price variance	5300.00F	
Sales margin total variance		6800F
Materials usage variance	2318.75A	
Materials price variance	596.75A	
Materials total variance		2915A
Labour efficiency variance	636.00F	
Labour rate variance	1272.00A	
Labour total variance		636A
Variable overhead variance		2014A
Fixed overhead expenditure variance		920F
Actual profit		7155

Note that the total cost variance for each component of cost corresponds to the flexed budget variance. The volume difference is accounted for by the sales volume variance.

Exercise 17.17   Reconciliation of profit

Corrolla Ltd produces ornaments with floral designs. The following profit statement relates to the company's annual results for last year.

	Actual (£)	Budget (£)
Sales	880000	874000
Costs		
Direct materials	32000	33915
Direct wages	435000	399000
Variable overheads	72000	69160
Total variable costs	539000	502075

Contribution	341000	371925
Fixed overhead	220000	210000
Net profit	121000	161925
Number of items produced and sold	40000	38000
Kilograms of material	8000	7980
Labour hours	60000	53200

Variable overheads are recovered on a labour hour basis.

Tasks

1   *Calculate all variances to budget as far as the information allows.*
2   *Use the variances to reconcile actual profit to budgeted profit.*

Summary

The objectives of a budgetary control system are to help co-ordinate, motivate and control operations. The budgeting process requires communication between the various parts of the business to plan future activities. The process ensures limiting factors are identified, that budgets remain relevant with revisions in line with actual activity, and that managers are made accountable for items within their control.

To ensure a building block approach to planning, standard costing helps quantify total resource requirements from standards for cost units. Standard cost variances can be used to reconcile actual profit to budgeted profit, and this highlights areas that require further investigation and appropriate management action.

Further reading

Management Accounting, published monthly by the Chartered Institute of Management Accounts.
Leslie Chadwick, *Management Accounting*, Routledge, 1993.
David Crowther, *Managing Accounting for Business,* Stanley Thornes, 1996.
Colin Drury, *Management Accounting Handbook*, Butterworth Heinemann, 1996.
Colin Drury, *Management and Cost Accounting*, 4th edition, International Thompson Business Press, 1996.
T. Lucey, *Management Accounting*, 4th edition, DP Publications, 1996.

18 Quantitative aids to planning

On completion of this chapter students should be able to:

- understand techniques used to quantify uncertainty
- use statistical methods to forecast data and evaluate the reliability of the predictions made
- identify and evaluate sources of published statistics
- understand the application of linear programming techniques to the solution of business problems.

.

Uncertainty

Uncertainty is a feature of private business, whether this is due to being part of a market economy or the dynamic processes that are internal to the firm. For effective planning it is imperative that uncertainty should be recognised and quantified where possible.

To plan, it is necessary to work with a description of future conditions that allows, with varying degrees of uncertainty, the anticipation of certain outcomes occurring. The term **probability** is used to describe the chances of an **event** happening or not happening. The term event is used to denote the outcome or group of outcomes that are being considered. Hence in considering the probability of getting a 1 with the throw of a dice, the event is to throw a 1. In considering the chance of throwing an odd number, the event is to throw a 1, 3 or 5.

Probability is measured on a scale from 0 to 1. A probability of zero indicates that an event has no chance of happening, whilst a probability of 1 applies to an event that is certain. It follows that the sum of probabilities for all possible events must therefore equal 1.

The probability of an event occurring is denoted by $P(event)$. So if the probability of a defective product being selected is 1 in 20 times then $P(\text{defective item}) = 1/20$ or 0.05. If the probability of something happening is $P(event)$ then the chance of something not happening $= 1 - P(event)$. From this it follows that $P(\text{good item}) = 1 - 0.05 = 0.95$.

There are three methods for assigning probabilities to possible outcomes.

Classical method of assigning probabilities

Where the outcomes of an uncertain situation are all equally likely to occur, then the probability of one of those outcomes occurring:

$$P(event) = \frac{1}{\text{number of possible outcomes}}$$

For example, if a dice is thrown there are six possible outcomes but each number is represented only once. Therefore, to throw a three:

$$P(\text{rolling a } 3) = \frac{1}{6} \text{ or } 0.1667$$

Relative frequency method

Where the probability cannot be calculated using the classical method, an experiment needs to be conducted to estimate the probability of an event occurring. Probability is estimated by comparing the number of events to the total number of outcomes.

$$P(\text{event}) = \frac{\text{Number of events}}{\text{Number of outcomes observed}}$$

For example, if a travel agency has sold 180 holidays in the last month and to those same customers 54 travel insurance policies were also sold, then the probability of selling an insurance policy to a customer is:

$$P(\text{insurance sold}) = \frac{54}{180} = 0.30$$

The number of occurrences for each outcome can usefully be presented in a frequency table or appropriate chart so as to aid understanding of the relative probabilities.

Subjective method

It may be more practical to estimate the probability of an event occurring, because the above methods are not possible or are too time consuming and costly in relation to the benefits to be gained. An informed estimate of chance is often used in business; for example:

- a pub landlord has to decide on how many additional bar staff to hire for the day of the town fete based on an estimate of likely customers
- a busy office of twenty workers has been hit by influenza and the manager is having to anticipate the temporary cover required for the next day based on a judgement of which individuals may be absent.

Combining probabilities

The **multiplication rule** applies to the combination of **independent events**. Where the occurrence of one event is unaffected by the occurrence of another, then the events are said to be independent. For example, subsequent dice throws are unaffected by previous throws, so they are independent events.

Where the combined probability of two or more independent events all occurring is required, then the probabilities of the individual events are multiplied.

$$P(A \text{ and } B) = P(A) \times P(B)$$

Using the dice throw example again, the probability of any one number being thrown is 1/6. So the probability of throwing a 1 followed by a 6 will be:

$$P(1 \text{ and } 6) = \frac{1}{6} \times \frac{1}{6} = \frac{1}{36}$$

This seems reasonable as there must be less chance of two events happening together compared to just one event.

The **addition rule** is used to combine probabilities that relate to mutually exclusive events. Mutually exclusive events are events that cannot occur together. For example, to throw a dice once and obtain either a 1 or a 6 are mutually exclusive events, as it is not possible to get both. However, to throw an odd number or a number over three are not mutually exclusive events, because a 5 would satisfy both events.

Where one outcome (A) or another (B) is required that are mutually exclusive events:

$$P(A \text{ or } B) = P(A) + P(B)$$

For example, the probability of throwing a 1 or a 6:

$$P(1 \text{ or } 6) = \frac{1}{6} + \frac{1}{6} = \frac{1}{3}$$

This seems reasonable as there must be a better chance of getting a 1 or a 6 compared to throwing one particular number.

So to summarise, provided the various conditions are fulfilled, for:

- one event *and* another then *multiply* probabilities
- one event *or* another then *add* probabilities.

Exercise 18.1   Combining probabilities

A leisure centre has undertaken a survey of customers on two different days to discover the usage of facilities.

Activity	Number of customers	
	Tuesday	Saturday
Swimming	50	70
Squash	20	30
Gym	30	20
Tennis	10	30
Total	110	150

Tasks

Required, for each day:

1   *What is the probability that a customer has come to play squash?*

2 *What is the probability that a customer came to play tennis?*

3 *What is the probability that a customer came to play squash or tennis?*

4 *Taking two customers at random, what is the probability that the first will have played squash and the second will have played tennis?*

5 *What is the probability that a customer came to swim or exercise in the gym?*

Expectation

In business, an event occurring usually results in a value being gained or lost. To calculate the expected value of an event, called its **expectation**, it is necessary to combine its value with its probability.

$$\text{Expectation} = \text{P(event)} \times \text{value of event}$$

For example, the success of a new product launch will depend on a number of market uncertainties, but the sales director has identified three scenarios for which he has assigned values and probabilities. There is a 40 per cent chance of £30 000 profits, 50 per cent chance of £40 000 profits and 10 per cent chance of £50 000 profits.

Profit expectation = (£30 000 × 0.40) + (£40 000 × 0.50) + (£50 000 × 0.10) = £37 000

Unfortunately the term expectation in this context is not the same as expected value. The expectation is the average value of possible outcomes. Like all average calculations it can be criticised for not indicating the dispersion of values around this central point.

Exercise 18.2   Expectation

A survey of people entering a travel agency produced the following data:

Observation	Numbers	Commission (£)	
Bookings:			
package holidays including flight	120	25	Of which 90 took out insurance
flight only	20	10	Of which 12 took out insurance
theatre tickets	10	2	
coach tour	30	5	
Left without a sale being made	180		
Total	360		

The travel agent earns a commission of £10 for every insurance policy sold.

Tasks

1 *Calculate the expected commission earned for a person entering the travel agency.*

2 *How could this information be used?*

Binomial distribution

There are many situations where the outcome of an experiment fits into just two categories. In statistical terms the outcome is often said to be a success or failure. Something has either happened or it has not happened. For example, someone entering a shop will either buy something or will not. A quality check will reveal that a product is acceptable or not acceptable.

The binomial distribution is a statistical tool for calculating the probability that a stated number of successes will occur on the basis of certain other information.

Binomial experiments have the following properties:

1 fixed number of n trials (observations)
2 trials are independent of one another
3 each trial has only two outcomes – success or failure
4 the probability of success p is the same for each trial.

To find the probability of x successes out of n trials:

$$P(x) = \frac{n!}{x!(n-x)!} \, p^x (1-p)^{n-x}$$

Note: $n! = n \times (n-1) \times (n-2) \times \dots \times 3 \times 2 \times 1.$

Illustration

From past experience a travel agency knows that 30 per cent of customers will buy travel insurance in addition to their holiday. What is the probability that three of the next four customers will purchase travel insurance?

$$P(3) = \frac{4!}{3!(4-3)!} 0.3^3 (1-0.3)^{4-3}$$

$$= \frac{24}{6} \times 0.027(0.7) = 0.0756$$

Exercise 18.3   Binomial distribution

A sales representative needs to make 4 sales from the next 8 customer visits to meet her monthly target. Experience has shown that the probability of a successful visit is 0.2. What is the probability that she will meet the target?

The number of times an event is expected to occur is measured by the **mean of the binomial distribution.** The calculation of the mean is a rearrangement of the relative frequency method of calculating probability.

$$\text{mean} = np$$

where n = number of trials and p = probability of an event occurring.

Illustration

From the travel agency example above:

$$\text{mean} = 4 \times 0.3 = 1.2$$

Therefore out of 4 customers it is expected that 1.2 will buy insurance, but it is also known that there is a 0.0756 chance of 3 customers buying insurance. Clearly a measure of the dispersion of the binomial distribution would be valuable for establishing how typical the mean is.

$$\text{Standard deviation} = \sqrt{npq}$$

where q = chance of the event not happening, i.e. $q = (1-p)$.

In this example, standard deviation = $4 \times 0.7 \times 0.3$ = 0.84.

Under most circumstances the binomial distribution can be approximated by the normal distribution (see next section) so it is possible to determine the probability of a range of values of success based on the number of standard deviations from the mean.

Normal distribution

The normal distribution is a continuous probability distribution. To allow frequencies to be summarised, values of the variable are grouped into categories and this allows data to be presented in the form of a frequency table or a histogram. If the mid-points of the histogram are joined by lines then Figure 18.1 is not untypical of many sets of data.

Figure 18.1   Histogram and distribution curve

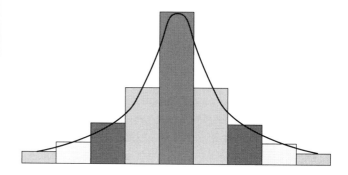

The normal probability distribution is valuable as it has been found that many practical situations appear to fit this distribution of outcomes. Like Figure 18.1, the normal distribution is bell shaped and symmetrical with a high proportion of frequencies grouped around the centre point.

Because the frequency distribution is symmetrical the highest point on the curve is the mean, which also equals the median and mode. The shape of the curve is described by the mean and standard deviation of the distribution. The larger the standard deviation the more spread out the data, and hence the flatter the curve.

As with the histograms from which it is often drawn, the area under the normal distribution curve equates to the density of frequencies for each grouping of the variable. Hence the area also equates to the probability of that range of values actually occurring.

Because the normal distribution approximates to so many situations in practice, a table has been constructed to give probabilities for what is called a **standard normal distribution** (Appendix I). This distribution has a mean = 0 and a horizontal scale measured in standard deviations.

For a given number of standard deviations the table gives the proportion of the curve to one side of the mean. The table is constructed so that standard deviations can be read to two decimal places using the table rows and columns.

Figure 18.2 Normal distribution and standard deviations

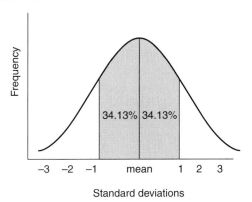

For example, a standard deviation of 1.11 would return 0.3665. The tables also show that 34.13 per cent of the frequencies above the mean are within 1.0 standard deviation. Therefore there are 68.26 per cent of frequencies either side of the mean that are within 1 standard deviation.

All that is needed for any distribution that displays normal distribution characteristics is the mean and standard deviation of the distribution. To use the normal distribution table any range of values for which probabilities are required must be converted into the number of standard deviations from the mean.

$$\text{Number of standard deviations} = \frac{\text{Maximum or minimum value} - \text{mean}}{\text{Standard deviation}}$$

Illustration

For a frequency distribution which is normally distributed with a mean of 10, a standard deviation of 5, find the probability of a value being 20 or below.

Solution

$$\text{Number of standard deviations above the mean} = \frac{20 - 10}{5} = 2$$

The normal distribution table gives a probability of 0.4772 for 2 standard deviations. This represents the probability of a value between 10 and 20. There is a 50 per cent chance of a value being below the mean so there is a 0.9772 probability of the value being 20 or less.

Knowing that the probability of all outcomes is 1, the normal distribution table can be adapted to particular circumstances. So using the data from the previous example, it is possible to calculate the probability of a value being above 20:

$$P(\text{over } 20) = 1 - 0.9772 = 0.0228$$

Because a standard deviation in the centre of a normal distribution covers more frequencies than one on the edge, it is important to appreciate that the normal distribution table gives probabilities for ranges that are adjacent to the mean. But by breaking down a problem into its constituent parts, it is possible to find the probability of a range that is distant from the mean.

Illustration

A frequency distribution displaying normal distribution characteristics has a mean of 20 and a standard deviation of 5. Find the probability of a value being between 16 and 18.

To find the number of standard deviations between 16 and the mean 20:

$$\text{Number of standard deviations} = \frac{20 - 16}{5} = 0.8$$

To find the number of standard deviations between 18 and 20:

$$\text{Number of standard deviations} = \frac{18 - 20}{5} = 0.4$$

Using the table for 0.4 and 0.8 standard deviations gives probabilities of 0.1554 and 0.2881 respectively. Hence the probability of being between 16 and 18:

$$P(\text{between } 16 \text{ and } 18) = 0.2881 - 0.1554 = 0.1327$$

Note that it was important to find the probability for each class boundary in relation to the mean separately. This is because the probability of 0.4 standard deviations depends on where it is in relation to the mean. There is a 0.1554 probability of a value within the first 0.4 standard deviations of the mean, but this decreases to 0.1327 for the next 0.4 standard deviations.

Exercise 18.4   Normal distribution

A manufacturer of machine tools wants to offer a guarantee on products it sells. The life of tools follows the normal distribution curve. The average life of a tool is 3 000 hours with a standard deviation of 200 hours. Calculate how many hours the tools should be guaranteed for to ensure no more than 1 per cent are returned.

Exercise 18.5   Normal distribution

The sizes of trousers manufactured by a clothing manufacturer are normally distributed around the stated nominal size. Jeans have a standard deviation of 0.2 inches and a new customer has stipulated that all trousers must be within 0.5 inches of the stated size. Calculate the number of jeans out of a batch of 1000 that would have to be rejected before shipping to the customer.

Sampling theory

The normal distribution is of particular value when using sampling to estimate the statistical characteristics of a population.

The mean of a sample is an estimation of the population mean. Further samples are likely to produce different mean values but they will tend to distribute themselves around the true population mean, with more sample means being near the population mean than being away from it. In fact, it is known that if every possible combination of samples were taken, the sample means of all the samples would be **normally distributed** around the actual population mean. The standard deviation of a sample means distribution is called the **standard error.**

For large samples of at least 30 items and where the sample represents no more than 5 per cent of the population:

$$\text{Standard error of the mean} = \frac{\text{standard deviation of the sample}}{\sqrt{\text{sample size}}}$$

In notation form $S_x = \dfrac{S}{\sqrt{n}}$

As the sample size increases, the standard error is reduced.

Illustration

A random sample of 50 items taken from the components store has a mean value of £6.00 with a sample standard deviation of £3.00. Find the standard error of the mean.

$$\text{Standard error of the mean} = \frac{3.00}{\sqrt{50}} = £0.42$$

Because of the properties of a normal distribution curve, it is known that 1.96 standard errors either side of the population mean covers 95 per cent of all samples and 2.58 standard errors either side covers 99 per cent of all samples.

It is therefore possible to state the probability that the actual population mean lies within a specified range (known as **confidence limits**) of the sample mean.

Taking the above example of stock items, it is possible to state:

that with 95 per cent confidence, the actual stock value mean is £6.00 + or − 1.96 × £0.42 = £5.17 to £6.83

or with 99 per cent confidence, the actual stock value mean is £6.00 + or − 2.58 × £0.42 = £4.91 to £7.09

Figure 18.3 1.96 Standard errors

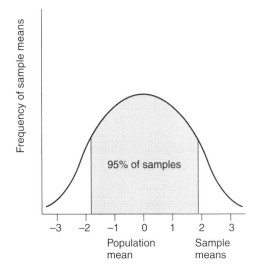

Figure 18.4 2.58 Standard errors

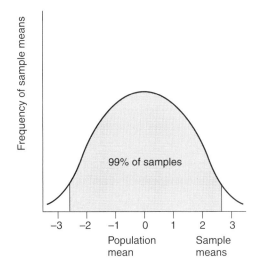

Exercise 18.6   Estimating the population mean

Product T2 has been manufactured 2 000 times. A sample of 35 units has provided a mean cost of £0.90 per unit with a standard deviation of £0.12. With 95 per cent and 99 per cent confidence levels, what is the actual mean cost of the component?

The calculation of the standard error accounts for the absolute sample size, and the bigger the sample the smaller the error. However, it is also true that if the sample is relatively large in relation to the population from which it is drawn, then the standard error will be further reduced.

Where the sample is more than 5 per cent of the total population then the standard error calculation is adjusted by multiplying it by the following factor:

$$\text{Finite population correction factor} = \sqrt{\frac{\text{Population size} - \text{sample size}}{\text{Population size} - 1}}$$

Exercise 18.7 Finite population correction factor

A sample of 40 purchase invoices has been randomly selected from 500 received during the past year. The mean value of the sample was £150 with a standard deviation of £50. With 95 per cent confidence what is the mean of all 500 invoices?

Where *samples are small*, i.e. are less than 30, the sample means are not normally distributed. In these cases the **Student's t distribution** table is used instead of the Normal distribution tables. In other respects the method is exactly the same. For 95 per cent confidence limits use 2.262 standard deviations, for 99 per cent use 3.250 standard deviations.

It is also possible to work back from a desired range of confidence limits to find the *size of sample* that should be selected.

Continuing with the components store illustration, if having taken the first sample it was decided that a sample mean was required, that would be within £0.50 of the actual mean. Then with a confidence level of 95 per cent:

$$\text{Standard error of the sample} = \frac{£0.50}{1.96} = £0.255$$

To find the sample size, using:

$$\text{Standard error of the mean} = \frac{\text{standard deviation of the sample}}{\sqrt{\text{sample size}}}$$

$$£0.255 = \frac{£3.00}{\sqrt{n}}$$

Sample size $= (3.00/0.255)^2 = 139$ items.

Exercise 18.8 Sampling with Student's t distribution

Contract Engineering Ltd produces mechanical components for the aerospace industry. It employs two banks of machines, the first group date from the firm's start-up 22 years ago, and a newer group of machines installed 4 years ago as part of an expansion plan. From the business's costing records it is known that the average cost of manufacturing the T7 component on the old machine is £7.45. The cost accountant has been asked by the production manager to support his assertion that producing the component on an old machine increases the average cost.

The cost accountant has ascertained that the component has been made on 500 occasions with the new machines and has randomly selected the following sample of costs:

£6.80, £7.20, £7.10, £7.60, £7.40, £7.50, £7.30, £7.90, £7.10, £7.80, £7.20, £7.20, £7.60, £7.50, £7.30, £7.20, £7.20, £7.00, £7.30, £7.20.

Tasks

1 *Calculate the mean, standard deviation and standard error of the sample.*
2 *Using 95 per cent confidence limits, can the cost accountant confirm that the new machines reduces the cost of the T7 component?*

Statistical methods

Correlation

Sometimes there is the need to measure the strength of the relationship between two variables. For example, it is hoped that increased advertising has led to increased sales. Where a change in one item has been affected by a change in another, there is said to be a **correlation** between the values of the two items. The variable that is being predicted is the dependent variable Y and its change is correlated to an independent variable X.

A scatter diagram can be prepared to give an initial view as to whether variables are correlated. The independent variable X is plotted on the horizontal axis and the dependent variable on the Y axis.

Illustration

The following data relates to sales made by an ice-cream firm during the past year.

	Jan.	Feb.	Mar	Apr.	May	June	July	Aug.	Sept.	Oct.	Nov.	Dec.
Average C°	3	5	8	11	13	18	21	22	18	11	6	4
Sales £'000s	12	13	12	16	18	30	45	50	28	14	8	9

A scatter diagram of the data is shown in Figure 18.5.

Figure 18.5 Ice-cream sales to temperatures

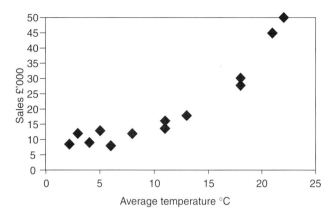

Clearly there appears to be some correlation between sales and average daily temperatures.

Exercise 18.9 Scatter diagram

Present the following data in the form of a suitable diagram to highlight a possible relationship between the variables of advertising and sales revenues.

(£'000)	Jan.	Feb.	Mar	Apr.	May	June	July	Aug.	Sept.	Oct.	Nov.	Dec.
Advertising	6	8	12	15	7	22	17	11	5	3	14	9
Sales	130	135	145	155	140	180	170	140	132	120	160	145

Evaluate the relationship between the two variables.

The **correlation coefficient** r is a measure of the linear relationship between two variables. It is calculated from n pairs of values of variables X and Y.

$$r = \frac{\sum xy - (\sum x \times \sum y) / n}{\sqrt{\sum x^2 - (\sum x)^2 / n} \times \sqrt{\sum y^2 - (\sum y)^2 / n}}$$

The coefficient is a value from -1 to 1. A value of zero indicates no linear relationship between the variables, whereas -1 shows a perfect negative linear relationship and 1 a perfect positive linear relationship. A positive coefficient indicates that as one variable increases or decreases in value, so does the other. A negative coefficient indicates that as one variable increases the other decreases, and vice versa. The coefficient will be at least 0.75 or -0.75 if there is a significant relationship between the variables. It is useful to combine a scatter diagram with the coefficient of correlation to provide a better understanding of the relationship. A diagram that produces a curve rather than a straight line can still provide a high coefficient if the relationship between the variables is strong.

Illustration

The ColorPress Ltd is a printing company specialising in wrappers for food products. The managing director believes there may be a relationship between the number of colours used on a print run and the resulting profitability of work done. For the last 10 print runs the number of colours (X) have been recorded with the job's respective profit margin percentage (Y). Three further columns have been produced to calculate XY, X^2 and Y^2. Calculate the correlation coefficient of number of colours to profit margin percentage.

Number of colours X	Profit margin % Y	XY	X^2	Y^2
4	15	60	16	225
5	12	60	25	144
4	11	44	16	121
6	16	96	36	256
3	9	27	9	81
5	16	80	25	256
7	18	126	49	324
6	16	96	36	256
8	20	160	64	400
6	17	102	36	289
Total 54	150	851	312	2352

$$n = 10$$

$$r = \frac{851 - (54 \times 150) / 10}{\sqrt{312 - 2916 / 10} \times \sqrt{2352 - 22500 / 10}}$$

$$= \frac{851 - 810}{\sqrt{20.4} \times \sqrt{102}} = \frac{41}{45.61} = 0.8987$$

The coefficient of correlation shows a fairly strong relationship between the two variables.

Exercise 18.10 Coefficient of correlation

Calculate the coefficient of correlation for the data tabled earlier in respect of:

1 temperature and ice-cream sales, and
2 advertising and sales.

The correlation coefficient can be calculated quickly and accurately using a *spreadsheet* function. The data relating to X and Y above could be keyed into columns B and C of a spreadsheet. The numerical data keyed into rows 2–11 can then be referred to by the following function keyed into a vacant cell:

$$=correl(b2:b11,c2:c11)$$

This function is in the format =correl(1st data range, 2nd data range).

Exercise 18.11 Coefficient of correlation with a spreadsheet

Cavetron UK Ltd manufactures on a batch production basis to customer orders. The following sales and profit figures relate to individual jobs completed in June.

Sales (£'000) 23 82 26 52 36 46 67 97 20 10 5 59

Profit (£'000)   4 22 5 11 7 11 15 29 3 1 0 14

The factory manager has noticed a possible relationship between the size of the job and the percentage profit earned.

Tasks

1 *Using a spreadsheet calculate the correlation coefficient of profit margin percentage to sales.*
2 *Comment on the relationship.*

Regression

The technique of regression analysis can be used to express the readings on a scatter diagram in terms of a straight line. This may be useful once it has been established that there is a linear correlation between two variables as the line could then be extrapolated to aid forecasting. The equation of a straight line is:

$$Y = a + bX$$

where *a* is where the line intercepts the vertical axis and *b* represents the gradient of the line, i.e. the changes in *Y* relative to *X*.

If the values of *a* and *b* are known, then the line can be drawn by inserting values of *X* into the formula and calculating the corresponding value of Y. The values of *X* used should be within the range of values contained in the data set.

Illustration

Given the equation $Y = 10 + X \times 1/20$ draw the corresponding straight line.

Solution

When $X = 0$ then $Y = 10$
When $X = 400$ then $Y = 30$

The line can now be drawn.

Figure 18.6 Illustration of a straight line graph

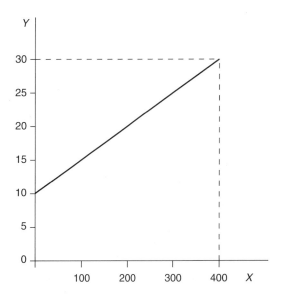

For a scatter diagram it is possible to draw a 'line of best fit' by eye. The process requires a line to be drawn that is as near as possible to each of the points plotted. Where there is a cluster of points the resulting line will tend to pass between them.

However, the values of *a* and *b* can be calculated where an accurate line is required for *n* pairs of observations. The values calculated are called **least squares estimates** because the resulting line minimises the sum of the squared distances away from each point.

$$a = \frac{\Sigma y - b\Sigma x}{n}$$

$$b = \frac{\Sigma xy - (\Sigma x \times \Sigma y)/n}{\Sigma x^2 - (\Sigma x)^2/n}$$

Illustration

Using the data from ColorPress, the values of *a* and *b* can be calculated.

$$b - \frac{851 - (54\ 3\ 150)/10}{312 - 54^2/10} = \frac{851 - 810}{20.4} = 2.01$$

$$a = \frac{150 - b54}{10} = 4.146$$

Using the values of *a* and *b* above, together with a value of say 8 for *X*, it is possible to find a corresponding value for *Y* using the general formula for a straight line.

$$Y = 4.146 + (2.01 \times 8) \quad = 20.2$$

The line drawn according to this formula is called a least squares line. It will pass through the following two points: where ($Y = 4.146$, $X = 0$) and ($Y = 20.2$ and $X = 8$).

The formula can now be used to predict a future value of *Y* for any value of *X* between 3 and 8.

Exercise 18.12 Least squares regression

1 Calculate least squares estimates for the data tabled earlier in respect of:
   ■ temperature and ice-cream sales,
   ■ advertising and sales.
2 Draw a line of best fit for advertising to sales using these estimates.

Time series

Many aspects of business can be usefully measured against time, for examples sales volumes, cost of resources used and staff absenteeism. The tabulation of a variable's value against a time period is called a **time series**. Values may be affected by various factors over time and for general analysis purposes it is generally accepted that there are four components of a time series:

1 **Trend** – There is an underlying trend in individual values being recorded. For example, the long-term change in sales may be a gradual increase despite volatile movements up and down each month.
2 **Seasonal variation** – Many businesses experience changes according to the seasons including sales of ice-cream, garden materials and seaside holidays. Less obvious situations may be confirmed with time series analysis, for example, many fish and chip shops experience falls in demand during hot summer spells.
3 **Cyclical variation** – Some businesses have variations in demand over periods of more than one year. Capital goods manufacturers and construction firms experience marked variations in their business activity depending on the phase of the economic cycle. Their fortunes are often a magnification of conditions in the general economy as they benefit early and disproportionately from an upswing in the economy, but suffer from a dearth of sales as the economic cycle turns from growth to maturity. There may be other cycles that affect particular types of businesses. A computer services company may have identified marked variations in demand corresponding to the periodic launch of new processing chips or the issue of new software releases. To measure the effect of cycles it is often necessary to have data covering a considerable number of years.
4 **Irregular or random variations** – This category contains variations that cannot be explained by any of the other three components of the time series.

In order to forecast future values, a time series must be analysed for its component parts. A forecast value will be the sum of items 1–3, with a qualification based on the range of irregular variations experienced to date.

The first step to understanding a time series is to remove variations due to seasonal and cyclical factors. This is done by smoothing individual values by a technique called moving averages.

The principle of the **moving average** technique is to find an average value during a cycle. Therefore to find the seasonal variation, values need to be averaged for a one year period on a moving basis. The same method applies to cyclical variations, except that the moving average will be based on the length of the cycle being considered.

The following illustration applies moving averages to seasonal variations.

Illustration

The Weary Traveller is situated in the heart of England and caters mainly for business travellers, but also enjoys some tourist trade. The hotel has recorded the following sales figures for the past four years with the first quarter starting on 1 January each year.

Year	Quarter	Sales (£'000)	Total for year (£'000)	Moving average (£'000)	Centred MA (£'000)
1	1	180			
	2	189			
			764	191.000	
	3	205			191.500
			768	192.000	
	4	190			192.500
			772	193.000	
2	1	184			193.875
			779	194.750	
	2	193			195.625
			786	196.500	
	3	212			196.750
			788	197.000	
	4	197			197.750
			794	198.500	
3	1	186			199.375
			801	200.250	
	2	199			200.500
			803	200.750	
	3	219			201.250
			807	201.750	
	4	199			202.625
			814	203.500	
4	1	190			204.125
			819	204.750	
	2	206			205.250
			823	205.750	
	3	224			
	4	203			

Method

1 Add the values for the first 12 months of sales. The total is recorded on the line between the second and third quarters as this is the middle point in the series.
2 Continue one quarter at a time down the series of values calculating the total for a moving 12-month period until the last quarter is reached. The second total will therefore include sales for quarters 2, 3, 4 and 5.
3 Calculate the quarterly moving average by taking the 12-month total and divide by 4.
4 It is necessary to identify the moving average figures against specific periods, so this is done by calculating a

centred moving average. The centred moving
average is not required where the moving average is
calculated from an odd number of values, e.g. where
the moving average is based on days in the week.

5 The next step is to estimate the **seasonal variation** for
each quarter. There are two widely recognised
methods of isolating the trend from seasonal and
cyclical variations. These are often referred to as the
additive model and the proportional model. The
additive model uses an absolute value for each
variation, whereas the proportional model relates the
size of the variation to the underlying trend.

Illustration

The current trend for umbrella sales indicates a weekly
sales figure of £1 000. However, because it is now winter,
the seasonal variation adds £500 to that figure giving total
sales of £1 500 per week. The underlying trend for
umbrella sales is forecast to be £1 200 per week for next
winter.

Using the **additive model,** the weekly sales forecast for
the same time next year will be £1 200 plus the seasonal
variation of £500, giving a total of £1 700.

The **proportional model,** however, requires the seasonal
variation to be stated as a proportion of the trend and is
therefore currently 50 per cent (£500/£1 000). For next
winter sales will therefore be forecast as £1 800 (£1 200 +
50 per cent).

The proportional model is often considered the most
appropriate for business applications and is the one
illustrated further here. Unless there is a steep underlying
trend, the results from each method will be similar.

Continuing with the data relating to the Weary Traveller,
we can isolate the seasonal effect.

Year	Quarter	Period number	Sales (£'000)	Centred M.Ave. (£'000)	Seasonal index (sales/ CM.Ave)	Average seasonal index	Deseasonal sales (£'000)
1	1	1	180				191.94
	2	2	189				190.05
	3	3	205	191.500	1.0705	1.0790	189.99
	4	4	190	192.500	0.9870	0.9887	192.19
2	1	5	184	193.875	0.9491	0.9378	196.20
	2	6	193	195.625	0.9866	0.9945	194.07
	3	7	212	196.750	1.0775	1.0790	196.48
	4	8	197	197.750	0.9962	0.9887	199.27
3	1	9	186	199.375	0.9329	0.9378	198.34
	2	10	199	200.500	0.9925	0.9945	200.10
	3	11	219	201.250	1.0882	1.0790	202.97
	4	12	199	202.625	0.9821	0.9887	201.29
4	1	13	190	204.125	0.9308	0.9378	202.60
	2	14	206	205.250	1.0037	0.9945	207.14
	3	15	224				207.60
	4	16	203				205.34

Method

1 Divide each quarter's sales by the centred moving
average to give a seasonal index. For example, the
index for quarter 3 of year 1 is 1.0705 (calculated
205/191.50), which shows that the seasonal variation
has contributed to more than average sales for this
quarter.

2 The seasonal variation is deemed to be explained by
the average of the indices for the same quarter each
year. Therefore, in this illustration the average seasonal
index is the average of 3 figures. If it is found that the
total of the seasonal indices does not quite add to 4, the
components are adjusted on a pro-rata basis.

Quarter	Calculation of average seasonal index	Average seasonal index	Adj. seasonal index
1	$\dfrac{0.9491 + 0.9329 + 0.9308}{3}$	0.9376	0.9378
2	$\dfrac{0.9866 + 0.9925 + 1.0037}{3}$	0.9943	0.9945
3	$\dfrac{1.0705 + 1.0775 + 1.0882}{3}$	1.0787	1.0790
4	$\dfrac{0.9870 + 0.9962 + 0.9821}{3}$	0.9884	0.9887
Total		3.9990	4.0000

3 Applying the average seasonal index to each quarter's
sales provides a deseasonalised sales figure. For
example, quarter 3 sales of £205 000 is divided by
1.0790 to give deseasonalised sales of £189 991.

If the deseasonalised sales show a linear relationship to
time, then the trend can be represented by a straight line
that can be extrapolated for future periods. The line of
best fit may be drawn by hand or more accurately by
calculating a least squares regression line. In this example,

the period number and the deseasonalised sales figures correspond to a correlation coefficient of 0.9647.

Using the above data

$$b = \frac{\Sigma xy - (\Sigma x \ 3 \ \Sigma y) / n}{\Sigma x^2 - (\Sigma x)^2 / n} = \frac{27393.15 - (136 \ 3 \ 3175.568) / 16\cdot}{1496 - 18496 / 16} = 1.1789$$

$$a = \frac{\Sigma y - b\Sigma x}{n} = \frac{3175.568 - 136b}{16} = 188.45$$

The equation of the trend line is therefore $Y = 188.45 + 1.1789X$ where X represents the time period number, and Y represents the trend sales figure.

The trend line can be extrapolated to enable forecasts for future periods to be made, or alternatively, the line formula allows trend sales figures to be calculated. The trend forecast is then adjusted for seasonal variations by multiplying by the seasonal component.

To forecast sales for year 5 for the Weary Traveller Lodge:

Year	Quarter number	Period	Trend using line equation component	Seasonal sales	Forecast (£'000)
5	1	17	Sales = 188.45 + (1.1789 × 17) = 208.49	0.9378	195.52
	2	18	Sales = 188.45 + (1.1789 × 18) = 209.67	0.9945	208.52
	3	19	Sales = 188.45 + (1.1789 × 19) = 210.85	1.0790	227.51
	4	20	Sales = 188.45 + (1.1789 × 20) = 212.03	0.9887	209.63
					841.18

Forecasts obtained by this method will only be accurate to the extent that past conditions apply to future periods. The trend may be affected by a cyclical variation that has not yet been identified, and of course the seasonal variation may change. Of particular significance is the fact that irregular variations have not been accounted for. These can be quantified as they are the differences between the deseasonalised figures and the trend (centred moving average). Future forecasts can be qualified with an error range based on these past irregular variations.

Exercise 18.13   Time series analysis

A clothes retailer has recorded the following sales for the past 4 years:

(£'000)	Jan.–Mar	Apr.–June	July–Sept.	Oct.–Dec.
19X5	552	640	610	630
19X6	540	635	580	615
19X7	530	614	575	608
19X8	522	611	565	601

Tasks

1 *Use moving averages to isolate the seasonal variation in the sales figures.*
2 *Calculate least squared estimates for the line representing the underlying sales trend.*
3 *Forecast sales for the four quarters of 19X9.*

Linear programming

Where competing activities make demands on limited resources, choices have to be made to optimise business objectives. Where there is just one limiting factor the contribution based approach as described in Chapter 15, can be used. However, some situations place more than one constraint on the decision maker, and so linear programming may be the appropriate technique to use.

For the technique to be used certain conditions must be present:

1 The problem requires an objective to be optimised. Typically exercises in this area are about allocating resources to minimise cost or to find the product mix that maximises profit.
2 There must be a linear relationship between the resources used and the outcome aimed for. Fortunately the usage of many resources is in proportion to output and in many other cases the simplification does not distort the outcome significantly. Examples include materials, labour hours and machine time.
3 There are a number of constraints affecting the stated objective. These may include limited amounts of physical resources, such as materials, labour and productive capacity. Other constraints include a limited market or inadequate finance to fund operations.

Linear programming problems can be solved by either the graphical approach or the simplex method. The graphical approach is described here, although it is only appropriate where there are just two variables to choose between. The simplex method uses matrices and has no restrictions on the number of alternatives for which values are required.

The objective and constraints of the decision maker are first expressed in mathematical form.

Illustration

Suitcase Ltd produces and sells two types of cases: holdalls and cabin bags. The two materials used, leather and silk, are in limited supply and so the company's management has to decide on the product mix that optimises profit from their usage.

	Leather	Silk
		(from a one metre roll)
One holdall uses	2 m²	20 cm
One cabin bag uses	1 m²	20 cm
Material available	100 m²	1400 cm

Holdalls and cabin bags contribute £16 and £12 respectively to overheads and profits. A maximum of 50 cabin bags can be sold.

Find the product mix that maximises contribution.

Solution

The objective is to maximise contribution. It is stated that for every holdall the firm makes £16 contribution, and for every cabin bag £12. The total contribution from holdalls will therefore be £16 multiplied by the number of holdalls. The total contribution from cabin bags will be £12 multiplied by the number of bags. In mathematical terms the **objective function** is therefore:

$$\text{Maximise } £16H + £12C$$

where H is the number of holdalls and C is the number of cabin bags.

Each **constraint** is also expressed in mathematical terms:

Leather usage is 2 m² for a holdall and 1 m² for a cabin bag but usage cannot be more than 100 m² in total. The formula is therefore:

Leather constraint $\qquad 2H + 1C \leq 100$ m²

Similarly, the silk constraint can be expressed as:

Silk constraint $\qquad 20H + 20C \leq 1400$ cm

In addition, the maximum number of cabin cases that can be sold is 50.

Sales constraint $\qquad C \leq 50$

The objective function and constraints are shown as lines on a graph. The axes represent the variables for which values are required. In the example of Suitcase Ltd the vertical axis can represent the number of holdalls and the horizontal axis the number of cabin bags. To find a suitable scale for the axes start by finding the maximum

value possible for each variable from the constraint equations. This is done by giving a value of zero to the other variable. In the case of the leather constraint, no more than 50 holdalls could be produced if the total 100 m² is divided by 2 m². It is useful to tabulate the results:

Constraint	Maximum number of holdalls	Maximum number of cases
Leather constraint	50	100
Silk constraint	70	70
Sales constraint		50

The horizontal axis should be scaled to 70 for holdalls and the vertical axis to 100 for cabin bags.

The constraint lines can now be drawn using the points already identified in the table above. In drawing the leather constraint line it is known that two extreme production possibilities exist: either 50 holdalls and no cabin bags or 100 cabin bags and no holdalls. The leather constraint can be drawn as a straight line between these two points, one on each axis. Taking any point along this line provides a product mix that uses all of the 100 m² of leather available. Any point below and to the left of this line is a feasible product mix although it will not make full use of the leather available. All points above the line relate to product mixes that require more leather than is available. The other constraint lines can also be drawn.

Figure 18.7 Suitcase Ltd – constraints

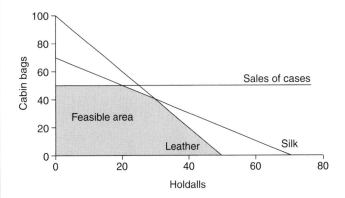

The shaded area represents the **feasible area.** Any point taken within this area corresponds to a product mix that is possible, as it is below and to the left of all the constraint lines. A point on a constraint line will maximise the usage of that constraint. The point where the leather and silk constraint lines intersect identifies the product mix that consumes all of both materials. However, this is not necessarily the mix that satisfies the objective function.

The objective function when drawn as a line needs to reflect the relative profitability of each of the products.

The objective function will be maximised the further it can be drawn away from the origin as that equates to more products being produced. The objective function is drawn so that any point along the line produces the same value (in this case contribution) even as product mix is changing.

It is necessary to find the number of each variable which, on its own, would achieve a given objective total.

Objective function

Maximise $£16H + £12C$

For a contribution of say $£480$

Value on the horizontal axis where $C = 0$	$£16H = £480$	$H = 30$
Value on the vertical axis where $H = 0$	$£12C = £480$	$C = 40$

For a contribution of say $£1\,200$

Value on the horizontal axis where $C = 0$	$£16H = £1\,200$	$H = 75$
Value on the vertical axis where $H = 0$	$£12C = £1\,200$	$C = 100$

The following diagram shows the objective function for these two different contribution levels.

Figure 18.8 Suitcase Ltd – objective function

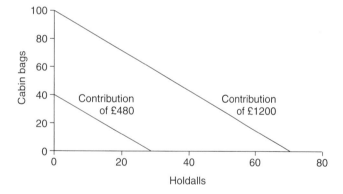

Notice that the gradient of each line is the same. It is this relationship between the profitability of one product and of the other that needs to be incorporated into the solution of the problem. To produce one fewer of one of the products requires a fixed amount of the other product to make up the contribution otherwise lost.

The point where the objective function is furthest from the origin but still on the boundary of the feasible area provides its maximum value. At this stage it is not important where the objective function is drawn on the diagram, provided the gradient is correct. Drawing an objective function equal to $£1\,200$ on the constraints diagram produces an objective function that is outside the feasible area (dotted line in Figure 18.9). By moving this line towards the feasible area the optimal mix of variables

Figure 18.9 Suitcase Ltd – solution

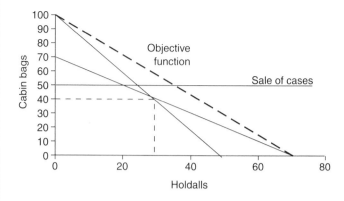

is identified where the boundary of the feasible area is first hit.

In this case the solution is where the leather and silk constraints also intersect, i.e. to produce 40 cabin bags and 30 holdalls. However, the optimal solution could have been at any of the points where the constraint lines intersect one another or intersect one of the axes. If the objective function had been steeper (i.e. holdalls were even more profitable, relative to cabin bags) the solution may have been to produce 50 holdalls and no cabin bags. If the objective function had been shallower (i.e. where cabin bags had been more profitable than holdalls) the solution may have been to produce 80 cabin bags and no holdalls, or to have produced 50 cabin bags and 20 holdalls.

The example of Suitcase Ltd involved maximising the objective function. The graphical approach can also be used to solve a minimisation problem. For example, the objective function may be to minimise cost by considering different mixes of factors of production. The same method is used as for maximising, except that the optimal point is furthest to the left of the feasible area.

The graphical approach to linear programming is simple in concept and provides an easily understandable representation of the problem. The effect of changes to underlying assumptions can easily be seen on the diagram and other solutions can be evaluated for their distance from the optimal point. It is also easy to see and measure the amount of each resource that is under-utilised, as this is represented by the distance between the optimal point and the appropriate constraint line.

The method has a number of disadvantages. It can only be used for two variables and the diagram becomes cluttered and confusing if there are many constraints. It also assumes that units of production can be split, so it is important that only whole numbers are read from the diagram scales.

Exercise 18.14   Graphical approach to linear programming

The Little Chip Choc Company is a small confectionery manufacturer that is preparing for Easter and is having to decide on the mix of chocolate eggs and chocolate rabbits which maximises the contribution to overheads and profit. Unfortunately, due to a mistake in purchase ordering, the chocolate and creme filling to be used are in limited supply.

	Chocolate	Creme filling
One egg uses	50 g	50 g
One rabbit uses	50 g	20 g
Material available	800 kg	500 kg

Product contribution is 6p for a rabbit and 10p for an egg.

Tasks

1 *Find the product mix that maximises contribution.*
2 *Calculate the maximum contribution and analyse the use of the material available between the two products.*

Exercise 18.15   Graphical approach to linear programming

St Mary's is a private college specialising in accountancy and business and finance courses. The college has experienced three main constraints in providing courses. There are 40 hours per week available to run courses in the computer suite, and the time of accountancy staff available is limited to a maximum of 90 hours per week.

Each type of course requires the following use of limited resources:

	Computer suite hours/week	Accountancy staff hours/week
Accountancy course	5	10
Business and finance	2	6

There is demand for a maximum of 3 accountancy courses and 14 business and finance courses. Accountancy courses contribute £10 000 to overheads and profits, business and finance courses contribute half that amount.

Tasks

1 *Find the product mix that maximises contribution.*
2 *Calculate the maximum contribution.*
3 *Quantify resources that are under-utilised.*

Exercise 18.16   Review of linear programming

B&T Woodworkers Ltd manufactures and sells two products, pine beds and tables. Each product goes through three stages of production: cutting, turning and assembly. There is limited capacity at each stage.

Production times:

	Cutting hours	Turning hours	Assembly hours
One bed	3	4	4
One table	2.25	4	2
Total hours available per week	54	64	48

Contribution to overheads and profit amounts to £120 for a bed and £80 for a table.

Tasks

1 *Find the product mix that maximises contribution.*
2 *Calculate the maximum contribution.*
3 *Quantify resources that will be under-utilised.*
4 *What type of decision-making problems is linear programming used for?*
5 *Problems that can be solved by linear programming must have certain characteristics. Describe two of them.*
6 *Explain the following terms: objective function, constraints and feasible region.*
7 *The graphical approach cannot solve all linear programming problems. What is the basic limitation to its use compared to the simplex method?*

Summary

Statistical techniques and methods are a valuable aid to the planning process. This chapter has considered: **uncertainty** – the calculation of probabilities, the use of the binomial and normal distributions; and sampling within desired confidence limits; **methods** for analysing relationships between variables including correlation, least squares regression, and time series analysis; and **linear programming** for solving limited factor problems.

Further reading

Audrey Curnock, *Quantitative Methods for Business*, Stanley Thornes, 1995.

K. Hoye and R. Ingram, *Statistics for Business*, Butterworth Heinemann, 1991.

T. Lucey, *Quantitative Techniques*, 5th edition, DP Publications, 1996.

Clare Morris, *Quantitative Approaches in Business Studies*, 4th edition, Pitman, 1996.

Frank Owen and Ron Jones, *Statistics*, 4th edition, Pitman, 1994.

Mik Wisniewski, *Foundation Quantitative Methods for Business*, Pitman, 1996.

On completion of this chapter students should be able to:

- evaluate the scope, key areas within and purposes of, a management information system
- review systems for monitoring and providing management information
- evaluate the relevance and appropriateness of information generated from a management information system.

Information needs

Vast amounts of data are gathered and stored about business activities.

Documentation for distribution alone includes sales orders, stock picking lists, sales invoices, delivery notes, customer complaint forms, marketing questionnaires, commission lists – to name a few.

Business records will show every single sale made, every supply ordered and every wage packet prepared. There will not be a movement of materials out of a store room or from one location of a factory to another, without the fact being recorded. The records will show how each worker spent every minute of time, when they were sick and when they went on holiday. There will be records about production volume, product rejects, deliveries made, the mileage and service history of motor vehicles and maintenance records for each item of plant. Responsibility for every event will have been assigned to an individual and every employee will have a personnel file and a payroll record.

Every event will be dated and quantified using money, weights and measures. Time may be measured in terms of labour hours, machine hours or just according to the ticking of the clock.

But the problem is, how can these vast stores of data be converted into a valuable resource to help manage the business?

Managing information is about designing and implementing a management information system (MIS) that turns raw data into something useful – information. Whereas data are facts that have been recorded and relate to the vast number of activities and transactions undertaken by the business, information is something that is useful to the person receiving it. In the business context information enables management to take action in the pursuit of business objectives.

Small businesses have the advantage that the manager is involved in the day-to-day activities of the business. The manager knows about and is able to decipher information from the numerous daily events. But for management to function as the business grows and becomes more complex, a formalised MIS is required that will provide information reliably and consistently.

The ideal MIS will convert data (from internal and external sources) into information that is relevant to the needs of individual managers. The system will enable managers to make timely and effective decisions in the execution of their duties to plan and control business activities. With this aim in mind, information is increasingly being viewed as a strategic resource to achieve corporate objectives.

Case study

Insurance

Insurance is about managing risk. For a motor insurer, the risk of a policy can be viewed in terms of claims history, age and occupation of the insured. A forty-year-old accountant who has never been caught speeding is a better bet than an eighteen-year-old student who crashed Dad's car last month.

But as all insurers have used the same formula this has resulted in tighter margins and little room for error. The cleverer firms are now using more sophisticated methods of sourcing and analysing information. The ability to search vast banks of data to find a link between a policyholder's risk and some other variable can be just the head start they need. For example, it has been found that people who install smoke detectors in their homes tend to have fewer motor accidents.

One problem is getting hold of all this information without the applicant having to fill in a questionnaire running into reams of paper. Although this is not a perfect method, the smoke detector question can be partly answered by looking at stored data sorted according to post code, as there are only about 6 homes to a post code. It may not be ideal, but knowing that the applicant lives in a house that has a 3 in 6 chance of having a smoke detector makes him or her a better risk than someone with a 1 in 6 chance.

Success in insurance is about managing information effectively.

Exercise 19.1   Airlines

Managing an airline is as much about filling seats as it is about flying planes. Describe how managing information is essential to success in the airline business.

The primary function of management is to *make decisions* to affect the future and achieve organisational objectives. Information, either historical or applying to the future, is a

vital ingredient to help management fulfil their responsibilities. Both types of information are important:

- *information about the future* – to plan, co-ordinate, lead and motivate;
- *historical information* – to monitor performance against some benchmark as a basis for controlling future activities.

Decision-making functions are performed by a large number of employees at all levels of the organisational structure. Therefore managers need information that is appropriate to their responsibilities, which must be:

- relevant
- timely
- reliable
- complete
- accurate enough for the task at hand.

Relevant information increases knowledge, reduces risk and enables management to take appropriate action. A particular piece of information may be more relevant to one manager than another because of the nature of their work and their relative position in the organisational hierarchy.

Senior managers make strategic decisions concerning marketing, procurement of resources and the financing of the business. They need to take a holistic view of the business within its environment over a number of years. The issues they have to address tend to be unpredictable, are difficult to quantify and concern the future. Information needs are often satisfied using external sources of data that relate to evolving conditions.

Exercise 19.2

Describe the role and information needs of a finance director.

Middle managers have functional responsibilities and specialise in areas such as marketing, production and finance. Tasks are split between those that are routine and others that are irregular but are sufficiently structured to be solved by a clearly defined decision making process. For a management accountant, a routine task would be to review the latest job cost report, but ad-hoc requests will occur, such as to evaluate a proposed investment in new plant.

For middle managers, a major responsibility is the control of current operations. Information is needed to highlight variances to plan, so that time is concentrated on the management of exceptions rather than being wasted on the interpretation of large volumes of data. In addition, by contributing to the formal budgeting process, middle managers also have a planning horizon of between one and three years. Information for control purposes is derived from internal sources, but information for planning will require greater information from outside the business, depending on the responsibilities of the individual manager.

Exercise 19.3

1 Explain the role of a management accountant as part of the management information system.
2 Describe the information that is demanded of a management accountant and hence what the information needs are for the management accountant to perform his or her role.
3 How are these information needs satisfied?

Junior managers supervise the day-to-day activities of the business. They work within the constraints of operational policy so conditions tend to be relatively stable. Information needs are predetermined and this facilitates the use of standard forms and, for computer systems, the use of data input screens. Information is almost entirely historical, relates to individual transactions and, apart from sales orders, comes mainly from internal sources.

Exercise 19.4

Describe the tasks and the information needs of a credit control supervisor who has responsibility for ten credit control clerks.

Exercise 19.5   Relevance

Match the most relevant items of information to the managers in the organisation.

Managers	Information
Quality controller	Cost to sales ratio of each sales team
Distribution manager	Cost per product delivered
Stock controller	Sales performance of individual salespersons
Sales director	Product returns
Sales manager – team A	Stock items below reorder level

In a commercial context, relevant information is information that can improve the profits and cash flow of the business.

The value of information = value of benefits – costs of information.

The costs of providing information include:

■ expenditure to investigate and design a system, including participation of users in the design stage
■ cost of procuring or writing the software
■ equipment purchases
■ possible increase in staffing to operate the system
■ expenditure on training
■ disruption to work flow during system implementation.

The benefits of information cannot always be measured easily, but as an example, consider how important it is to have knowledge about business costs. Product costs enable important decisions to be made concerning pricing, product viability and make or buy situations. Process costs keep the focus on efficiency and its continual improvement as cost overruns can trigger management action for controlling future cost levels.

Information can also improve the utilisation of capital employed in the business. By forecasting levels of revenues and costs against the capital to be employed, financial resources can be allocated to the most rewarding projects.

Information that facilitates good customer service and identifies problems promptly is clearly valuable. Products delivered to customers on time, and to the desired quality, maximise the chance of repeat orders and minimise product returns and the cost of reworking.

Exercise 19.6   Value of information

Credito Ltd is a wholesaler of electrical components that does business with 100 new customers every year. Each customer spends an average £500 per annum but bad debts have been running at 5 per cent of annual new business sales.

The accounts manager believes that if the company carried out a credit check on each new customer, bad debts could be reduced to 2 per cent of sales. The credit reference company requires £20 for every search and it is estimated that internal administration costs would add a further £5 to that.

Tasks

1 *Calculate the net value per annum of having the credit information.*
2 *Should Credito run a credit check on new customers?*

For information to be appropriate, it also needs to be **timely**. Information is like a perishable good, it loses value over time. In fact information that is superseded by events may become mis-information as managers react to yesterday's rather than today's problems. Information must also be received at the right frequency. For example, most businesses prepare management accounts on a monthly basis but lists of customers going over their credit limits may be required daily.

Exercise 19.7   Time value of information

1   A customer requires a delivery of goods next week that will give profit of £2 000. How valuable is that information if received (i) now or (ii) in 8 days' time?
2   A fault in a production process, which occurs on average once a week, costs £1000 in wasted resources every hour it remains undetected. What is the value of an MIS system that reports within 15 minutes as opposed to one that provides feedback after 2 hours?

Of course information only has value if it is acted upon. An effective MIS is a combination of technology and organisational culture. There must be sufficient motivation to act as a team to allow activities to be co-ordinated. A culture that does not foster a team spirit will undermine the system's use, as individuals will fail to relate to group performance.

Exercise 19.8   Football team

Teamwork is arguably the most important ingredient for a successful football team.

1   Why is communication important on the football pitch?
2   Identify the methods of communication used on the pitch.
3   What are the factors that motivate players to communicate with one another?
4   What are the implications for a team that loses the desire to communicate?

The MIS should provide information to an appropriate level of **accuracy** but sometimes accuracy has to be compromised in the interests of cost.

Whilst it is important for the financial accountant to know that the bank statement and the accounting records can be reconciled to the very last penny, there are other areas where that level of accuracy may not be justified. For example, to know that sales orders for next month are around £50 000 after just 2 hours of work would seem appropriate if it would take a further 2 hours to establish the true figure to be £49 871.

Managers should be initiating change in response to changes in circumstance, whether these are external influences such as technological change or internal conditions such as plant breakdown. An important indicator of an MIS's effectiveness is that appropriate action is being taken in response to the information provided. It shows that the information is not only relevant and timely but that it is being received and understood correctly by management. Inaction could be due to:

- inappropriateness of message – not relevant, not timely, not accurate;
- interference with or distortion of the message – incorrect mode of communication or incorrect format (for example, user interfaces with a computer system, such as screen and printout formats, should be user friendly to help accurate data input and understanding of information output);
- problems with the receiver of the information – lack of motivation or inability to act, perhaps because of insufficient training and skills;
- information is not being received by the right person.

It is vital that reports to managers are designed only after their precise information requirements have been established. In a system of 'management by objectives', individual managers at all levels are set objectives that support corporate objectives. But a failure to support managers with appropriate information will undermine their attainment of the targets set. For example, a parcel courier may promise that 95 per cent of deliveries will be within the estimated drop-off time. If the distribution co-ordinator is unaware that major roadworks on the M1 are currently delaying 25 per cent of journeys made, then the business will fail to meet a crucial objective and the eventual cost may be significant.

It is important, therefore, that the MIS should be market- not production-orientated. It is there to satisfy the needs of its internal customers, not to produce reports for which a circulation list is then designed.

Figure 19.1 Outline of a management information system

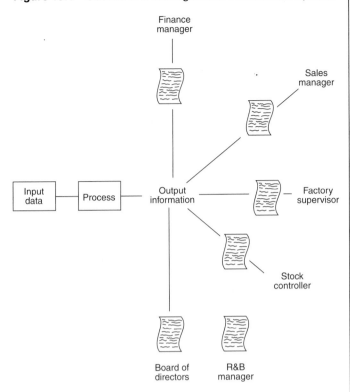

- Finance manager
- Sales manager
- Factory supervisor
- Stock controller
- Board of directors
- R&B manager
- Input data → Process → Output information

Exercise 19.9   MIS specifications

Consider the following needs for information:

- A factory manager who has a £5 000 budget for labour each month needs to know his *actual wages spend*.
- A manager who leads a sales team that has a total sales target of £5 million per year required historical *sales performance* figures.
- The directors of an engineering company require *financial projections* to the end of the year to monitor their budget of £20 million sales and £2 million profit. Previous forecasts have been within 30 per cent of the actual outcome but to get nearer in 5 per cent steps would require more staff time at a cost of £10 000. It is considered that a forecasting error of 10 per cent either way will have to be tolerated, however sophisticated the reporting system.

Task

Suggest possible levels of accuracy, timeliness and frequency that would be appropriate in each case.

Once a system has been introduced it should be periodically evaluated against organisational goals. The review process should encompass the flows of information

with suppliers and customers, particularly for those organisations strong enough to harness the whole vertical process for competitive advantage, e.g. the information interface between Marks and Spencer and its suppliers.

Elements of a management information system

Management information systems consist of three parts: physical resources, human resources and the methods of bringing these resources together.

Although computers are often used, MISs are more than just computer systems. The physical resources of an MIS will also include such items as communication lines, manual records and manual filing systems.

The human resources used by the system will include all those involved from collecting data to those who actually use the information that is generated. Workers who record their activities on time sheets and stores personnel who complete stores documentation are as much part of the system as the computer operator who oversees the processing of the data. Where a system requires interaction between a human resource and a computer system, this is called a **user interface**.

It is how the physical and human resources are brought together as a working system that will determine the quality of information that is produced. The work of the systems analyst is to ensure the systems design meets the information needs of the business and makes efficient and effective use of the resources available.

In a formalised MIS the three system elements will be documented and the roles of individual staff will be defined as part of their job descriptions.

Control systems

Managers should be monitoring and controlling operational performance. Where conditions are predictable and quantifiable, the actual outcome of a business activity can be compared with an expected or previous outcome. A **closed loop control system** can then provide a feedback loop to control future operational activities. Because the system reports on conditions that do not conform to a predetermined standard it permits 'management by exception'. Examples include quality failures, stock turnover and departmental expenses.

Systems that provide information concerning volumes of work passing through the business also require feedback mechanisms if they are to have any value. Volumes need to be reported in units of measure that are most meaningful to those involved in the operating process. For example, a car manufacturer may use the number of vehicles produced each day, and this measure would be supported by other performance indicators concerning utilisation of resources. Where throughput is inadequate, the feedback by management should be in the form of decisions that will correct the situation. The need for this type of system is particularly acute for businesses with high fixed costs, such as an airline where utilisation of capacity is paramount for success.

To understand the roles of the different parts of the MIS, consider the budgetary control example outlined in Figure 19.2. For the stages of data input, data processing and information output there will be a combination of human and physical resources to produce a management report, in this case probably in a printed form. However, for a budgetary control system to be effective there has to be action that controls the costs being incurred. Because this feedback loop requires decisions that depend upon the circumstances, the loop cannot be pre-programmed.

Where a response to a situation can be predetermined it may be possible to design an **automatic closed loop** that requires no further action by management or staff. Some of the procedures used in controlling the credit afforded to customers are automatic closed loops. Depending on the age of overdue sales invoices, a computerised credit control system can automatically produce the appropriate standard letter without any action by a credit controller.

However, whilst many operational systems are best served with a control mechanism, automatic loops are not appropriate where conditions are unpredictable or relate to big issues. Take the case of capital expenditure as an example. Although there may be a formal system that identifies company cars due for renewal, the actual purchase may require the authorisation of the managing director. This is because the expenditure is discretionary and would not be essential if the business currently had cash flow problems.

If no action is taken despite the information produced, or there is a failure in the communication of the desired action, there will be no control loop and the system will become an **open loop system**. For a financial reporting system this would imply that there is no budgetary control. The control of expenditure will depend on some influence outside the system, perhaps the self control of the purchasing manager.

Figure 19.2 A closed loop system – budgetary control

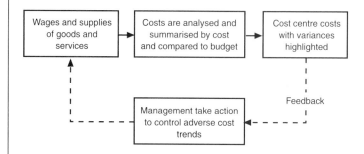

Exercise 19.10 Information systems

The following information is generated by a food retailer.

Purchasing	Central stores and retail outlet	Customer
About deliveries: timeliness, accuracy and quality	Stock orders	Reasons for shopping here and what new
	Operating costs	products they would like
Relative prices of different suppliers	Sales	Customer complaints
		Product returns

Tasks

Categorise the various systems that report the information into:

- automatic closed loop
- closed loop
- open loop.

Operating environment

The characteristics of the MIS must suit the system's operating environment. Stable environments can have formal systems that are highly structured, but if conditions are likely to change, then the MIS must be flexible enough to adapt to new needs.

Consideration has already been given to the possible automation of the feedback loop above, but changing conditions mean that other aspects of the system also need to be flexible. For example, in dealing with customer complaints, the process of gathering information may need human intuition rather than standard form filling.

Operating environments may change due to changes in technology, politics, society, legislation, economic growth and relative competitive advantage. Figure 19.3 looks at an example of a change in business environment and the resulting change in information requirements.

Figure 19.3 Business environment change

	New information needs
The railways in Britain have been privatised and to survive they have had to become more commercially aware	✓ On competitors, e.g. coach and air operators. ✓ Financial appraisal and control requires management accounting information. ✓ Financial accounts to comply with the Companies Acts.

Information flows

Being a manager is largely about communicating information, whether passing instructions down the line of command or receiving feedback from below. But as a channel for information, managers can also be an obstacle to its flow, so organisational structure is an important determinant of an MIS's effectiveness. In realising this, many organisations have undertaken rationalisation programmes (called **downsizing** or **delayering**) that have removed whole layers of middle management. Figure 19.4 illustrates the flow of information up and down a

Figure 19.4 Management information flows

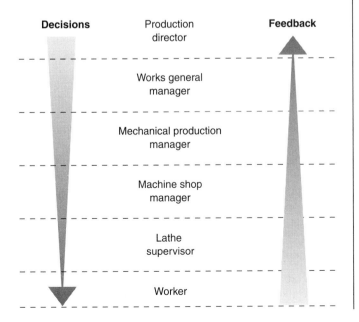

| Decisions | Production director | Feedback |
| Works general manager |
| Mechanical production manager |
| Machine shop manager |
| Lathe supervisor |
| Worker |

management hierarchy where the possibility of message distortion and information hold-ups increases with the number of layers in the structure.

Exercise 19.11 Organisation structure

In recent years there has been a move away from highly structured, hierarchical organisations to flatter organisational structures, to promote greater flexibility in the face of environmental change.

Task

Suggest how management information systems have had to adapt to this change.

For the conversion of data into information, data have to flow through certain processes. Unfortunately the free flow of data is often obstructed because individual managers solve their own local information needs without taking a corporate perspective for the MIS.

The free flow of information is more assured if all systems development work is co-ordinated by one senior manager. Standards can then be agreed for hardware, software and data-file structure that apply to the whole business. Very often the output from one system is manually keyed into another because of system incompatibility. The result is a delay in the flow of information, greater cost and the possibility of errors. Equally important is the need to break down the political barriers to data sharing. People may be reluctant to share data because information gives power, and the ignorant depend on those with knowledge for the effective performance of their duties.

Exercise 19.12 Information is power

For an organisation with which you are familiar, identify and describe the role of an individual who exercises authority because of the information he or she possesses.

The management information system of a business should ideally operate as a working whole, without barriers to data flows caused by the operation of functional systems. For example, data stored concerning a direct worker may include personal details, training undertaken, skills developed, wages paid, holidays taken, sick leave, hours worked and details of work done in that time. These data will have been input by different business functions, including production control, personnel department, the payroll section and the costing department. If all these data can be stored in one accessible place (called a **data**

Figure 19.5 Information flows

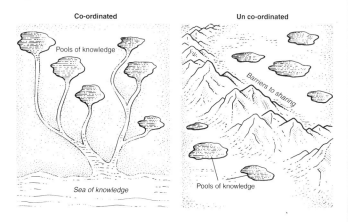

warehouse) management information reports can be designed without a constraint on where the data are stored. The ideal situation is for a seamless management information system that does not recognise functional boundaries.

The desirability of using common data stores, of course, does not replace the need for specialised application software for the collection of data. Even in a co-ordinated

system there will be distinct elements focused on particular business functions. For the finance and accounting department, the elements detailed in Figure 19.6 will be discernible.

It should not be forgotten that informal information channels, often through personal contacts in the organisation, can make a valuable contribution to the information available to management. Some businesses encourage informal channels with an open organisation culture and relatively flat hierarchical structure. Informal systems can also be useful for obtaining external information, and managers may be encouraged to participate in industry associations and local chambers of commerce where informal contacts can be built up.

Data capture

Most of the information that flows through a business comes from the recording of financial transactions and the monitoring of business activities, although this may be augmented by data obtained from outside sources.

The methods adopted for the collection of data will depend upon the nature of the items being recorded and

Figure 19.6 Accounting elements of a management information system

	Data: individual transactions	Information: summary figures
Customer accounting (sales ledger)	sales invoices	analysis of sales age analysis of debtor balances
Supplier accounting (purchase ledger)	purchase invoices	analysis of purchases liabilities to suppliers
Payroll	pay rates hours worked	wages paid analysed by work done
Bank and cash	receipts payments	analysis of receipts and payments current bank and cash balances
Stock accounting	stock receipts stock issues	stock turnover rates stock balances
Product costing	materials, labour expenses standard costs	total job costs cost variances
Planning	functional relationships forecast activity resource requirements	functional budgets forecast profit and loss account, balance sheet and cash flow statement simulation and sensitivity analysis
Financial reporting	actual transactions budget comparisons	financial statements with variances to budget departmental expense reports

the relative costs of manual procedures and computer systems. They include the following.

- Keyboard entry to a computer system.
- Manual recording, for example onto a time sheet or stores issue note, although this data may also be keyed into a computer system at a later stage.
- Electronic Data Interchange (EDI), which enables data to be transferred from one computer system to another. Problems of compatibility between systems have so far restricted the use of EDI although it is widely used in the retail sector where large retailers can pass stock requirement details to suppliers.
- Electronic input with transactions recorded by scanning equipment, including optical character recognition (used with utility bill counterfoils), magnetic ink character recognition (used for the clearance of bank cheques), optical mark readers (used for questionnaire boxes), electronic point of sale (bar codes used in retailing).

Processing and storing information

The processes of the MIS maintain structured data stores that can be accessed to produce management information. The production of information often requires data to be searched, sorted, and for calculations to be made. The principles are the same whether the system is manual or computerised. A manual system will maintain filing cabinets of paper records, whereas a computerised system will use electronic storage media to store files in digital form.

Where data are stored in a computer file, each record is usually structured into fields. A data field stores a certain type of information concerning each data subject, such as ages of employees, their addresses, etc. Data records stored in this highly structured manner are known as **databases** and are a basis for sharing data between different applications.

For example, a computer file containing details of jobs being worked on in a factory may be structured like the one below. This is an example of a **master file** because it relates to permanent data concerning a data subject, e.g. job number 19005.

A file that is used to record costs incurred may have the following file structure:

Date	Reference	Job number	Cost category	Value (£)
24/04/X3	I12004	19004	Materials	20.00
24/04/X3	I12005	19010	Materials	44.00
25/04/X3	P5087	19001	Payroll	123.00

This record of individual cost items is an example of a **transaction file**. The job number is the common field that will enable details from the master file and the transaction file to be combined for the production of a cost report. For example, if a report of total cost analysed between different cost categories was required for job 19004, the system would locate, analyse and accumulate all the items on the transaction file with a job number of 19004. That information could be combined with appropriate fields from the master file, such as customer name and sales value.

Communicating information

Management information systems should communicate information to end users using an appropriate medium. Traditionally reports have been paper based, but other means are now in wide use to suit the needs of managers.

Floppy disks, distributed to users, allow them to access and analyse files of summarised transactions using software packages such as spreadsheets. Managers can also use them to print hard copies of what really interests them rather than receiving hundreds of pages of facts that they rarely read.

In recent years systems have been developed that allow users to access electronic files in real time, i.e. as they are being updated with the very latest transactions. These systems have become possible with the widespread use of networked computers and mobile telecommunications.

The choice of medium and the frequency of reporting should reflect the nature of the information, the audience it is to reach and the use to which the information is to be

Job number	Date of order	Date of delivery	Sales order	Customer code	Customer	Work	Sales value (£)
19004	19/04/X3	20/06/X3	S10088	Tre001	Treett	Drilling	2 200.00
19005	20/04/X3	15/06/X3	S10089	Dea018	Deacon & Co	Fabrication	1 250.00
19006	20/04/X3	24/06/X3	S10090	Pre041	Preston Ltd	Painting	600.00

put. Routine expense reports are usually produced in printed form on a monthly basis. However, certain activities require the latest situation to be reported, such as stock and credit control, so on-line facilities are most appropriate.

Defining the system

During a systems review it is useful to adopt a pictorial view of the MIS. This helps to identify data flows by considering information needs, data sources and possible system constraints. A **data flow diagram** (DFD) is good for establishing the system fundamentals without preconceived ideas about specific methods and physical resources. The DFD represents the problem in a logical and comprehensible manner and the systems designer should not be afraid to represent pictures of everyday office objects on the diagrams if this facilitates understanding for all those concerned.

The DFD becomes a basis for discussion between the analyst and user, allowing the user to participate in the system's design. During a systems review new ideas may develop and users may become more specific about their needs, as their understanding of what is possible also develops. This has the advantage of confirming the analyst's understanding of the system, thus minimising errors that may be costly to rectify later.

Figure 19.7 Data flow diagrams – symbols

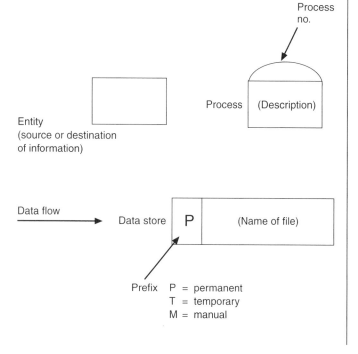

Figure 19.8 Data flow diagram for a product costing system

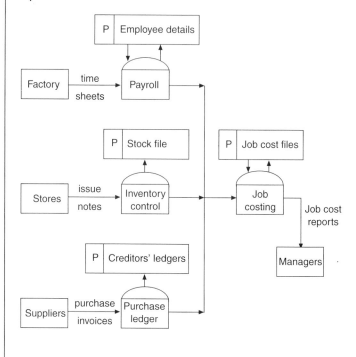

Case study

Net Educational Resources

A group of college lecturers plan to set up a publishing company to sell classroom resource packs to colleges and schools throughout the English-speaking world. The members of the group have identified that teachers tend to 'reinvent the wheel' in creating teaching material and that many hours could be saved if the best of classroom resources were available to all teachers. The resource packs are to be marketed via the Internet as most colleges and an increasing number of schools are connected.

Net Educational Resources would provide a service bringing together those who had good resources to sell and those who wanted to buy them. Initially the group would concentrate on business-related subjects. They have contacted colleagues who either have good resources already or would like the opportunity to develop them. Authors are to be paid a royalty based on the cash receipts for a particular period.

For the business to have any significant growth potential, other authors will be required and the Internet is again considered the most focused and cost-effective form of communication to potential authors.

It has been decided that to minimise overheads and to reduce the financial risk, a fairly simple administration system will be used to provide management information. For similar reasons, a resource pack will only be produced once a firm order has been placed, so there will be no stocks to control other than relatively inexpensive stationery.

At first all tasks are be undertaken by all members of the group in their spare time, so it will be particularly important that work is controlled in a methodical way to ensure continuity. On Sunday afternoons the members will meet to review progress and to consider new resource packs submitted to them.

Sales orders are be placed in a series of in-trays depending on the progress of work:

1 order received
2 order completed
3 order despatched
4 invoice raised
5 invoice paid

The invoices will be recorded on a spreadsheet called a sales journal and coded according to the particular resource pack supplied. The product code will be the basis for accumulating information on product sales and for the calculation of royalties payable to the authors. This information should also be useful for monitoring the relative success of different packs and for identifying organisations that purchase regularly.

Tasks

1 *Is the sales journal a master file or a transaction file?*
2 *Produce a possible database structure for the sales journal.*
3 *What other information store will be of strategic importance to the business?*
4 *Would this information store be in the form of a master file or a transaction file?*
5 *Suggest possible sources of information for this file.*
6 *Prepare a data flow diagram for the sales order processing system from the receipt of the order to the provision of management reports.*
7 *Design management reports for (i) royalties earned and (ii) an analysis of sales.*

Exercise 19.13 Data flow diagram

The Wymington College runs 400 courses with a total teaching staff of 150 lecturers. The college is experiencing problems reconciling names of students who attend classes with those who have actually registered and paid fees. The administration director has decided that student records should be computerised, which would help generate class registers pre-printed with names of students who had registered and paid. However, an added complication is that some students are sponsored by employers who pay the college some time after the registration process. It has not been easy ensuring that all students' fees have subsequently been paid.

Tasks

1 *Describe the college's information needs.*
2 *Design a database to record student details.*
3 *Produce an outline design for a possible system making use of a data flow diagram.*

Once information needs have been defined, specific requirements and constraints can be incorporated so that a more detailed system emerges. In particular, ideas should be forming on how data can be collected and the appropriate user interfaces for inputting data and receiving information. At this stage a series of flow charts will show the systems logic in greater detail than a DFD.

Case study

Glossy Printing Ltd

Glossy Printing Ltd operates a relatively old computerised financial accounting system on two networked personal computers with 386 Intel processing chips. Unfortunately not all of the software modules link automatically so, for example, although a sales invoice links with the sales ledger it does not link with job costing. This has also created hold-ups in the accounts office as staff wait for a computer to become free. Additionally the directors have been complaining about the lack of comprehensive historical information, and also that the reports they do receive are not always in an appropriate format.

Because of the current problems the firm's accountant has chosen a new software package that requires computers with Pentium processing chips and greater memory and disk space. A local hardware supplier can upgrade the existing machines at significantly lower cost than buying new machines although she requires two days to complete the work.

The system will require some changes to office procedures, and the keying in of historical file data would take a clerk one week to complete. The accountant believes that the other staff could be sent on training courses while the data were being transferred.

Tasks

1 *Explain the costs and benefits of the new system.*
2 *When would be the most convenient time to implement the new system?*
3 *What should have been the accountant's main considerations when selecting a software package?*

Managing accounting systems

The accounts department is an integral part of the management information system. It produces information to enable finance managers to manage the financial resources of the business and it is also a major source of information for other departments. How accounting data are used to produce management information is described in Chapters 12 to 18.

The effectiveness of the accounts function is in part due to how it is organised and the quality of its staff members. The organisational structure of an accounts department depends on the size and nature of the business. There tends to be greater complexity in the accounting records of a manufacturing business compared to those of a retailer for instance, but the retailer may have branches in more locations. It follows that when it comes to role specialisation, the manufacturing business may have greater skill specialisation (e.g. costing for manufacturing and for service work would use distinct costing techniques), whereas staff for the retailer may have responsibility for specific geographical areas (e.g. management accountants for each region).

Examples of management positions within the finance and accounting function including the following:

Management position	Responsibilities
Finance director	The most senior finance specialist with a place on the board of directors. Has a major role in the strategic direction of the business and is ultimately responsible for the finance and accounting function.
Financial controller	A senior role, where responsibilities could be very wide or may relate specifically to the financial management of the business. Duties will include identifying and satisfying finance needs and making financial investments.
Treasurer	May have duties similar to those of a financial controller but tends to have a narrower role, with particular emphasis on cash management. In a business context the post is unlikely to have responsibility for the financial reporting process.
Chief accountant	In charge of the accounts department with specific responsibility for financial reporting, both internally and for publication. May also be in charge of purchase and sales accounting if a treasurer is not employed.
Financial accountant	Maintenance of the nominal ledger and the production of financial statements. There is an emphasis on historical information but the position may involve budgeting, particularly cash forecasts.
Cost accountant	Maintenance of cost records and the production of cost reports.
Management accountant	Production of information relevant for the management of the business. This will include routine performance reports and guidance in the production of budgets and other ad-hoc financial forecasts and evaluations.
Credit control manager	Manages the credit given to customers and may also oversee the administration of the sales ledger.
Cashier	Recording and controlling of bank and cash receipts and payments.
Sales ledger manager	Recording credit sales and payments from customers.
Purchase ledger manager	Recording credit purchases and paying suppliers' invoices.
Payroll manager	Maintaining payroll records and paying wages to employees.
Accounts manager	A general accounting role, often within a smaller business, which may encompass many of the individual responsibilities described above.

The staff employed in an accounts department should be suitably qualified by experience and, where appropriate, by membership to one of the professional accounting bodies. Senior accounting positions in business are

Figure 19.9 Organisation structure of an accounts department – for a medium-sized business

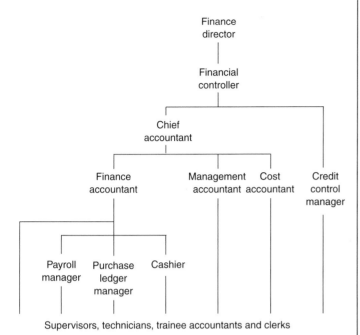

Supervisors, technicians, trainee accountants and clerks

usually, but not necessarily, filled by members of one of the main accountancy bodies. These are the Chartered Institute of Management Accountants, the Association of Chartered Certified Accountants and the three Institutes of Chartered Accountants. Other relevant qualifications include the Institute of Credit Managers and the Association of Accounting Technicians.

Quality control of information

All except the smallest of limited companies are required to have their annual accounts audited by an independent firm of accountants. The role of an independent accountant is to ensure that management have adequate financial controls in place, that financial transactions are being recorded accurately, and that the financial statements are in accordance with the accounting records.

Many large businesses also employ accountants as internal auditors. Unlike external auditors who are answerable to the company's shareholders, internal auditors are employees of the business and report to management. The internal audit department can play an important role in controlling the activities of the business and ensuring that management information is of a high quality. An essential element of the work is the checking of financial transactions.

The scope of internal audits varies greatly and can encompass the whole operation of the business. Typically the department will concentrate on testing and developing the internal controls of the business. Other duties may include reviewing compliance with laws and regulations and reporting on the efficiency and effectiveness of operations.

In addition to ensuring that management policies are being adhered to in respect of the authorisation of transactions and the safeguard of business assets, the internal auditors may be required specifically to review the relevance, reliability, completeness and accuracy of information.

The safeguard of resources and the provision of quality information will be improved if there are adequate internal controls within the information system. The internal audit function is one such control but others can be incorporated into business procedures, including the following:

- *Segregation of duties* – so that a single employee is unable to manipulate the information system. An example, relating to the receipt of cash, would require two people to open the post and list the cheques received, another person to record the receipt on the sales ledger, and another to make bank deposits.
- *Authorisation* – all transactions should be appropriately authorised according to an approval policy. This should include journal entries that do not relate directly to amounts received and paid as they can be used to cover up a fraud as well as to distort financial reports.
- *Supervision* – all staff should be supervised where control by documentation is difficult.
- *Organisation* – clear job boundaries and lines of reporting.
- *Arithmetical* – control totals and reconciliations should be built into the system. For example, the regular reconciliation of the cash book to the bank statement and the nominal ledger to the personal ledgers.

Testing

Internal auditors use two main types of tests:

- *control testing* – evaluation of control procedures
- *substantive testing* – direct evidence that systems have worked or have failed

Control tests will require evidence that an internal control is working effectively. Examples include correct authorisation signatures on purchase invoices and effective passwords on computer systems.

Where system controls are found to be working well, the amount of **substantive testing** can be reduced which is important because it can be very time consuming. But in areas where it is difficult to operate a control procedure or where there is little confidence in its operation, it may be necessary to check a significant number of documents and/or physical items. Substantive testing includes checking:

- individual sales transactions from sales orders and goods leaving the warehouse through to receipt of monies at the bank
- individual purchases from payments out of the bank, working back to the raising of purchase orders and the receiving of items into the stores
- the physical existence of assets that have been recorded in the accounts.

Independence

The independence of the internal audit department is very important if its work is to be of value. Although many internal auditors report to the finance director, this is a questionable practice when a significant amount of the work involves checking the director's own department. In recent years many businesses have set up audit committees where non-executive directors are strongly represented. Internal auditors should report to this high-level committee where executive directors have less direct influence.

Computerised systems

Computers can be valuable tools in the operation of a management information system. Reports that at one time were tedious and time consuming to prepare can now be produced at the press of a button.

The main advantages of a computerised system are:

- it is relatively cheap to run
- it speeds up the process of data capture, analysis and reporting
- it improves the accuracy and presentation of reports
- it allows information to be shared throughout the business for multiple use
- it offers a fast, easy-to-access and compact facility for the storage of information.

As computers continue to become cheaper to buy but workers become more costly to employ, they will increasingly replace human resources in the workplace.

Historically computers have been more useful at the operational rather than executive level, but the introduction of user-friendly data access and decision-support applications has extended the computer's use up the management hierarchy. Computers are now found on the desks of most managers.

Monthly financial reporting often combines the integrity and discipline of highly structured accounting packages for data stores, with the flexibility of spreadsheets for generating management reports. However, the spreadsheets tend to be complex and difficult to maintain, partly because information is required concerning different products, geographical regions, management teams and time scales. Additionally, values are required for actual performance and budget.

A number of software firms are now offering products that use multi-dimensional databases and high level analytical tools to permit flexible reporting. Databases are specifically designed for holding time-series data such as sales by month, by product, by region, by customer, etc. The software provides interfaces which allow users to manipulate and analyse the data, with the ability to 'drill down' to levels of greater detail if required (see Figure 19.10). The software allows managers to evaluate information themselves as a basis for decision making. The users can develop solutions to ad-hoc problems using such facilities as 'what-if' to simulate the effects of decisions.

Figure 19.10 Accounting information structure

Total business expenses		Actual (£'000)	Budget (£'000)	Variance (£'000)
		587	545	42

Total branch expenses		Actual (£'000)	Budget (£'000)	Variance (£'000)
	South East	85	74	(11)

South East department expenses		Actual (£'000)	Budget (£'000)	Variance (£'000)
	Service	33	34	1
	Distribution	15	14	(1)
	Administration	37	26	(11)

South East administration expenses		Actual (£'000)	Budget (£'000)	Variance (£'000)
	Salaries	8	8	0
	Utilities	4	5	1
	Depreciation	5	5	0
	Motor	6	5	(1)
	Repairs and maintenance	14	3	(11)

Repairs and maintenance individual transactions	Invoice number	Supplier	Amount (£'000)	Comment
	1247	ACC	2	Computer
	1287	Reagan	10	Roofing
	1321	Cornell	2	Plumbing

Drill down

Exercise 19.14 Buzz words

The developments in computer software have introduced a host of new terms to the list of information technology buzz words. Consider the following terms:

- Data warehousing
- Graphical user interface
- Internet
- E mail
- Intranet
- On-line analytical processing (OLAP)

Tasks

1 *Investigate and explain the meaning of these terms.*
2 *Explain their relevance for the management of information.*

Case study

Banking

Only a few years ago a bank required an extensive network of grand buildings in prime locations. Today those buildings are being converted into pubs and restaurants as the banks batten down the hatches in the face of new competition. They are not having an easy time in this age of information technology.

Retailers like Marks and Spencer have offered store cards for some years, but they are now also offering financial products like unit trusts and pensions. When Tesco gave its 'loyalty' card holders high interest on card deposits it shocked more than just the likes of Sainsbury's and Safeway.

Any organisation with a large database of customers and plenty of processing power has the essential ingredients to turn itself into a bank. The overheads of running a back office with a telephone for a direct banking service are minimal compared to a branch network.

But the retailers cannot be complacent. If a pension can be bought down the telephone, why not a tin of baked beans?

Tasks

1 *Investigate and explain how managing information has replaced the role of branch management in the approval of bank lending.*

2 *Describe the information that you would consider necessary in the management of a bank branch.*
3 *Identify the role of electronic equipment in satisfying the needs described in 2.*

Case study

Marks and Spencer plc

Extract from 1996 Annual Report *reproduced by kind permission*

Marks and Spencer invested some £51m during 1995/6 in information technology systems in stores, warehouses and at head office to assist in making the business more efficient and reduce costs. In recent years we have aimed to minimise non-selling activities in our stores. Wherever possible we carry out stock preparation in our warehouses and we are increasingly consolidating administrative activities at regional or divisional level.

The next stage is to strengthen further the computer and communication links with our suppliers. We are currently developing an inter-company database for managing contracts with several clothing suppliers. The initial goals are to improve commercial practice and reduce the paperwork associated with placing orders, planning production and arranging delivery schedules but the system is also capable of interactive image transfer and this could prove of immense benefit in cutting product development lead times.

Our distribution centres are using point-of-sale data transmitted directly from the central mainframe computer to drive a paperless stock-picking and replenishment system. The system uses the latest radio data transmission technology to support a dynamic inter-active database that allows us to move merchandise quickly and accurately around the business. During the Christmas period our improved ability to fine-tune allocation, without cumbersome and labour intensive paperwork, allowed us to move over £40m of merchandise to satisfy last-minute customer demand.

A major systems development programme is under way to support the expansion of our food business in Europe. Over £10m has been committed to bring Europe up to date with the UK's best standards of computerised sales floor stock replenishment systems and to extend our supply chain to ensure that chilled foods with short shelf-life reach our stores quickly and in peak condition, an issue which increases in complexity as the lines of supply become longer.

Improving customer care continues to be a priority.

Having provided a nation-wide customer ordering system, we are now developing more sophisticated systems with enhanced data capture capabilities to automate administrative tasks like reserving merchandise and confirming delivery arrangements. This equipment will also service customer orders for home delivery of furniture, flowers and wines. We shall run a trial of new electronic-point-of-sale systems which offer scope for improving service, for example making it simpler for customers to combine related purchases, such as shirts and ties, and not limiting special offers to items physically packaged together. These systems incorporate user-friendly help screens to reduce operator training time.

Tasks

1 *List the various IT systems and associated technology innovations.*
2 *Describe the benefits for each system and how these help provide M&S with a competitive advantage in the market place.*
3 *Draw a data flow diagram, showing, where possible, how data is captured and in what form information is output.*

Summary

Management information systems convert data into information to enable managers to make decisions. It is important that information needs are ascertained before considering how they might be satisfied. Management information systems may harness the processing power of computers, although systems design should not be hampered by preconceived views of hardware and software resources. As with other management issues, managing information should be on a contingency basis, with a corporate perspective of costs and benefits.

Further reading

Mike Harry, *Information Systems in Business*, Pitman, 1994.

Jane Knight, *Management Information Systems*, Pitman, 1996.

T. Lucey, *Management Information Systems*, 6th edition, DP Publications, 1991.

Wendy Robson, *Strategic Management and Information Systems*, 2nd edition, Pitman, 1996.

David A. Wilson, *Managing Information*, Butterworth Heinemann, 1993.

Appendix I: Normal distribution

The table gives the area under the normal distribution curve between the mean and a point measured in standard deviations (z) from the mean.

z	0.00	0.01	0.02	0.03	0.04	0.05	0.06	0.07	0.08	0.09
0.0	0.0000	0.0040	0.0080	0.0120	0.0160	0.0199	0.0239	0.0279	0.0319	0.0359
0.1	0.0398	0.0438	0.0478	0.0517	0.0557	0.0596	0.0636	0.0675	0.0714	0.0753
0.2	0.0793	0.0832	0.0871	0.0910	0.0948	0.0987	0.1026	0.1064	0.1103	0.1141
0.3	0.1179	0.1217	0.1255	0.1293	0.1331	0.1368	0.1406	0.1443	0.1480	0.1517
0.4	0.1554	0.1591	0.1628	0.1664	0.1700	0.1736	0.1772	0.1808	0.1844	0.1879
0.5	0.1915	0.1950	0.1985	0.2019	0.2054	0.2088	0.2123	0.2157	0.2190	0.2224
0.6	0.2257	0.2291	0.2324	0.2357	0.2389	0.2422	0.2454	0.2486	0.2517	0.2549
0.7	0.2580	0.2611	0.2642	0.2673	0.2704	0.2734	0.2764	0.2794	0.2823	0.2852
0.8	0.2881	0.2910	0.2939	0.2967	0.2995	0.3023	0.3051	0.3078	0.3106	0.3133
0.9	0.3159	0.3186	0.3212	0.3238	0.3264	0.3289	0.3315	0.3340	0.3365	0.3389
1.0	0.3413	0.3438	0.3461	0.3485	0.3508	0.3531	0.3554	0.3577	0.3599	0.3621
1.1	0.3643	0.3665	0.3686	0.3708	0.3729	0.3749	0.3770	0.3790	0.3810	0.3830
1.2	0.3849	0.3869	0.3888	0.3907	0.3925	0.3944	0.3962	0.3980	0.3997	0.4015
1.3	0.4032	0.4049	0.4066	0.4082	0.4099	0.4115	0.4131	0.4147	0.4162	0.4177
1.4	0.4192	0.4207	0.4222	0.4236	0.4251	0.4265	0.4279	0.4292	0.4306	0.4319
1.5	0.4332	0.4345	0.4357	0.4370	0.4382	0.4394	0.4406	0.4418	0.4429	0.4441
1.6	0.4452	0.4463	0.4474	0.4484	0.4495	0.4505	0.4515	0.4525	0.4535	0.4545
1.7	0.4554	0.4564	0.4573	0.4582	0.4591	0.4599	0.4608	0.4616	0.4625	0.4633
1.8	0.4641	0.4649	0.4656	0.4664	0.4671	0.4678	0.4686	0.4693	0.4699	0.4706
1.9	0.4713	0.4719	0.4726	0.4732	0.4738	0.4744	0.4750	0.4756	0.4761	0.4767
2.0	0.4772	0.4778	0.4783	0.4788	0.4793	0.4798	0.4803	0.4808	0.4812	0.4817
2.1	0.4821	0.4826	0.4830	0.4834	0.4838	0.4842	0.4846	0.4850	0.4854	0.4857
2.2	0.4861	0.4864	0.4868	0.4871	0.4875	0.4878	0.4881	0.4884	0.4887	0.4890
2.3	0.4893	0.4896	0.4898	0.4901	0.4904	0.4906	0.4909	0.4911	0.4913	0.4916
2.4	0.4918	0.4920	0.4922	0.4925	0.4927	0.4929	0.4931	0.4932	0.4934	0.4936
2.5	0.4938	0.4940	0.4941	0.4943	0.4945	0.4946	0.4948	0.4949	0.4951	0.4952
2.6	0.4953	0.4955	0.4956	0.4957	0.4959	0.4960	0.4961	0.4962	0.4963	0.4964
2.7	0.4965	0.4966	0.4967	0.4968	0.4969	0.4970	0.4971	0.4972	0.4973	0.4974
2.8	0.4974	0.4975	0.4976	0.4977	0.4977	0.4978	0.4979	0.4979	0.4980	0.4981
2.9	0.4981	0.4982	0.4982	0.4983	0.4984	0.4984	0.4985	0.4985	0.4986	0.4986
3.0	0.4987	0.4987	0.4987	0.4988	0.4988	0.4989	0.4989	0.4989	0.4990	0.4990

Appendix II: Random number table

23 46	69 49	07 79	04 30	57 04	92 47	80 45	76 15	09 57	54 82
19 98	14 02	08 61	84 80	06 40	38 83	55 04	14 87	38 83	06 23
90 27	57 32	87 03	95 63	75 46	09 57	31 98	62 38	20 13	08 24
10 24	54 22	56 15	68 68	69 74	44 97	60 54	70 75	17 99	64 88
67 04	59 25	62 13	37 81	68 75	23 57	65 92	83 09	48 39	69 32
39 27	73 36	12 87	05 51	25 39	96 33	38 31	58 19	25 47	28 28
31 96	70 20	33 52	23 24	59 13	55 92	18 20	10 82	55 97	05 21
19 02	98 36	30 04	80 99	70 37	70 18	97 35	49 48	74 40	68 82
04 72	58 53	59 40	15 59	62 91	43 48	17 10	52 27	14 25	02 44
60 07	25 77	59 26	54 98	19 62	83 20	75 32	35 60	93 49	69 90
33 15	32 32	47 26	44 60	03 89	46 40	98 43	46 43	55 39	73 44
13 87	96 57	90 84	38 28	44 78	03 61	11 80	63 80	04 60	91 66
10 03	55 86	02 20	23 66	59 26	82 58	69 28	12 34	60 03	24 07
11 94	39 62	06 12	58 92	61 59	63 09	28 84	47 01	47 26	28 74
12 12	04 56	29 45	56 21	61 65	71 63	24 96	50 99	94 97	01 14
48 61	95 93	82 87	24 08	82 93	59 91	59 30	90 26	29 62	60 76
23 82	44 31	83 81	16 85	00 68	05 69	20 56	86 38	18 37	70 26
19 93	28 02	10 77	01 13	81 87	15 02	04 90	66 82	38 48	80 29
06 11	25 65	13 53	08 06	89 02	31 35	94 70	38 62	37 97	78 98
97 57	86 64	84 02	02 76	91 14	06 45	16 82	23 07	31 44	71 05

Appendix III: Present value table

Years Interest rates %

	5	6	7	8	9	10	11	12	13	14	15
1	0.9524	0.9434	0.9346	0.9259	0.9174	0.9091	0.9009	0.8929	0.8850	0.8772	0.8696
2	0.9070	0.8900	0.8734	0.8573	0.8417	0.8264	0.8116	0.7972	0.7831	0.7695	0.7561
3	0.8638	0.8396	0.8163	0.7938	0.7722	0.7513	0.7312	0.7118	0.6931	0.6750	0.6575
4	0.8227	0.7921	0.7629	0.7350	0.7084	0.6830	0.6587	0.6355	0.6133	0.5921	0.5718
5	0.7835	0.7473	0.7130	0.6806	0.6499	0.6209	0.5935	0.5674	0.5428	0.5194	0.4972
6	0.7462	0.7050	0.6663	0.6302	0.5963	0.5645	0.5346	0.5066	0.4803	0.4556	0.4323
7	0.7107	0.6651	0.6227	0.5835	0.5470	0.5132	0.4817	0.4523	0.4251	0.3996	0.3759
8	0.6768	0.6274	0.5820	0.5403	0.5019	0.4665	0.4339	0.4039	0.3762	0.3506	0.3269
9	0.6446	0.5919	0.5439	0.5002	0.4604	0.4241	0.3909	0.3606	0.3329	0.3075	0.2843
10	0.6139	0.5584	0.5083	0.4632	0.4224	0.3855	0.3522	0.3220	0.2946	0.2697	0.2472
11	0.5847	0.5268	0.4751	0.4289	0.3875	0.3505	0.3173	0.2875	0.2607	0.2366	0.2149
12	0.5568	0.4970	0.4440	0.3971	0.3555	0.3186	0.2858	0.2567	0.2307	0.2076	0.1869
13	0.5303	0.4688	0.4150	0.3677	0.3262	0.2897	0.2575	0.2292	0.2042	0.1821	0.1625
14	0.5051	0.4423	0.3878	0.3405	0.2992	0.2633	0.2320	0.2046	0.1807	0.1597	0.1413
15	0.4810	0.4173	0.3624	0.3152	0.2745	0.2394	0.2090	0.1827	0.1599	0.1401	0.1229
16	0.4581	0.3936	0.3387	0.2919	0.2519	0.2176	0.1883	0.1631	0.1415	0.1229	0.1069
17	0.4363	0.3714	0.3166	0.2703	0.2311	0.1978	0.1696	0.1456	0.1252	0.1078	0.0929
18	0.4155	0.3503	0.2959	0.2502	0.2120	0.1799	0.1528	0.1300	0.1108	0.0946	0.0808
19	0.3957	0.3305	0.2765	0.2317	0.1945	0.1635	0.1377	0.1161	0.0981	0.0829	0.0703
20	0.3769	0.3118	0.2584	0.2145	0.1784	0.1486	0.1240	0.1037	0.0868	0.0728	0.0611

Index